CLOSED

VOLUME 57

Gosho Aoyama

Case Briefing:

Subject:
Occupation:
Special Skills:
Equipment:

Jimmy Kudo, a.k.a. Conan Edogawa
High School Student/Detective
Analytical thinking and deductive reasoning, Soccer
Bow Tie Voice Transmitter, Super Sneakers,
Homing Glasses, Stretchy Suspenders

The subject is hot on the trail of a pair of suspicious men in black when he is attacked from behind and administered a strange substance which physically transforms him into a first grader. When the subject confides in the eccentric inventor Dr. Agasa, they decide to keep the subject's true identity a secret for the safety of everyone around him. Assuming the new identity of first-grader Conan Edogawa, the subject continues to assist the police force on their most baffling cases. The only problem is that most crime-solving professionals won't take a little kid's advice!

Table of Contents

CASE CLOSED

Volume 57
Shonen Sunday Edition

Story and Art by GOSHO AOYAMA

MEITANTEI CONAN Vol. 57
by Gosho AOYAMA
© 1994 Gosho AOYAMA
All rights reserved.
Original Japanese edition published by SHOGAKUKAN.
English translation rights in the United States of America, Canada,
the United Kingdom and Ireland arranged with SHOGAKUKAN.

Translation
Tetsuichiro Miyaki

Touch-up & Lettering
Freeman Wong

Cover & Graphic Design
Andrea Rice

Editor
Shaenon K. Garrity

Printed in the U.S.A.

Published by VIZ Media, LLC
P.O. Box 77010
San Francisco, CA 94107

10 9 8 7 6 5 4 3 2 1
First printing, January 2016

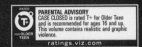

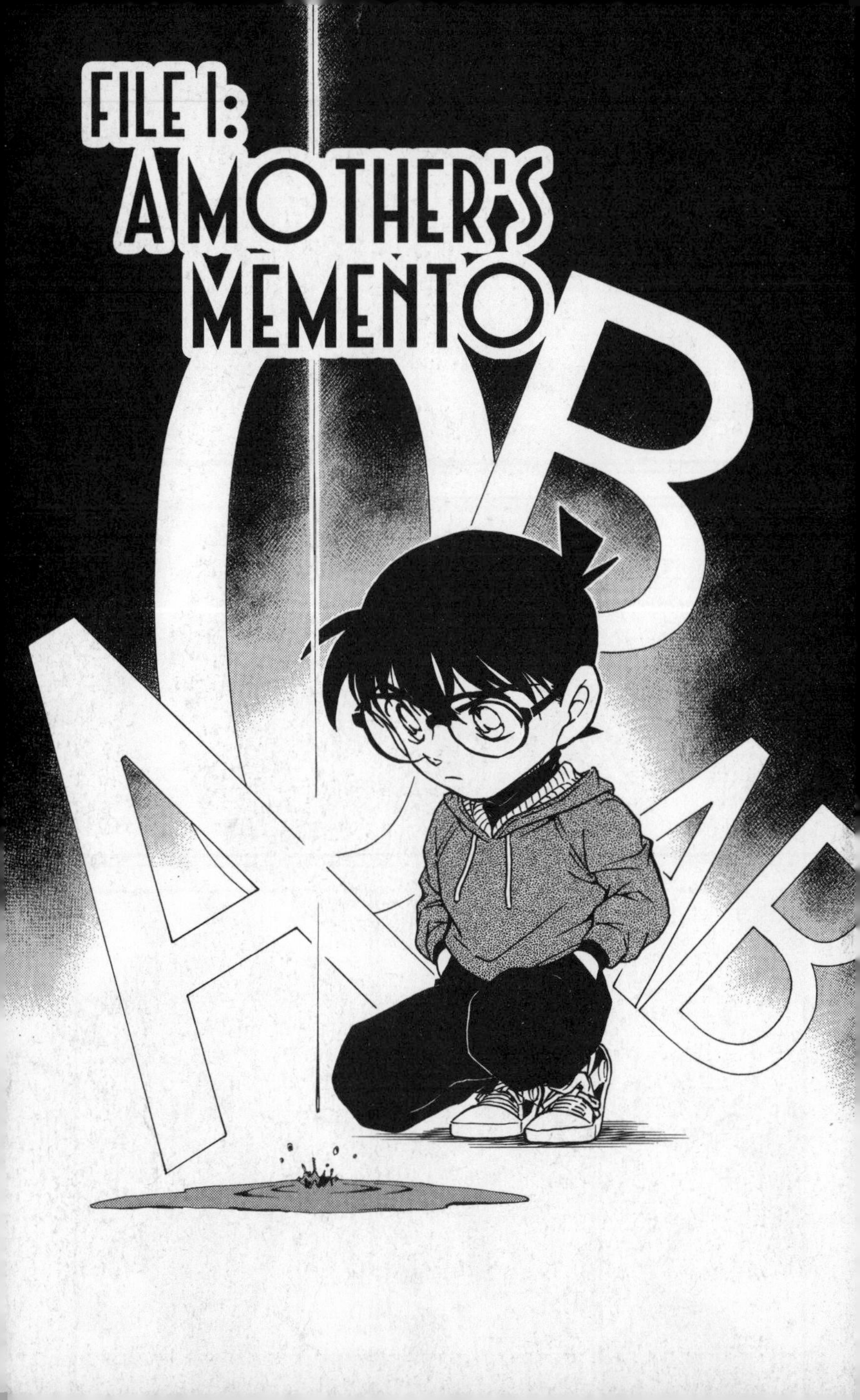
FILE 1:
A MOTHER'S MEMENTO

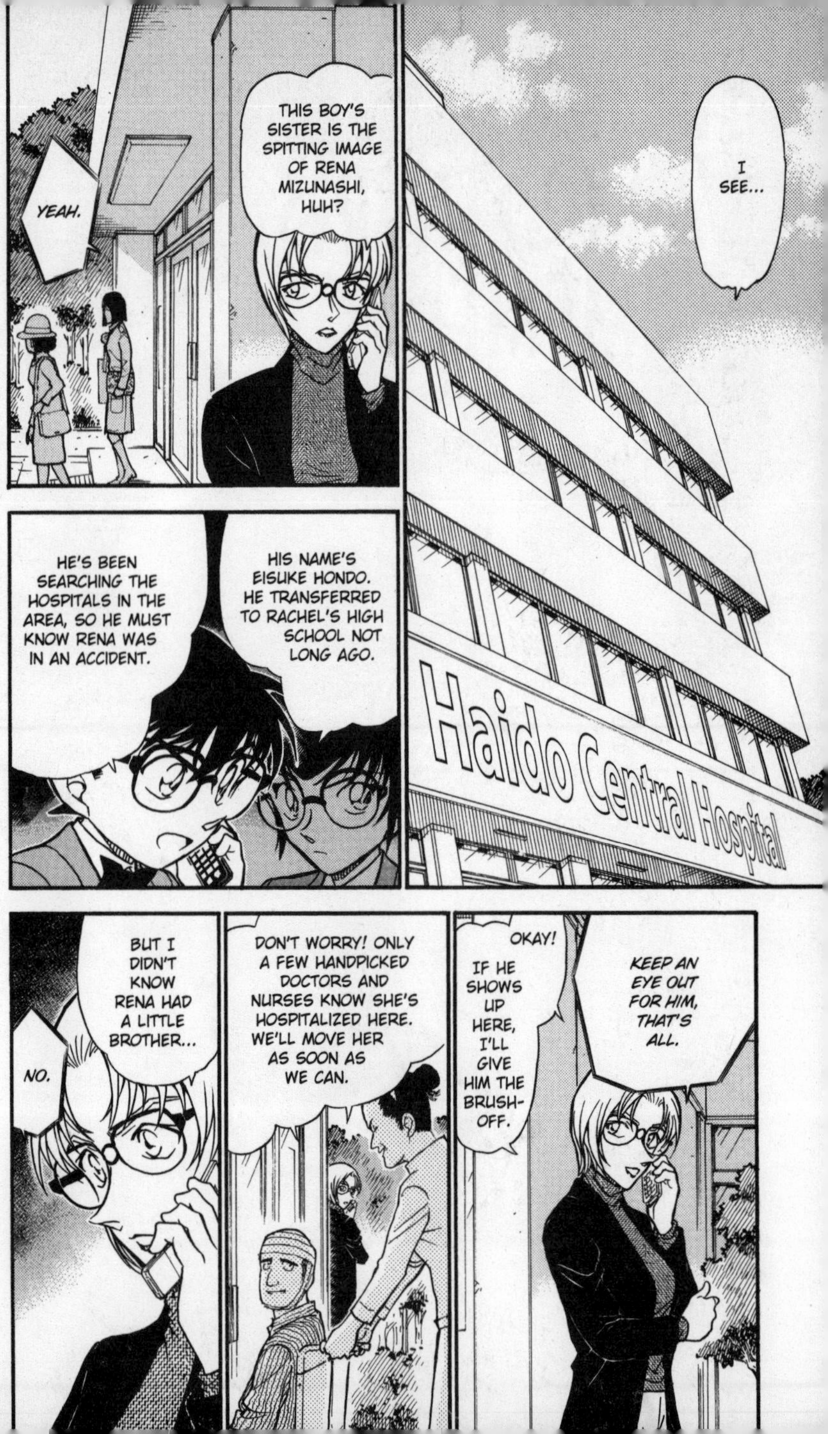
I SEE...
Haido Central Hospital
THIS BOY'S SISTER IS THE SPITTING IMAGE OF RENA MIZUNASHI, HUH?
YEAH.
HIS NAME'S EISUKE HONDO. HE TRANSFERRED TO RACHEL'S HIGH SCHOOL NOT LONG AGO.
HE'S BEEN SEARCHING THE HOSPITALS IN THE AREA, SO HE MUST KNOW RENA WAS IN AN ACCIDENT.
KEEP AN EYE OUT FOR HIM, THAT'S ALL.
OKAY!
IF HE SHOWS UP HERE, I'LL GIVE HIM THE BRUSH-OFF.
DON'T WORRY! ONLY A FEW HANDPICKED DOCTORS AND NURSES KNOW SHE'S HOSPITALIZED HERE. WE'LL MOVE HER AS SOON AS WE CAN.
BUT I DIDN'T KNOW RENA HAD A LITTLE BROTHER...
NO.

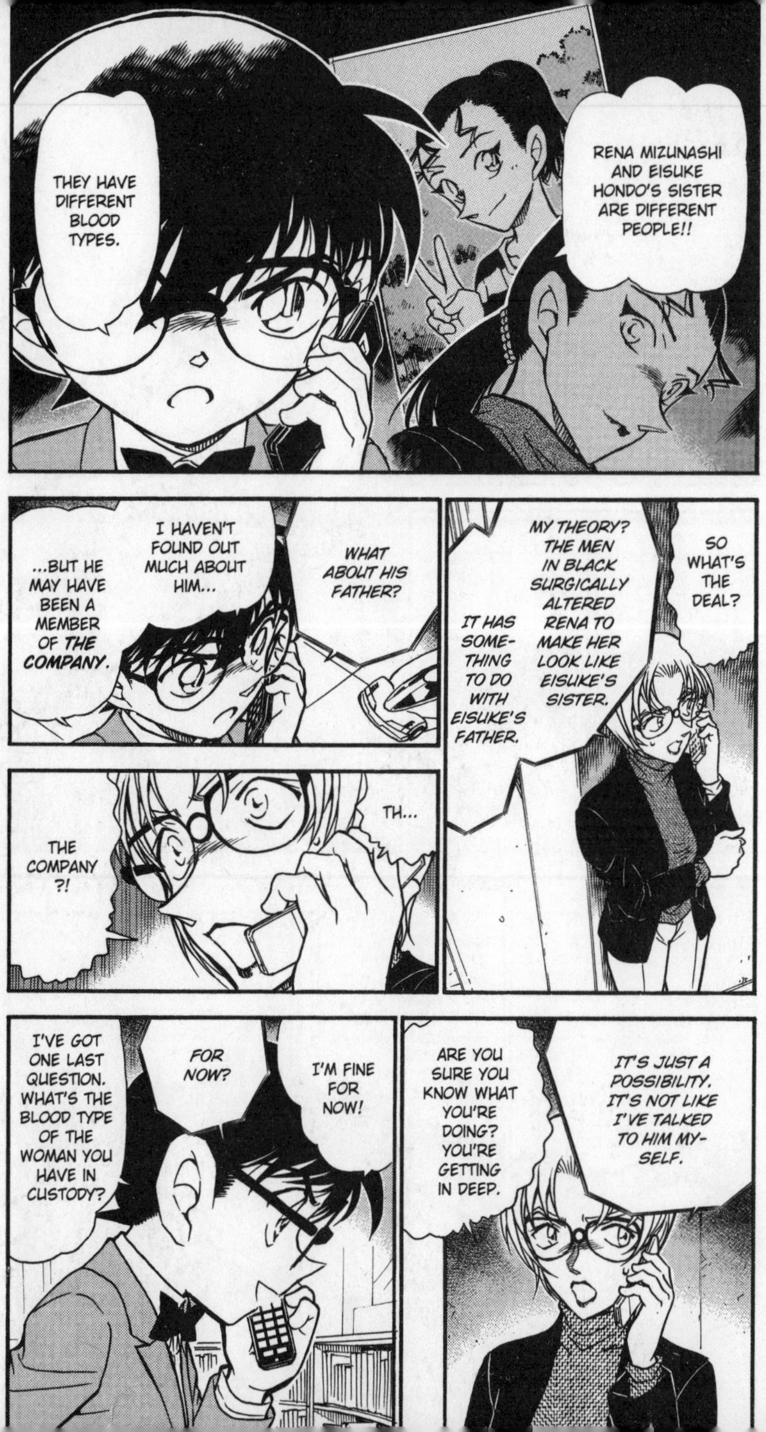
RENA MIZUNASHI AND EISUKE HONDO'S SISTER ARE DIFFERENT PEOPLE!!
THEY HAVE DIFFERENT BLOOD TYPES.
SO WHAT'S THE DEAL?
MY THEORY? THE MEN IN BLACK SURGICALLY ALTERED RENA TO MAKE HER LOOK LIKE EISUKE'S SISTER.
IT HAS SOME-THING TO DO WITH EISUKE'S FATHER.
WHAT ABOUT HIS FATHER?
I HAVEN'T FOUND OUT MUCH ABOUT HIM...
...BUT HE MAY HAVE BEEN A MEMBER OF **THE COMPANY**.
TH...
THE COMPANY ?!
IT'S JUST A POSSIBILITY. IT'S NOT LIKE I'VE TALKED TO HIM MY-SELF.
ARE YOU SURE YOU KNOW WHAT YOU'RE DOING? YOU'RE GETTING IN DEEP.
I'M FINE FOR NOW!
FOR NOW?
I'VE GOT ONE LAST QUESTION. WHAT'S THE BLOOD TYPE OF THE WOMAN YOU HAVE IN CUSTODY?

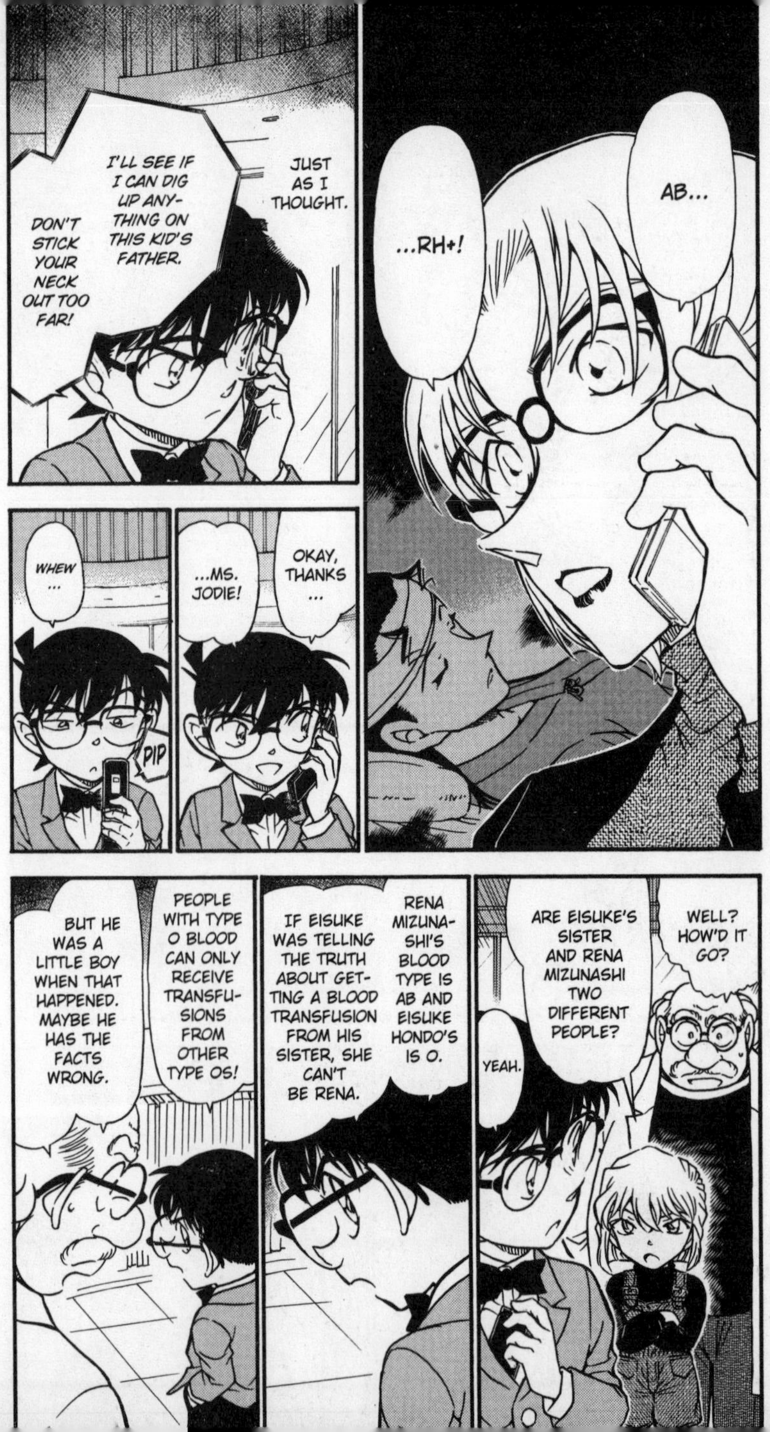
AB...
...RH+!
JUST AS I THOUGHT.
I'LL SEE IF I CAN DIG UP ANY-THING ON THIS KID'S FATHER.
DON'T STICK YOUR NECK OUT TOO FAR!
OKAY, THANKS...
...MS. JODIE!
WHEW...
PIP
WELL? HOW'D IT GO?
ARE EISUKE'S SISTER AND RENA MIZUNASHI TWO DIFFERENT PEOPLE?
YEAH.
RENA MIZUNA-SHI'S BLOOD TYPE IS AB AND EISUKE HONDO'S IS O.
IF EISUKE WAS TELLING THE TRUTH ABOUT GET-TING A BLOOD TRANSFUSION FROM HIS SISTER, SHE CAN'T BE RENA.
PEOPLE WITH TYPE O BLOOD CAN ONLY RECEIVE TRANSFU-SIONS FROM OTHER TYPE OS!
BUT HE WAS A LITTLE BOY WHEN THAT HAPPENED. MAYBE HE HAS THE FACTS WRONG.

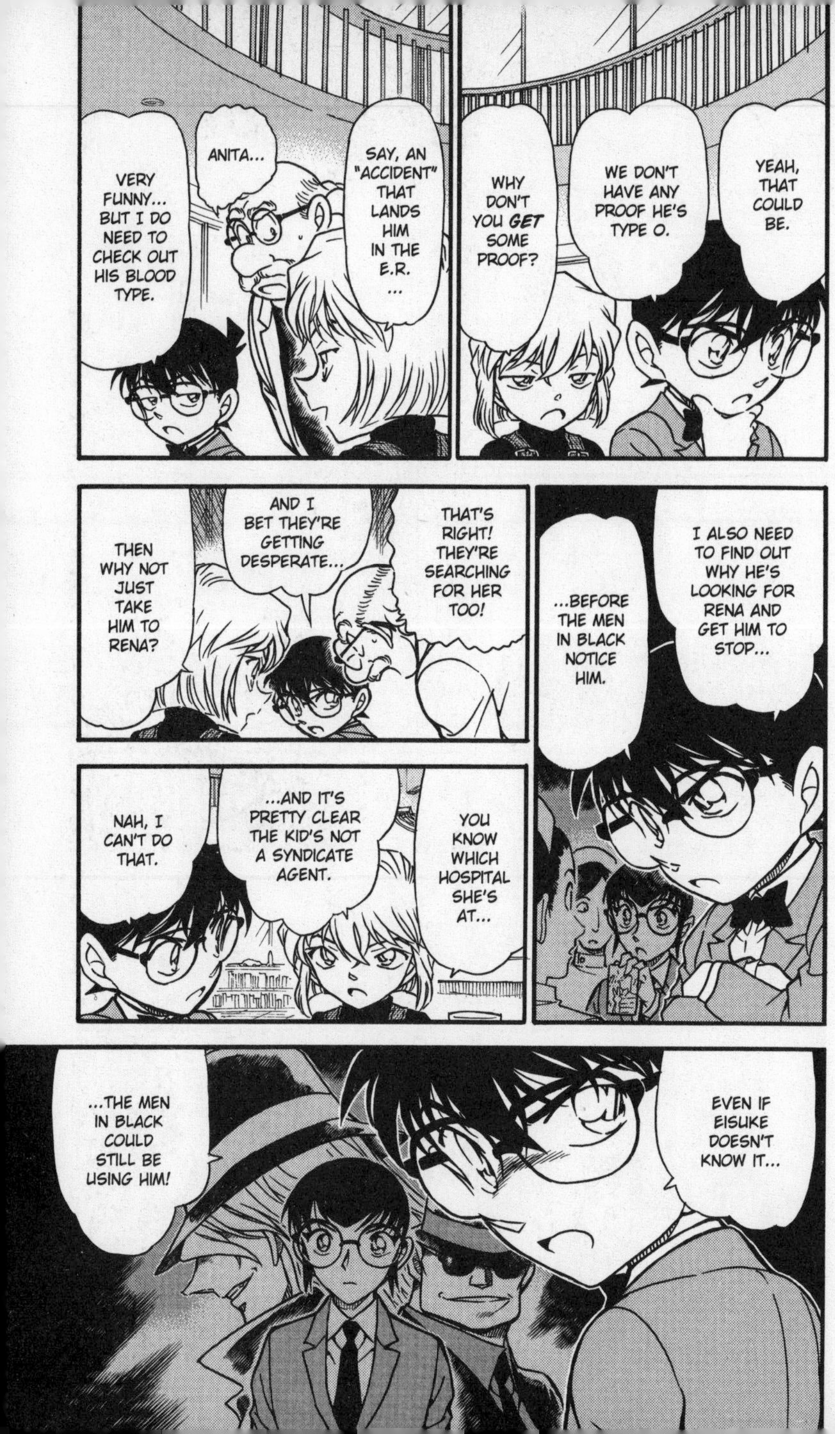
YEAH, THAT COULD BE.
WE DON'T HAVE ANY PROOF HE'S TYPE O.
WHY DON'T YOU *GET* SOME PROOF?
SAY, AN "ACCIDENT" THAT LANDS HIM IN THE E.R. ...
ANITA...
VERY FUNNY... BUT I DO NEED TO CHECK OUT HIS BLOOD TYPE.
I ALSO NEED TO FIND OUT WHY HE'S LOOKING FOR RENA AND GET HIM TO STOP...
...BEFORE THE MEN IN BLACK NOTICE HIM.
THAT'S RIGHT! THEY'RE SEARCHING FOR HER TOO!
AND I BET THEY'RE GETTING DESPERATE...
THEN WHY NOT JUST TAKE HIM TO RENA?
YOU KNOW WHICH HOSPITAL SHE'S AT...
...AND IT'S PRETTY CLEAR THE KID'S NOT A SYNDICATE AGENT.
NAH, I CAN'T DO THAT.
EVEN IF EISUKE DOESN'T KNOW IT...
...THE MEN IN BLACK COULD STILL BE USING HIM!

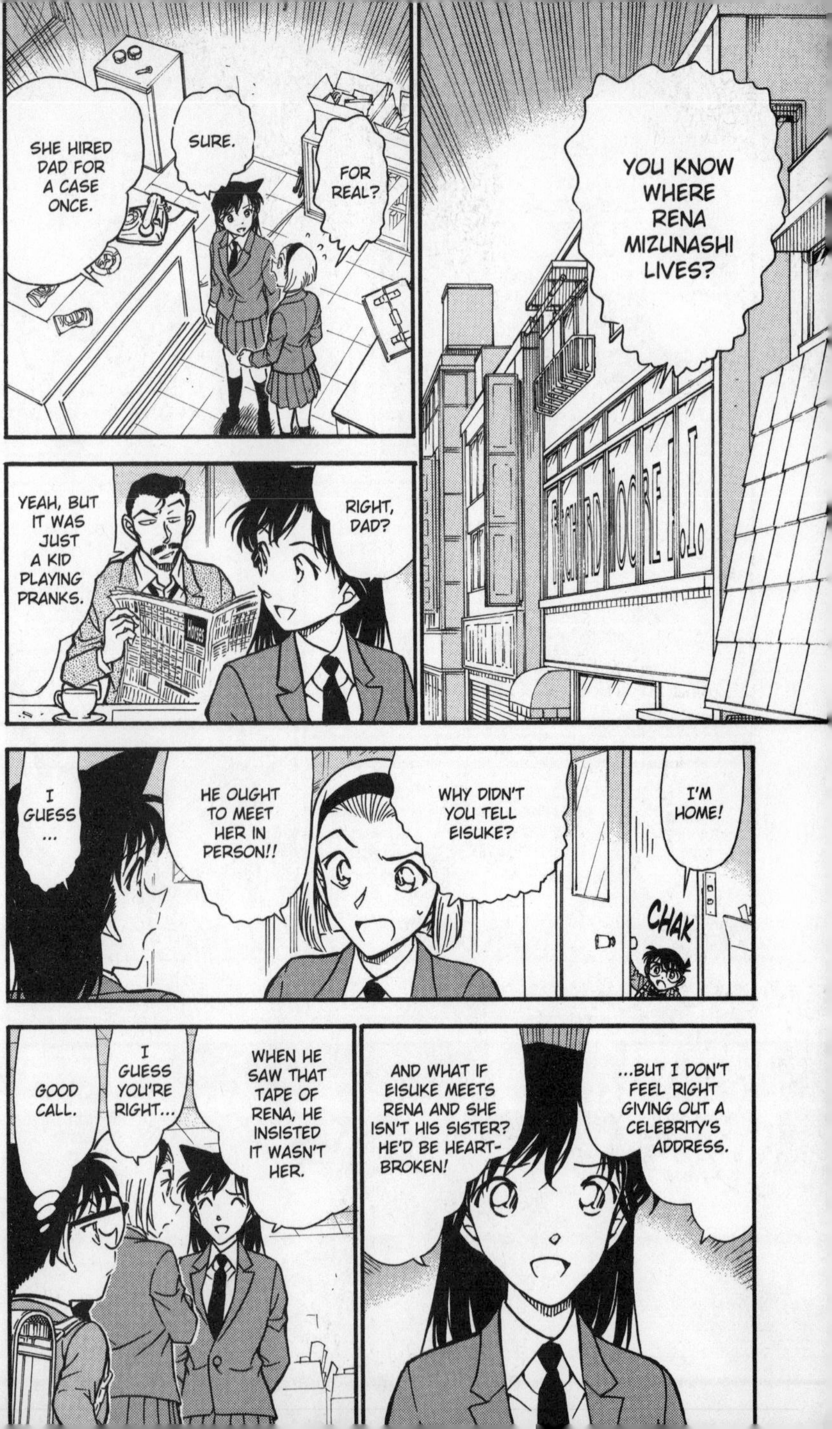
YOU KNOW WHERE RENA MIZUNASHI LIVES?
RICHARD MOORE P.I.
FOR REAL?
SURE.
SHE HIRED DAD FOR A CASE ONCE.
RIGHT, DAD?
YEAH, BUT IT WAS JUST A KID PLAYING PRANKS.
Horses
I'M HOME!
CHAK
WHY DIDN'T YOU TELL EISUKE?
HE OUGHT TO MEET HER IN PERSON!!
I GUESS ...
...BUT I DON'T FEEL RIGHT GIVING OUT A CELEBRITY'S ADDRESS.
AND WHAT IF EISUKE MEETS RENA AND SHE ISN'T HIS SISTER? HE'D BE HEART-BROKEN!
WHEN HE SAW THAT TAPE OF RENA, HE INSISTED IT WASN'T HER.
I GUESS YOU'RE RIGHT...
GOOD CALL.

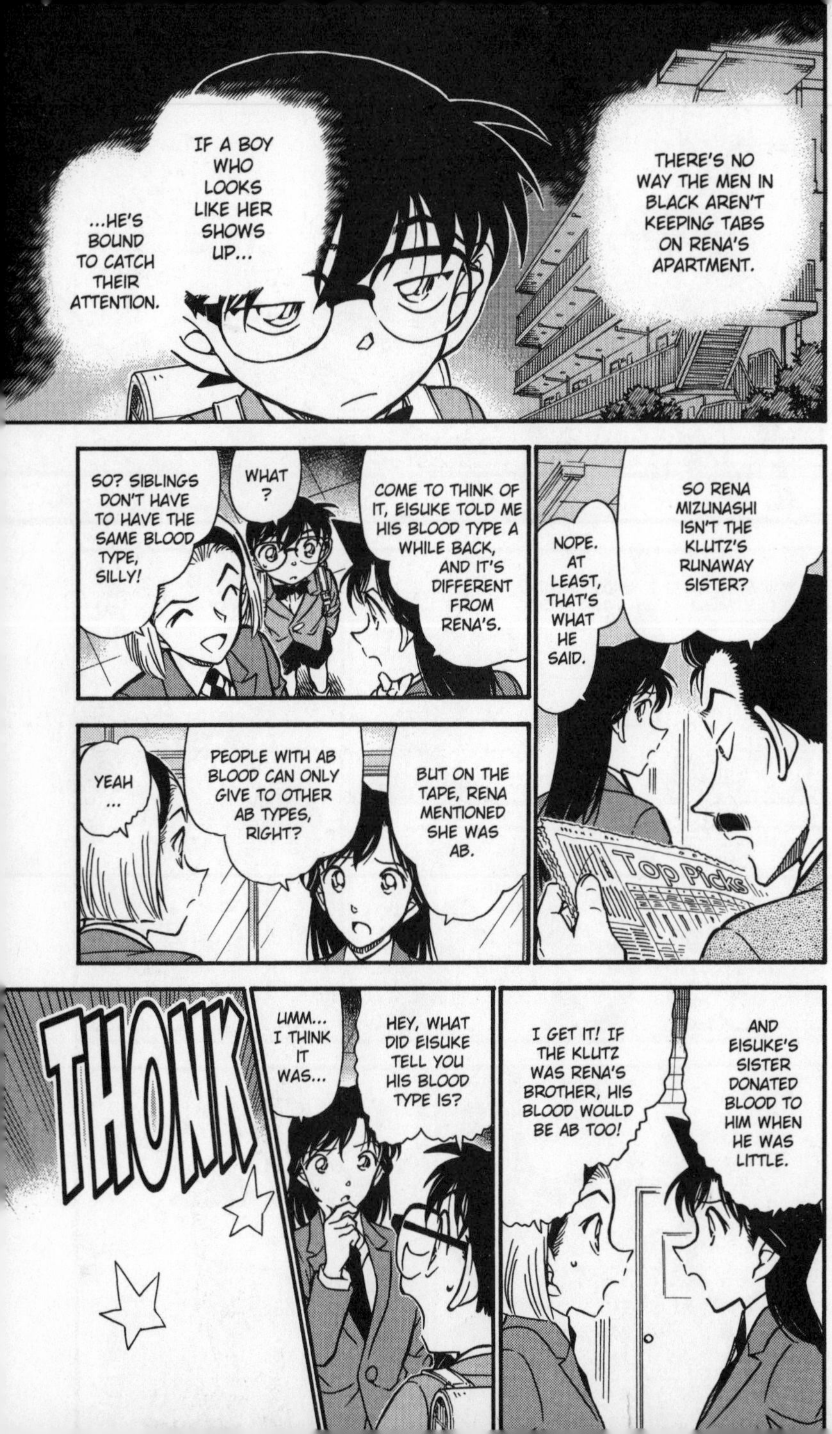
THERE'S NO WAY THE MEN IN BLACK AREN'T KEEPING TABS ON RENA'S APARTMENT.
IF A BOY WHO LOOKS LIKE HER SHOWS UP...
...HE'S BOUND TO CATCH THEIR ATTENTION.
SO RENA MIZUNASHI ISN'T THE KLUTZ'S RUNAWAY SISTER?
NOPE. AT LEAST, THAT'S WHAT HE SAID.
Top Picks
COME TO THINK OF IT, EISUKE TOLD ME HIS BLOOD TYPE A WHILE BACK, AND IT'S DIFFERENT FROM RENA'S.
WHAT?
SO? SIBLINGS DON'T HAVE TO HAVE THE SAME BLOOD TYPE, SILLY!
BUT ON THE TAPE, RENA MENTIONED SHE WAS AB.
PEOPLE WITH AB BLOOD CAN ONLY GIVE TO OTHER AB TYPES, RIGHT?
YEAH...
AND EISUKE'S SISTER DONATED BLOOD TO HIM WHEN HE WAS LITTLE.
I GET IT! IF THE KLUTZ WAS RENA'S BROTHER, HIS BLOOD WOULD BE AB TOO!
HEY, WHAT DID EISUKE TELL YOU HIS BLOOD TYPE IS?
UMM... I THINK IT WAS...
THONK

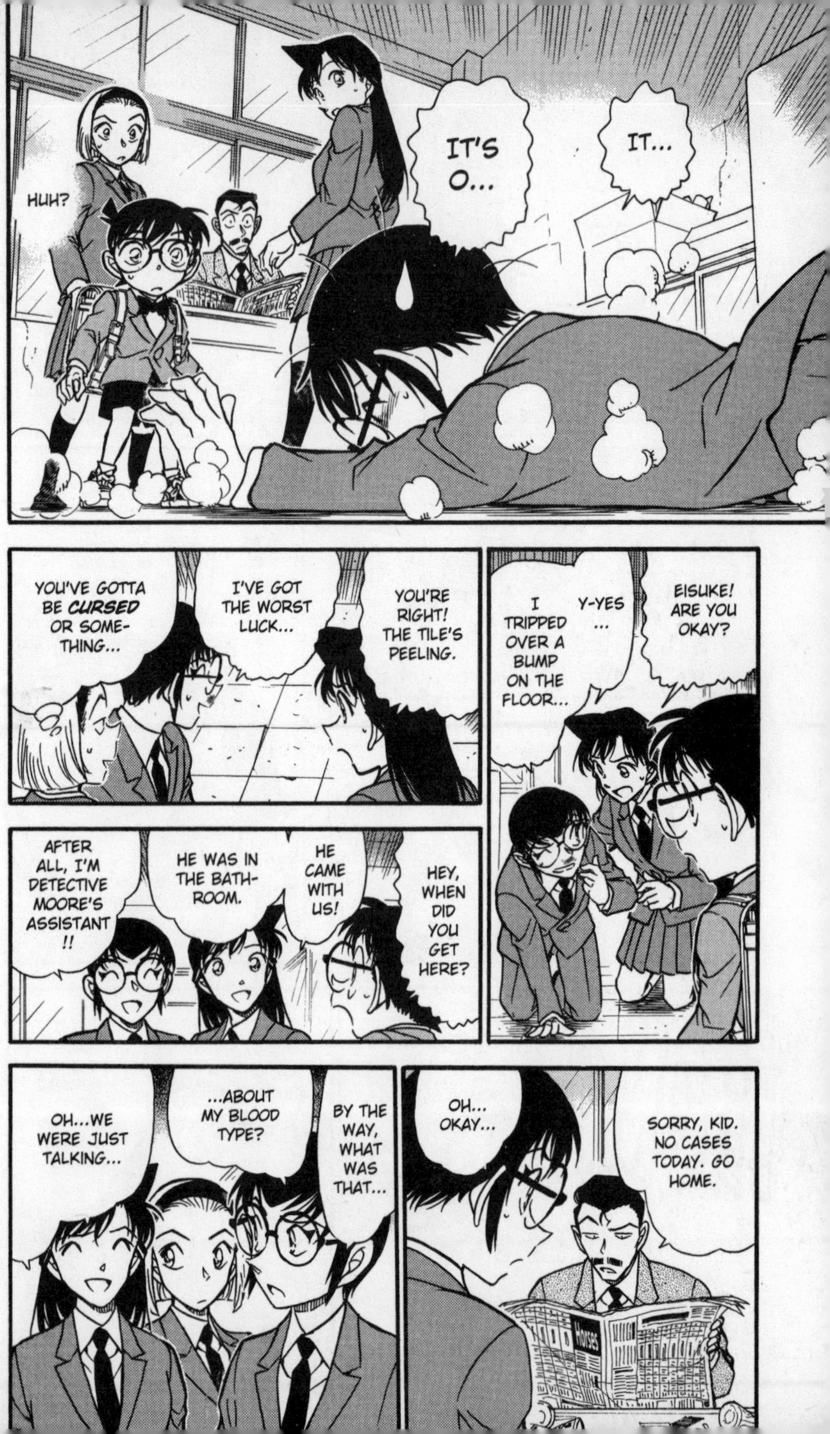
IT...
IT'S O...
HUH?
EISUKE! ARE YOU OKAY?
Y-YES ...
I TRIPPED OVER A BUMP ON THE FLOOR...
YOU'RE RIGHT! THE TILE'S PEELING.
I'VE GOT THE WORST LUCK...
YOU'VE GOTTA BE *CURSED* OR SOME-THING...
HEY, WHEN DID YOU GET HERE?
HE CAME WITH US!
HE WAS IN THE BATH-ROOM.
AFTER ALL, I'M DETECTIVE MOORE'S ASSISTANT !!
SORRY, KID. NO CASES TODAY. GO HOME.
OH... OKAY...
BY THE WAY, WHAT WAS THAT...
...ABOUT MY BLOOD TYPE?
OH...WE WERE JUST TALKING...

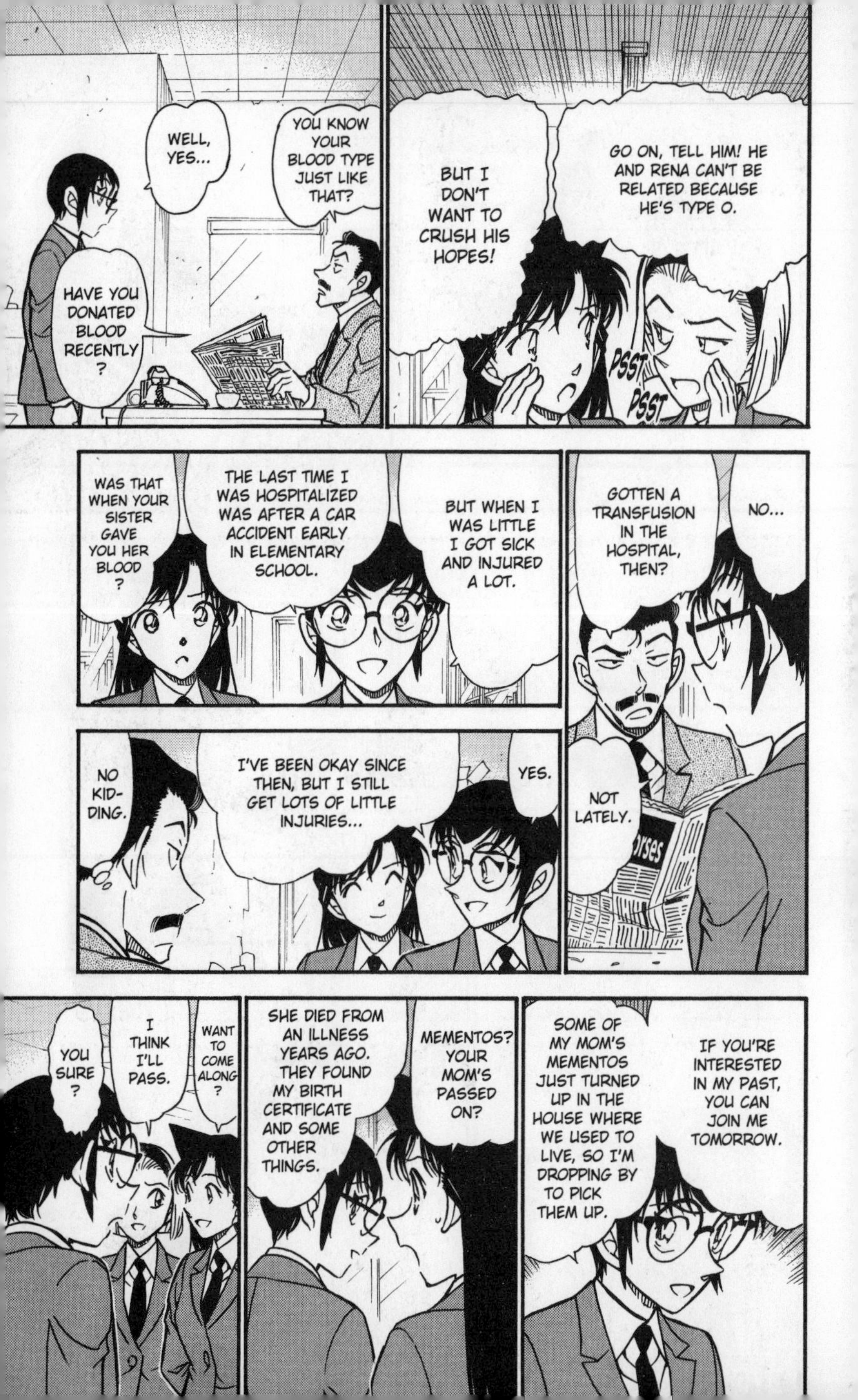
GO ON, TELL HIM! HE AND RENA CAN'T BE RELATED BECAUSE HE'S TYPE O.
BUT I DON'T WANT TO CRUSH HIS HOPES!
PSST
PSST
YOU KNOW YOUR BLOOD TYPE JUST LIKE THAT?
WELL, YES...
HAVE YOU DONATED BLOOD RECENTLY?
NO...
GOTTEN A TRANSFUSION IN THE HOSPITAL, THEN?
NOT LATELY.
BUT WHEN I WAS LITTLE I GOT SICK AND INJURED A LOT.
THE LAST TIME I WAS HOSPITALIZED WAS AFTER A CAR ACCIDENT EARLY IN ELEMENTARY SCHOOL.
WAS THAT WHEN YOUR SISTER GAVE YOU HER BLOOD?
YES.
I'VE BEEN OKAY SINCE THEN, BUT I STILL GET LOTS OF LITTLE INJURIES...
NO KIDDING.
IF YOU'RE INTERESTED IN MY PAST, YOU CAN JOIN ME TOMORROW.
SOME OF MY MOM'S MEMENTOS JUST TURNED UP IN THE HOUSE WHERE WE USED TO LIVE, SO I'M DROPPING BY TO PICK THEM UP.
MEMENTOS? YOUR MOM'S PASSED ON?
SHE DIED FROM AN ILLNESS YEARS AGO. THEY FOUND MY BIRTH CERTIFICATE AND SOME OTHER THINGS.
WANT TO COME ALONG?
I THINK I'LL PASS.
YOU SURE?

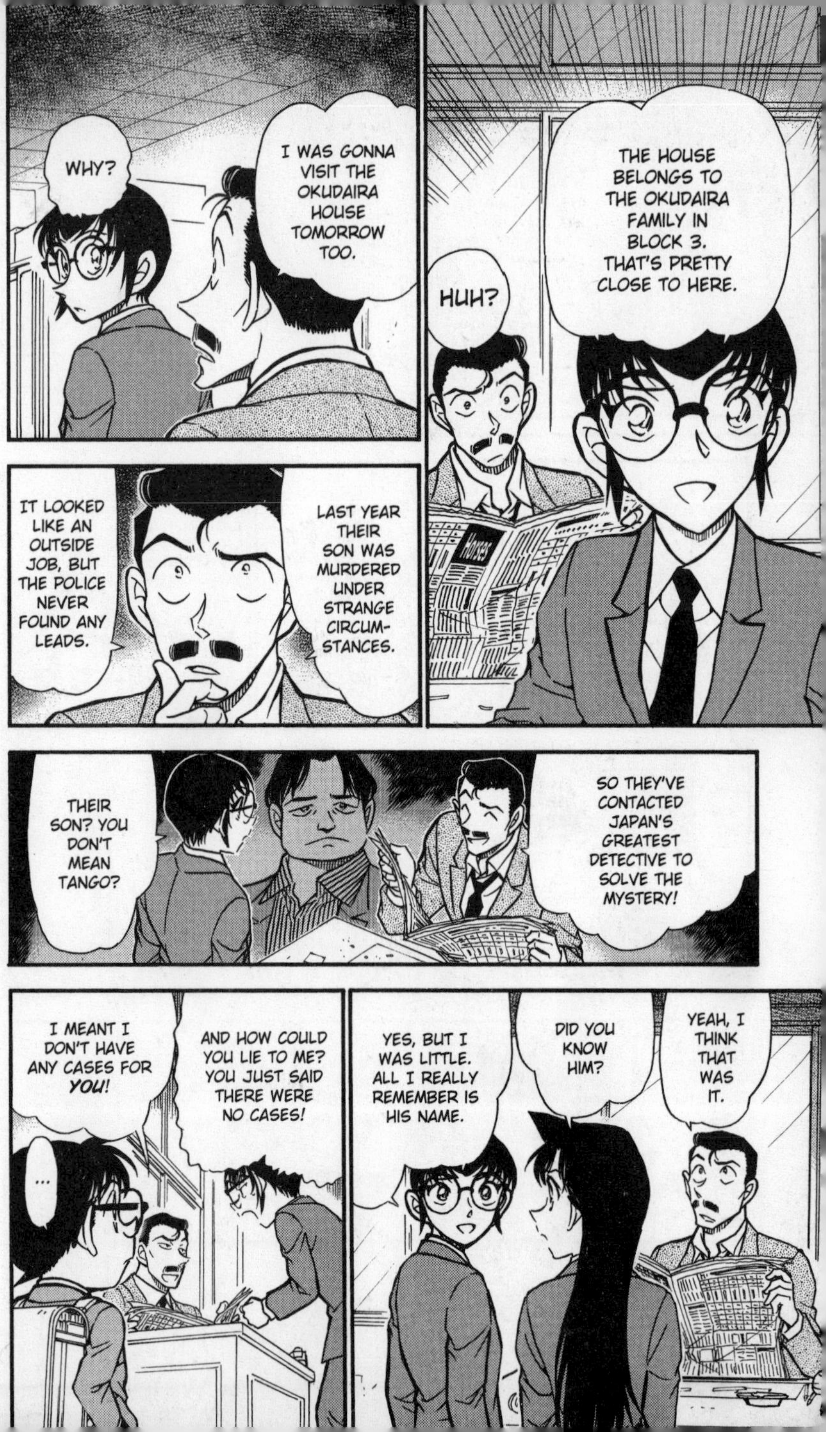
THE HOUSE BELONGS TO THE OKUDAIRA FAMILY IN BLOCK 3. THAT'S PRETTY CLOSE TO HERE.
HUH?
Horses
I WAS GONNA VISIT THE OKUDAIRA HOUSE TOMORROW TOO.
WHY?
LAST YEAR THEIR SON WAS MURDERED UNDER STRANGE CIRCUM-STANCES.
IT LOOKED LIKE AN OUTSIDE JOB, BUT THE POLICE NEVER FOUND ANY LEADS.
SO THEY'VE CONTACTED JAPAN'S GREATEST DETECTIVE TO SOLVE THE MYSTERY!
THEIR SON? YOU DON'T MEAN TANGO?
YEAH, I THINK THAT WAS IT.
DID YOU KNOW HIM?
YES, BUT I WAS LITTLE. ALL I REALLY REMEMBER IS HIS NAME.
AND HOW COULD YOU LIE TO ME? YOU JUST SAID THERE WERE NO CASES!
I MEANT I DON'T HAVE ANY CASES FOR *YOU*!
...

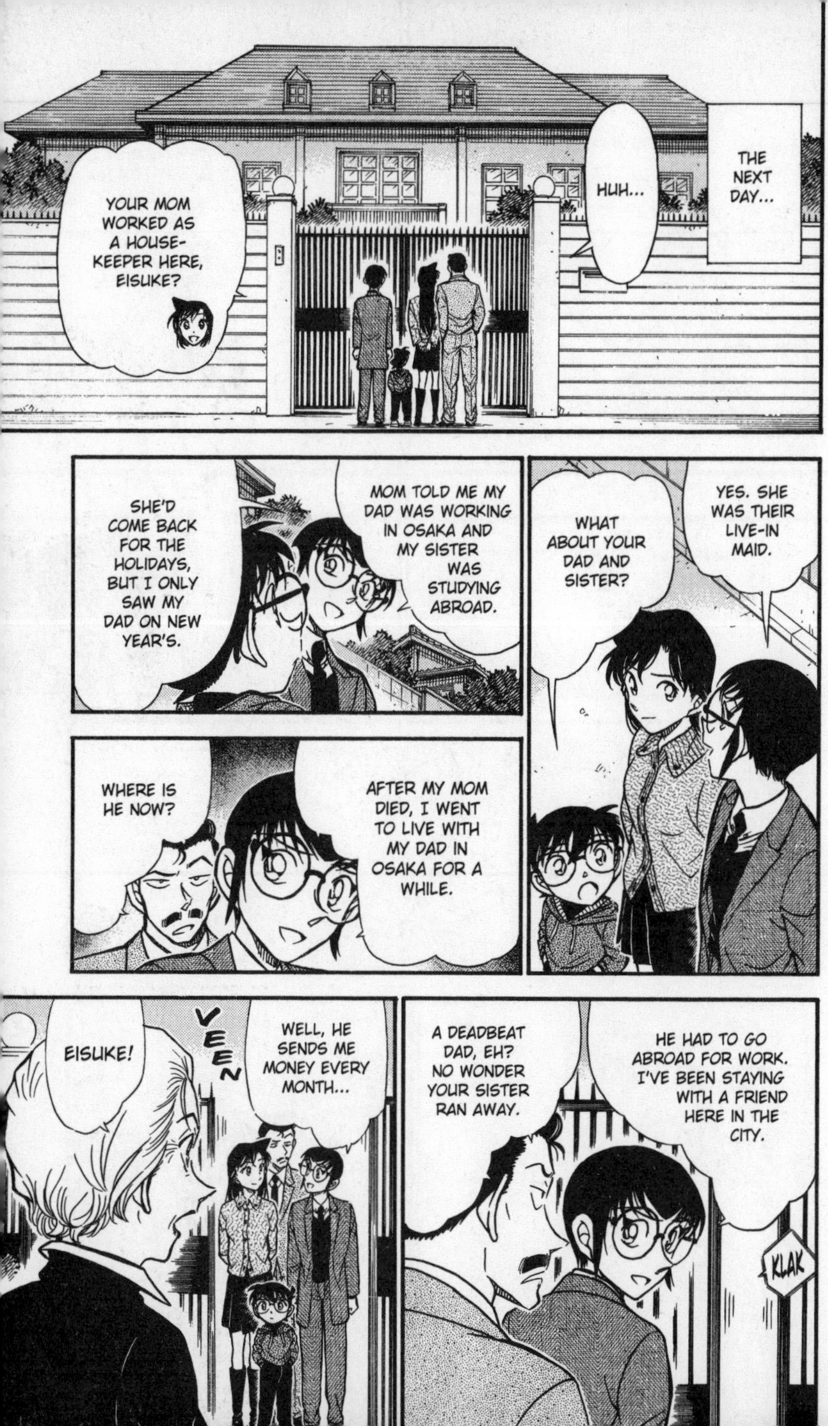
THE NEXT DAY...
HUH...
YOUR MOM WORKED AS A HOUSE-KEEPER HERE, EISUKE?
YES. SHE WAS THEIR LIVE-IN MAID.
WHAT ABOUT YOUR DAD AND SISTER?
MOM TOLD ME MY DAD WAS WORKING IN OSAKA AND MY SISTER WAS STUDYING ABROAD.
SHE'D COME BACK FOR THE HOLIDAYS, BUT I ONLY SAW MY DAD ON NEW YEAR'S.
AFTER MY MOM DIED, I WENT TO LIVE WITH MY DAD IN OSAKA FOR A WHILE.
WHERE IS HE NOW?
HE HAD TO GO ABROAD FOR WORK. I'VE BEEN STAYING WITH A FRIEND HERE IN THE CITY.
KLAK
A DEADBEAT DAD, EH? NO WONDER YOUR SISTER RAN AWAY.
WELL, HE SENDS ME MONEY EVERY MONTH...
VEEN
EISUKE!

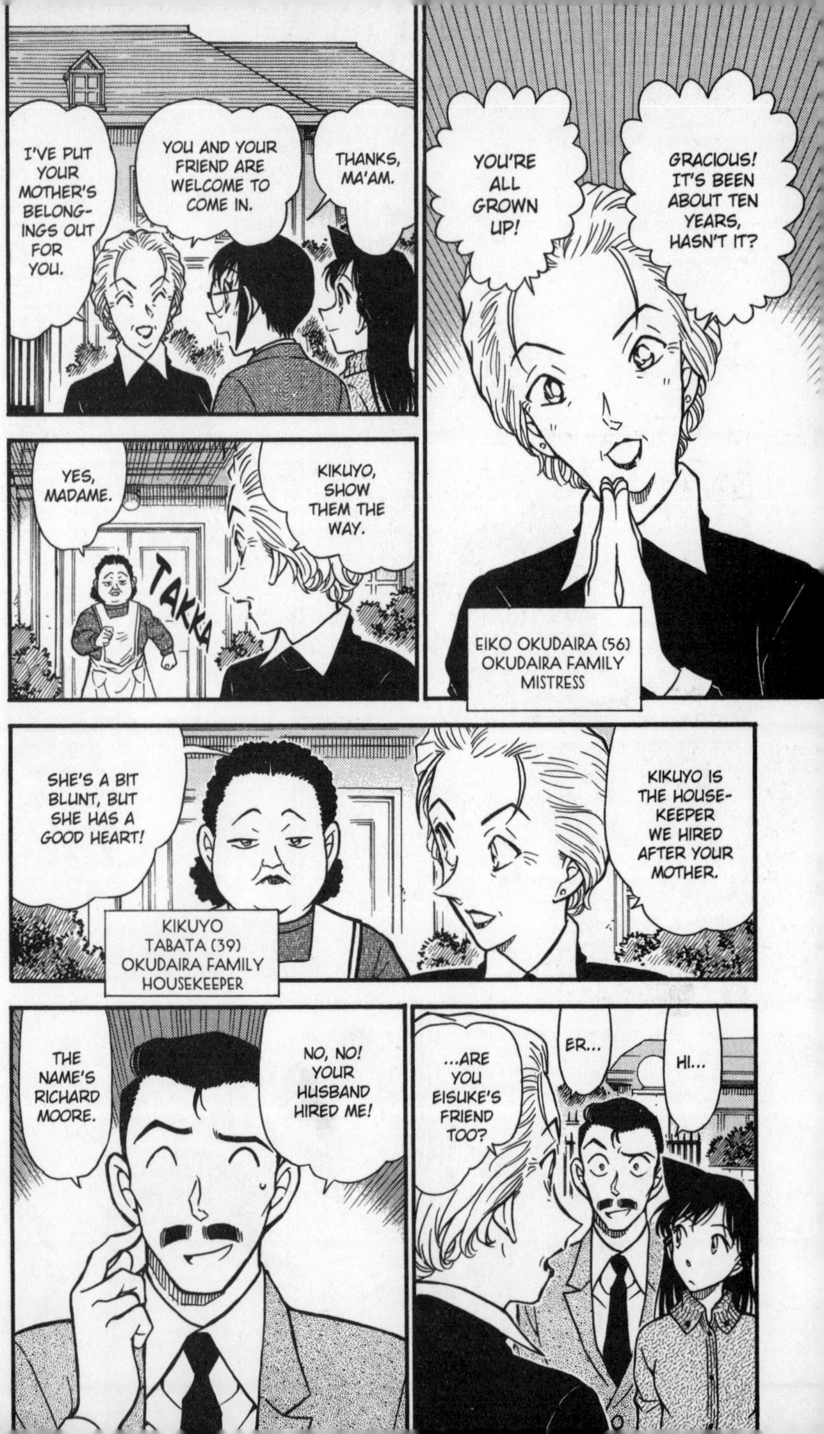
GRACIOUS! IT'S BEEN ABOUT TEN YEARS, HASN'T IT?
YOU'RE ALL GROWN UP!
EIKO OKUDAIRA (56) OKUDAIRA FAMILY MISTRESS
THANKS, MA'AM.
YOU AND YOUR FRIEND ARE WELCOME TO COME IN.
I'VE PUT YOUR MOTHER'S BELONG-INGS OUT FOR YOU.
KIKUYO, SHOW THEM THE WAY.
YES, MADAME.
TAKKA
KIKUYO IS THE HOUSE-KEEPER WE HIRED AFTER YOUR MOTHER.
SHE'S A BIT BLUNT, BUT SHE HAS A GOOD HEART!
KIKUYO TABATA (39) OKUDAIRA FAMILY HOUSEKEEPER
HI...
ER...
...ARE YOU EISUKE'S FRIEND TOO?
NO, NO! YOUR HUSBAND HIRED ME!
THE NAME'S RICHARD MOORE.

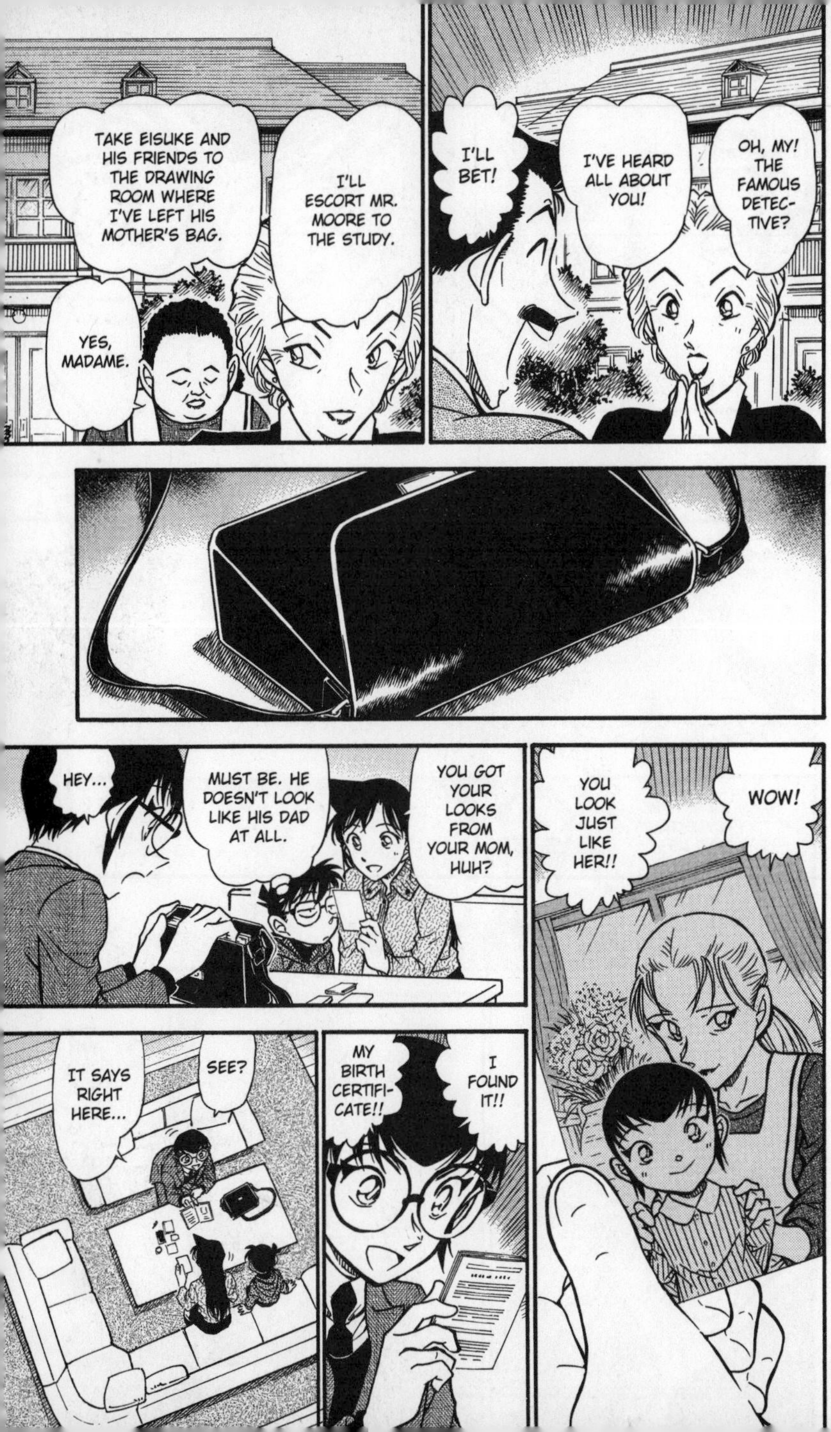
OH, MY! THE FAMOUS DETEC-TIVE?
I'VE HEARD ALL ABOUT YOU!
I'LL BET!
I'LL ESCORT MR. MOORE TO THE STUDY.
TAKE EISUKE AND HIS FRIENDS TO THE DRAWING ROOM WHERE I'VE LEFT HIS MOTHER'S BAG.
YES, MADAME.
WOW!
YOU LOOK JUST LIKE HER!!
YOU GOT YOUR LOOKS FROM YOUR MOM, HUH?
MUST BE. HE DOESN'T LOOK LIKE HIS DAD AT ALL.
HEY...
I FOUND IT!!
MY BIRTH CERTIFI-CATE!!
SEE?
IT SAYS RIGHT HERE...

THERE ARE MY VITAL STATISTICS!

HEY, YEAH.

...EISUKE HONDO, BLOOD TYPE O!

Name Eisuke Hondo

| Gender | Male | Blood Type | O | Weight | 6 lbs 15 oz |
| Length | 19.25 inches | Head | | Chest | 13 inches |

NOW I JUST NEED TO CONFIRM THAT STORY ABOUT GETTING A TRANSFUSION FROM HIS SISTER ...

WHEN WE SHOWED IT TO THE MISTRESS, SHE TOLD US IT BELONGED TO THE PREVIOUS HOUSE-KEEPER. THAT'S WHEN WE CALLED YOU.

IT WAS STUCK IN THE BACK OF A DRAWER IN MY ROOM.

SORRY THE BAG'S A LITTLE CRUSHED.

YOU'RE MISTAKEN. WHEN YOU WERE HERE, MY *OLDER BROTHER* WAS THE BUTLER.

LONG TIME NO SEE! YOU'VE HARDLY CHANGED, MR. SEGAWA!

THE MISTRESS SAID HIS SPIRIT MUST BE CALLING OUT TO OLD FRIENDS.

IT WAS ONE YEAR AGO TODAY THAT YOUNG MASTER TANGO DIED.

HATARO SEGAWA (48) OKUDAIRA FAMILY BUTLER

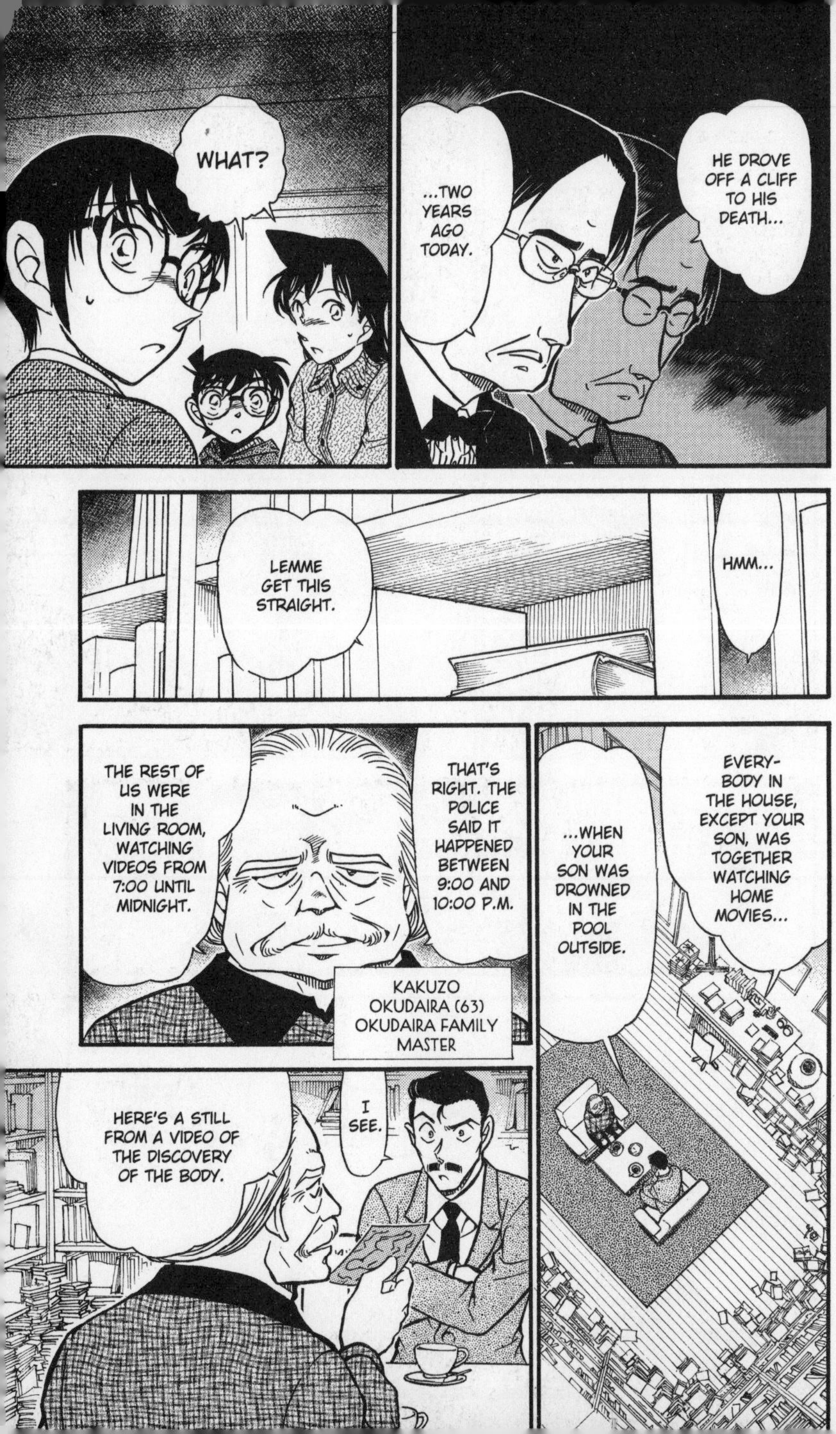
HE DROVE OFF A CLIFF TO HIS DEATH...
...TWO YEARS AGO TODAY.
WHAT?
HMM...
LEMME GET THIS STRAIGHT.
EVERY-BODY IN THE HOUSE, EXCEPT YOUR SON, WAS TOGETHER WATCHING HOME MOVIES...
...WHEN YOUR SON WAS DROWNED IN THE POOL OUTSIDE.
THAT'S RIGHT. THE POLICE SAID IT HAPPENED BETWEEN 9:00 AND 10:00 P.M.
THE REST OF US WERE IN THE LIVING ROOM, WATCHING VIDEOS FROM 7:00 UNTIL MIDNIGHT.
KAKUZO OKUDAIRA (63) OKUDAIRA FAMILY MASTER
I SEE.
HERE'S A STILL FROM A VIDEO OF THE DISCOVERY OF THE BODY.

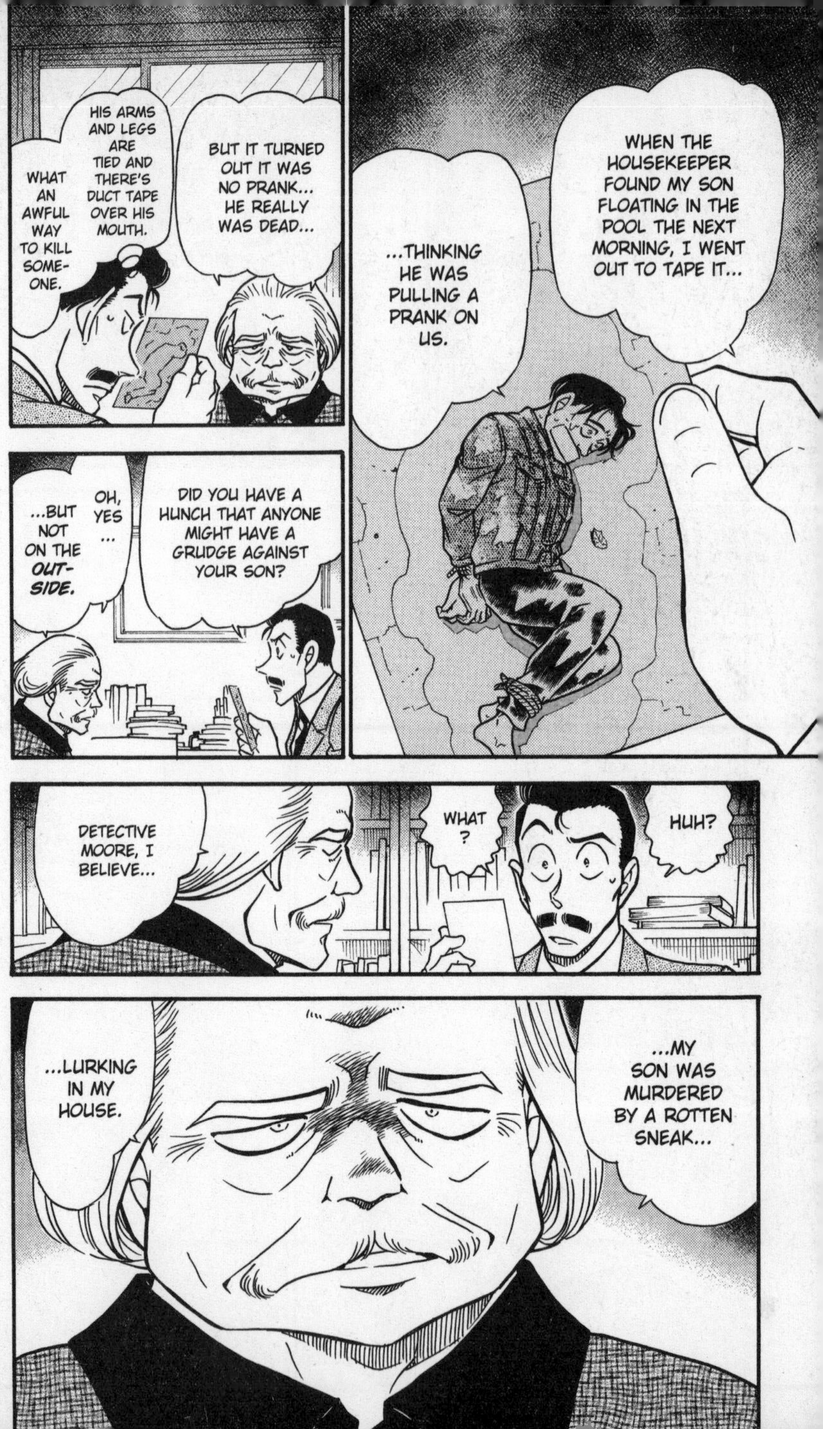
WHEN THE HOUSEKEEPER FOUND MY SON FLOATING IN THE POOL THE NEXT MORNING, I WENT OUT TO TAPE IT...
...THINKING HE WAS PULLING A PRANK ON US.
BUT IT TURNED OUT IT WAS NO PRANK... HE REALLY WAS DEAD...
HIS ARMS AND LEGS ARE TIED AND THERE'S DUCT TAPE OVER HIS MOUTH.
WHAT AN AWFUL WAY TO KILL SOME-ONE.
DID YOU HAVE A HUNCH THAT ANYONE MIGHT HAVE A GRUDGE AGAINST YOUR SON?
OH, YES...
...BUT NOT ON THE OUT-SIDE.
HUH?
WHAT?
DETECTIVE MOORE, I BELIEVE...
...MY SON WAS MURDERED BY A ROTTEN SNEAK...
...LURKING IN MY HOUSE.

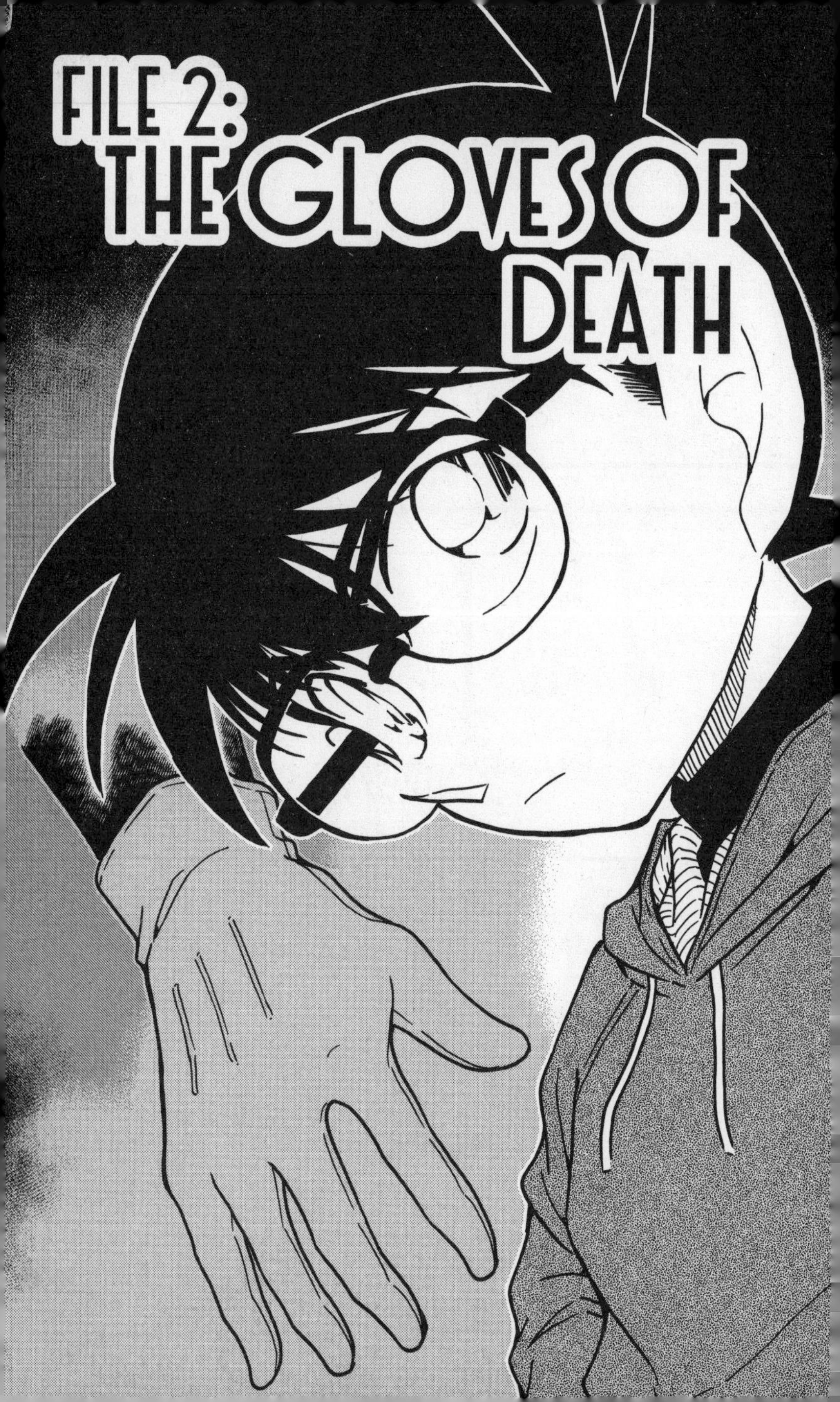
FILE 2:
THE GLOVES OF
DEATH

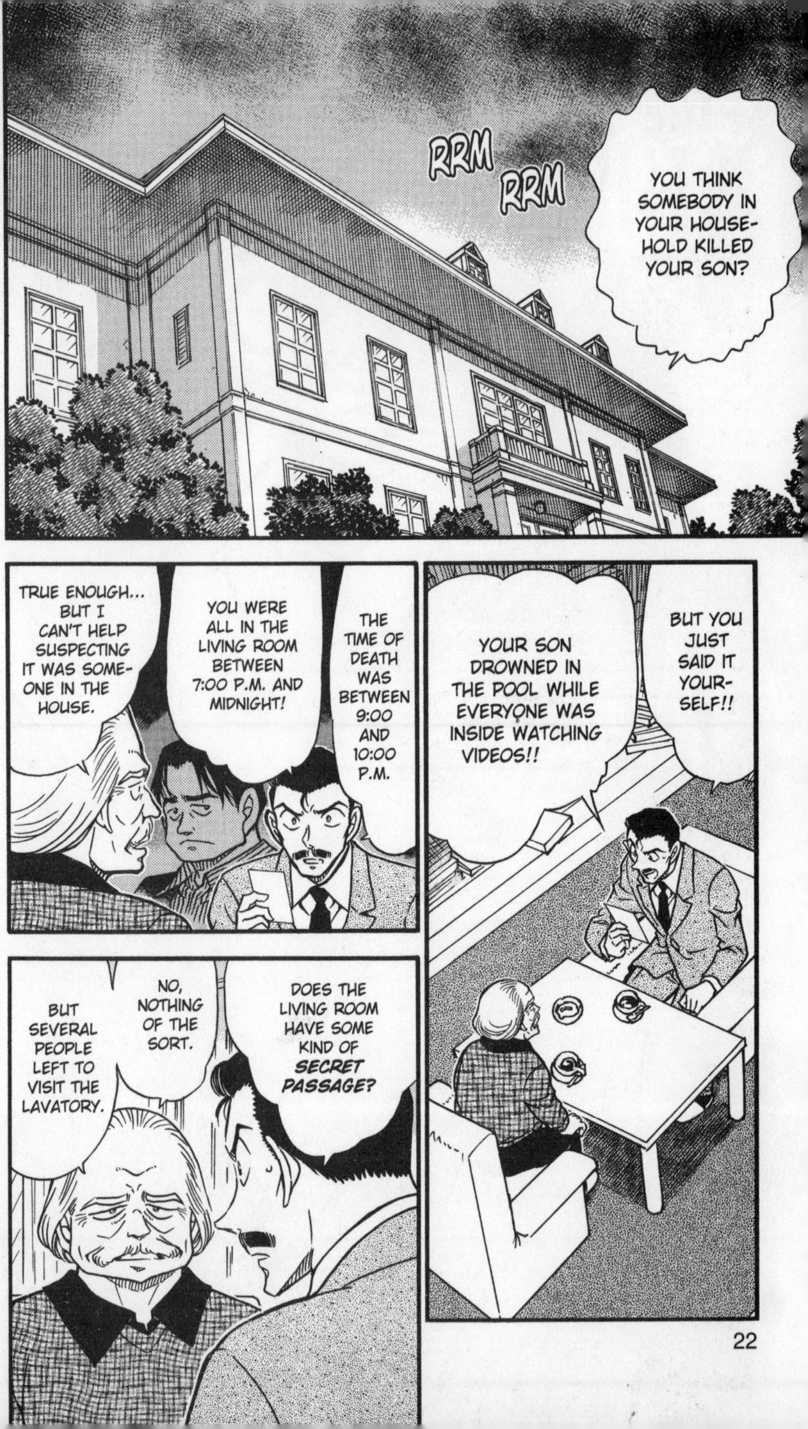
RRM
RRM
YOU THINK SOMEBODY IN YOUR HOUSE-HOLD KILLED YOUR SON?
BUT YOU JUST SAID IT YOUR-SELF!!
YOUR SON DROWNED IN THE POOL WHILE EVERYONE WAS INSIDE WATCHING VIDEOS!!
THE TIME OF DEATH WAS BETWEEN 9:00 AND 10:00 P.M.
YOU WERE ALL IN THE LIVING ROOM BETWEEN 7:00 P.M. AND MIDNIGHT!
TRUE ENOUGH... BUT I CAN'T HELP SUSPECTING IT WAS SOME-ONE IN THE HOUSE.
DOES THE LIVING ROOM HAVE SOME KIND OF *SECRET PASSAGE?*
NO, NOTHING OF THE SORT.
BUT SEVERAL PEOPLE LEFT TO VISIT THE LAVATORY.

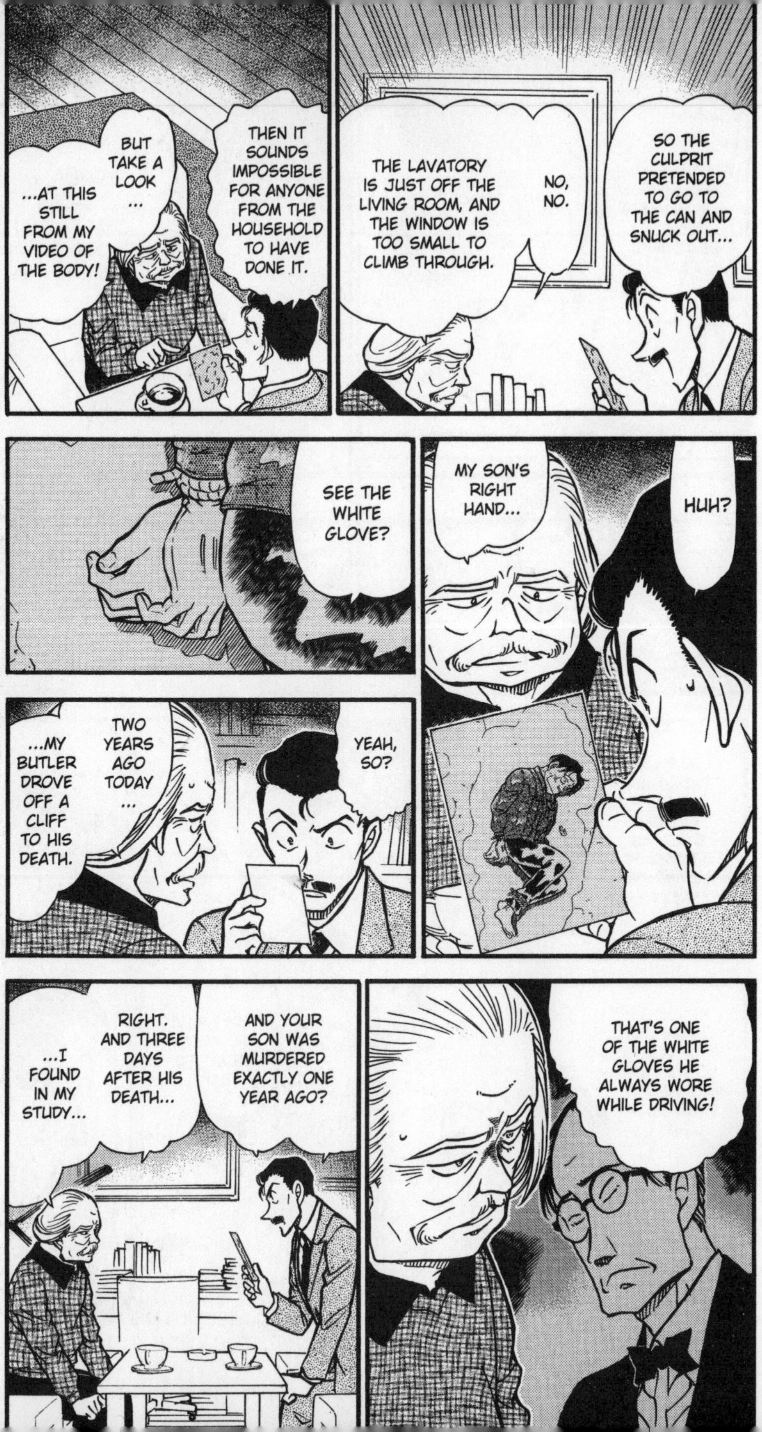
SO THE CULPRIT PRETENDED TO GO TO THE CAN AND SNUCK OUT...
NO, NO.
THE LAVATORY IS JUST OFF THE LIVING ROOM, AND THE WINDOW IS TOO SMALL TO CLIMB THROUGH.
THEN IT SOUNDS IMPOSSIBLE FOR ANYONE FROM THE HOUSEHOLD TO HAVE DONE IT.
BUT TAKE A LOOK ...
...AT THIS STILL FROM MY VIDEO OF THE BODY!
HUH?
MY SON'S RIGHT HAND...
SEE THE WHITE GLOVE?
YEAH, SO?
TWO YEARS AGO TODAY ...
...MY BUTLER DROVE OFF A CLIFF TO HIS DEATH.
THAT'S ONE OF THE WHITE GLOVES HE ALWAYS WORE WHILE DRIVING!
AND YOUR SON WAS MURDERED EXACTLY ONE YEAR AGO?
RIGHT. AND THREE DAYS AFTER HIS DEATH...
...I FOUND IN MY STUDY...

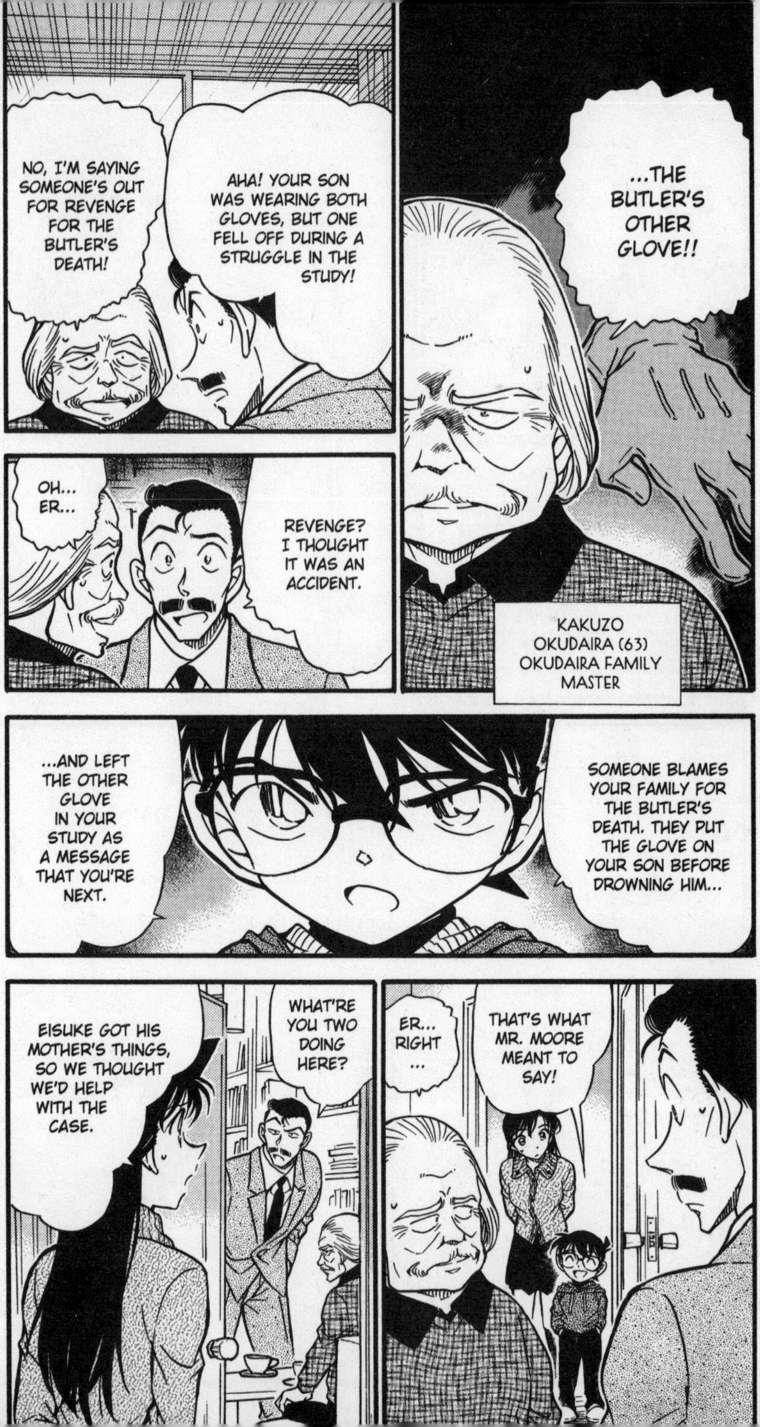
...THE BUTLER'S OTHER GLOVE!!
KAKUZO OKUDAIRA (63) OKUDAIRA FAMILY MASTER
AHA! YOUR SON WAS WEARING BOTH GLOVES, BUT ONE FELL OFF DURING A STRUGGLE IN THE STUDY!
NO, I'M SAYING SOMEONE'S OUT FOR REVENGE FOR THE BUTLER'S DEATH!
REVENGE? I THOUGHT IT WAS AN ACCIDENT.
OH... ER...
SOMEONE BLAMES YOUR FAMILY FOR THE BUTLER'S DEATH. THEY PUT THE GLOVE ON YOUR SON BEFORE DROWNING HIM...
...AND LEFT THE OTHER GLOVE IN YOUR STUDY AS A MESSAGE THAT YOU'RE NEXT.
THAT'S WHAT MR. MOORE MEANT TO SAY!
ER... RIGHT ...
WHAT'RE YOU TWO DOING HERE?
EISUKE GOT HIS MOTHER'S THINGS, SO WE THOUGHT WE'D HELP WITH THE CASE.

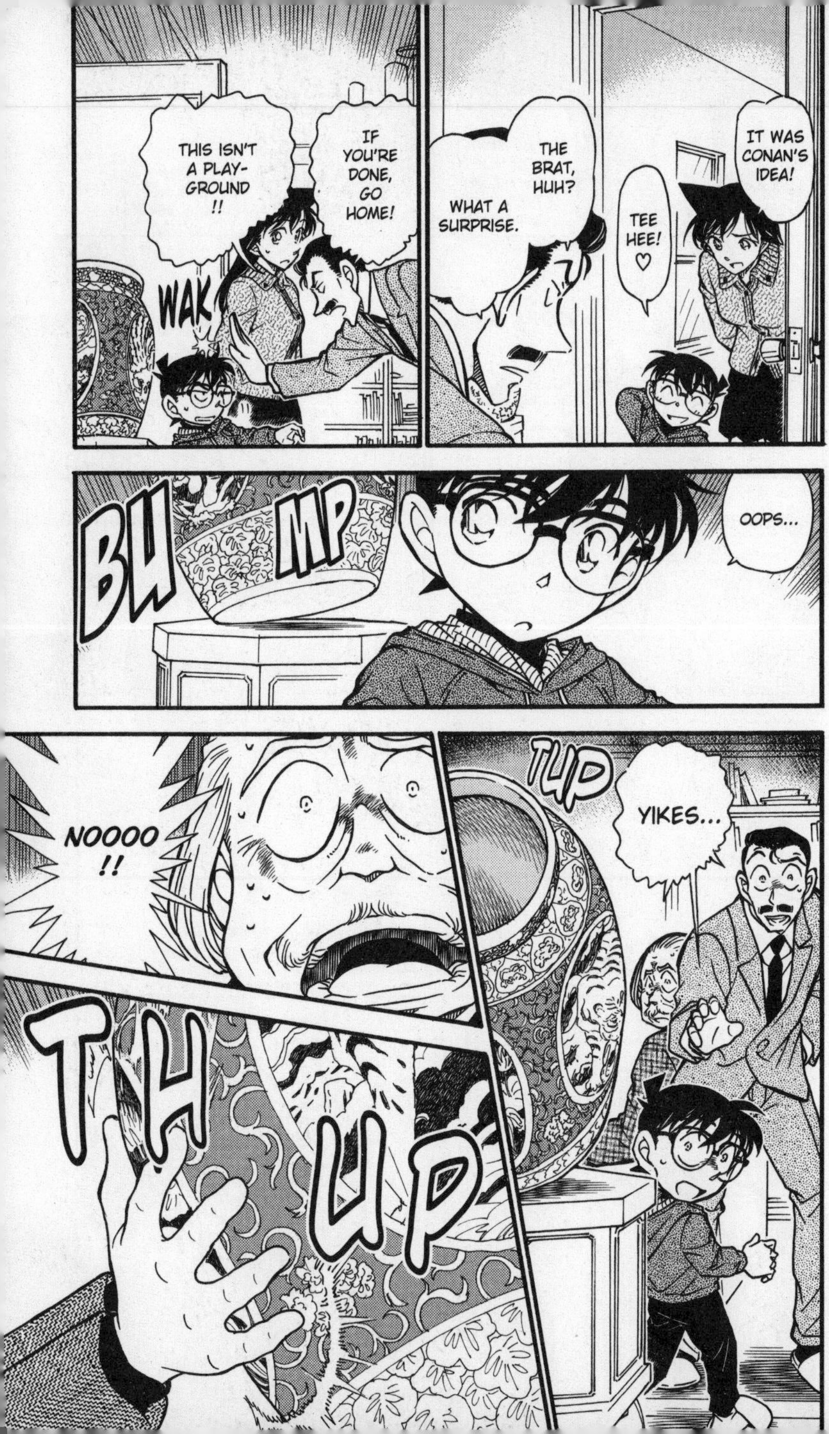
IT WAS CONAN'S IDEA!
TEE HEE! ♡
THE BRAT, HUH?
WHAT A SURPRISE.
IF YOU'RE DONE, GO HOME!
THIS ISN'T A PLAY-GROUND!!
WAK
OOPS...
BUMP
TUP
YIKES...
NOOOO!!
THUP

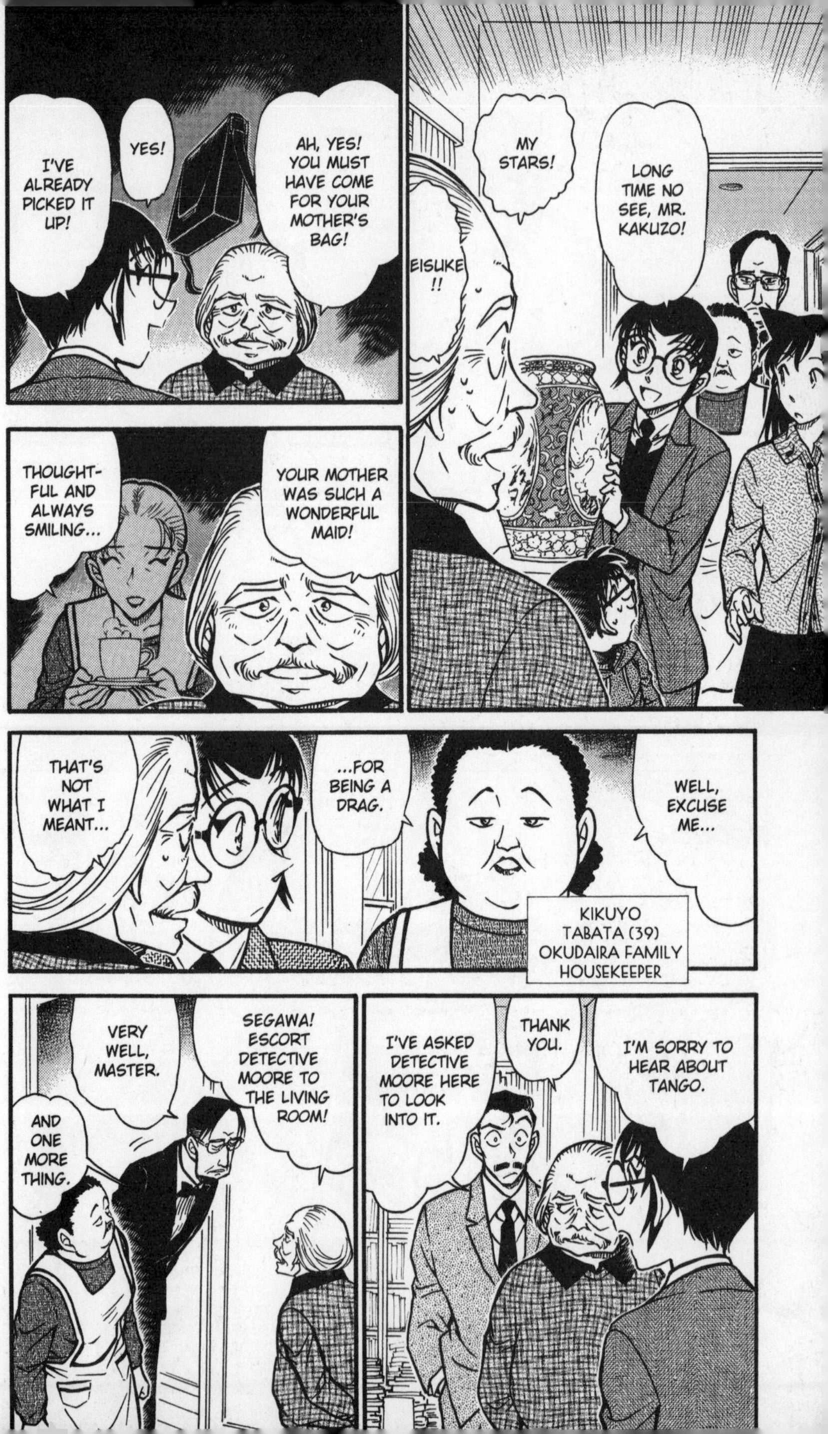
LONG TIME NO SEE, MR. KAKUZO!
MY STARS!
EISUKE !!
AH, YES! YOU MUST HAVE COME FOR YOUR MOTHER'S BAG!
YES!
I'VE ALREADY PICKED IT UP!
YOUR MOTHER WAS SUCH A WONDERFUL MAID!
THOUGHTFUL AND ALWAYS SMILING...
WELL, EXCUSE ME...
KIKUYO TABATA (39) OKUDAIRA FAMILY HOUSEKEEPER
...FOR BEING A DRAG.
THAT'S NOT WHAT I MEANT...
I'M SORRY TO HEAR ABOUT TANGO.
THANK YOU.
I'VE ASKED DETECTIVE MOORE HERE TO LOOK INTO IT.
SEGAWA! ESCORT DETECTIVE MOORE TO THE LIVING ROOM!
VERY WELL, MASTER.
AND ONE MORE THING.

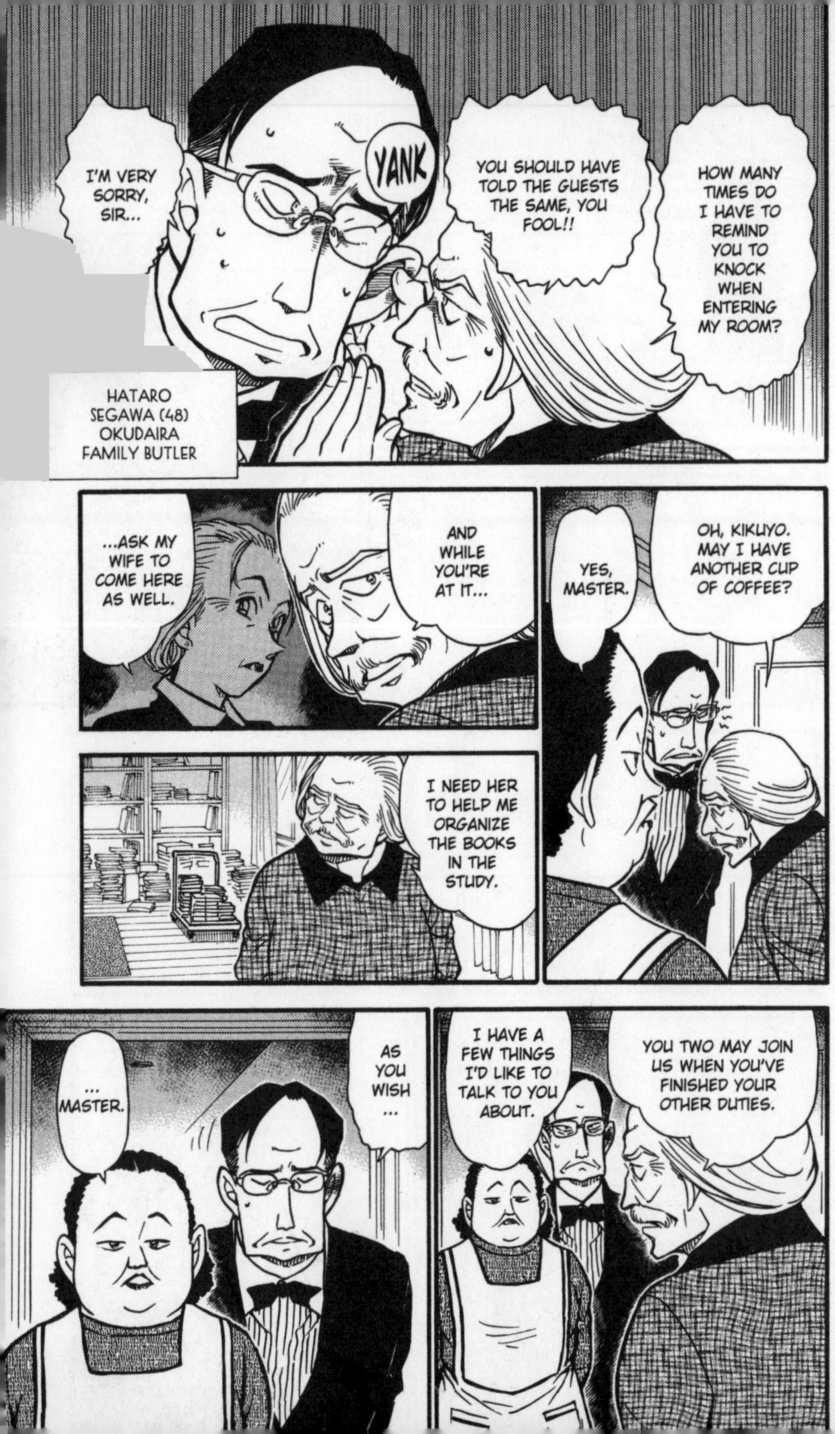
HOW MANY TIMES DO I HAVE TO REMIND YOU TO KNOCK WHEN ENTERING MY ROOM?
YOU SHOULD HAVE TOLD THE GUESTS THE SAME, YOU FOOL!!
YANK
I'M VERY SORRY, SIR...
HATARO SEGAWA (48) OKUDAIRA FAMILY BUTLER
OH, KIKUYO. MAY I HAVE ANOTHER CUP OF COFFEE?
YES, MASTER.
AND WHILE YOU'RE AT IT...
...ASK MY WIFE TO COME HERE AS WELL.
I NEED HER TO HELP ME ORGANIZE THE BOOKS IN THE STUDY.
YOU TWO MAY JOIN US WHEN YOU'VE FINISHED YOUR OTHER DUTIES.
I HAVE A FEW THINGS I'D LIKE TO TALK TO YOU ABOUT.
AS YOU WISH ...
... MASTER.

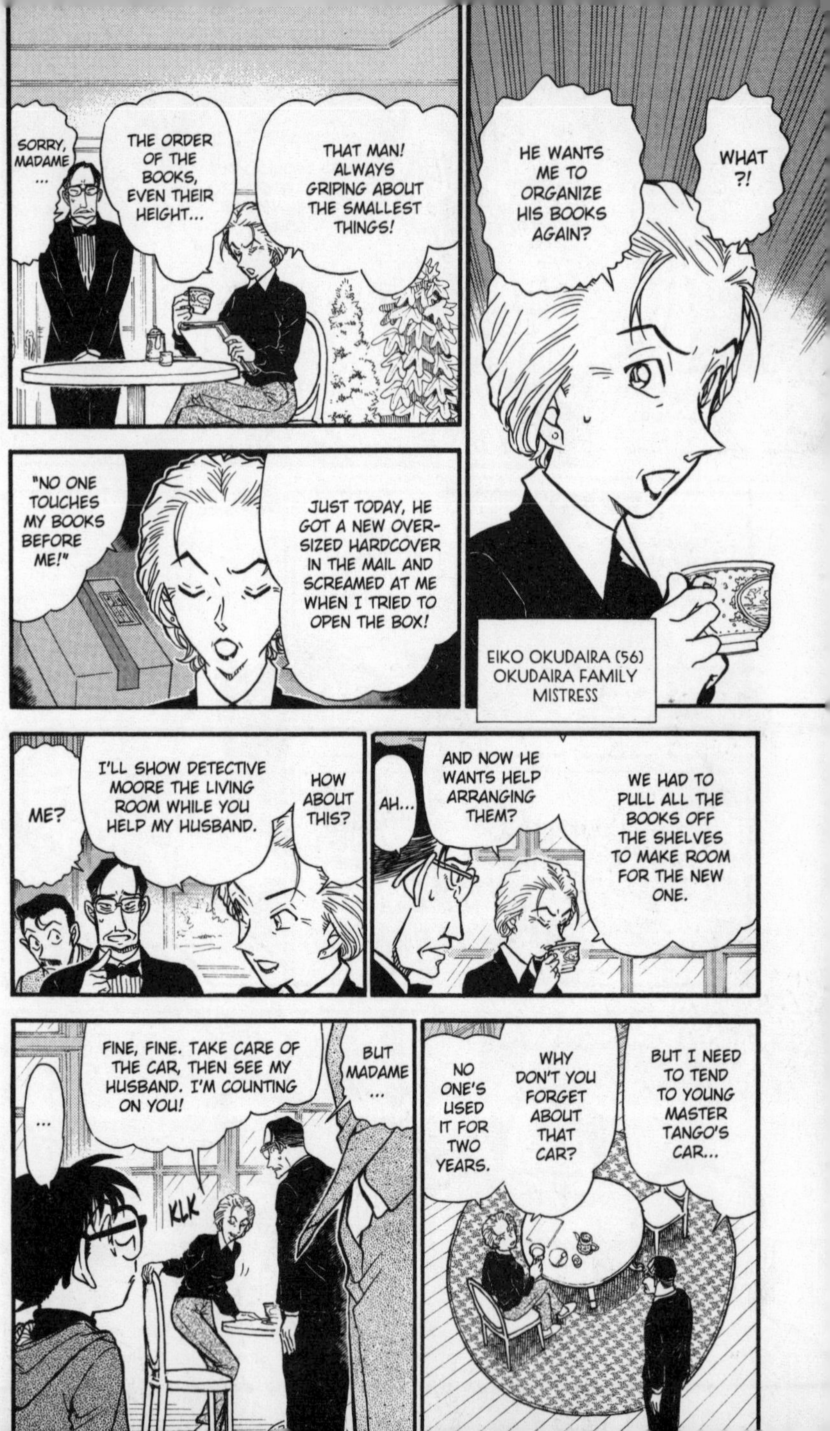
WHAT ?!
HE WANTS ME TO ORGANIZE HIS BOOKS AGAIN?
EIKO OKUDAIRA (56) OKUDAIRA FAMILY MISTRESS
THAT MAN! ALWAYS GRIPING ABOUT THE SMALLEST THINGS!
THE ORDER OF THE BOOKS, EVEN THEIR HEIGHT...
SORRY, MADAME ...
JUST TODAY, HE GOT A NEW OVER-SIZED HARDCOVER IN THE MAIL AND SCREAMED AT ME WHEN I TRIED TO OPEN THE BOX!
"NO ONE TOUCHES MY BOOKS BEFORE ME!"
WE HAD TO PULL ALL THE BOOKS OFF THE SHELVES TO MAKE ROOM FOR THE NEW ONE.
AND NOW HE WANTS HELP ARRANGING THEM?
AH...
HOW ABOUT THIS?
I'LL SHOW DETECTIVE MOORE THE LIVING ROOM WHILE YOU HELP MY HUSBAND.
ME?
BUT I NEED TO TEND TO YOUNG MASTER TANGO'S CAR...
WHY DON'T YOU FORGET ABOUT THAT CAR?
NO ONE'S USED IT FOR TWO YEARS.
BUT MADAME ...
FINE, FINE. TAKE CARE OF THE CAR, THEN SEE MY HUSBAND. I'M COUNTING ON YOU!
KLK
...

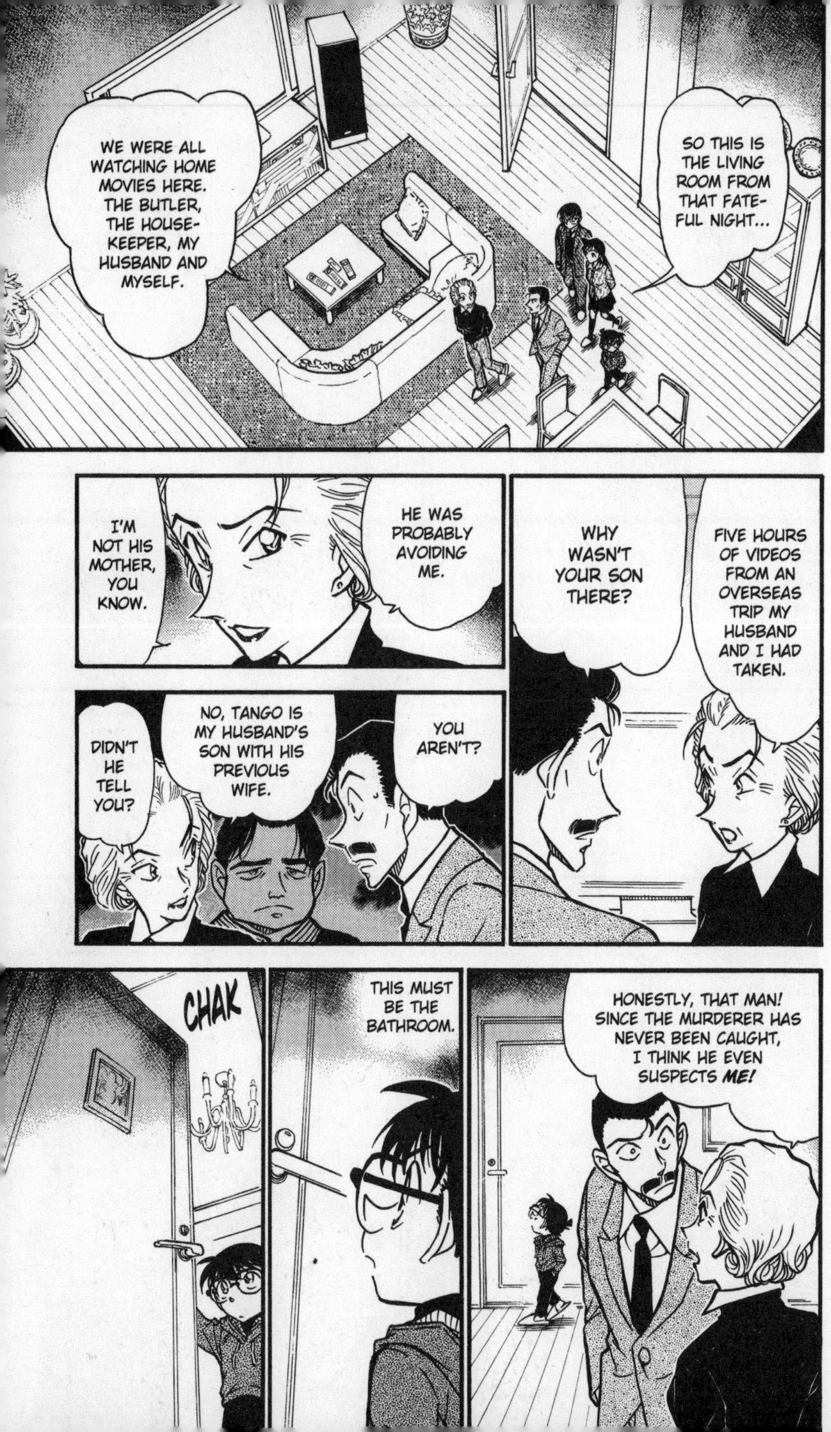
SO THIS IS THE LIVING ROOM FROM THAT FATEFUL NIGHT...
WE WERE ALL WATCHING HOME MOVIES HERE. THE BUTLER, THE HOUSEKEEPER, MY HUSBAND AND MYSELF.
FIVE HOURS OF VIDEOS FROM AN OVERSEAS TRIP MY HUSBAND AND I HAD TAKEN.
WHY WASN'T YOUR SON THERE?
HE WAS PROBABLY AVOIDING ME.
I'M NOT HIS MOTHER, YOU KNOW.
YOU AREN'T?
NO, TANGO IS MY HUSBAND'S SON WITH HIS PREVIOUS WIFE.
DIDN'T HE TELL YOU?
HONESTLY, THAT MAN! SINCE THE MURDERER HAS NEVER BEEN CAUGHT, I THINK HE EVEN SUSPECTS ***ME!***
THIS MUST BE THE BATHROOM.
CHAK

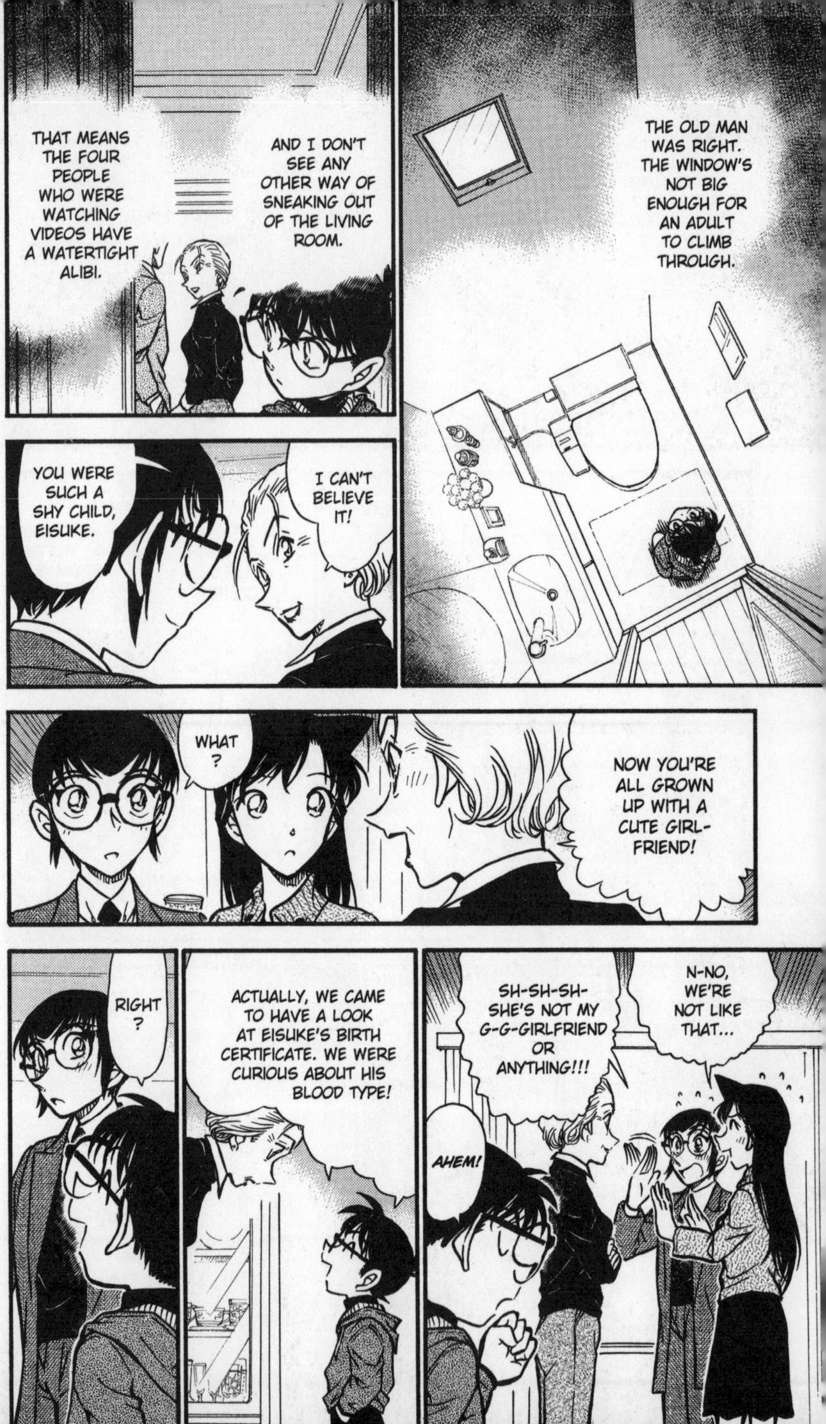
THE OLD MAN WAS RIGHT. THE WINDOW'S NOT BIG ENOUGH FOR AN ADULT TO CLIMB THROUGH.
AND I DON'T SEE ANY OTHER WAY OF SNEAKING OUT OF THE LIVING ROOM.
THAT MEANS THE FOUR PEOPLE WHO WERE WATCHING VIDEOS HAVE A WATERTIGHT ALIBI.
I CAN'T BELIEVE IT!
YOU WERE SUCH A SHY CHILD, EISUKE.
NOW YOU'RE ALL GROWN UP WITH A CUTE GIRL-FRIEND!
WHAT?
N-NO, WE'RE NOT LIKE THAT...
SH-SH-SH-SHE'S NOT MY G-G-GIRLFRIEND OR ANYTHING!!!
AHEM!
ACTUALLY, WE CAME TO HAVE A LOOK AT EISUKE'S BIRTH CERTIFICATE. WE WERE CURIOUS ABOUT HIS BLOOD TYPE!
RIGHT?

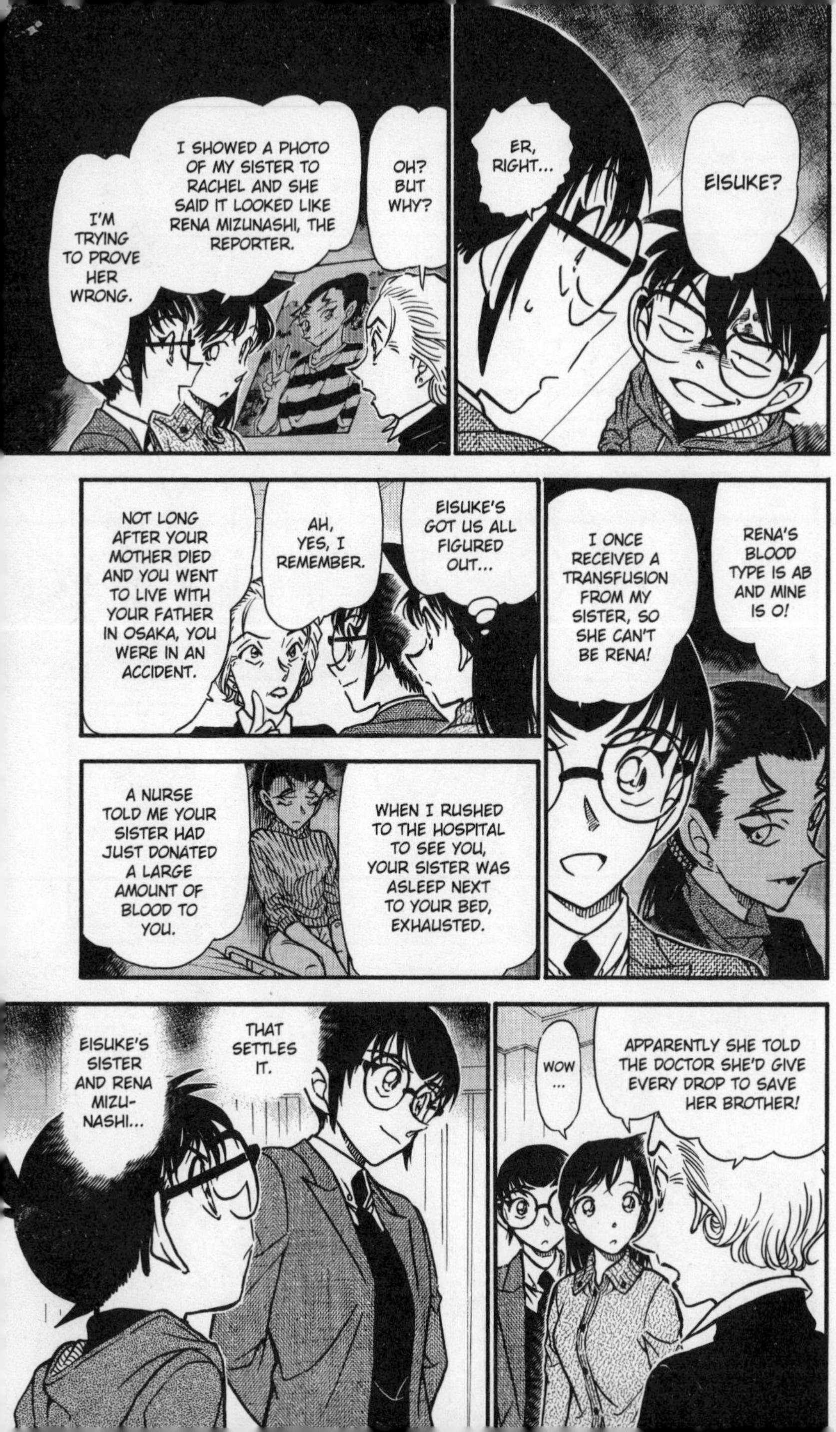
EISUKE?
ER, RIGHT...
OH? BUT WHY?
I SHOWED A PHOTO OF MY SISTER TO RACHEL AND SHE SAID IT LOOKED LIKE RENA MIZUNASHI, THE REPORTER.
I'M TRYING TO PROVE HER WRONG.
RENA'S BLOOD TYPE IS AB AND MINE IS O!
I ONCE RECEIVED A TRANSFUSION FROM MY SISTER, SO SHE CAN'T BE RENA!
EISUKE'S GOT US ALL FIGURED OUT...
AH, YES, I REMEMBER.
NOT LONG AFTER YOUR MOTHER DIED AND YOU WENT TO LIVE WITH YOUR FATHER IN OSAKA, YOU WERE IN AN ACCIDENT.
WHEN I RUSHED TO THE HOSPITAL TO SEE YOU, YOUR SISTER WAS ASLEEP NEXT TO YOUR BED, EXHAUSTED.
A NURSE TOLD ME YOUR SISTER HAD JUST DONATED A LARGE AMOUNT OF BLOOD TO YOU.
APPARENTLY SHE TOLD THE DOCTOR SHE'D GIVE EVERY DROP TO SAVE HER BROTHER!
WOW ...
THAT SETTLES IT.
EISUKE'S SISTER AND RENA MIZUNASHI...

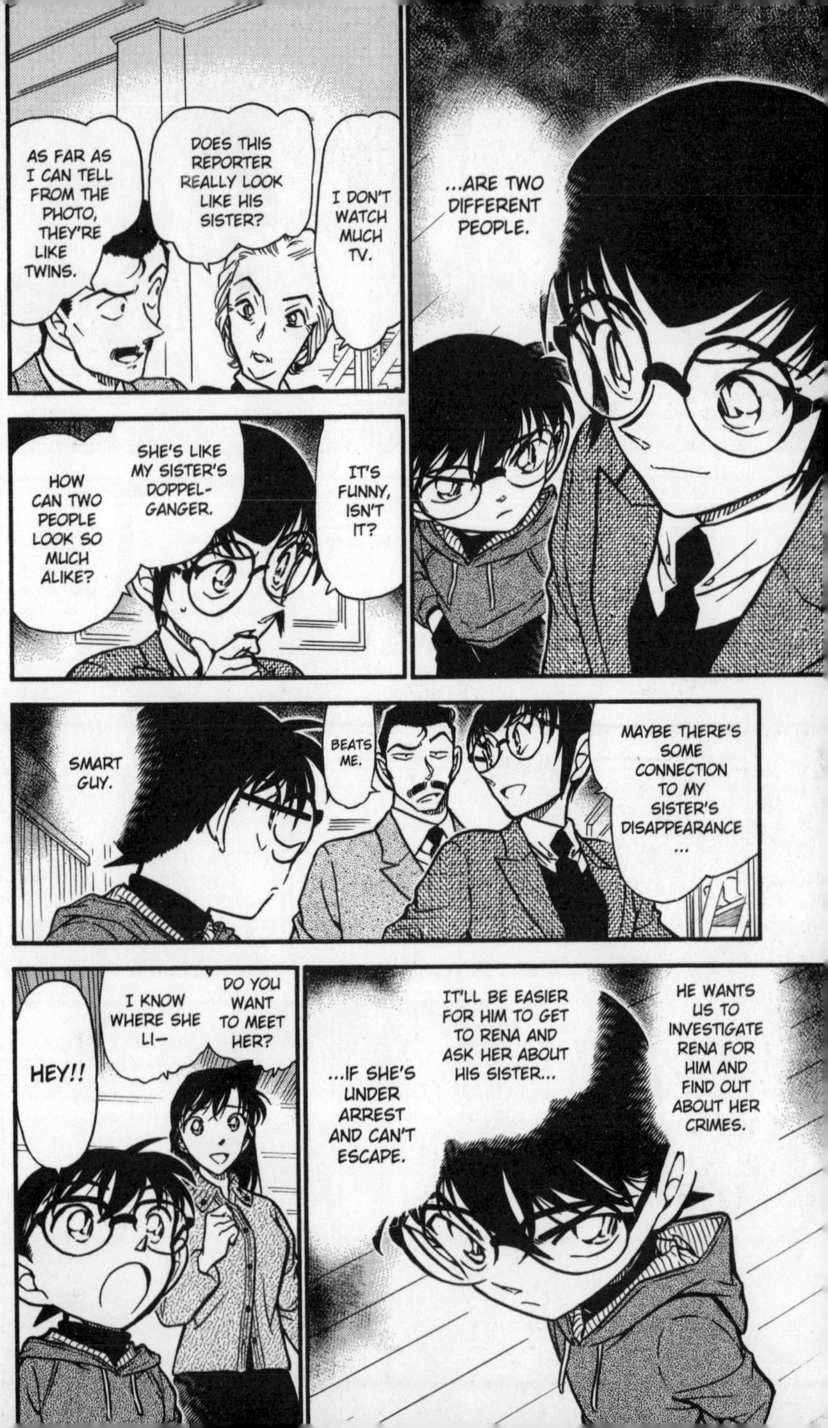
...ARE TWO DIFFERENT PEOPLE.
I DON'T WATCH MUCH TV.
DOES THIS REPORTER REALLY LOOK LIKE HIS SISTER?
AS FAR AS I CAN TELL FROM THE PHOTO, THEY'RE LIKE TWINS.
IT'S FUNNY, ISN'T IT?
SHE'S LIKE MY SISTER'S DOPPEL-GANGER.
HOW CAN TWO PEOPLE LOOK SO MUCH ALIKE?
MAYBE THERE'S SOME CONNECTION TO MY SISTER'S DISAPPEARANCE ...
BEATS ME.
SMART GUY.
HE WANTS US TO INVESTIGATE RENA FOR HIM AND FIND OUT ABOUT HER CRIMES.
IT'LL BE EASIER FOR HIM TO GET TO RENA AND ASK HER ABOUT HIS SISTER...
...IF SHE'S UNDER ARREST AND CAN'T ESCAPE.
DO YOU WANT TO MEET HER?
I KNOW WHERE SHE LI—
HEY!!

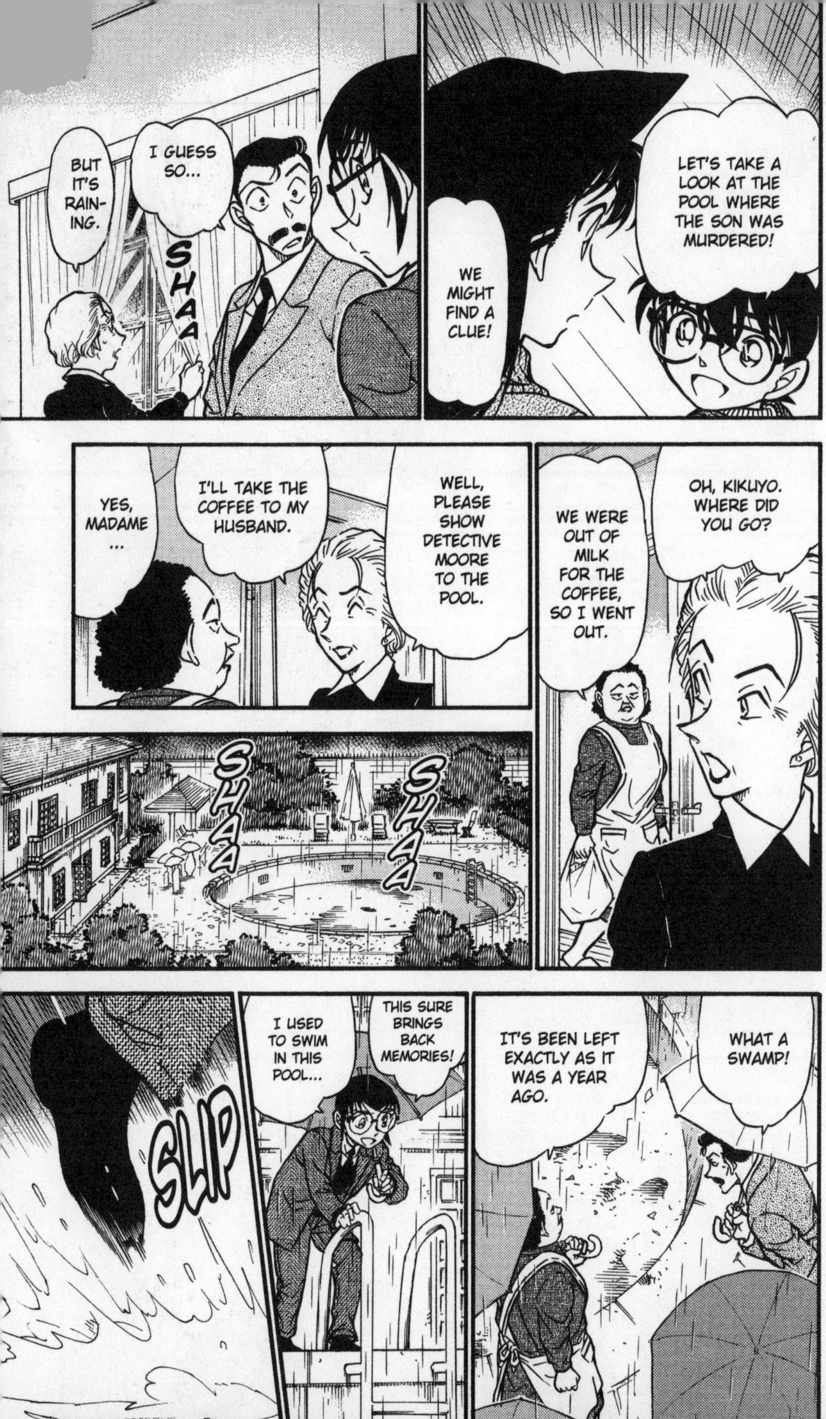
LET'S TAKE A LOOK AT THE POOL WHERE THE SON WAS MURDERED!
WE MIGHT FIND A CLUE!
I GUESS SO...
BUT IT'S RAINING.
SHAA
OH, KIKUYO. WHERE DID YOU GO?
WE WERE OUT OF MILK FOR THE COFFEE, SO I WENT OUT.
WELL, PLEASE SHOW DETECTIVE MOORE TO THE POOL.
I'LL TAKE THE COFFEE TO MY HUSBAND.
YES, MADAME ...
SHAA
SHAA
WHAT A SWAMP!
IT'S BEEN LEFT EXACTLY AS IT WAS A YEAR AGO.
THIS SURE BRINGS BACK MEMORIES!
I USED TO SWIM IN THIS POOL...
SLIP

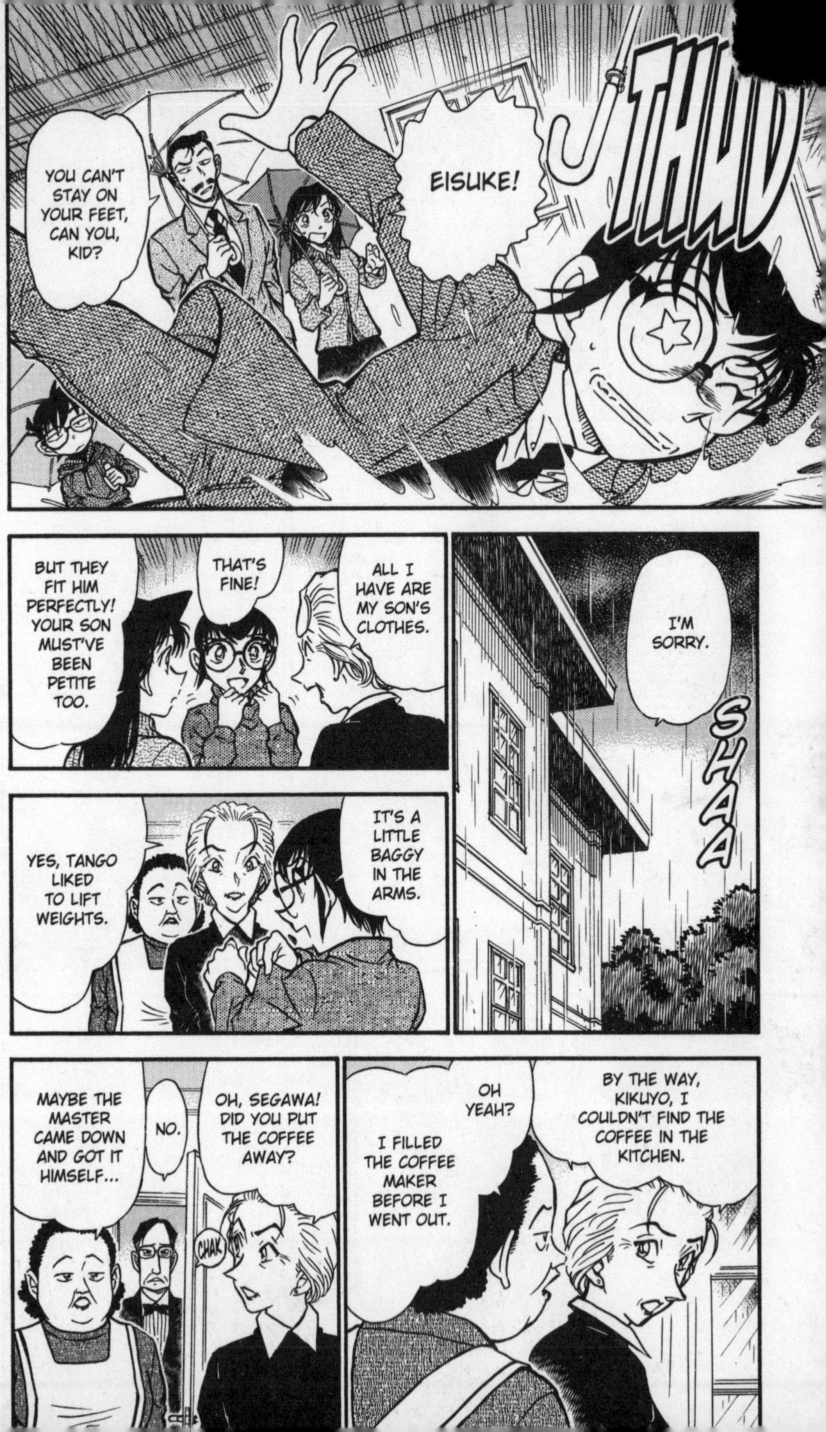
THUD
EISUKE!
YOU CAN'T STAY ON YOUR FEET, CAN YOU, KID?
I'M SORRY.
SHAA
ALL I HAVE ARE MY SON'S CLOTHES.
THAT'S FINE!
BUT THEY FIT HIM PERFECTLY! YOUR SON MUST'VE BEEN PETITE TOO.
IT'S A LITTLE BAGGY IN THE ARMS.
YES, TANGO LIKED TO LIFT WEIGHTS.
BY THE WAY, KIKUYO, I COULDN'T FIND THE COFFEE IN THE KITCHEN.
OH YEAH?
I FILLED THE COFFEE MAKER BEFORE I WENT OUT.
OH, SEGAWA! DID YOU PUT THE COFFEE AWAY?
CHAK
NO.
MAYBE THE MASTER CAME DOWN AND GOT IT HIMSELF...

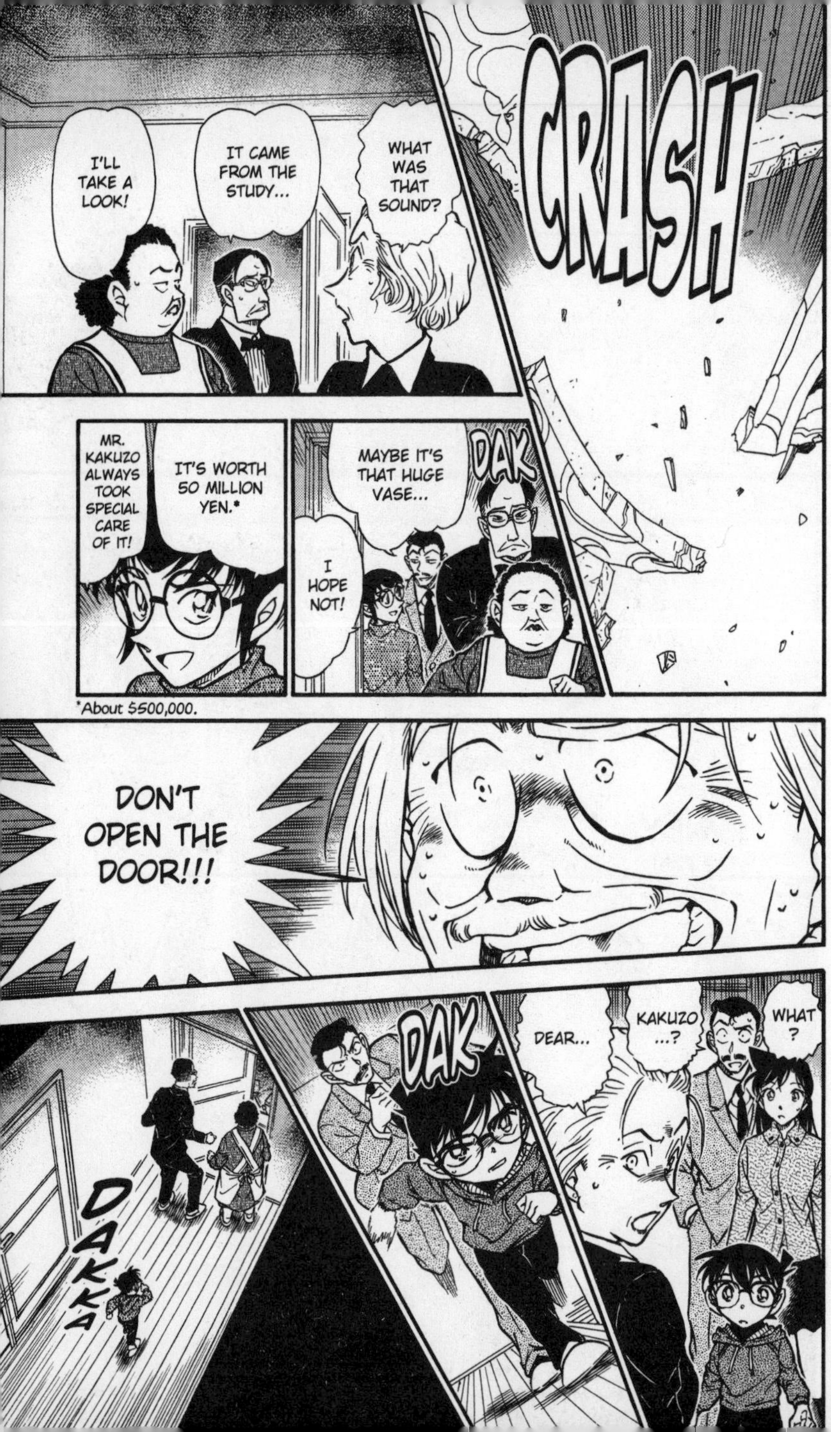
CRASH
WHAT WAS THAT SOUND?
IT CAME FROM THE STUDY...
I'LL TAKE A LOOK!
DAK
MAYBE IT'S THAT HUGE VASE...
I HOPE NOT!
IT'S WORTH 50 MILLION YEN.*
MR. KAKUZO ALWAYS TOOK SPECIAL CARE OF IT!
DON'T OPEN THE DOOR!!!
WHAT ?
KAKUZO ...?
DEAR...
DAK
DAKKA

*About $500,000.

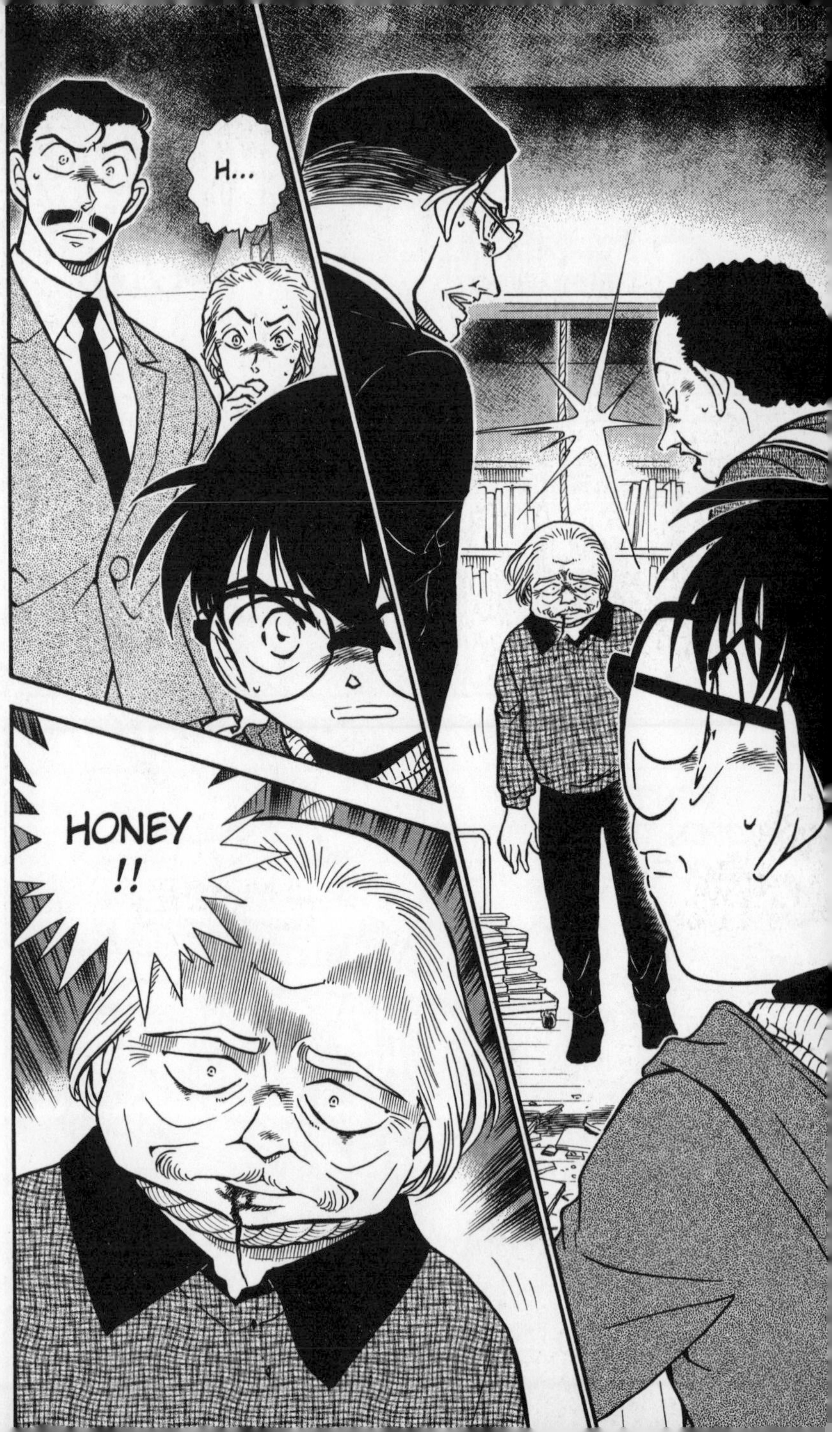
H...
HONEY !!

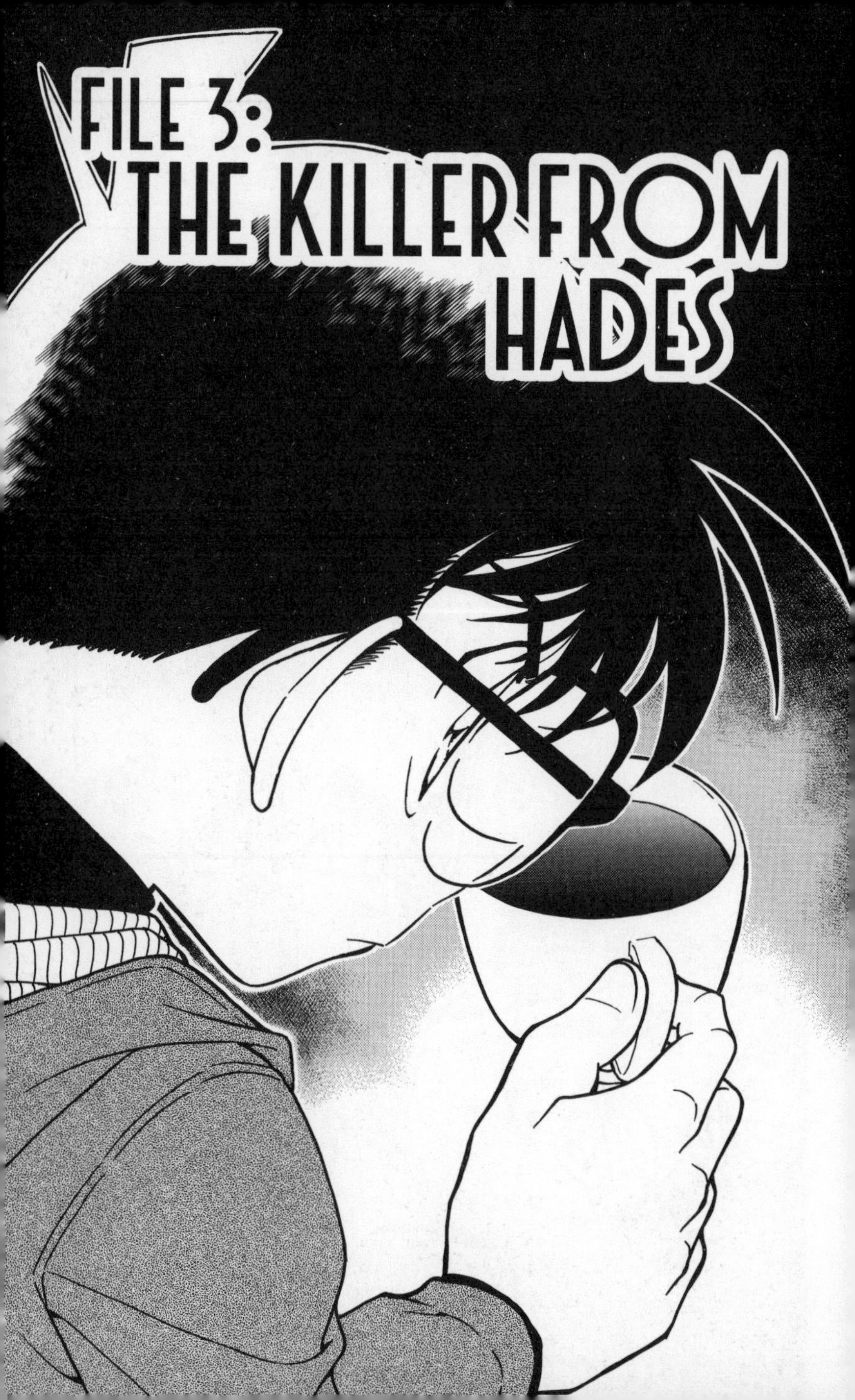
FILE 3:
THE KILLER FROM HADES

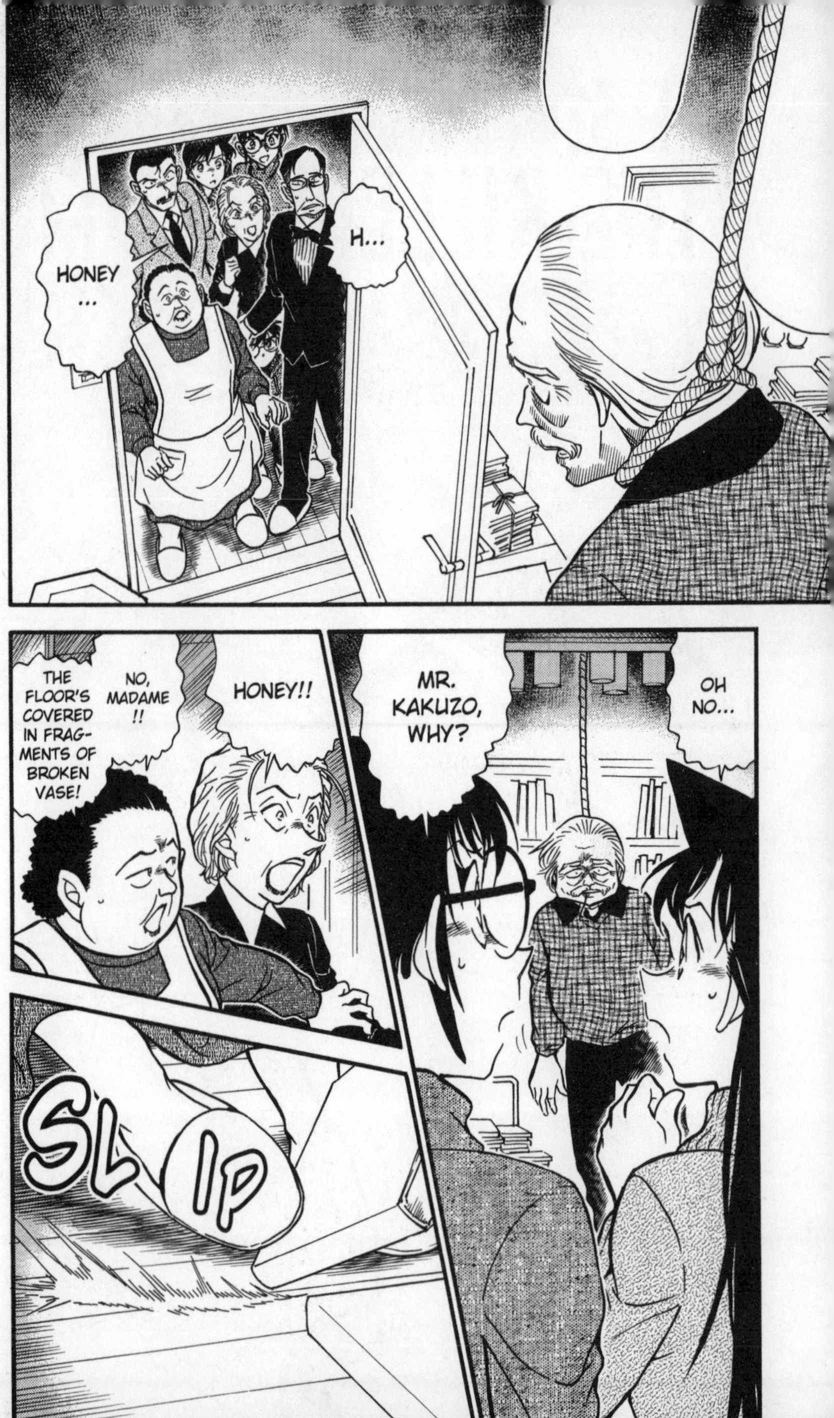
H...
HONEY ...
OH NO...
MR. KAKUZO, WHY?
HONEY!!
NO, MADAME !!
THE FLOOR'S COVERED IN FRAG-MENTS OF BROKEN VASE!
SLIP

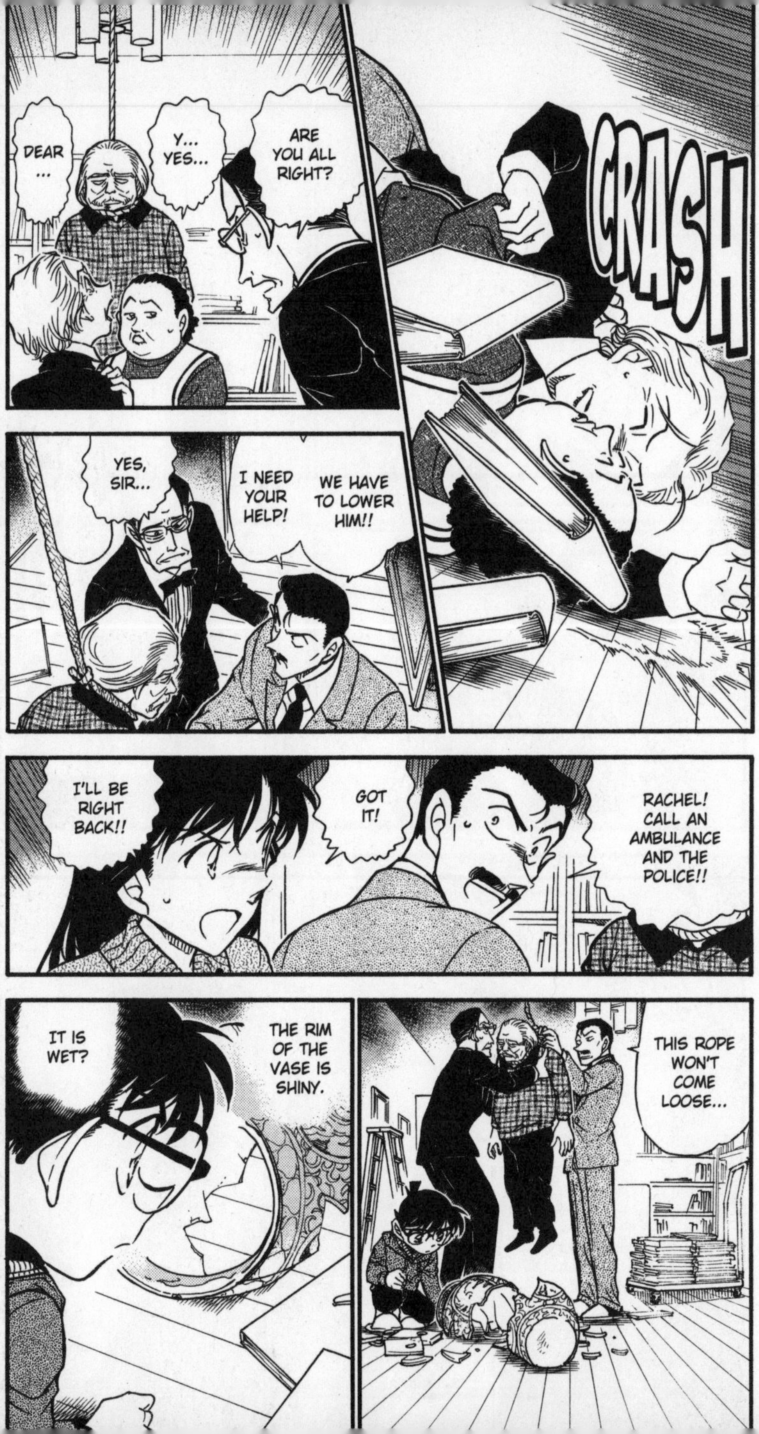
CRASH
ARE YOU ALL RIGHT?
Y... YES...
DEAR ...
WE HAVE TO LOWER HIM!!
I NEED YOUR HELP!
YES, SIR...
RACHEL! CALL AN AMBULANCE AND THE POLICE!!
GOT IT!
I'LL BE RIGHT BACK!!
THIS ROPE WON'T COME LOOSE...
THE RIM OF THE VASE IS SHINY.
IT IS WET?

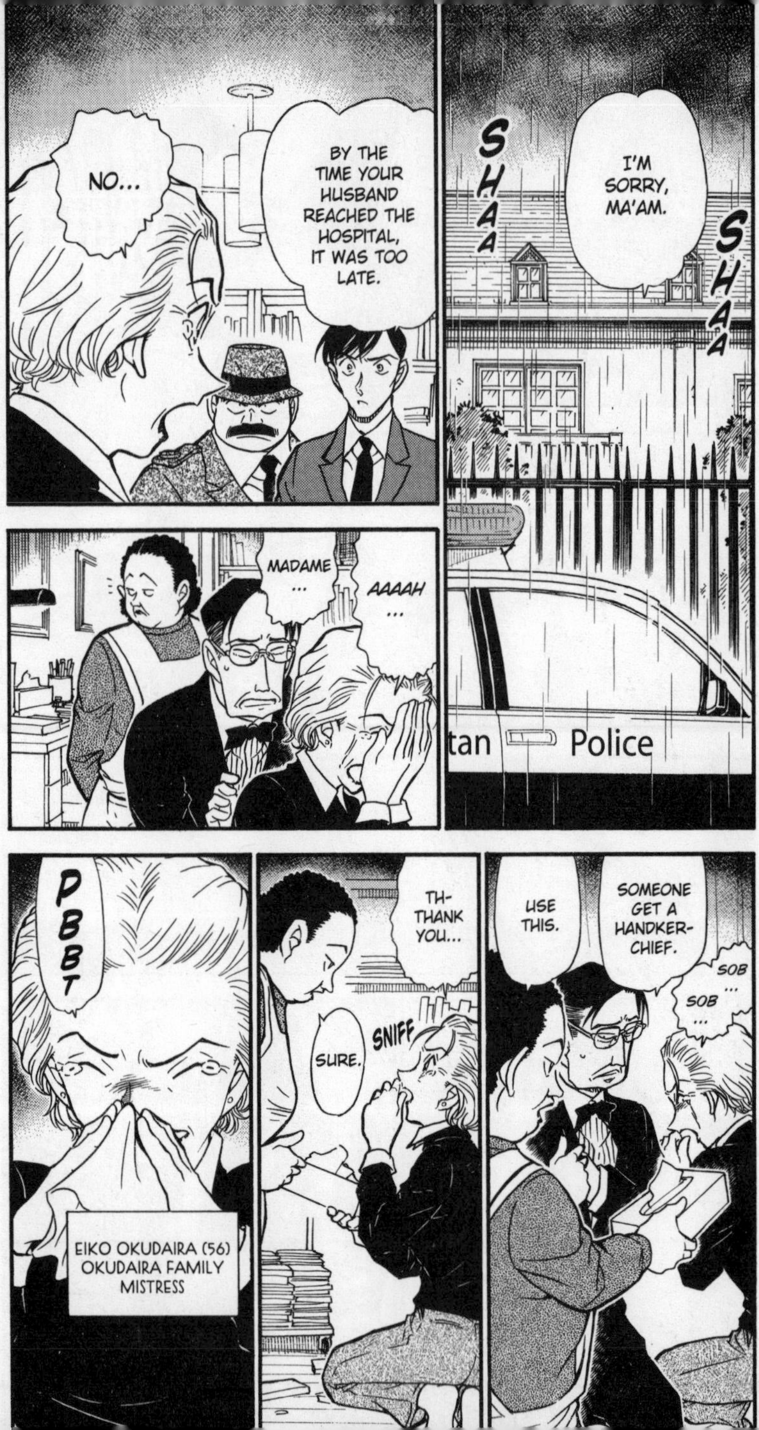
I'M SORRY, MA'AM.
SHAA
SHAA
tan Police
BY THE TIME YOUR HUSBAND REACHED THE HOSPITAL, IT WAS TOO LATE.
NO...
AAAAH...
MADAME...
SOMEONE GET A HANDKER-CHIEF.
USE THIS.
SOB... SOB...
TH-THANK YOU...
SNIFF
SURE.
PBBT
EIKO OKUDAIRA (56) OKUDAIRA FAMILY MISTRESS

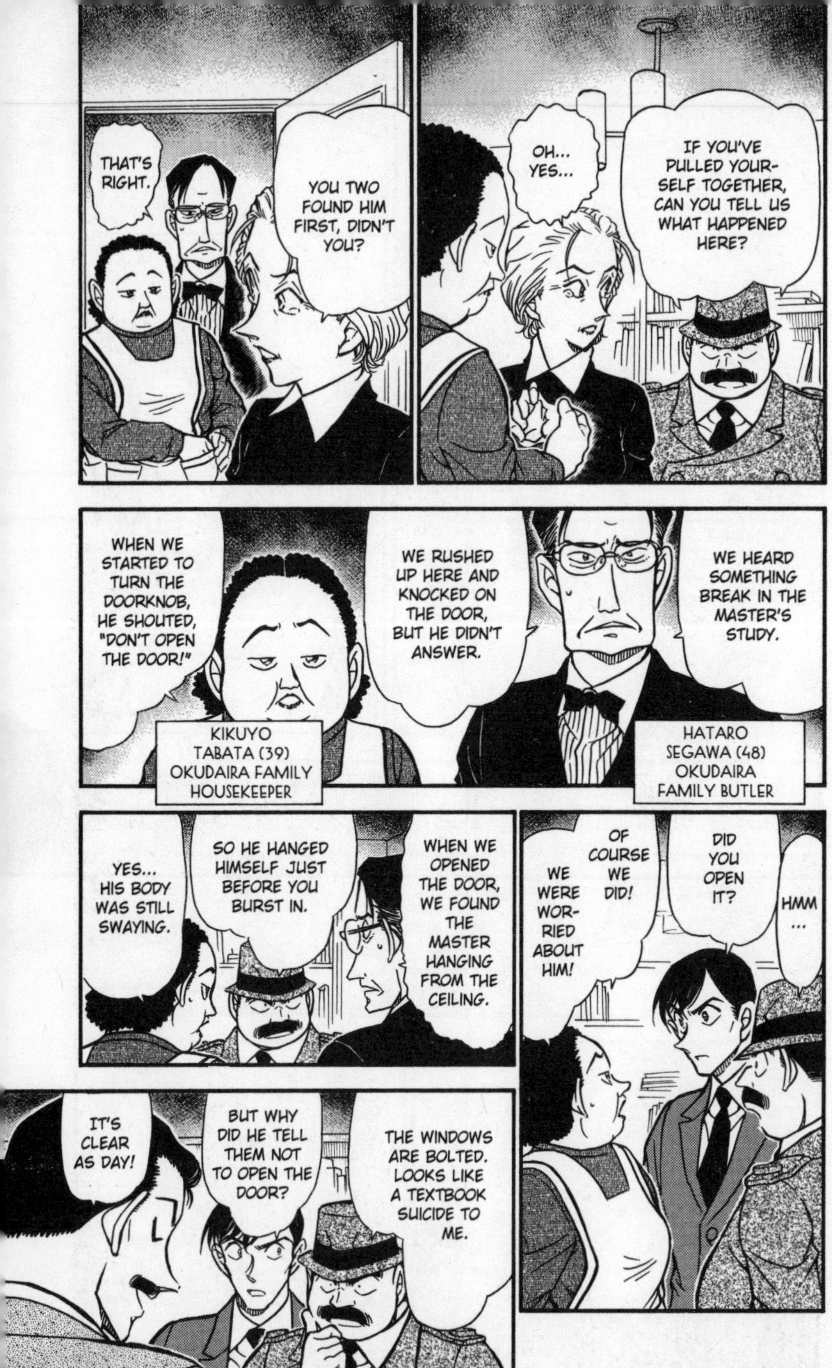
IF YOU'VE PULLED YOURSELF TOGETHER, CAN YOU TELL US WHAT HAPPENED HERE?
OH... YES...
YOU TWO FOUND HIM FIRST, DIDN'T YOU?
THAT'S RIGHT.
WE HEARD SOMETHING BREAK IN THE MASTER'S STUDY.
HATARO SEGAWA (48) OKUDAIRA FAMILY BUTLER
WE RUSHED UP HERE AND KNOCKED ON THE DOOR, BUT HE DIDN'T ANSWER.
WHEN WE STARTED TO TURN THE DOORKNOB, HE SHOUTED, "DON'T OPEN THE DOOR!"
KIKUYO TABATA (39) OKUDAIRA FAMILY HOUSEKEEPER
HMM ...
DID YOU OPEN IT?
OF COURSE WE DID!
WE WERE WORRIED ABOUT HIM!
WHEN WE OPENED THE DOOR, WE FOUND THE MASTER HANGING FROM THE CEILING.
SO HE HANGED HIMSELF JUST BEFORE YOU BURST IN.
YES... HIS BODY WAS STILL SWAYING.
THE WINDOWS ARE BOLTED. LOOKS LIKE A TEXTBOOK SUICIDE TO ME.
BUT WHY DID HE TELL THEM NOT TO OPEN THE DOOR?
IT'S CLEAR AS DAY!

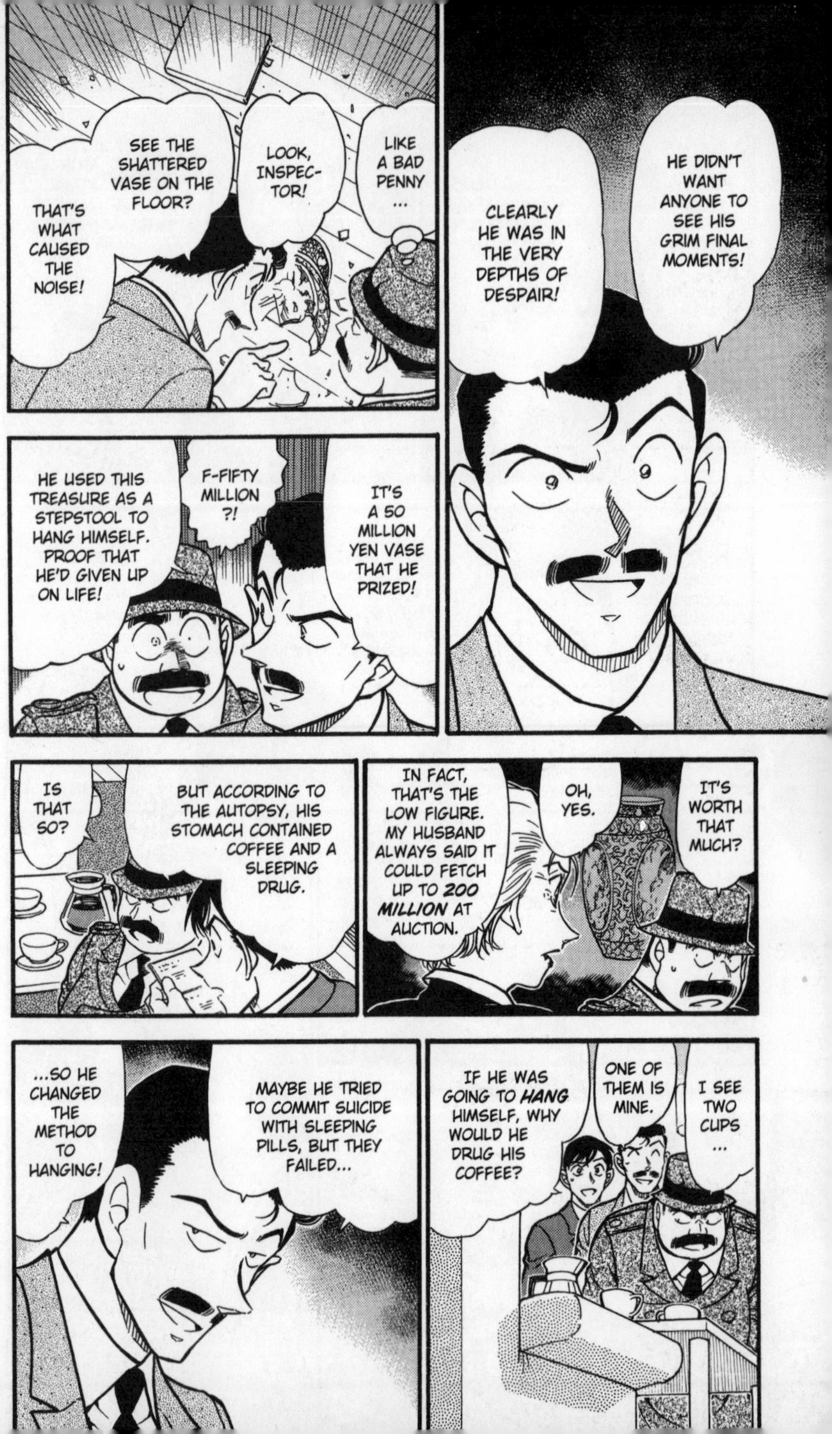
HE DIDN'T WANT ANYONE TO SEE HIS GRIM FINAL MOMENTS!
CLEARLY HE WAS IN THE VERY DEPTHS OF DESPAIR!
LIKE A BAD PENNY ...
LOOK, INSPECTOR!
SEE THE SHATTERED VASE ON THE FLOOR?
THAT'S WHAT CAUSED THE NOISE!
IT'S A 50 MILLION YEN VASE THAT HE PRIZED!
F-FIFTY MILLION ?!
HE USED THIS TREASURE AS A STEPSTOOL TO HANG HIMSELF. PROOF THAT HE'D GIVEN UP ON LIFE!
IT'S WORTH THAT MUCH?
OH, YES.
IN FACT, THAT'S THE LOW FIGURE. MY HUSBAND ALWAYS SAID IT COULD FETCH UP TO ***200 MILLION*** AT AUCTION.
BUT ACCORDING TO THE AUTOPSY, HIS STOMACH CONTAINED COFFEE AND A SLEEPING DRUG.
IS THAT SO?
I SEE TWO CUPS ...
ONE OF THEM IS MINE.
IF HE WAS GOING TO ***HANG*** HIMSELF, WHY WOULD HE DRUG HIS COFFEE?
MAYBE HE TRIED TO COMMIT SUICIDE WITH SLEEPING PILLS, BUT THEY FAILED...
...SO HE CHANGED THE METHOD TO HANGING!

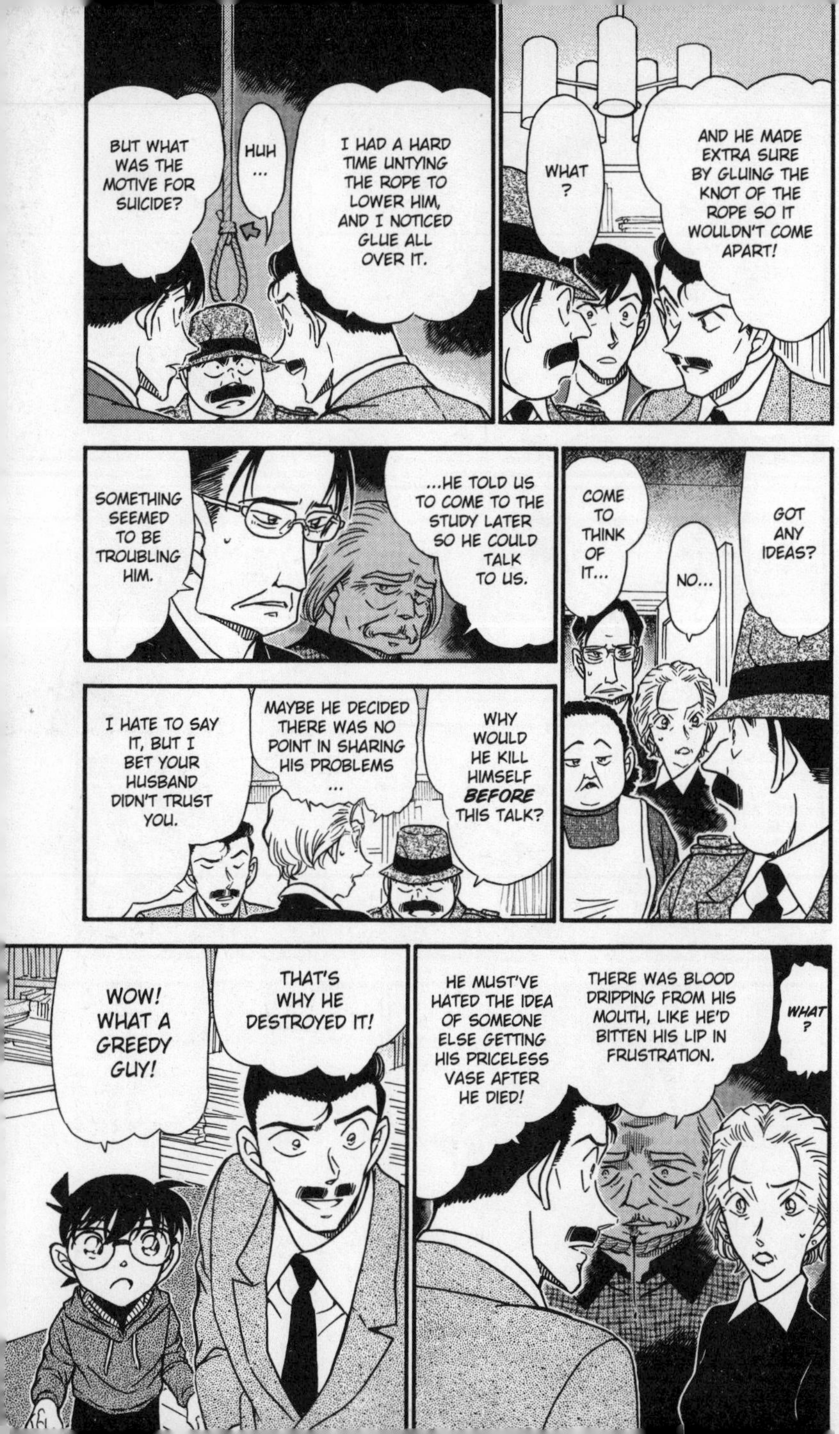
AND HE MADE EXTRA SURE BY GLUING THE KNOT OF THE ROPE SO IT WOULDN'T COME APART!
WHAT?
I HAD A HARD TIME UNTYING THE ROPE TO LOWER HIM, AND I NOTICED GLUE ALL OVER IT.
HUH...
BUT WHAT WAS THE MOTIVE FOR SUICIDE?
GOT ANY IDEAS?
NO...
COME TO THINK OF IT...
...HE TOLD US TO COME TO THE STUDY LATER SO HE COULD TALK TO US.
SOMETHING SEEMED TO BE TROUBLING HIM.
WHY WOULD HE KILL HIMSELF *BEFORE* THIS TALK?
MAYBE HE DECIDED THERE WAS NO POINT IN SHARING HIS PROBLEMS...
I HATE TO SAY IT, BUT I BET YOUR HUSBAND DIDN'T TRUST YOU.
WHAT?
THERE WAS BLOOD DRIPPING FROM HIS MOUTH, LIKE HE'D BITTEN HIS LIP IN FRUSTRATION.
HE MUST'VE HATED THE IDEA OF SOMEONE ELSE GETTING HIS PRICELESS VASE AFTER HE DIED!
THAT'S WHY HE DESTROYED IT!
WOW! WHAT A GREEDY GUY!

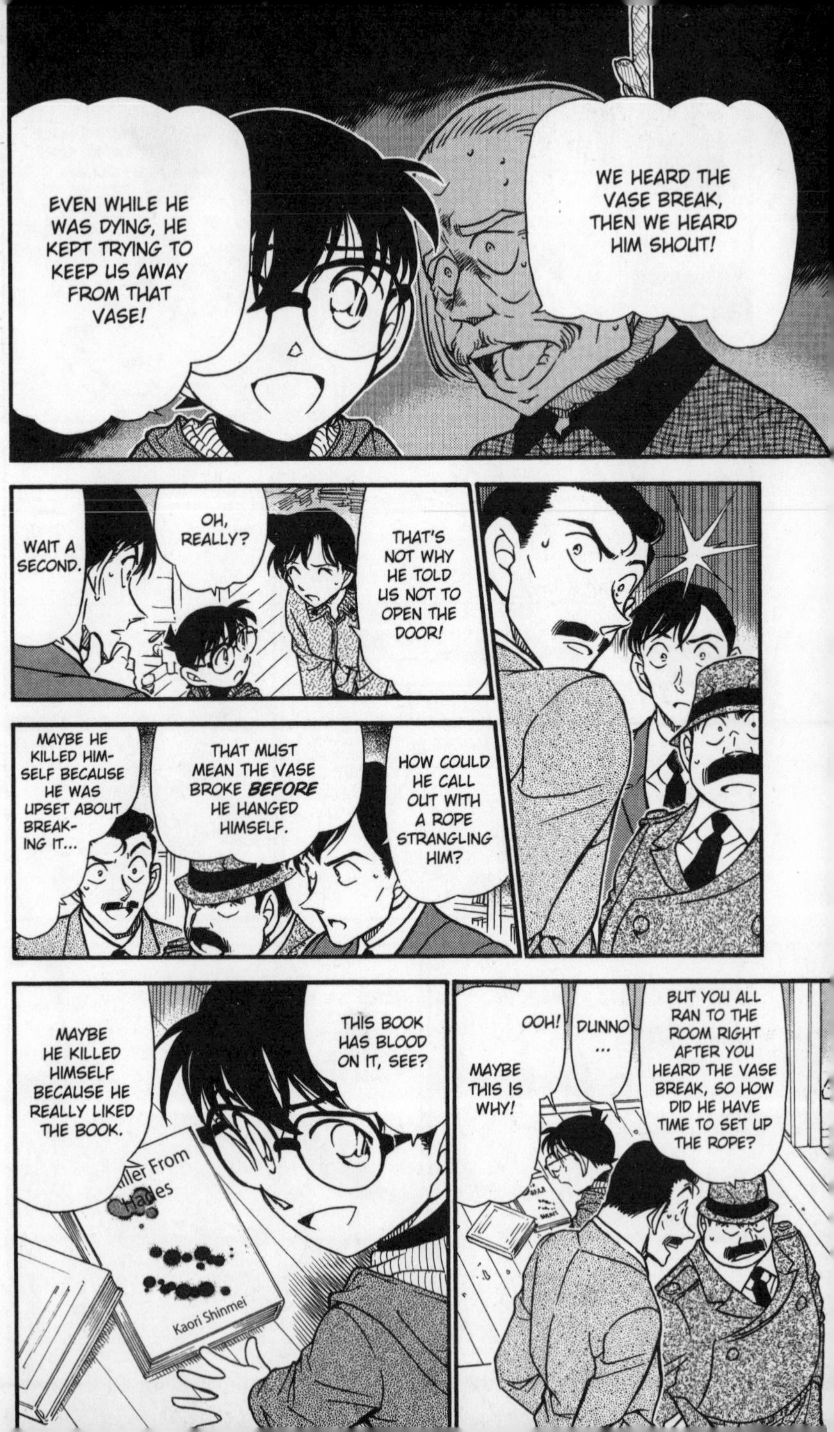
WE HEARD THE VASE BREAK, THEN WE HEARD HIM SHOUT!
EVEN WHILE HE WAS DYING, HE KEPT TRYING TO KEEP US AWAY FROM THAT VASE!
THAT'S NOT WHY HE TOLD US NOT TO OPEN THE DOOR!
OH, REALLY?
WAIT A SECOND.
HOW COULD HE CALL OUT WITH A ROPE STRANGLING HIM?
THAT MUST MEAN THE VASE BROKE ***BEFORE*** HE HANGED HIMSELF.
MAYBE HE KILLED HIM-SELF BECAUSE HE WAS UPSET ABOUT BREAK-ING IT...
BUT YOU ALL RAN TO THE ROOM RIGHT AFTER YOU HEARD THE VASE BREAK, SO HOW DID HE HAVE TIME TO SET UP THE ROPE?
DUNNO...
OOH!
MAYBE THIS IS WHY!
THIS BOOK HAS BLOOD ON IT, SEE?
MAYBE HE KILLED HIMSELF BECAUSE HE REALLY LIKED THE BOOK.
Kaori Shinmei

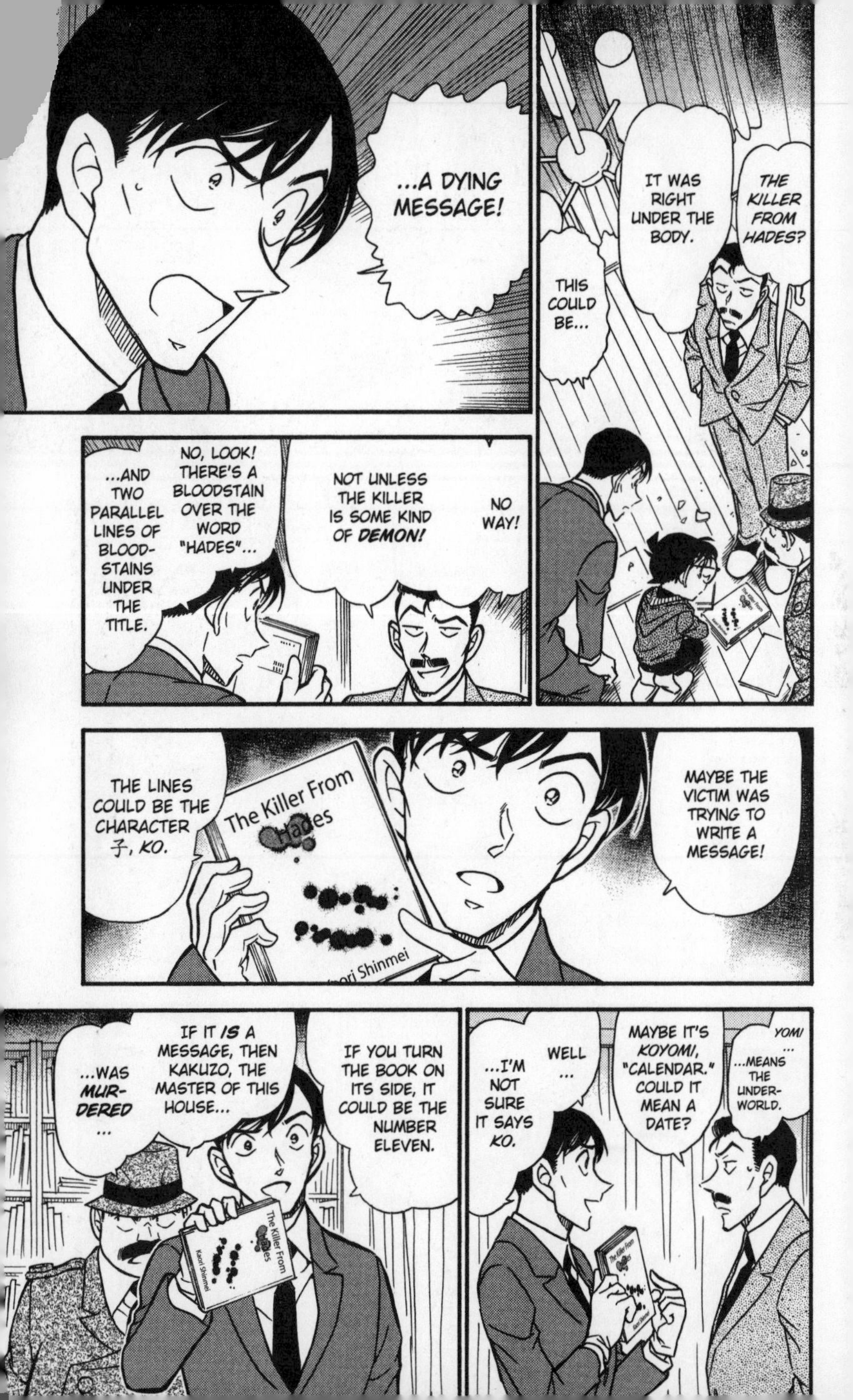
THE KILLER FROM HADES?
IT WAS RIGHT UNDER THE BODY.
THIS COULD BE...
...A DYING MESSAGE!
NO WAY!
NOT UNLESS THE KILLER IS SOME KIND OF ***DEMON!***
NO, LOOK! THERE'S A BLOODSTAIN OVER THE WORD "HADES"...
...AND TWO PARALLEL LINES OF BLOOD-STAINS UNDER THE TITLE.
MAYBE THE VICTIM WAS TRYING TO WRITE A MESSAGE!
The Killer From Hades
Kaori Shinmei
THE LINES COULD BE THE CHARACTER 子, *KO.*
YOMI ... ...MEANS THE UNDER-WORLD.
MAYBE IT'S *KOYOMI,* "CALENDAR." COULD IT MEAN A DATE?
WELL ...
...I'M NOT SURE IT SAYS *KO.*
IF YOU TURN THE BOOK ON ITS SIDE, IT COULD BE THE NUMBER ELEVEN.
IF IT ***IS*** A MESSAGE, THEN KAKUZO, THE MASTER OF THIS HOUSE...
...WAS ***MUR-DERED*** ...

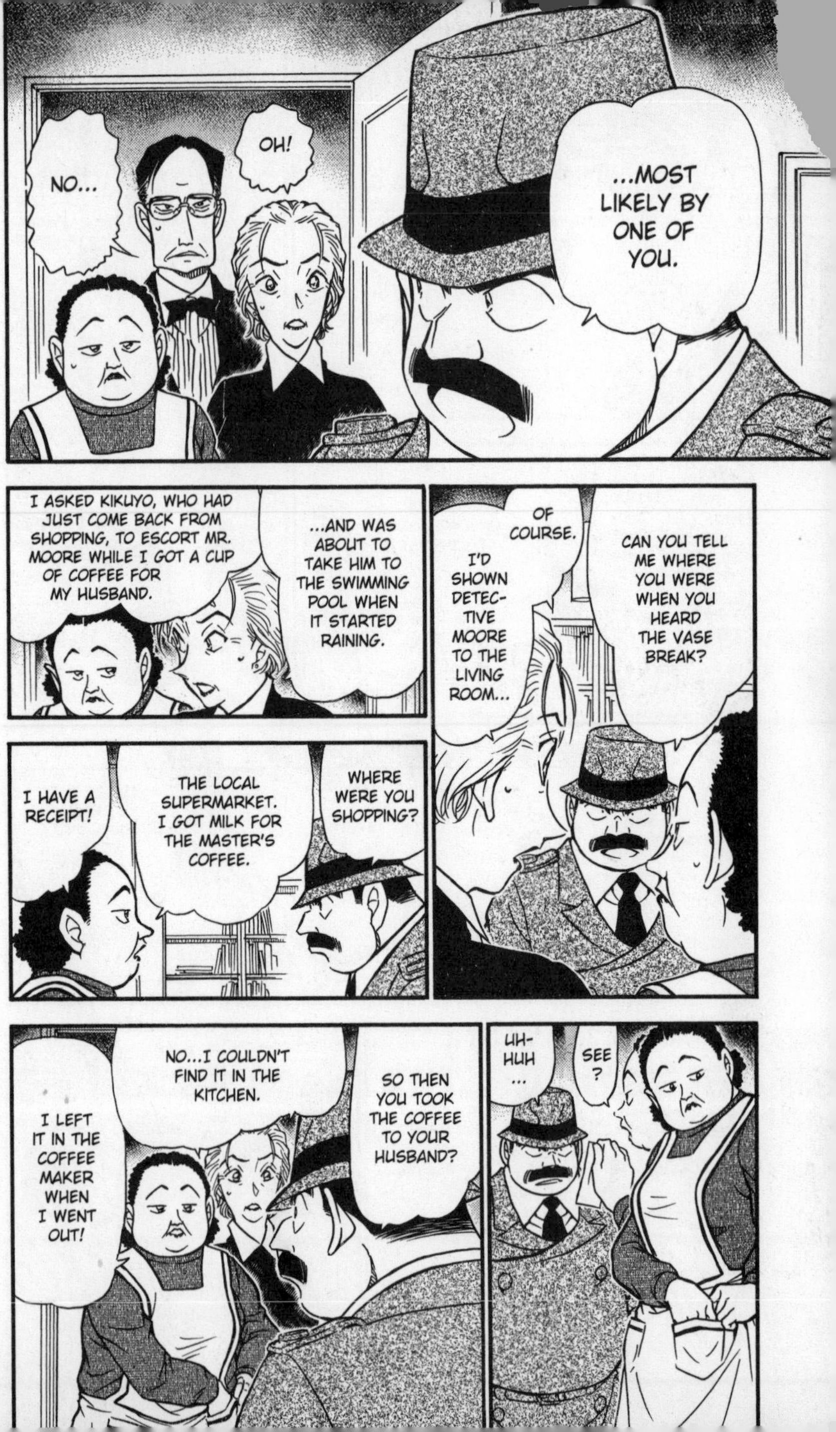

...MOST LIKELY BY ONE OF YOU.
OH!
NO...
CAN YOU TELL ME WHERE YOU WERE WHEN YOU HEARD THE VASE BREAK?
OF COURSE.
I'D SHOWN DETEC-TIVE MOORE TO THE LIVING ROOM...
...AND WAS ABOUT TO TAKE HIM TO THE SWIMMING POOL WHEN IT STARTED RAINING.
I ASKED KIKUYO, WHO HAD JUST COME BACK FROM SHOPPING, TO ESCORT MR. MOORE WHILE I GOT A CUP OF COFFEE FOR MY HUSBAND.
WHERE WERE YOU SHOPPING?
THE LOCAL SUPERMARKET. I GOT MILK FOR THE MASTER'S COFFEE.
I HAVE A RECEIPT!
SEE?
UH-HUH...
SO THEN YOU TOOK THE COFFEE TO YOUR HUSBAND?
NO...I COULDN'T FIND IT IN THE KITCHEN.
I LEFT IT IN THE COFFEE MAKER WHEN I WENT OUT!

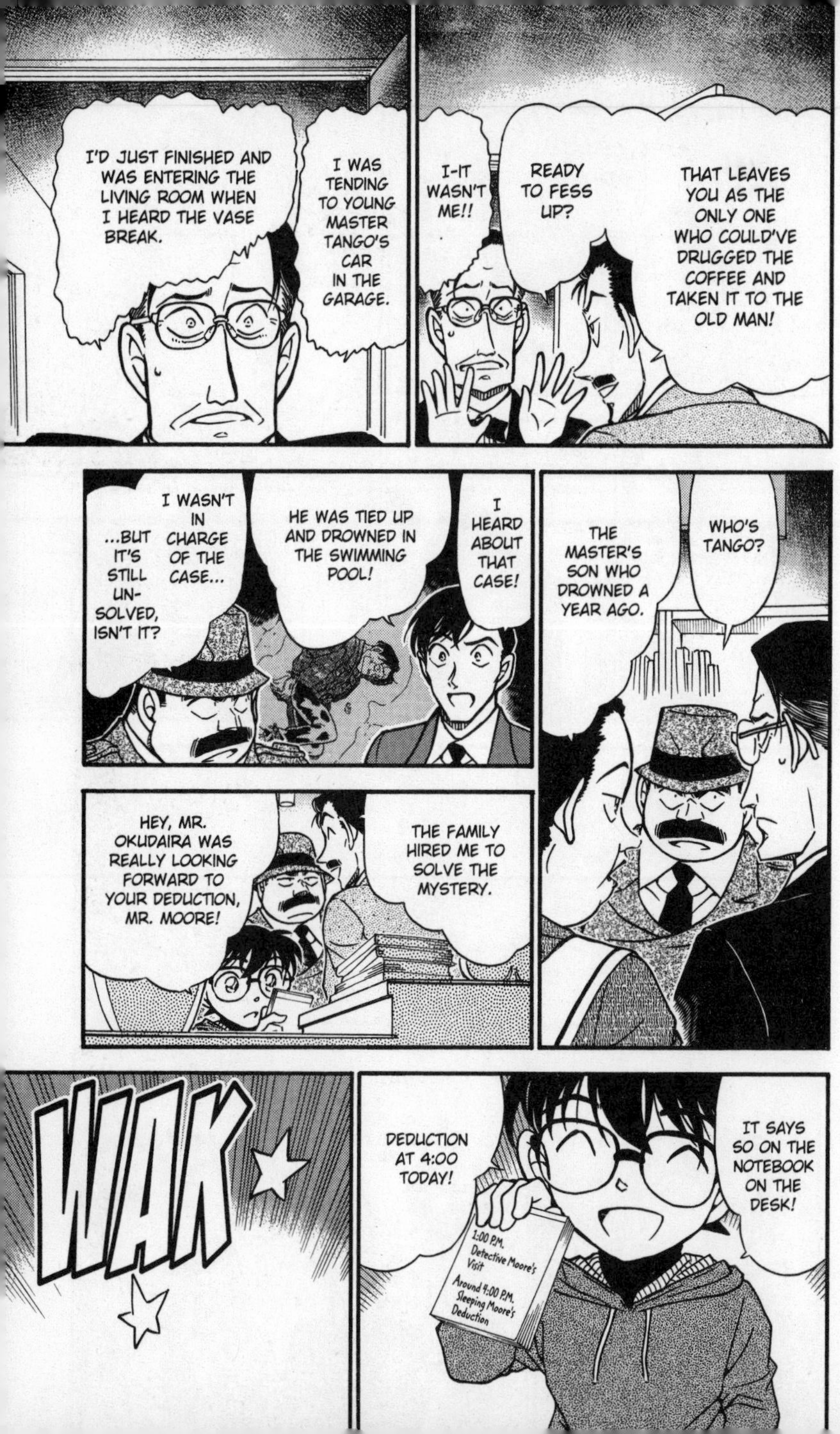
THAT LEAVES YOU AS THE ONLY ONE WHO COULD'VE DRUGGED THE COFFEE AND TAKEN IT TO THE OLD MAN!
READY TO FESS UP?
I-IT WASN'T ME!!
I WAS TENDING TO YOUNG MASTER TANGO'S CAR IN THE GARAGE.
I'D JUST FINISHED AND WAS ENTERING THE LIVING ROOM WHEN I HEARD THE VASE BREAK.
WHO'S TANGO?
THE MASTER'S SON WHO DROWNED A YEAR AGO.
I HEARD ABOUT THAT CASE!
HE WAS TIED UP AND DROWNED IN THE SWIMMING POOL!
I WASN'T IN CHARGE OF THE CASE...
...BUT IT'S STILL UN-SOLVED, ISN'T IT?
THE FAMILY HIRED ME TO SOLVE THE MYSTERY.
HEY, MR. OKUDAIRA WAS REALLY LOOKING FORWARD TO YOUR DEDUCTION, MR. MOORE!
IT SAYS SO ON THE NOTEBOOK ON THE DESK!
DEDUCTION AT 4:00 TODAY!
1:00 P.M. Detective Moore's Visit
Around 4:00 P.M. Sleeping Moore's Deduction
WAK

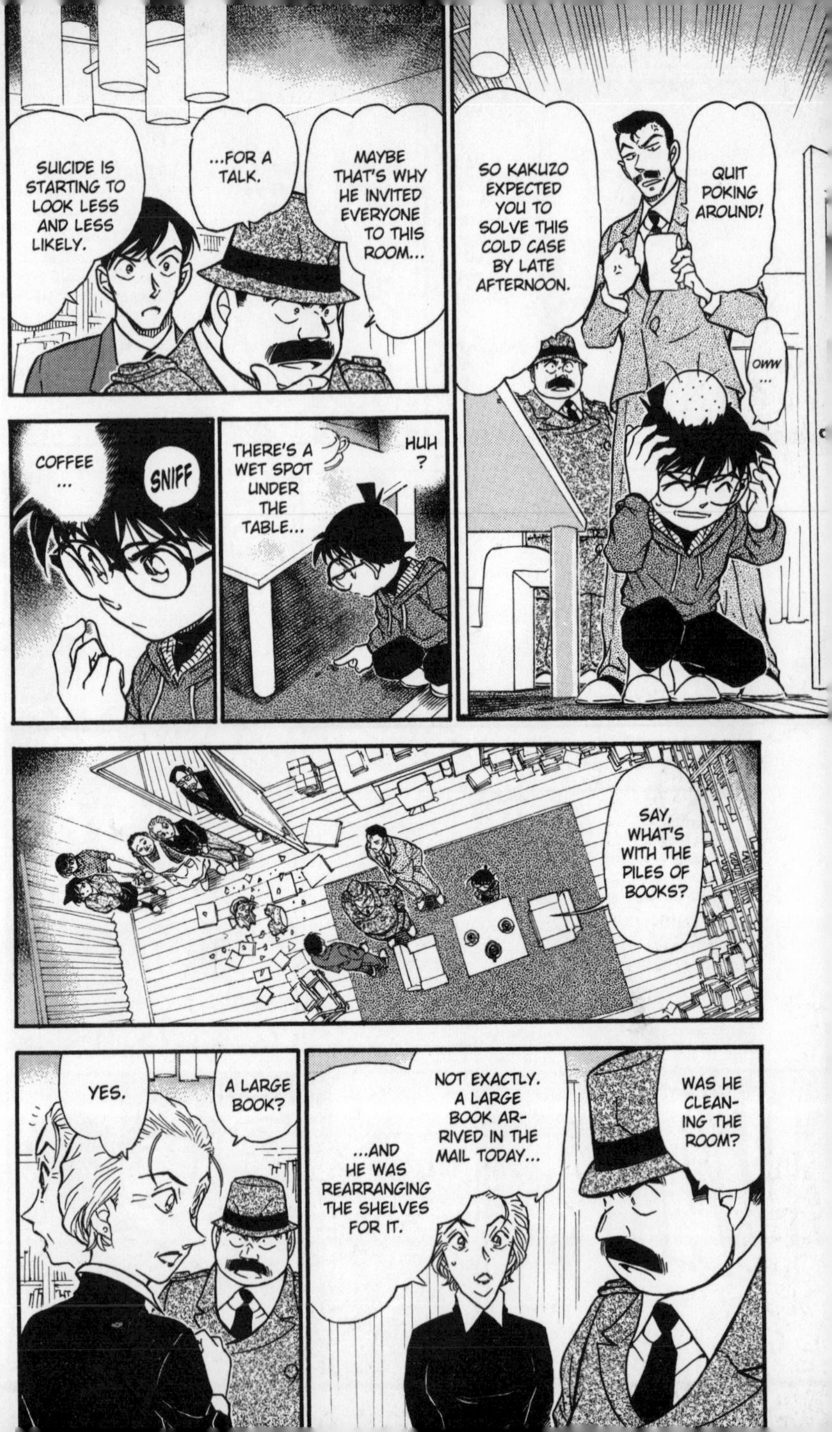
QUIT POKING AROUND!
SO KAKUZO EXPECTED YOU TO SOLVE THIS COLD CASE BY LATE AFTERNOON.
OWW ...
MAYBE THAT'S WHY HE INVITED EVERYONE TO THIS ROOM...
...FOR A TALK.
SUICIDE IS STARTING TO LOOK LESS AND LESS LIKELY.
HUH ?
THERE'S A WET SPOT UNDER THE TABLE...
SNIFF
COFFEE ...
SAY, WHAT'S WITH THE PILES OF BOOKS?
WAS HE CLEANING THE ROOM?
NOT EXACTLY. A LARGE BOOK ARRIVED IN THE MAIL TODAY...
...AND HE WAS REARRANGING THE SHELVES FOR IT.
A LARGE BOOK?
YES.

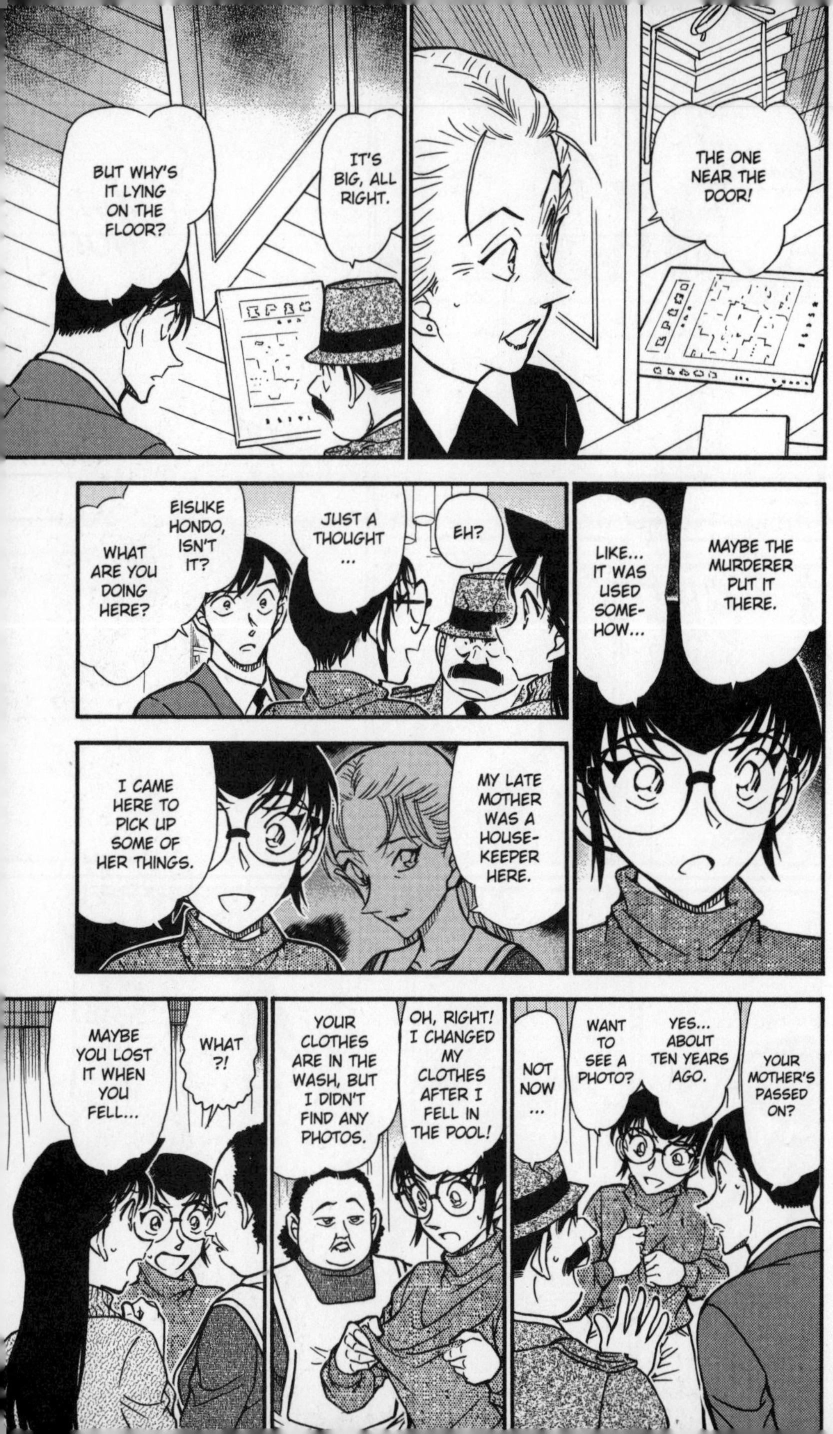
THE ONE NEAR THE DOOR!
IT'S BIG, ALL RIGHT.
BUT WHY'S IT LYING ON THE FLOOR?
MAYBE THE MURDERER PUT IT THERE.
LIKE... IT WAS USED SOME-HOW...
EH?
JUST A THOUGHT ...
EISUKE HONDO, ISN'T IT?
WHAT ARE YOU DOING HERE?
MY LATE MOTHER WAS A HOUSE-KEEPER HERE.
I CAME HERE TO PICK UP SOME OF HER THINGS.
YOUR MOTHER'S PASSED ON?
YES... ABOUT TEN YEARS AGO.
WANT TO SEE A PHOTO?
NOT NOW ...
OH, RIGHT! I CHANGED MY CLOTHES AFTER I FELL IN THE POOL!
YOUR CLOTHES ARE IN THE WASH, BUT I DIDN'T FIND ANY PHOTOS.
WHAT ?!
MAYBE YOU LOST IT WHEN YOU FELL...

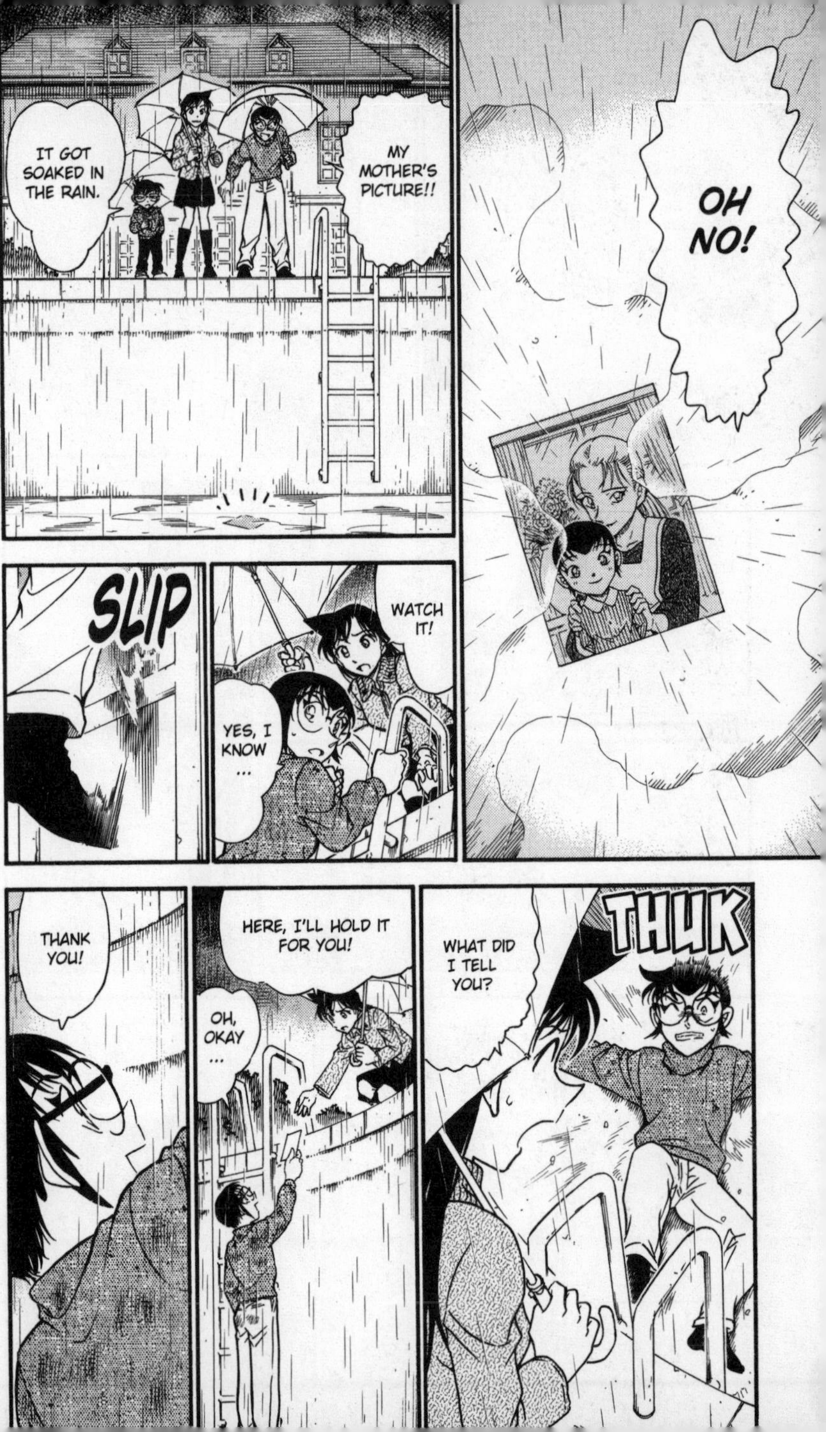
OH NO!
MY MOTHER'S PICTURE!!
IT GOT SOAKED IN THE RAIN.
WATCH IT!
YES, I KNOW ...
SLIP
THUK
WHAT DID I TELL YOU?
HERE, I'LL HOLD IT FOR YOU!
OH, OKAY ...
THANK YOU!

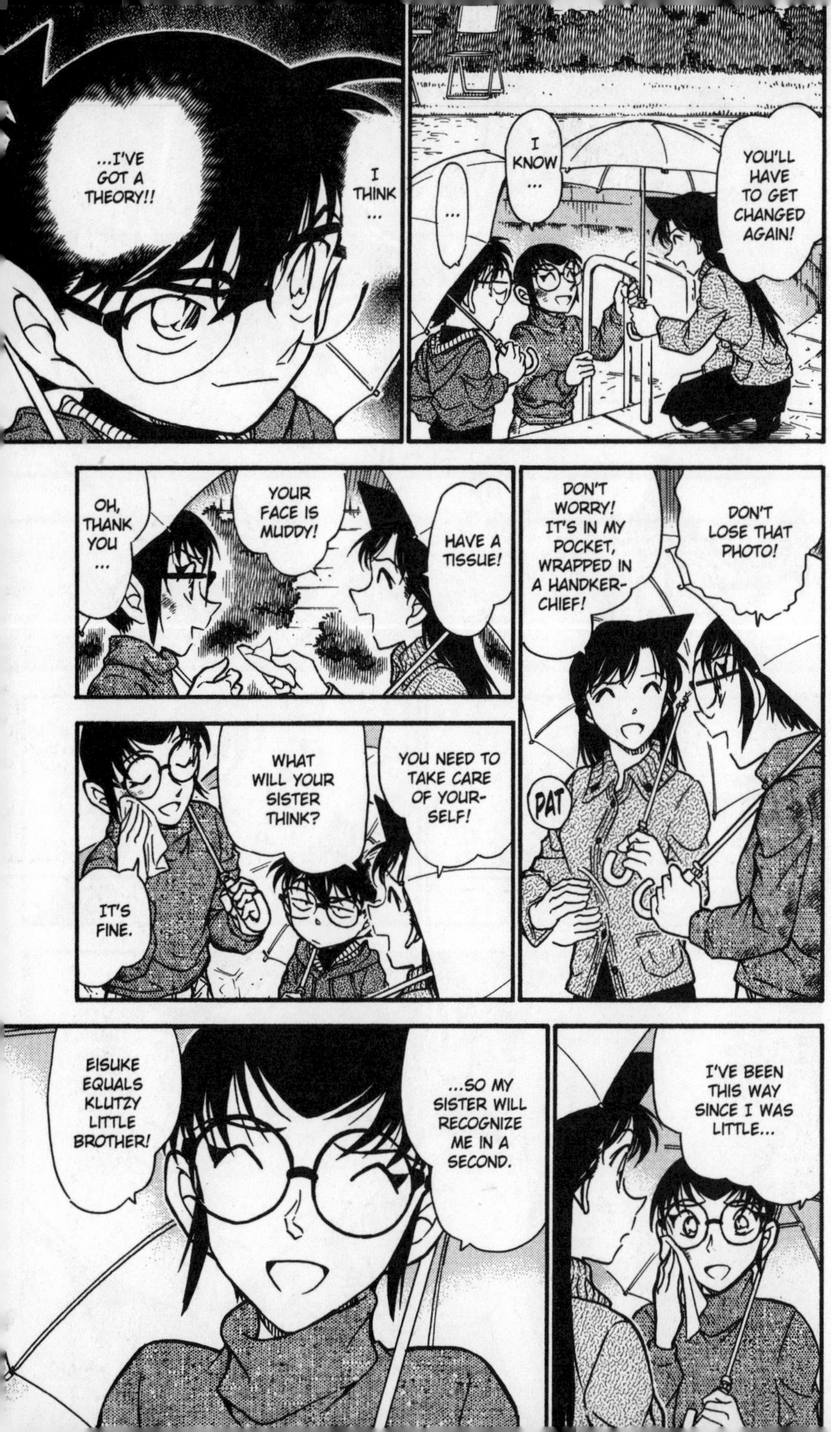
YOU'LL HAVE TO GET CHANGED AGAIN!
I KNOW ...
...
I THINK ...
...I'VE GOT A THEORY!!
DON'T LOSE THAT PHOTO!
DON'T WORRY! IT'S IN MY POCKET, WRAPPED IN A HANDKERCHIEF!
PAT
HAVE A TISSUE!
YOUR FACE IS MUDDY!
OH, THANK YOU ...
YOU NEED TO TAKE CARE OF YOURSELF!
WHAT WILL YOUR SISTER THINK?
IT'S FINE.
I'VE BEEN THIS WAY SINCE I WAS LITTLE...
...SO MY SISTER WILL RECOGNIZE ME IN A SECOND.
EISUKE EQUALS KLUTZY LITTLE BROTHER!

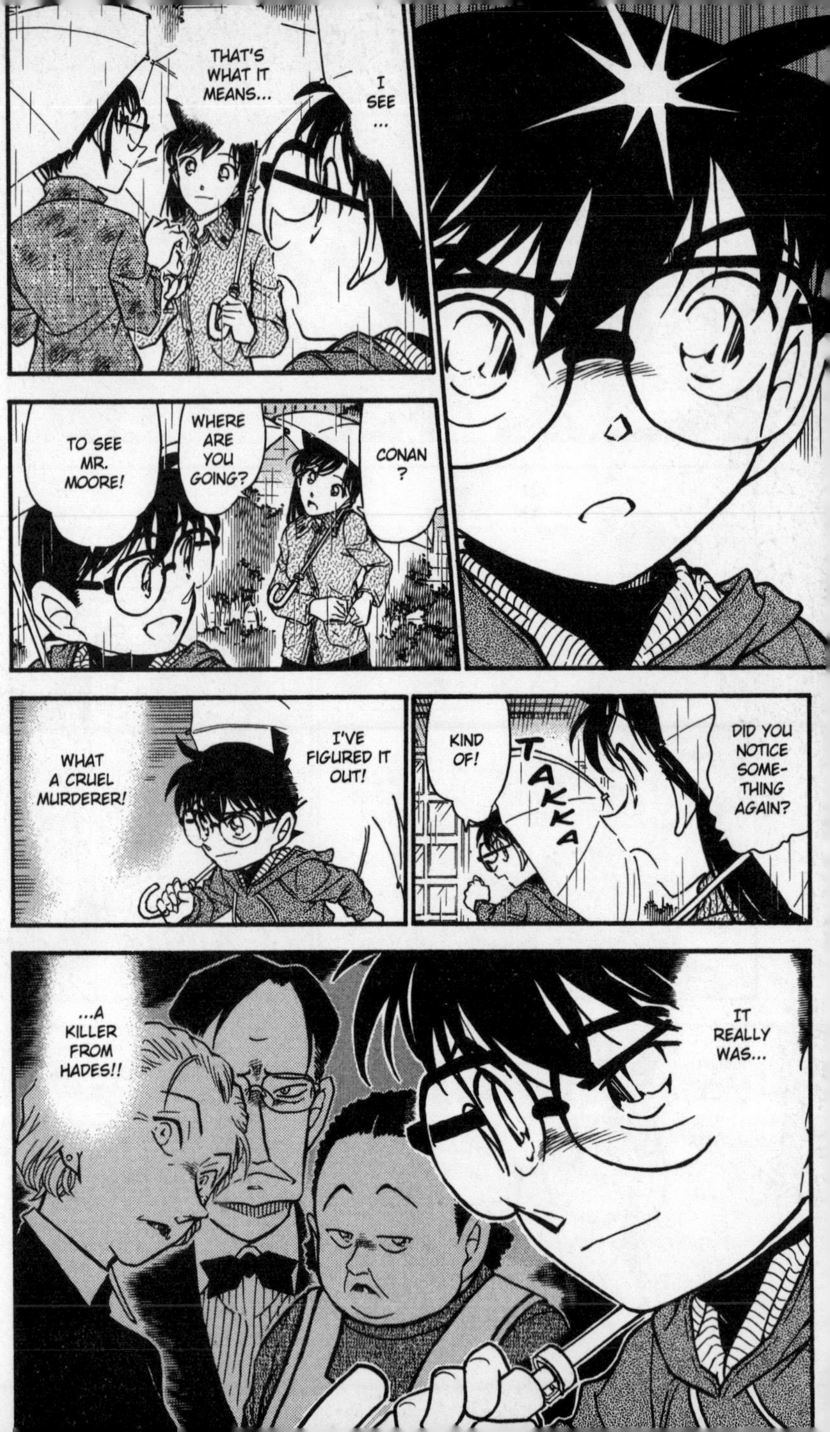

I SEE ...
THAT'S WHAT IT MEANS...
CONAN ?
WHERE ARE YOU GOING?
TO SEE MR. MOORE!
DID YOU NOTICE SOME-THING AGAIN?
TAKKA
KIND OF!
I'VE FIGURED IT OUT!
WHAT A CRUEL MURDERER!
IT REALLY WAS...
...A KILLER FROM HADES!!

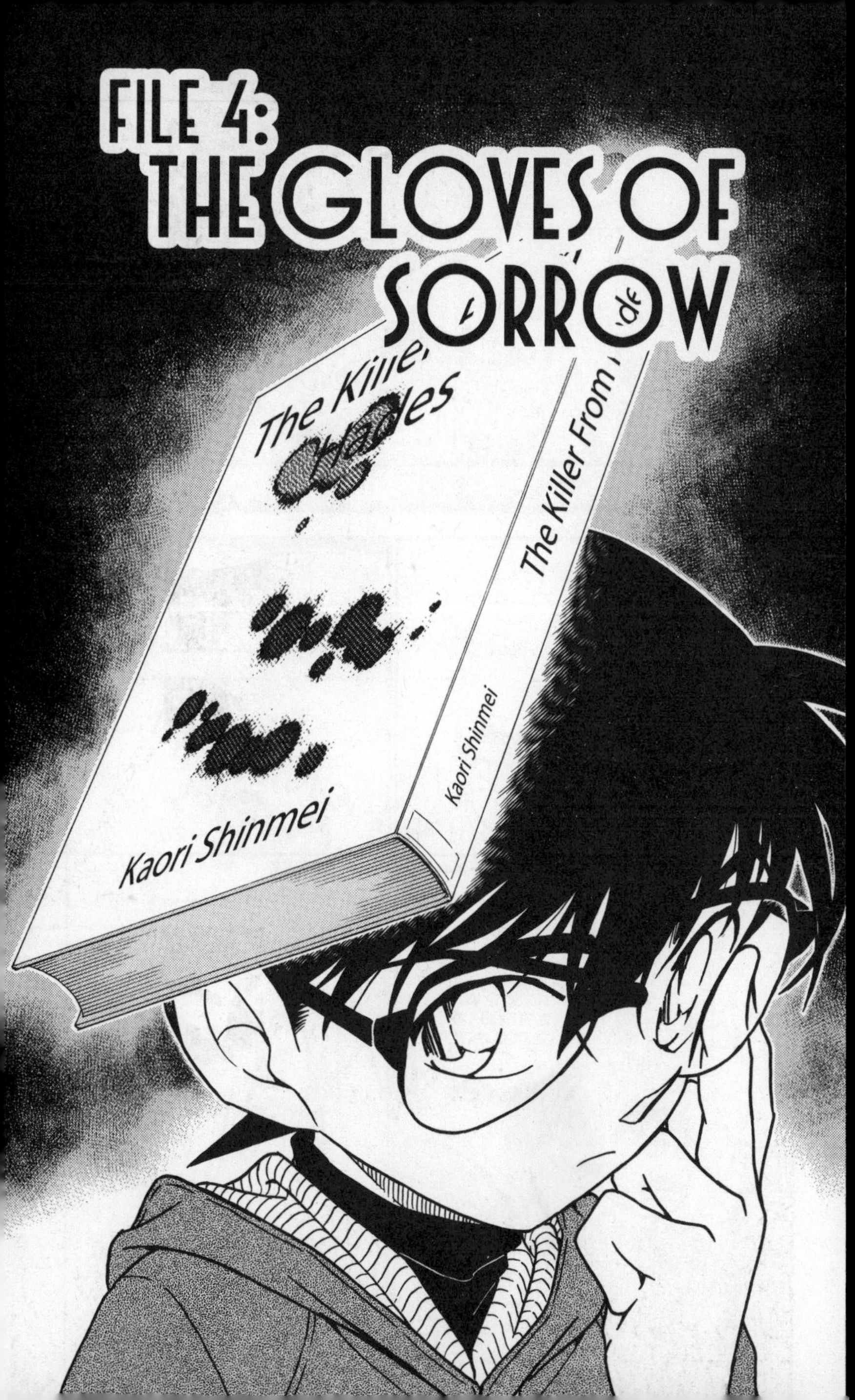
FILE 4:
THE GLOVES OF SORROW
The Kille
ades
Kaori Shinmei
The Killer From
Kaori Shinmei

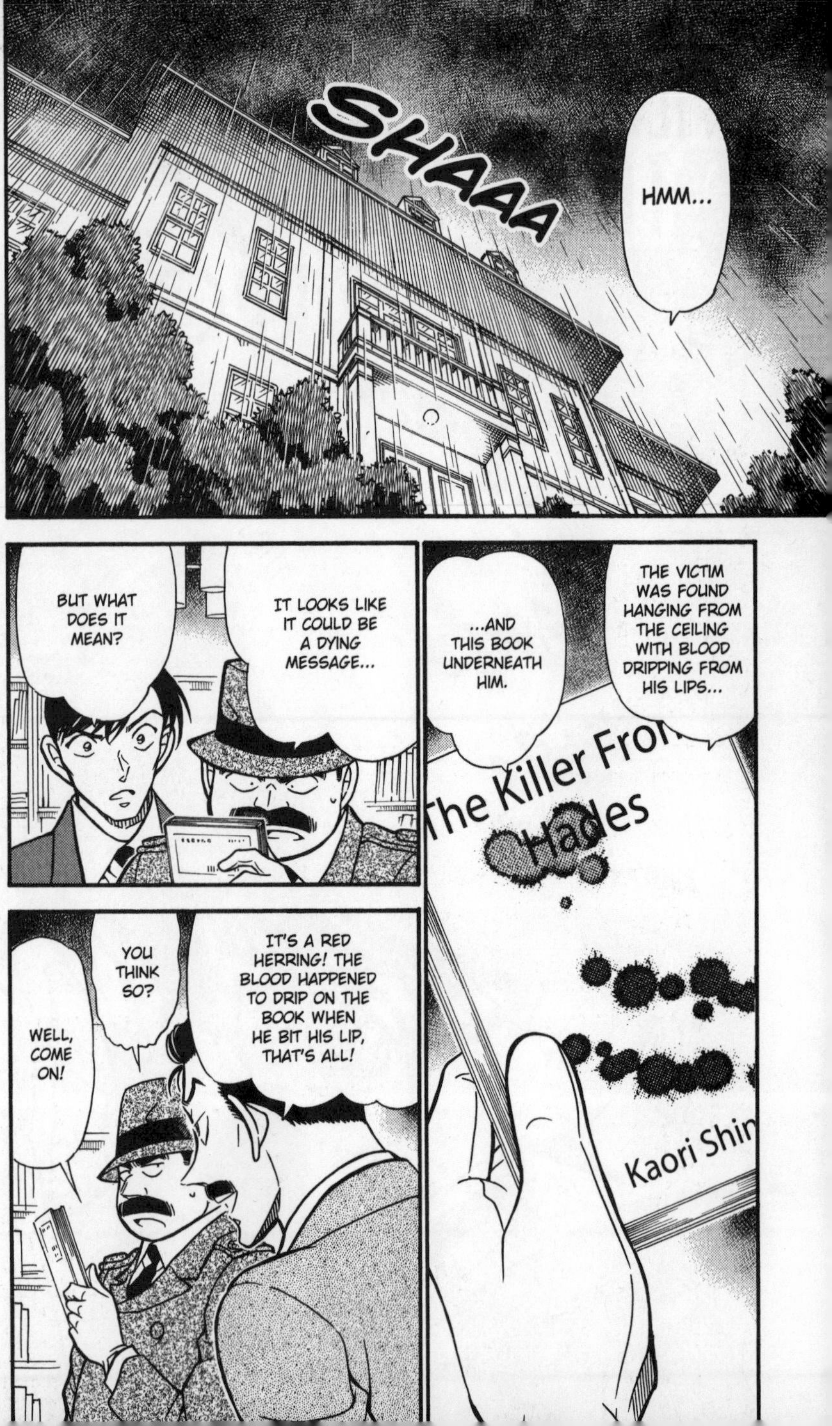
SHAAA
HMM...
THE VICTIM WAS FOUND HANGING FROM THE CEILING WITH BLOOD DRIPPING FROM HIS LIPS...
...AND THIS BOOK UNDERNEATH HIM.
The Killer Fro
Hades
Kaori Shin
IT LOOKS LIKE IT COULD BE A DYING MESSAGE...
BUT WHAT DOES IT MEAN?
IT'S A RED HERRING! THE BLOOD HAPPENED TO DRIP ON THE BOOK WHEN HE BIT HIS LIP, THAT'S ALL!
YOU THINK SO?
WELL, COME ON!

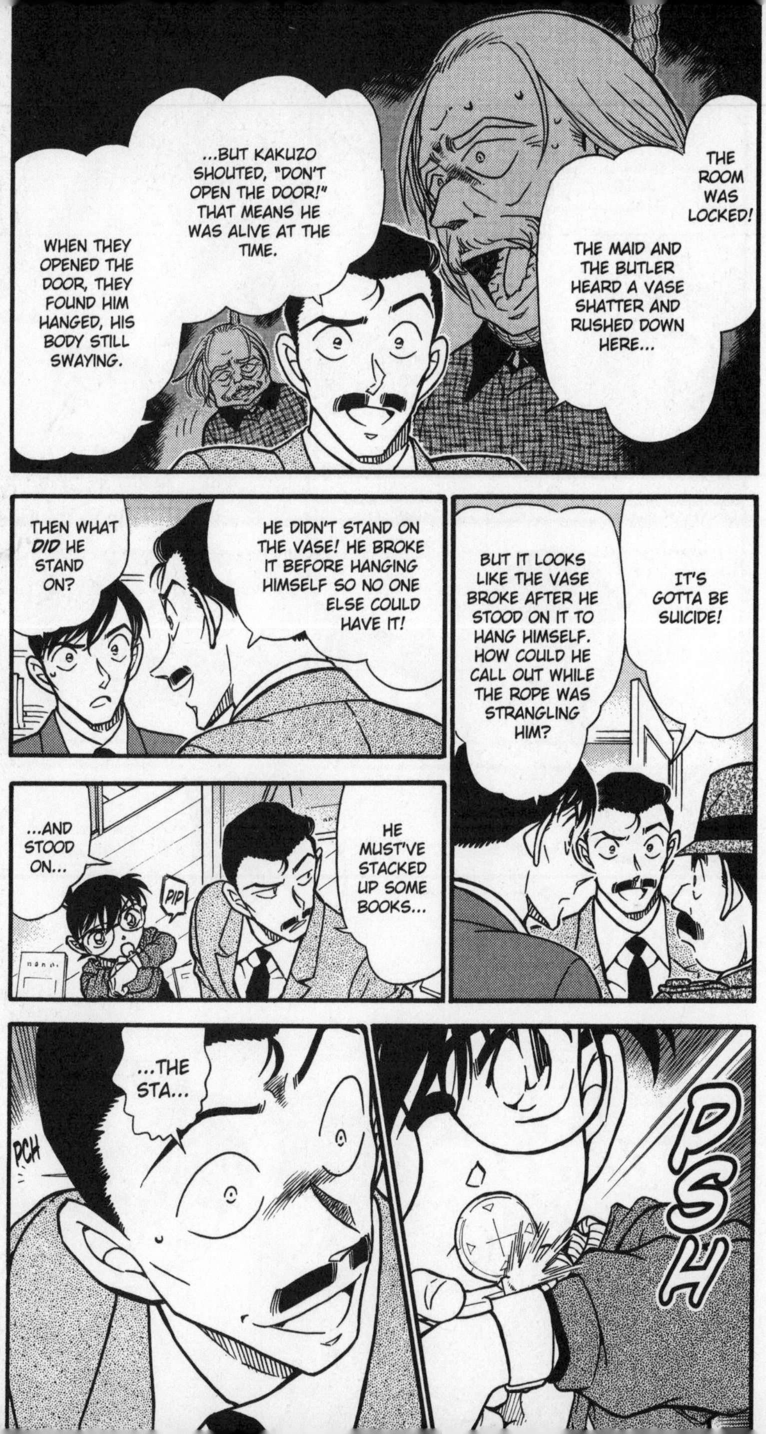
THE ROOM WAS LOCKED!
THE MAID AND THE BUTLER HEARD A VASE SHATTER AND RUSHED DOWN HERE...
...BUT KAKUZO SHOUTED, "DON'T OPEN THE DOOR!" THAT MEANS HE WAS ALIVE AT THE TIME.
WHEN THEY OPENED THE DOOR, THEY FOUND HIM HANGED, HIS BODY STILL SWAYING.
IT'S GOTTA BE SUICIDE!
BUT IT LOOKS LIKE THE VASE BROKE AFTER HE STOOD ON IT TO HANG HIMSELF. HOW COULD HE CALL OUT WHILE THE ROPE WAS STRANGLING HIM?
HE DIDN'T STAND ON THE VASE! HE BROKE IT BEFORE HANGING HIMSELF SO NO ONE ELSE COULD HAVE IT!
THEN WHAT *DID* HE STAND ON?
HE MUST'VE STACKED UP SOME BOOKS...
PIP
...AND STOOD ON...
PSH
...THE STA...
PCH

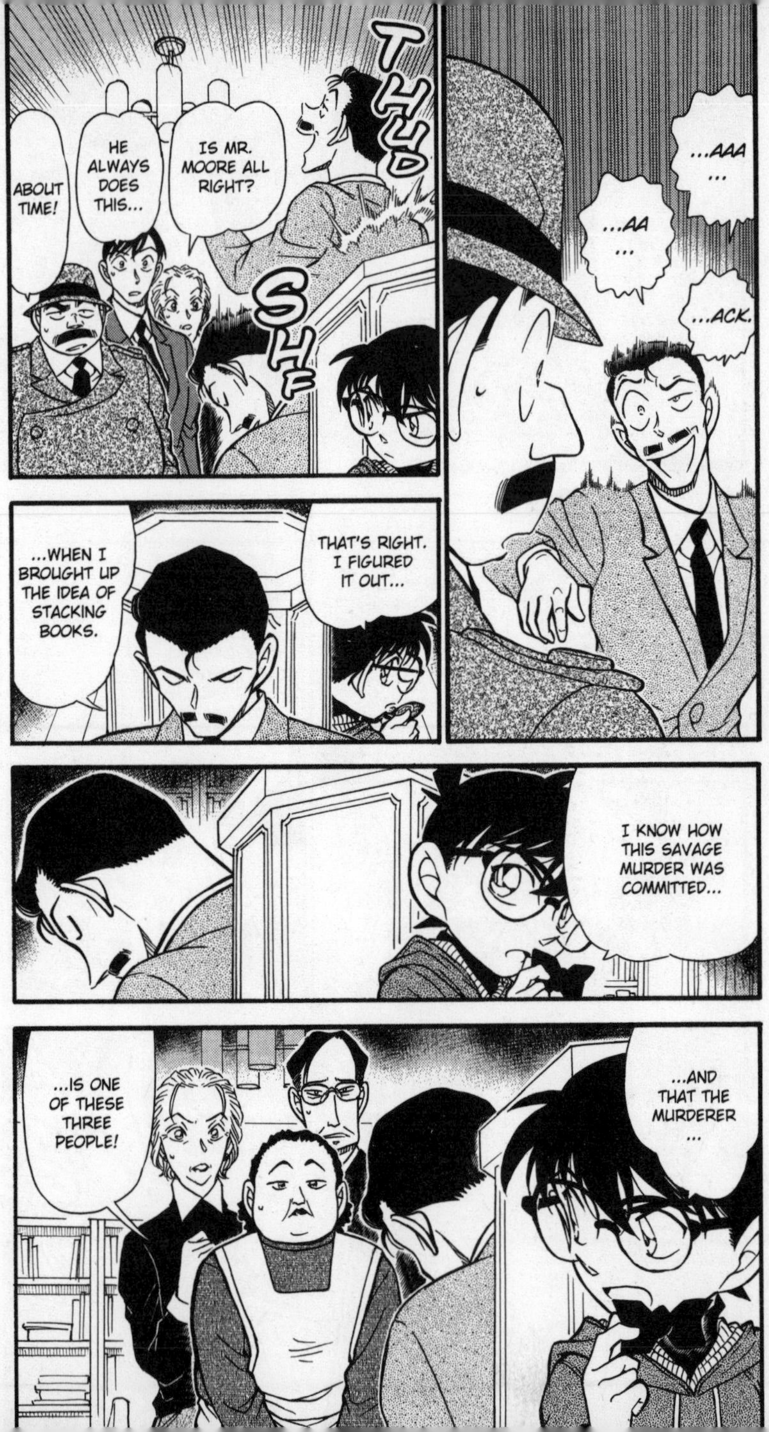

...AAA ...
...AA ...
...ACK.
THUD
IS MR. MOORE ALL RIGHT?
HE ALWAYS DOES THIS...
ABOUT TIME!
SHF
THAT'S RIGHT. I FIGURED IT OUT...
...WHEN I BROUGHT UP THE IDEA OF STACKING BOOKS.
I KNOW HOW THIS SAVAGE MURDER WAS COMMITTED...
...AND THAT THE MURDERER ...
...IS ONE OF THESE THREE PEOPLE!

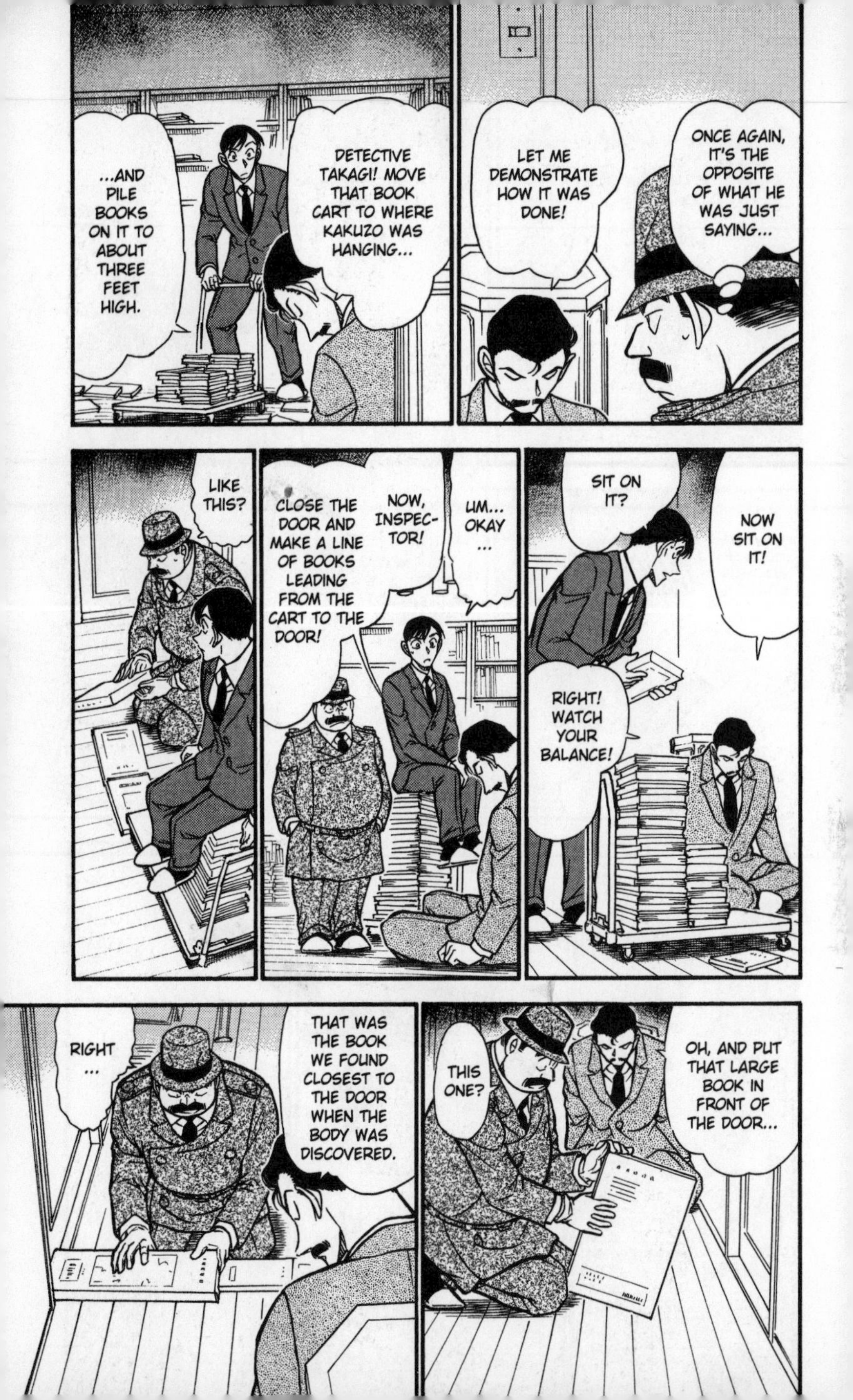
ONCE AGAIN, IT'S THE OPPOSITE OF WHAT HE WAS JUST SAYING...
LET ME DEMONSTRATE HOW IT WAS DONE!
DETECTIVE TAKAGI! MOVE THAT BOOK CART TO WHERE KAKUZO WAS HANGING...
...AND PILE BOOKS ON IT TO ABOUT THREE FEET HIGH.
NOW SIT ON IT!
SIT ON IT?
RIGHT! WATCH YOUR BALANCE!
NOW, INSPECTOR!
CLOSE THE DOOR AND MAKE A LINE OF BOOKS LEADING FROM THE CART TO THE DOOR!
UM... OKAY ...
LIKE THIS?
OH, AND PUT THAT LARGE BOOK IN FRONT OF THE DOOR...
THIS ONE?
THAT WAS THE BOOK WE FOUND CLOSEST TO THE DOOR WHEN THE BODY WAS DISCOVERED.
RIGHT ...

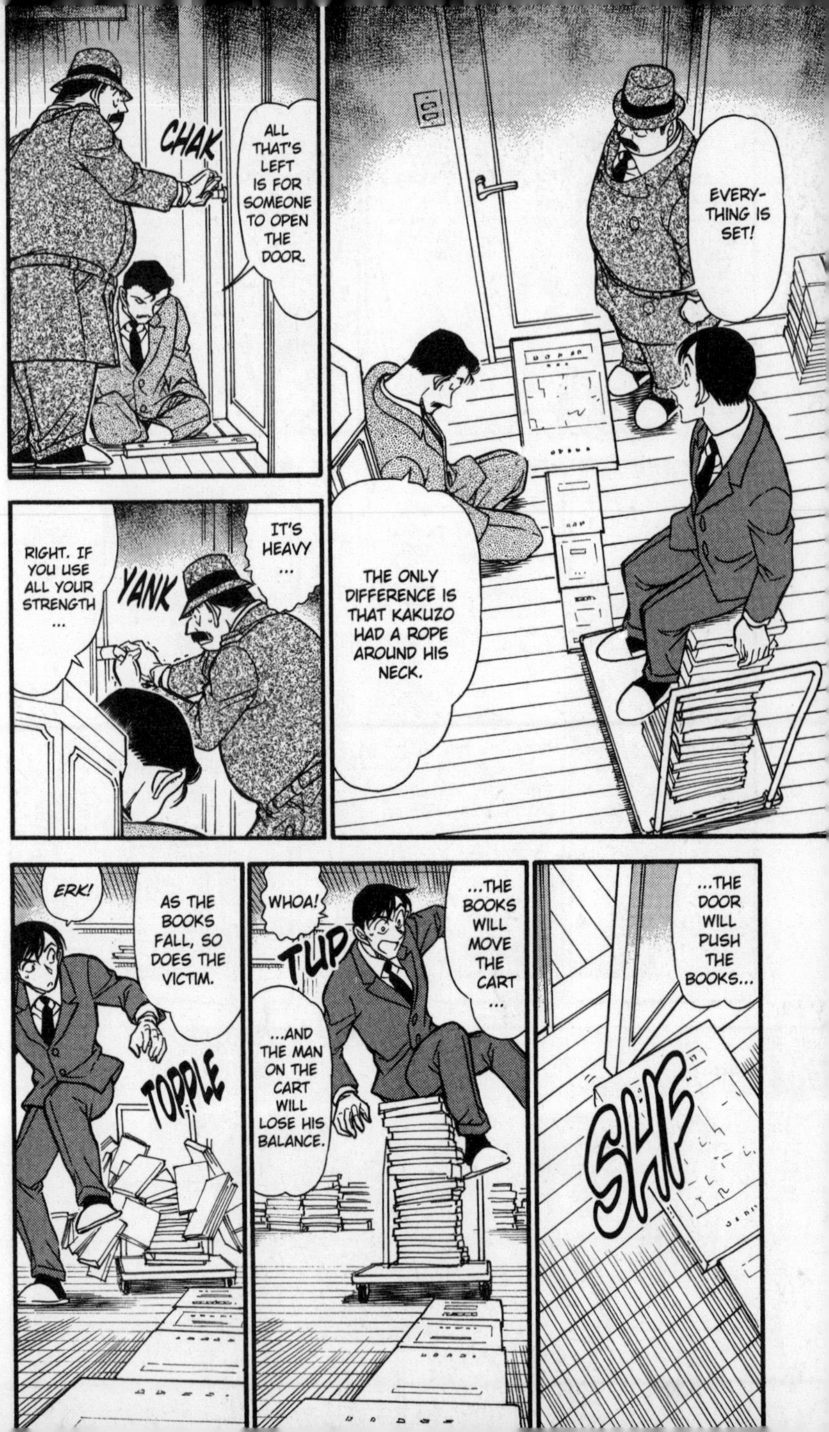
EVERY-THING IS SET!
THE ONLY DIFFERENCE IS THAT KAKUZO HAD A ROPE AROUND HIS NECK.
CHAK
ALL THAT'S LEFT IS FOR SOMEONE TO OPEN THE DOOR.
IT'S HEAVY ...
YANK
RIGHT. IF YOU USE ALL YOUR STRENGTH ...
...THE DOOR WILL PUSH THE BOOKS...
SHF
...THE BOOKS WILL MOVE THE CART ...
WHOA!
TUP
...AND THE MAN ON THE CART WILL LOSE HIS BALANCE.
AS THE BOOKS FALL, SO DOES THE VICTIM.
ERK!
TOPPLE

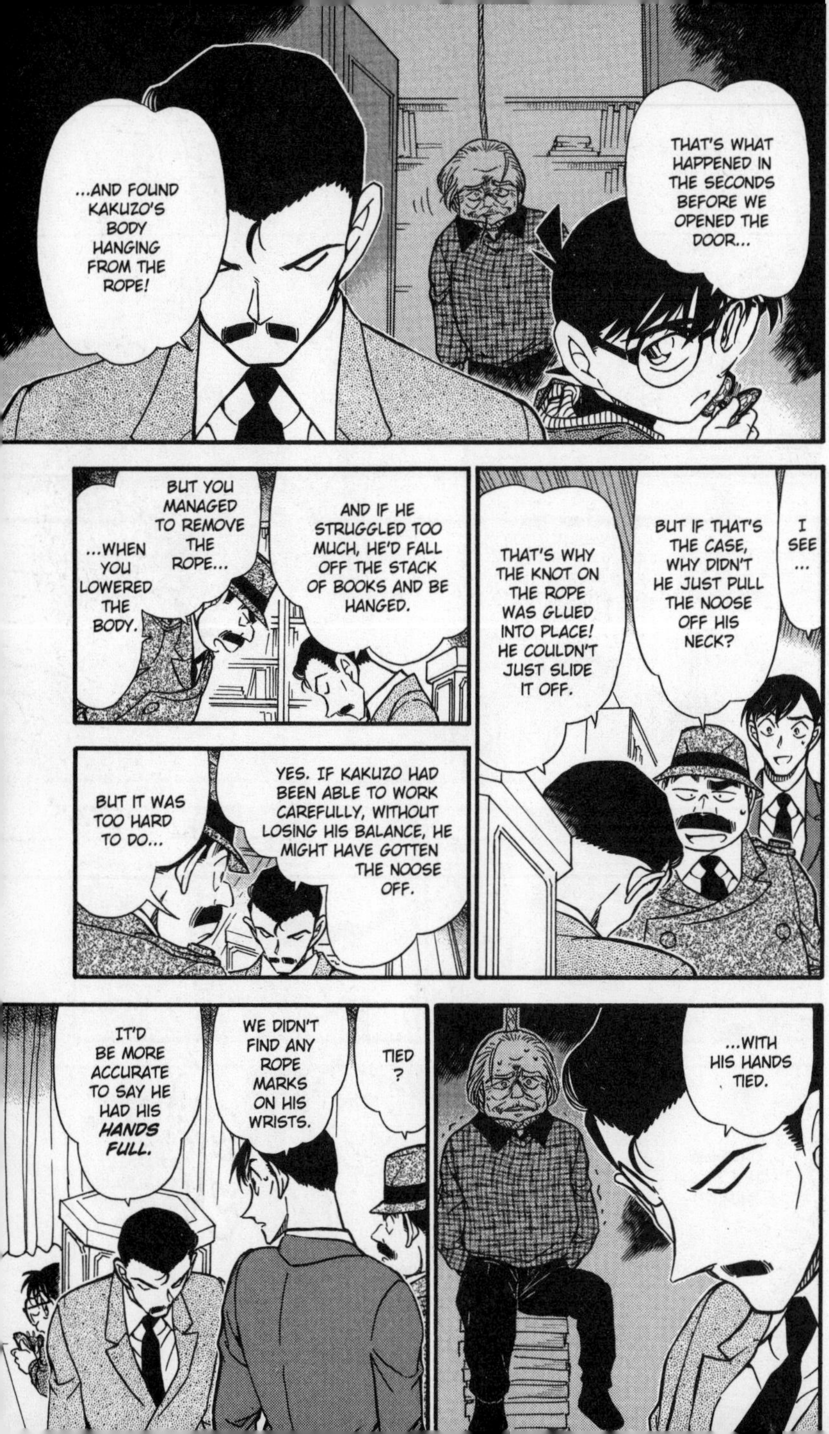
THAT'S WHAT HAPPENED IN THE SECONDS BEFORE WE OPENED THE DOOR...
...AND FOUND KAKUZO'S BODY HANGING FROM THE ROPE!
I SEE...
BUT IF THAT'S THE CASE, WHY DIDN'T HE JUST PULL THE NOOSE OFF HIS NECK?
THAT'S WHY THE KNOT ON THE ROPE WAS GLUED INTO PLACE! HE COULDN'T JUST SLIDE IT OFF.
AND IF HE STRUGGLED TOO MUCH, HE'D FALL OFF THE STACK OF BOOKS AND BE HANGED.
BUT YOU MANAGED TO REMOVE THE ROPE...
...WHEN YOU LOWERED THE BODY.
YES. IF KAKUZO HAD BEEN ABLE TO WORK CAREFULLY, WITHOUT LOSING HIS BALANCE, HE MIGHT HAVE GOTTEN THE NOOSE OFF.
BUT IT WAS TOO HARD TO DO...
...WITH HIS HANDS TIED.
TIED?
WE DIDN'T FIND ANY ROPE MARKS ON HIS WRISTS.
IT'D BE MORE ACCURATE TO SAY HE HAD HIS ***HANDS FULL.***

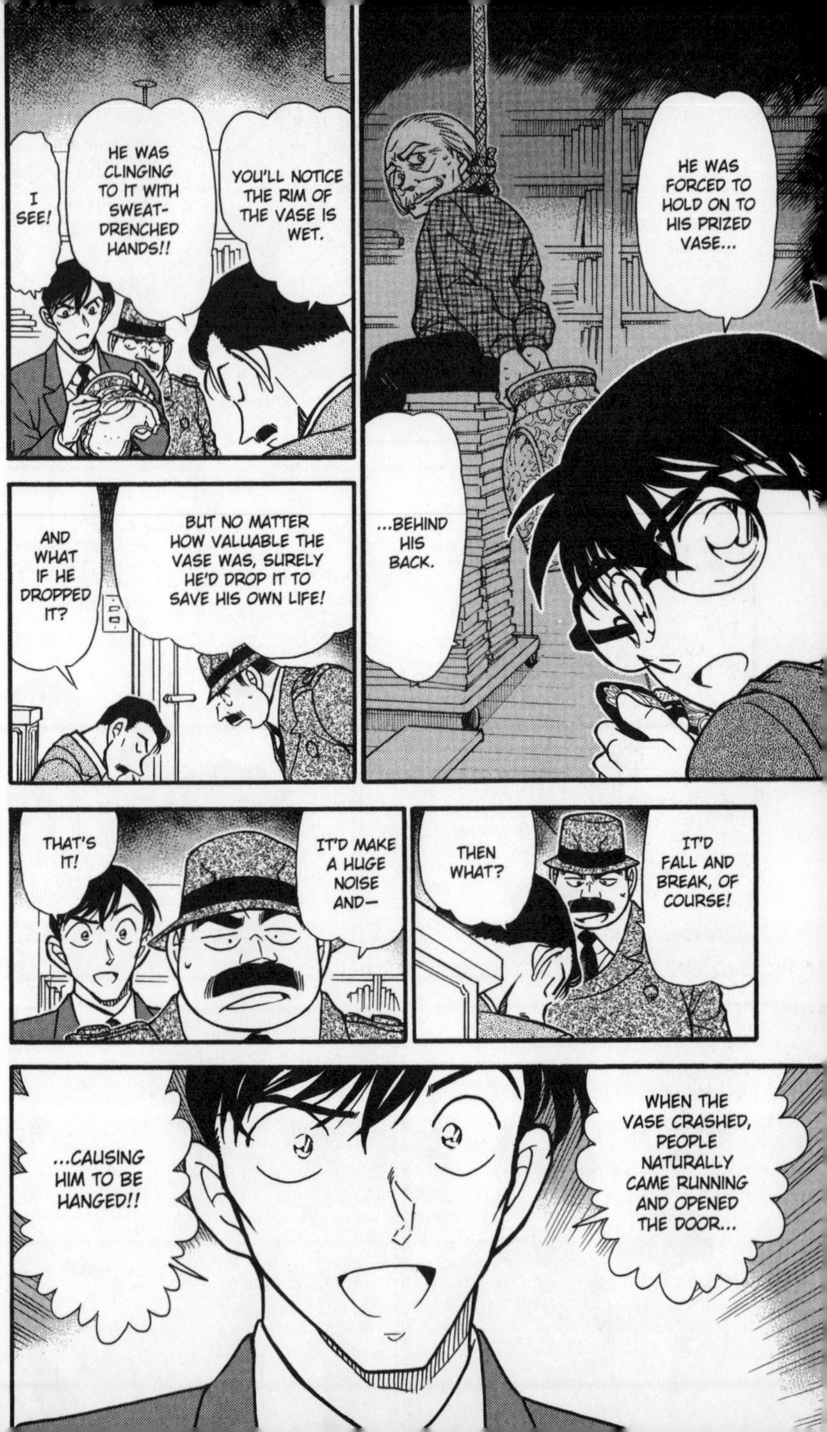
HE WAS FORCED TO HOLD ON TO HIS PRIZED VASE...
...BEHIND HIS BACK.
YOU'LL NOTICE THE RIM OF THE VASE IS WET.
HE WAS CLINGING TO IT WITH SWEAT-DRENCHED HANDS!!
I SEE!
BUT NO MATTER HOW VALUABLE THE VASE WAS, SURELY HE'D DROP IT TO SAVE HIS OWN LIFE!
AND WHAT IF HE DROPPED IT?
IT'D FALL AND BREAK, OF COURSE!
THEN WHAT?
IT'D MAKE A HUGE NOISE AND—
THAT'S IT!
WHEN THE VASE CRASHED, PEOPLE NATURALLY CAME RUNNING AND OPENED THE DOOR...
...CAUSING HIM TO BE HANGED!!

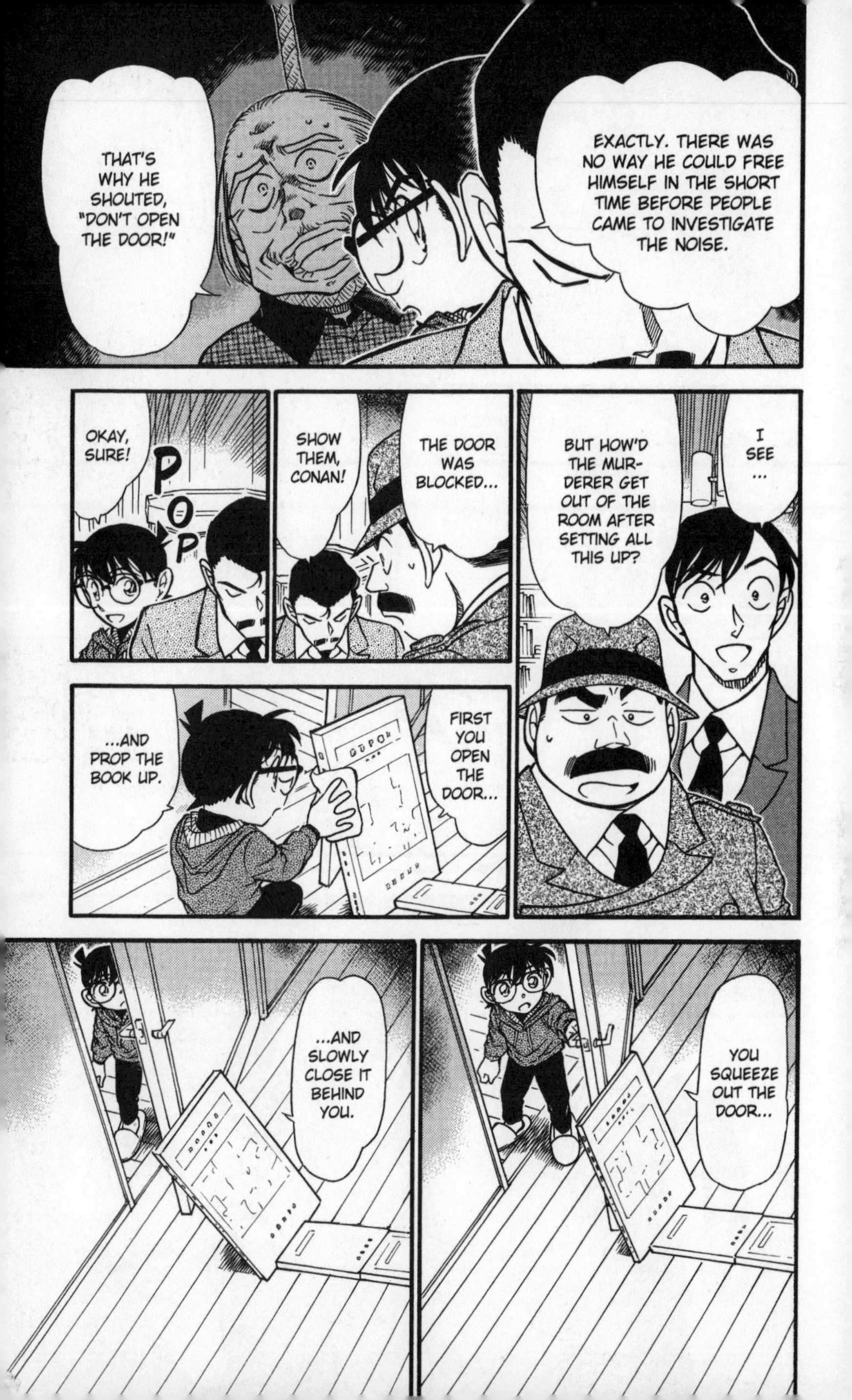
EXACTLY. THERE WAS NO WAY HE COULD FREE HIMSELF IN THE SHORT TIME BEFORE PEOPLE CAME TO INVESTIGATE THE NOISE.
THAT'S WHY HE SHOUTED, "DON'T OPEN THE DOOR!"
I SEE...
BUT HOW'D THE MUR-DERER GET OUT OF THE ROOM AFTER SETTING ALL THIS UP?
THE DOOR WAS BLOCKED...
SHOW THEM, CONAN!
OKAY, SURE!
POP POP
FIRST YOU OPEN THE DOOR...
...AND PROP THE BOOK UP.
YOU SQUEEZE OUT THE DOOR...
...AND SLOWLY CLOSE IT BEHIND YOU.

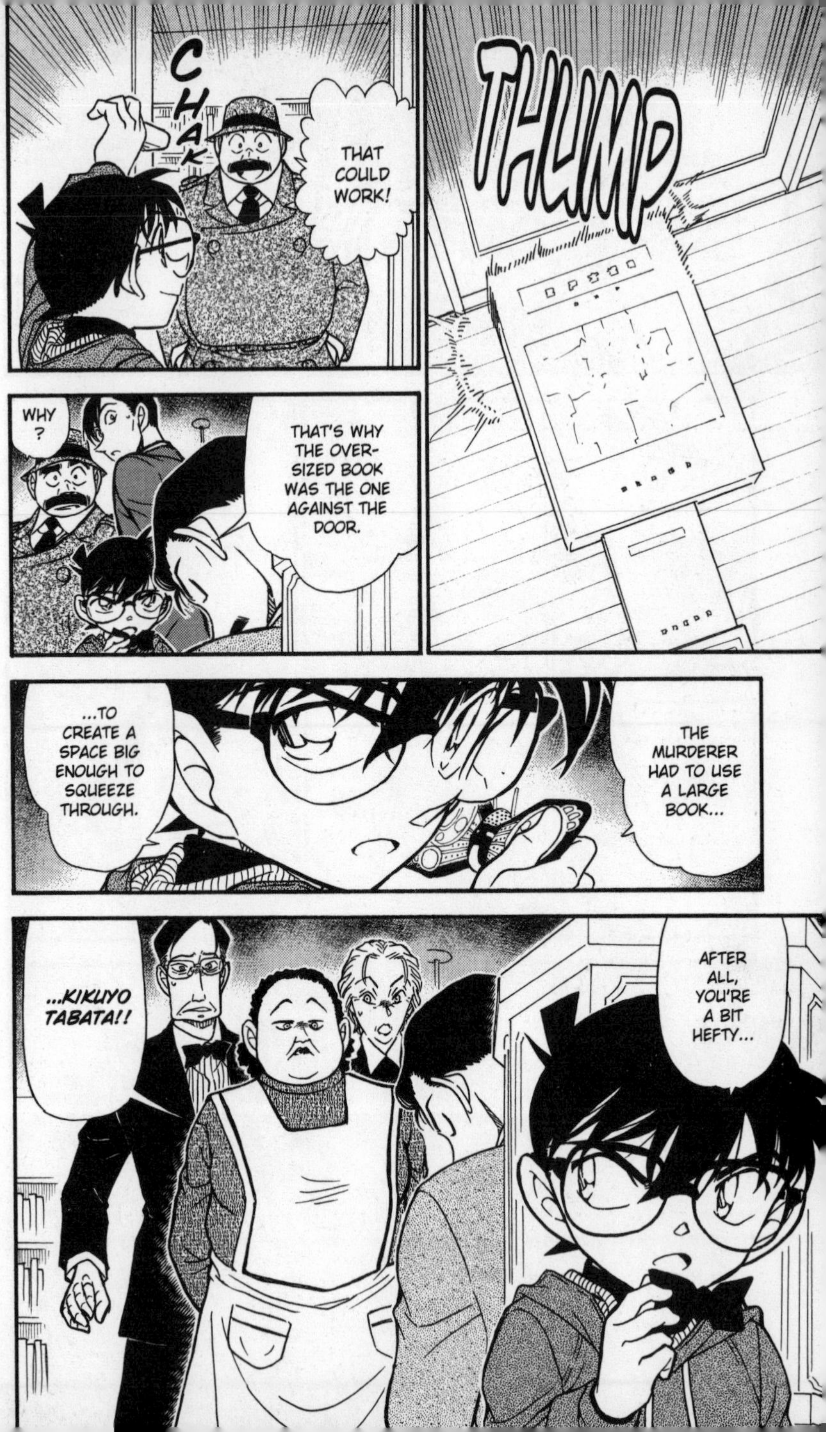
THUMP
CHAK
THAT COULD WORK!
THAT'S WHY THE OVER-SIZED BOOK WAS THE ONE AGAINST THE DOOR.
WHY?
THE MURDERER HAD TO USE A LARGE BOOK...
...TO CREATE A SPACE BIG ENOUGH TO SQUEEZE THROUGH.
AFTER ALL, YOU'RE A BIT HEFTY...
...KIKUYO TABATA!!

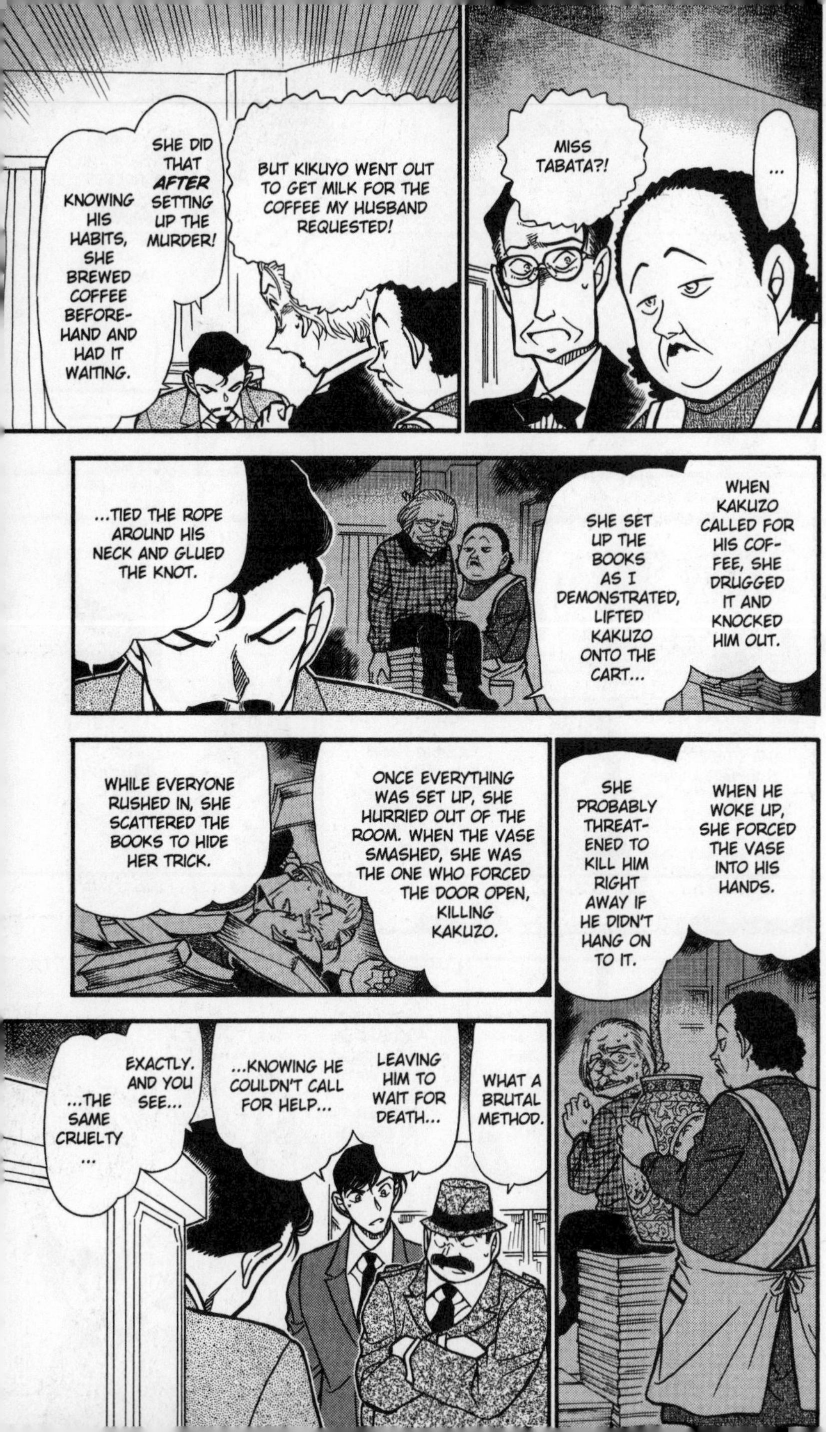
...
MISS TABATA?!
BUT KIKUYO WENT OUT TO GET MILK FOR THE COFFEE MY HUSBAND REQUESTED!
SHE DID THAT AFTER SETTING UP THE MURDER!
KNOWING HIS HABITS, SHE BREWED COFFEE BEFOREHAND AND HAD IT WAITING.
WHEN KAKUZO CALLED FOR HIS COFFEE, SHE DRUGGED IT AND KNOCKED HIM OUT.
SHE SET UP THE BOOKS AS I DEMONSTRATED, LIFTED KAKUZO ONTO THE CART...
...TIED THE ROPE AROUND HIS NECK AND GLUED THE KNOT.
WHEN HE WOKE UP, SHE FORCED THE VASE INTO HIS HANDS.
SHE PROBABLY THREATENED TO KILL HIM RIGHT AWAY IF HE DIDN'T HANG ON TO IT.
ONCE EVERYTHING WAS SET UP, SHE HURRIED OUT OF THE ROOM. WHEN THE VASE SMASHED, SHE WAS THE ONE WHO FORCED THE DOOR OPEN, KILLING KAKUZO.
WHILE EVERYONE RUSHED IN, SHE SCATTERED THE BOOKS TO HIDE HER TRICK.
WHAT A BRUTAL METHOD.
LEAVING HIM TO WAIT FOR DEATH...
...KNOWING HE COULDN'T CALL FOR HELP...
EXACTLY. AND YOU SEE...
...THE SAME CRUELTY ...

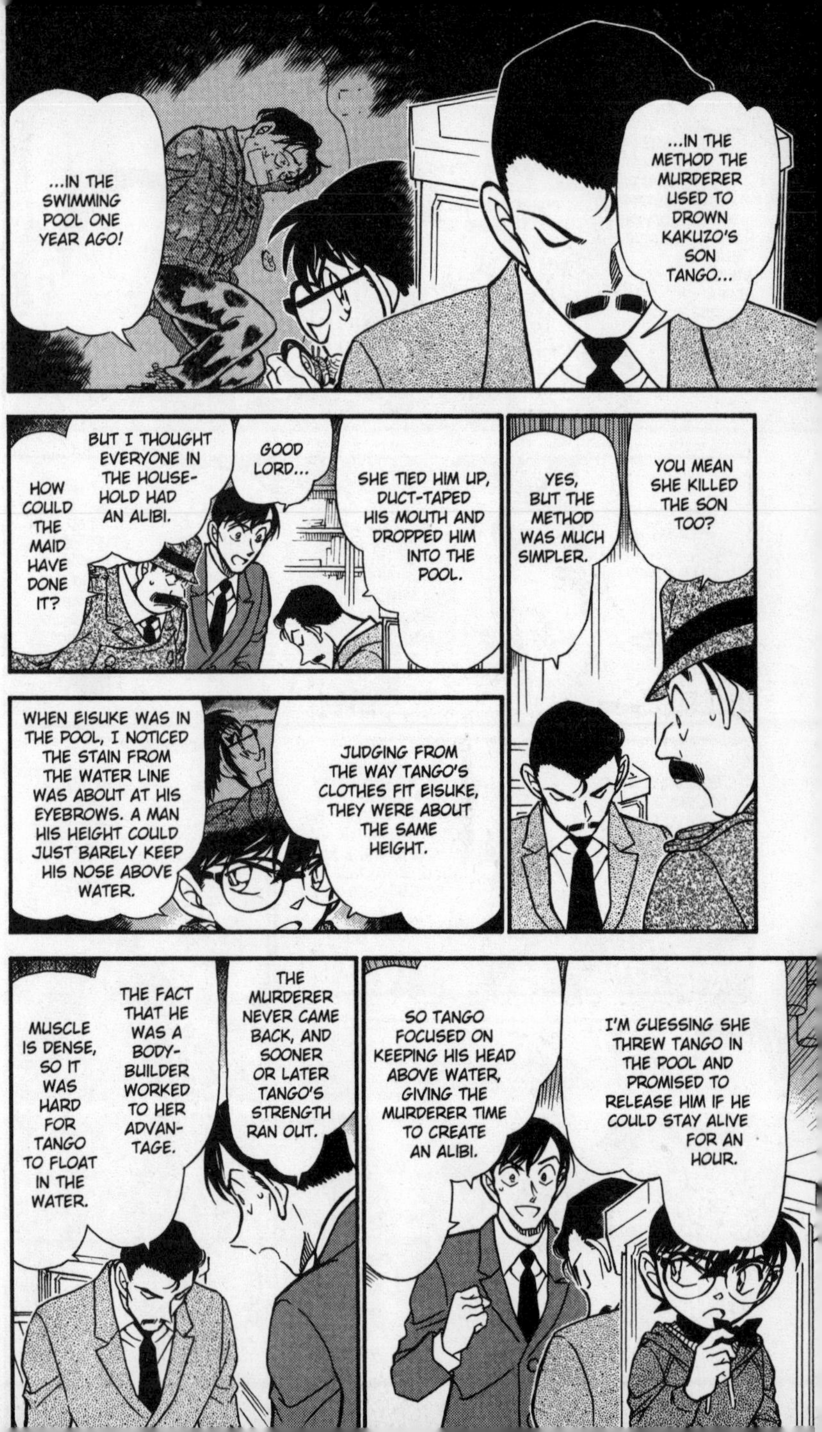
...IN THE METHOD THE MURDERER USED TO DROWN KAKUZO'S SON TANGO...
...IN THE SWIMMING POOL ONE YEAR AGO!
YOU MEAN SHE KILLED THE SON TOO?
YES, BUT THE METHOD WAS MUCH SIMPLER.
SHE TIED HIM UP, DUCT-TAPED HIS MOUTH AND DROPPED HIM INTO THE POOL.
GOOD LORD...
BUT I THOUGHT EVERYONE IN THE HOUSE-HOLD HAD AN ALIBI.
HOW COULD THE MAID HAVE DONE IT?
JUDGING FROM THE WAY TANGO'S CLOTHES FIT EISUKE, THEY WERE ABOUT THE SAME HEIGHT.
WHEN EISUKE WAS IN THE POOL, I NOTICED THE STAIN FROM THE WATER LINE WAS ABOUT AT HIS EYEBROWS. A MAN HIS HEIGHT COULD JUST BARELY KEEP HIS NOSE ABOVE WATER.
I'M GUESSING SHE THREW TANGO IN THE POOL AND PROMISED TO RELEASE HIM IF HE COULD STAY ALIVE FOR AN HOUR.
SO TANGO FOCUSED ON KEEPING HIS HEAD ABOVE WATER, GIVING THE MURDERER TIME TO CREATE AN ALIBI.
THE MURDERER NEVER CAME BACK, AND SOONER OR LATER TANGO'S STRENGTH RAN OUT.
THE FACT THAT HE WAS A BODY-BUILDER WORKED TO HER ADVAN-TAGE.
MUSCLE IS DENSE, SO IT WAS HARD FOR TANGO TO FLOAT IN THE WATER.

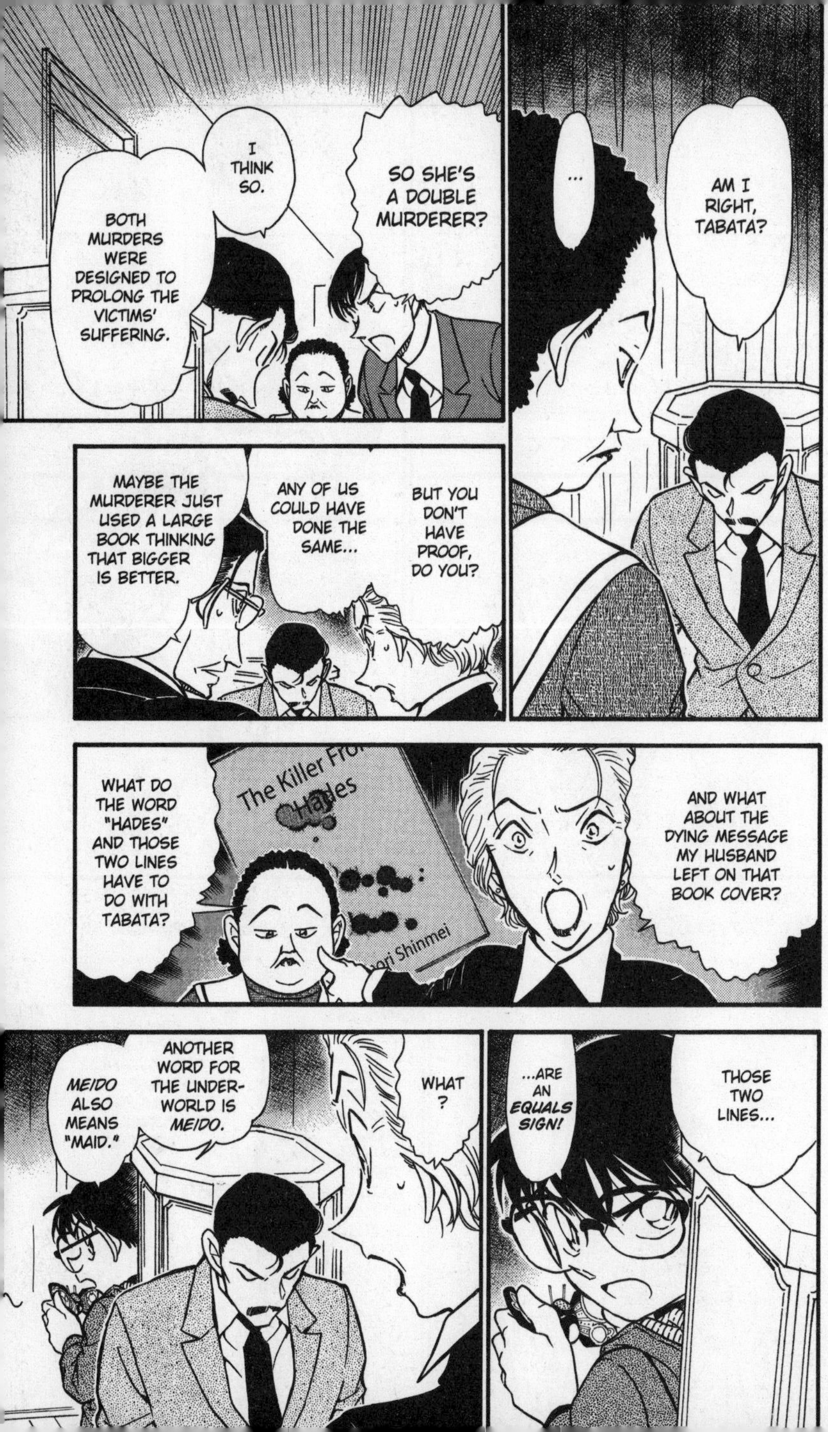
AM I RIGHT, TABATA?
...
SO SHE'S A DOUBLE MURDERER?
I THINK SO.
BOTH MURDERS WERE DESIGNED TO PROLONG THE VICTIMS' SUFFERING.
BUT YOU DON'T HAVE PROOF, DO YOU?
ANY OF US COULD HAVE DONE THE SAME...
MAYBE THE MURDERER JUST USED A LARGE BOOK THINKING THAT BIGGER IS BETTER.
AND WHAT ABOUT THE DYING MESSAGE MY HUSBAND LEFT ON THAT BOOK COVER?
Hades
WHAT DO THE WORD "HADES" AND THOSE TWO LINES HAVE TO DO WITH TABATA?
THOSE TWO LINES...
...ARE AN *EQUALS SIGN!*
WHAT?
ANOTHER WORD FOR THE UNDER-WORLD IS *MEIDO.*
MEIDO ALSO MEANS "MAID."

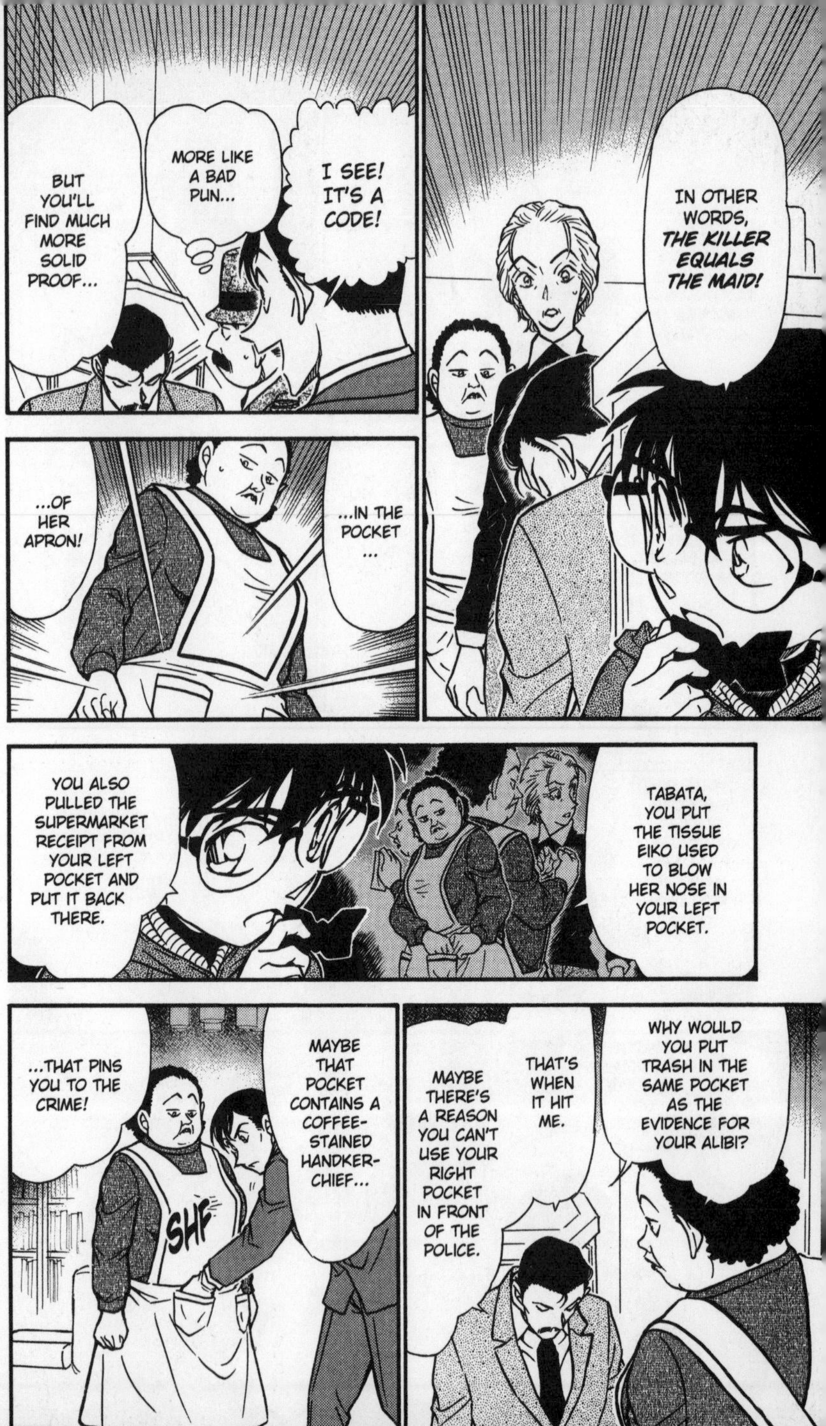
IN OTHER WORDS, *THE KILLER EQUALS THE MAID!*
I SEE! IT'S A CODE!
MORE LIKE A BAD PUN...
BUT YOU'LL FIND MUCH MORE SOLID PROOF...
...IN THE POCKET...
...OF HER APRON!
TABATA, YOU PUT THE TISSUE EIKO USED TO BLOW HER NOSE IN YOUR LEFT POCKET.
YOU ALSO PULLED THE SUPERMARKET RECEIPT FROM YOUR LEFT POCKET AND PUT IT BACK THERE.
WHY WOULD YOU PUT TRASH IN THE SAME POCKET AS THE EVIDENCE FOR YOUR ALIBI?
THAT'S WHEN IT HIT ME.
MAYBE THERE'S A REASON YOU CAN'T USE YOUR RIGHT POCKET IN FRONT OF THE POLICE.
MAYBE THAT POCKET CONTAINS A COFFEE-STAINED HANDKER-CHIEF...
...THAT PINS YOU TO THE CRIME!

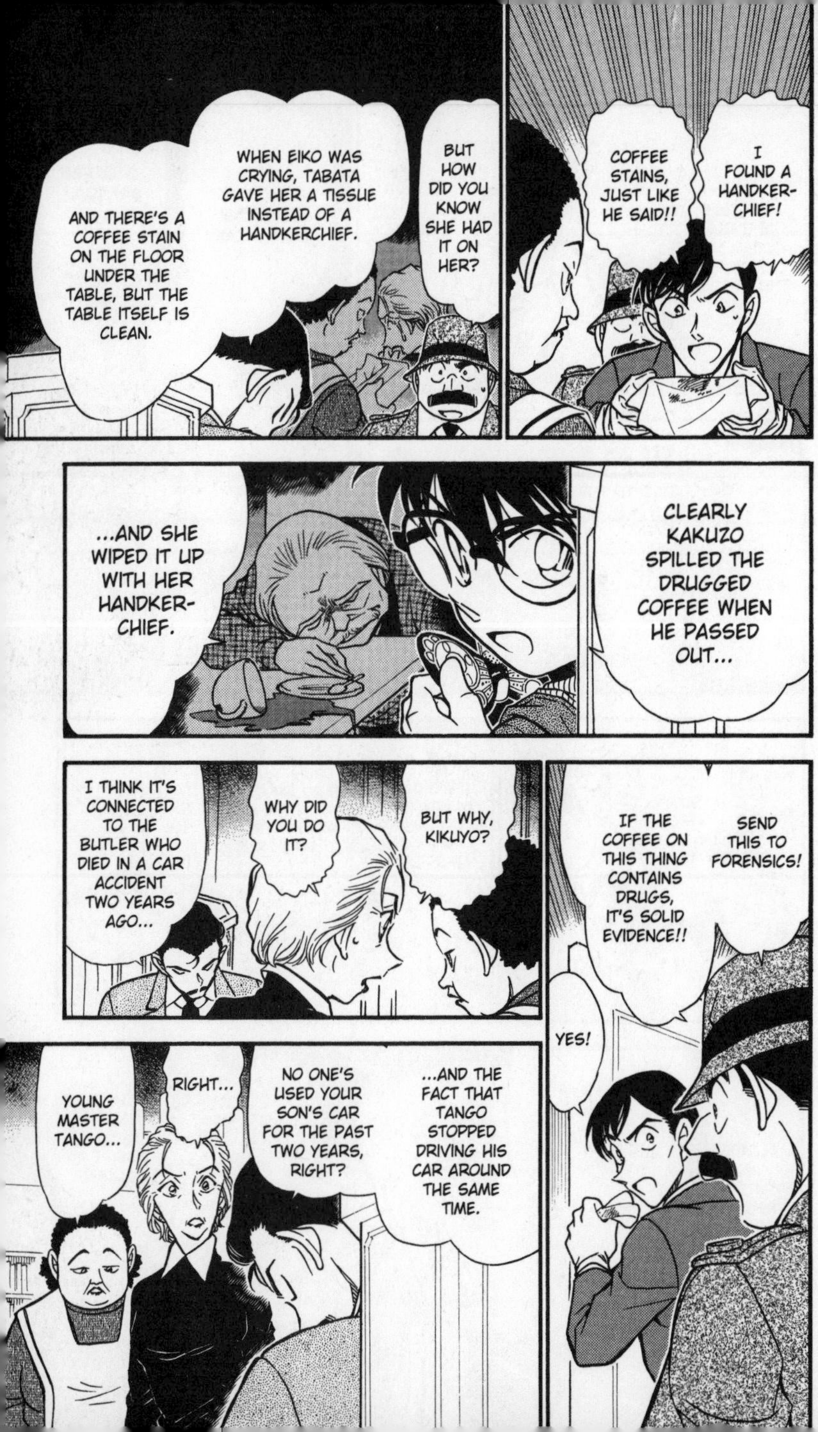
I FOUND A HANDKERCHIEF!
COFFEE STAINS, JUST LIKE HE SAID!!
BUT HOW DID YOU KNOW SHE HAD IT ON HER?
WHEN EIKO WAS CRYING, TABATA GAVE HER A TISSUE INSTEAD OF A HANDKERCHIEF.
AND THERE'S A COFFEE STAIN ON THE FLOOR UNDER THE TABLE, BUT THE TABLE ITSELF IS CLEAN.
CLEARLY KAKUZO SPILLED THE DRUGGED COFFEE WHEN HE PASSED OUT...
...AND SHE WIPED IT UP WITH HER HANDKERCHIEF.
SEND THIS TO FORENSICS!
IF THE COFFEE ON THIS THING CONTAINS DRUGS, IT'S SOLID EVIDENCE!!
YES!
BUT WHY, KIKUYO?
WHY DID YOU DO IT?
I THINK IT'S CONNECTED TO THE BUTLER WHO DIED IN A CAR ACCIDENT TWO YEARS AGO...
...AND THE FACT THAT TANGO STOPPED DRIVING HIS CAR AROUND THE SAME TIME.
NO ONE'S USED YOUR SON'S CAR FOR THE PAST TWO YEARS, RIGHT?
RIGHT...
YOUNG MASTER TANGO...

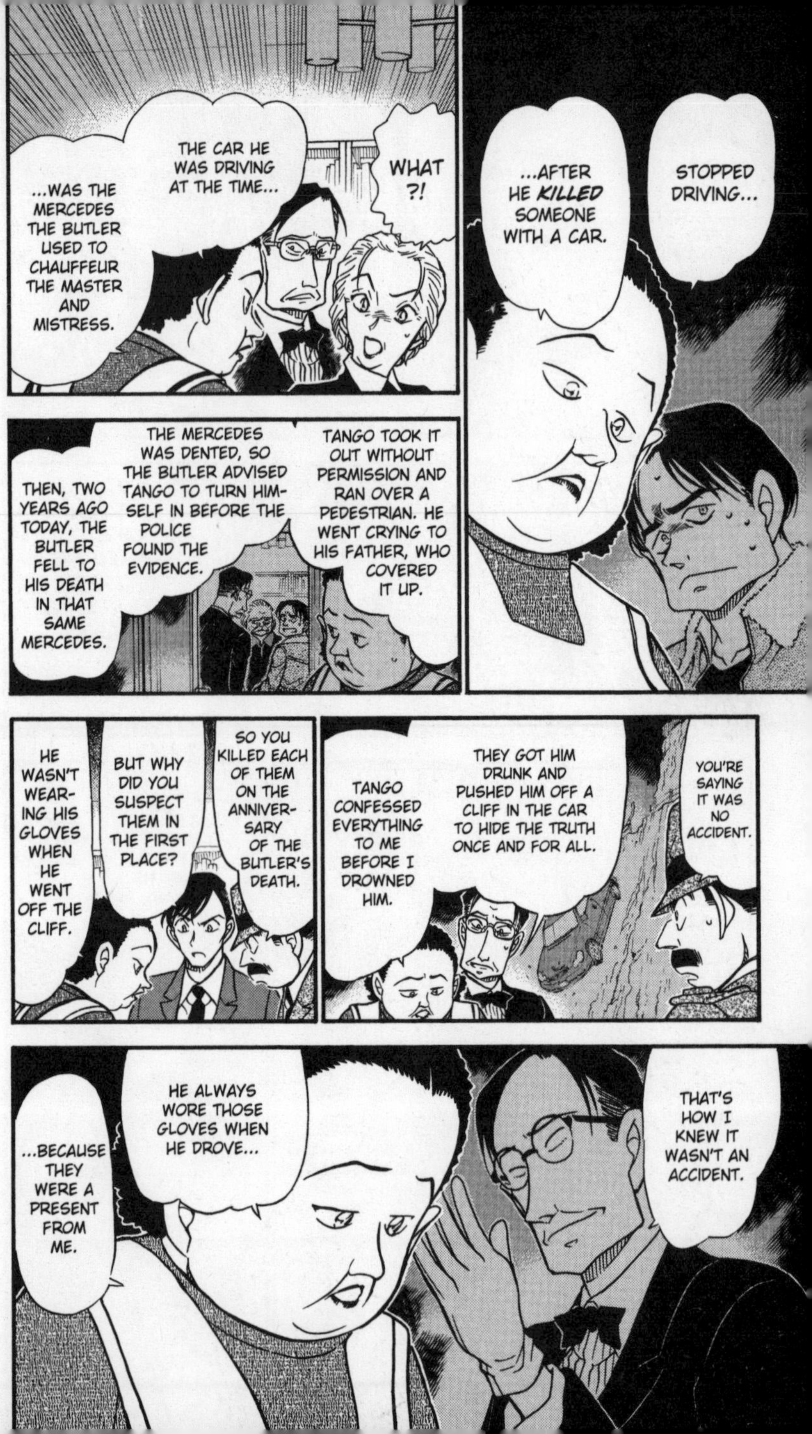
STOPPED DRIVING...
...AFTER HE KILLED SOMEONE WITH A CAR.
WHAT?!
THE CAR HE WAS DRIVING AT THE TIME...
...WAS THE MERCEDES THE BUTLER USED TO CHAUFFEUR THE MASTER AND MISTRESS.
TANGO TOOK IT OUT WITHOUT PERMISSION AND RAN OVER A PEDESTRIAN. HE WENT CRYING TO HIS FATHER, WHO COVERED IT UP.
THE MERCEDES WAS DENTED, SO THE BUTLER ADVISED TANGO TO TURN HIMSELF IN BEFORE THE POLICE FOUND THE EVIDENCE.
THEN, TWO YEARS AGO TODAY, THE BUTLER FELL TO HIS DEATH IN THAT SAME MERCEDES.
YOU'RE SAYING IT WAS NO ACCIDENT.
THEY GOT HIM DRUNK AND PUSHED HIM OFF A CLIFF IN THE CAR TO HIDE THE TRUTH ONCE AND FOR ALL.
TANGO CONFESSED EVERYTHING TO ME BEFORE I DROWNED HIM.
SO YOU KILLED EACH OF THEM ON THE ANNIVERSARY OF THE BUTLER'S DEATH.
BUT WHY DID YOU SUSPECT THEM IN THE FIRST PLACE?
HE WASN'T WEARING HIS GLOVES WHEN HE WENT OFF THE CLIFF.
THAT'S HOW I KNEW IT WASN'T AN ACCIDENT.
HE ALWAYS WORE THOSE GLOVES WHEN HE DROVE...
...BECAUSE THEY WERE A PRESENT FROM ME.

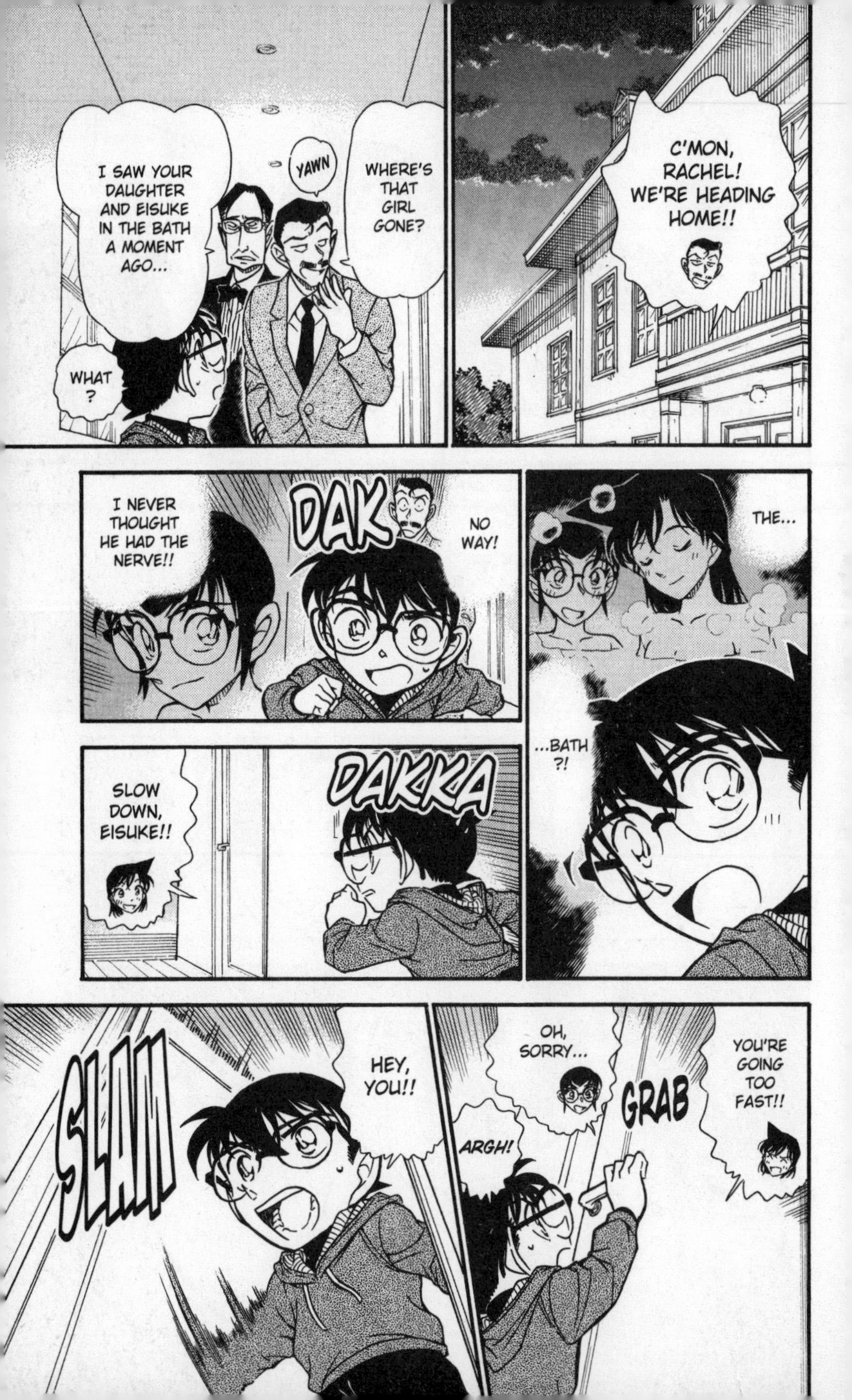
C'MON, RACHEL! WE'RE HEADING HOME!!
WHERE'S THAT GIRL GONE?
YAWN
I SAW YOUR DAUGHTER AND EISUKE IN THE BATH A MOMENT AGO...
WHAT?
THE...
...BATH?!
NO WAY!
DAK
I NEVER THOUGHT HE HAD THE NERVE!!
DAKKA
SLOW DOWN, EISUKE!!
YOU'RE GOING TOO FAST!!
GRAB
OH, SORRY...
ARGH!
HEY, YOU!!
SLAM

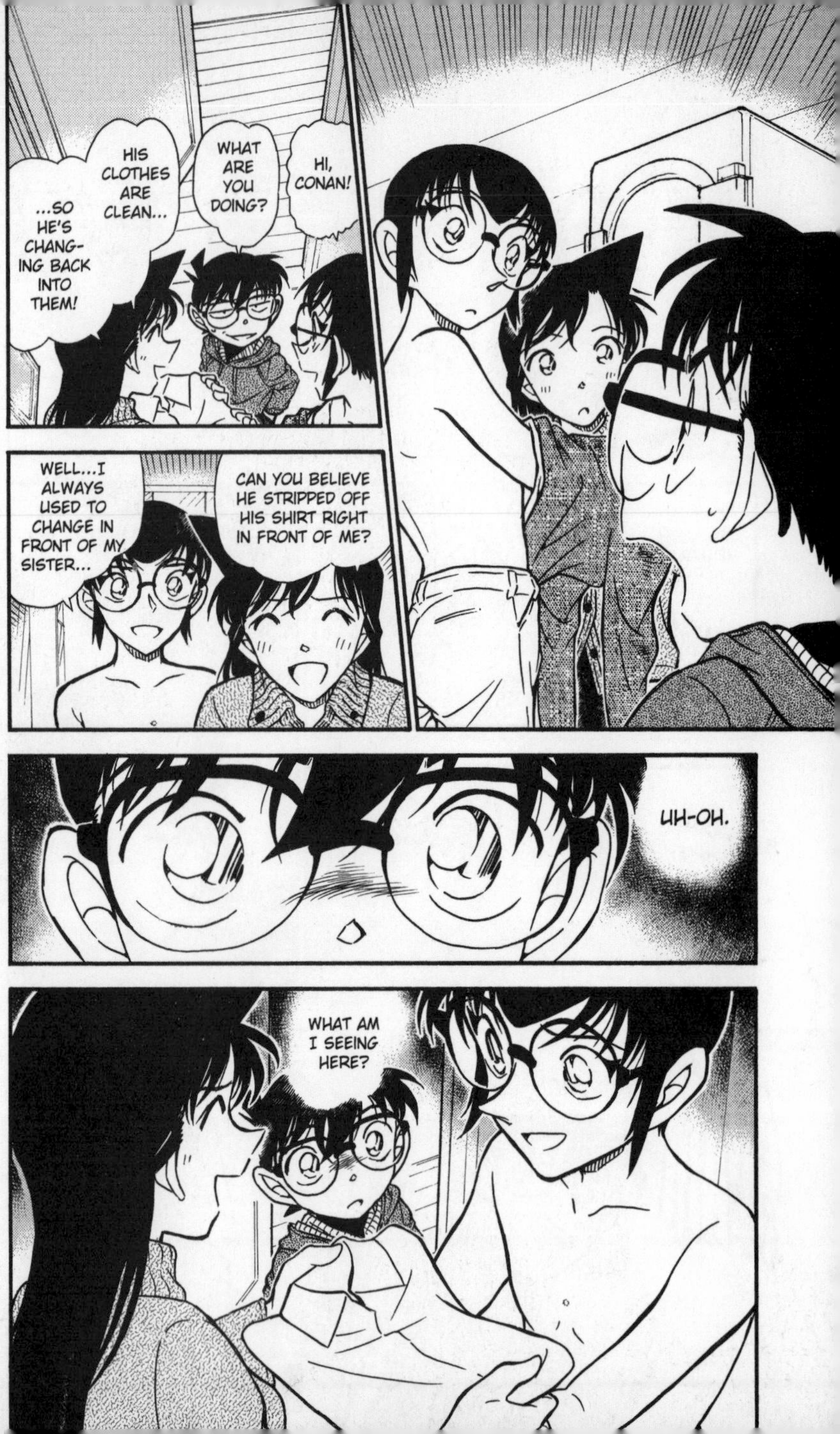

HI, CONAN!
WHAT ARE YOU DOING?
HIS CLOTHES ARE CLEAN...
...SO HE'S CHANGING BACK INTO THEM!
CAN YOU BELIEVE HE STRIPPED OFF HIS SHIRT RIGHT IN FRONT OF ME?
WELL...I ALWAYS USED TO CHANGE IN FRONT OF MY SISTER...
UH-OH.
WHAT AM I SEEING HERE?

FILE 5: THE DEMON COMETH

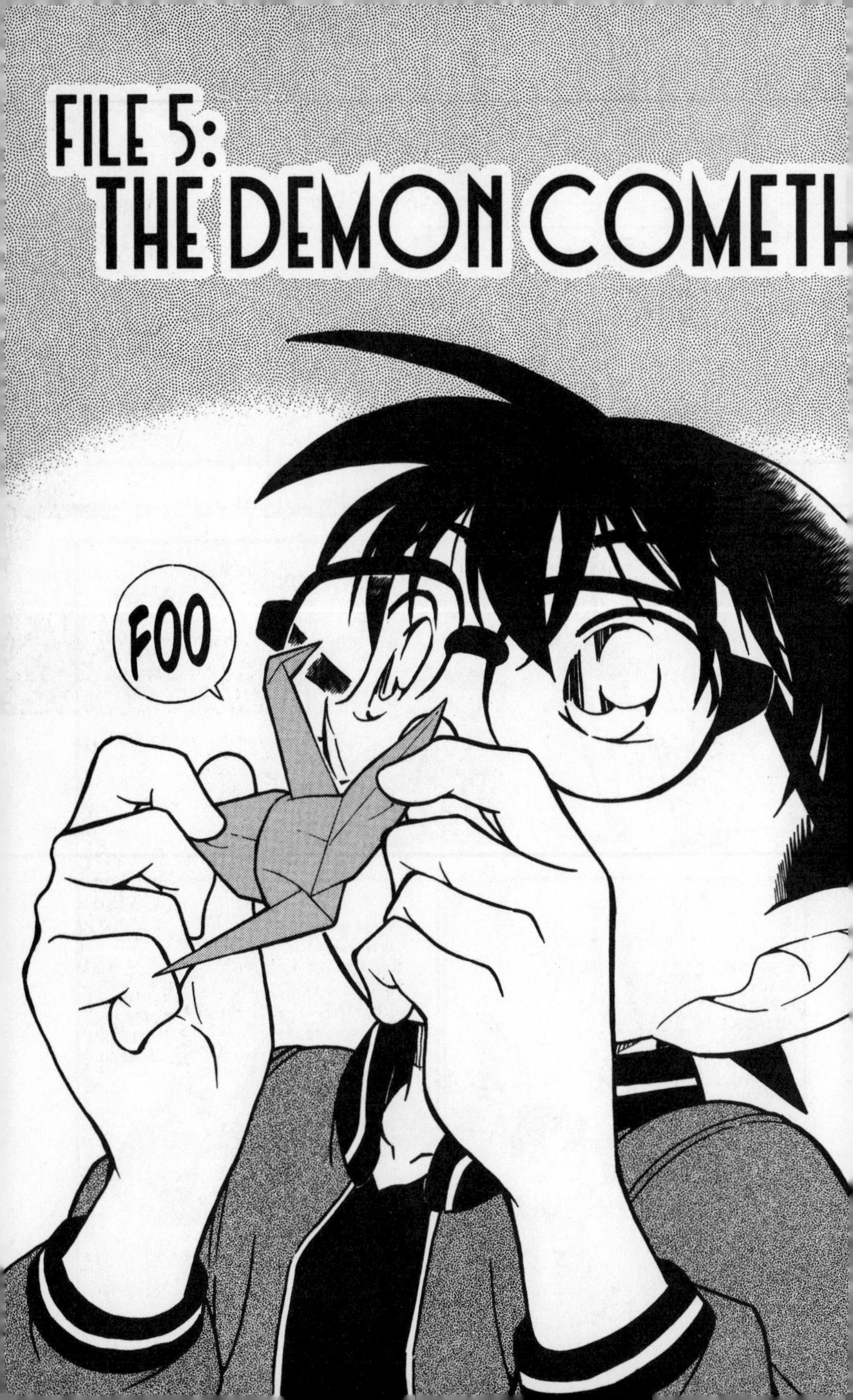
FOO

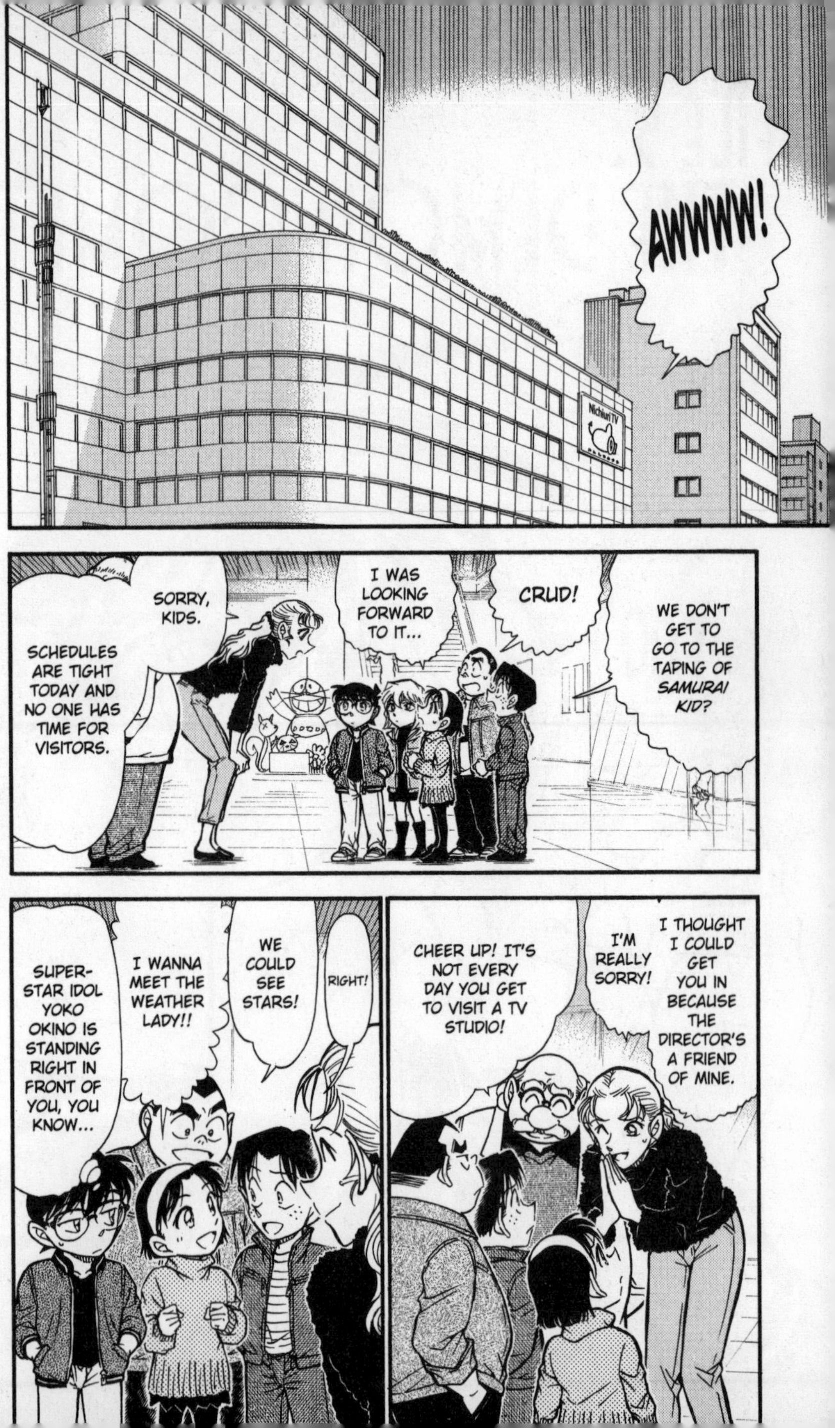
AWWWW!
Nichiuri TV
WE DON'T GET TO GO TO THE TAPING OF SAMURAI KID?
CRUD!
I WAS LOOKING FORWARD TO IT...
SORRY, KIDS.
SCHEDULES ARE TIGHT TODAY AND NO ONE HAS TIME FOR VISITORS.
I THOUGHT I COULD GET YOU IN BECAUSE THE DIRECTOR'S A FRIEND OF MINE.
I'M REALLY SORRY!
CHEER UP! IT'S NOT EVERY DAY YOU GET TO VISIT A TV STUDIO!
RIGHT!
WE COULD SEE STARS!
I WANNA MEET THE WEATHER LADY!!
SUPER-STAR IDOL YOKO OKINO IS STANDING RIGHT IN FRONT OF YOU, YOU KNOW...

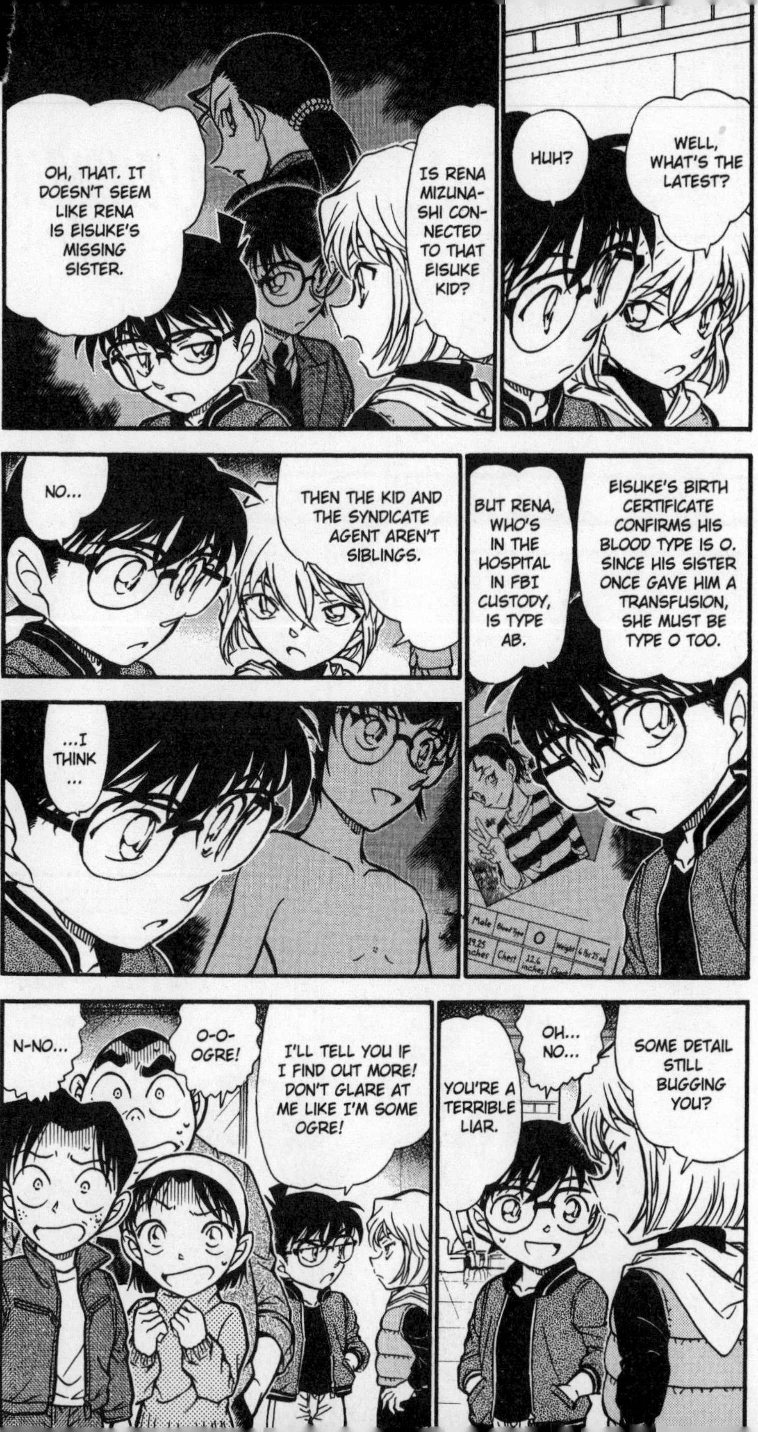
WELL, WHAT'S THE LATEST?
HUH?
IS RENA MIZUNASHI CONNECTED TO THAT EISUKE KID?
OH, THAT. IT DOESN'T SEEM LIKE RENA IS EISUKE'S MISSING SISTER.
EISUKE'S BIRTH CERTIFICATE CONFIRMS HIS BLOOD TYPE IS O. SINCE HIS SISTER ONCE GAVE HIM A TRANSFUSION, SHE MUST BE TYPE O TOO.
BUT RENA, WHO'S IN THE HOSPITAL IN FBI CUSTODY, IS TYPE AB.
THEN THE KID AND THE SYNDICATE AGENT AREN'T SIBLINGS.
NO...
...I THINK...
SOME DETAIL STILL BUGGING YOU?
OH... NO...
YOU'RE A TERRIBLE LIAR.
I'LL TELL YOU IF I FIND OUT MORE! DON'T GLARE AT ME LIKE I'M SOME OGRE!
O-O-OGRE!
N-NO...

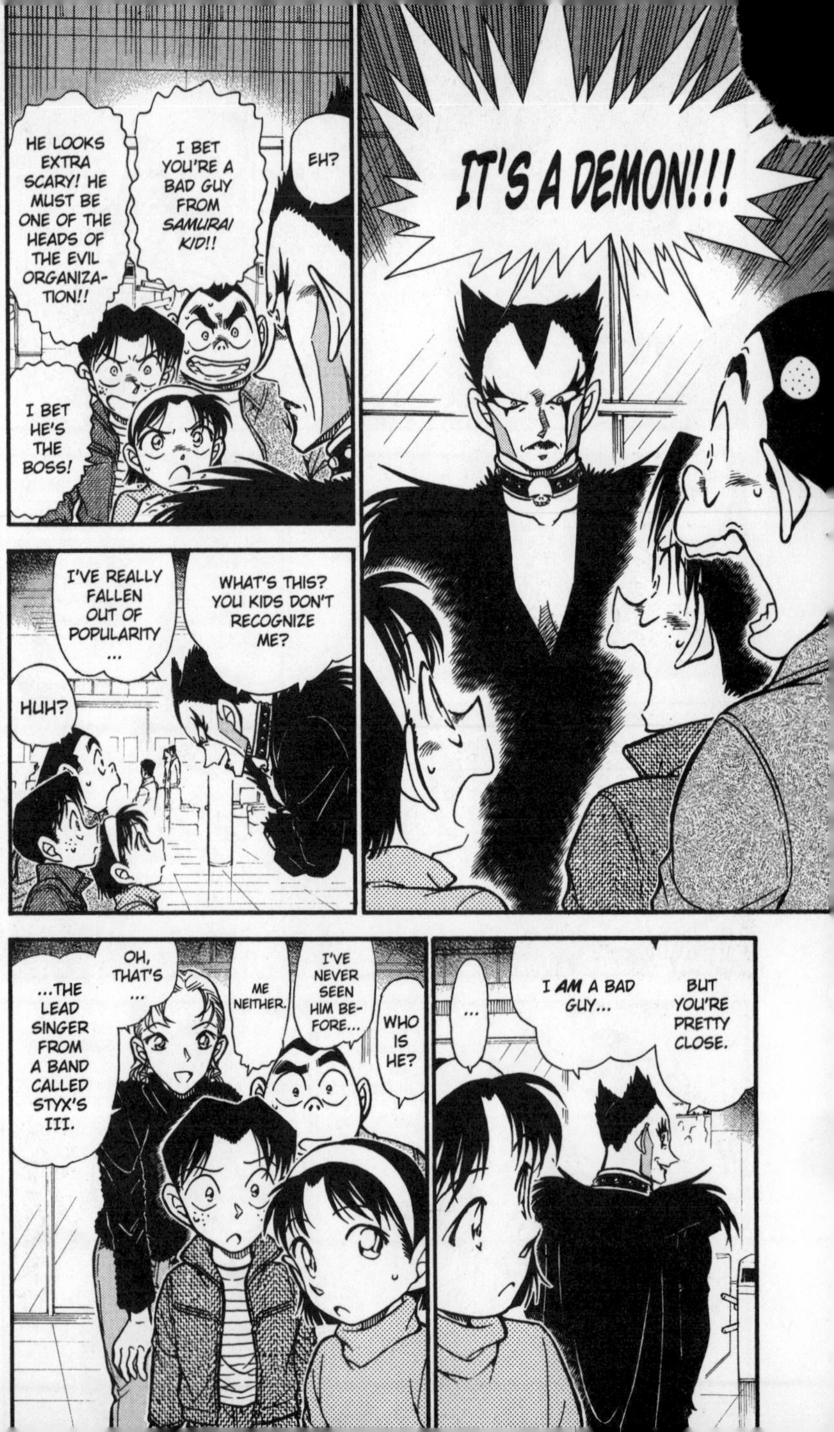
IT'S A DEMON!!!
EH?
I BET YOU'RE A BAD GUY FROM SAMURAI KID!!
HE LOOKS EXTRA SCARY! HE MUST BE ONE OF THE HEADS OF THE EVIL ORGANIZA-TION!!
I BET HE'S THE BOSS!
WHAT'S THIS? YOU KIDS DON'T RECOGNIZE ME?
I'VE REALLY FALLEN OUT OF POPULARITY ...
HUH?
...
I *AM* A BAD GUY...
BUT YOU'RE PRETTY CLOSE.
WHO IS HE?
I'VE NEVER SEEN HIM BE-FORE...
ME NEITHER.
OH, THAT'S ...
...THE LEAD SINGER FROM A BAND CALLED STYX'S III.

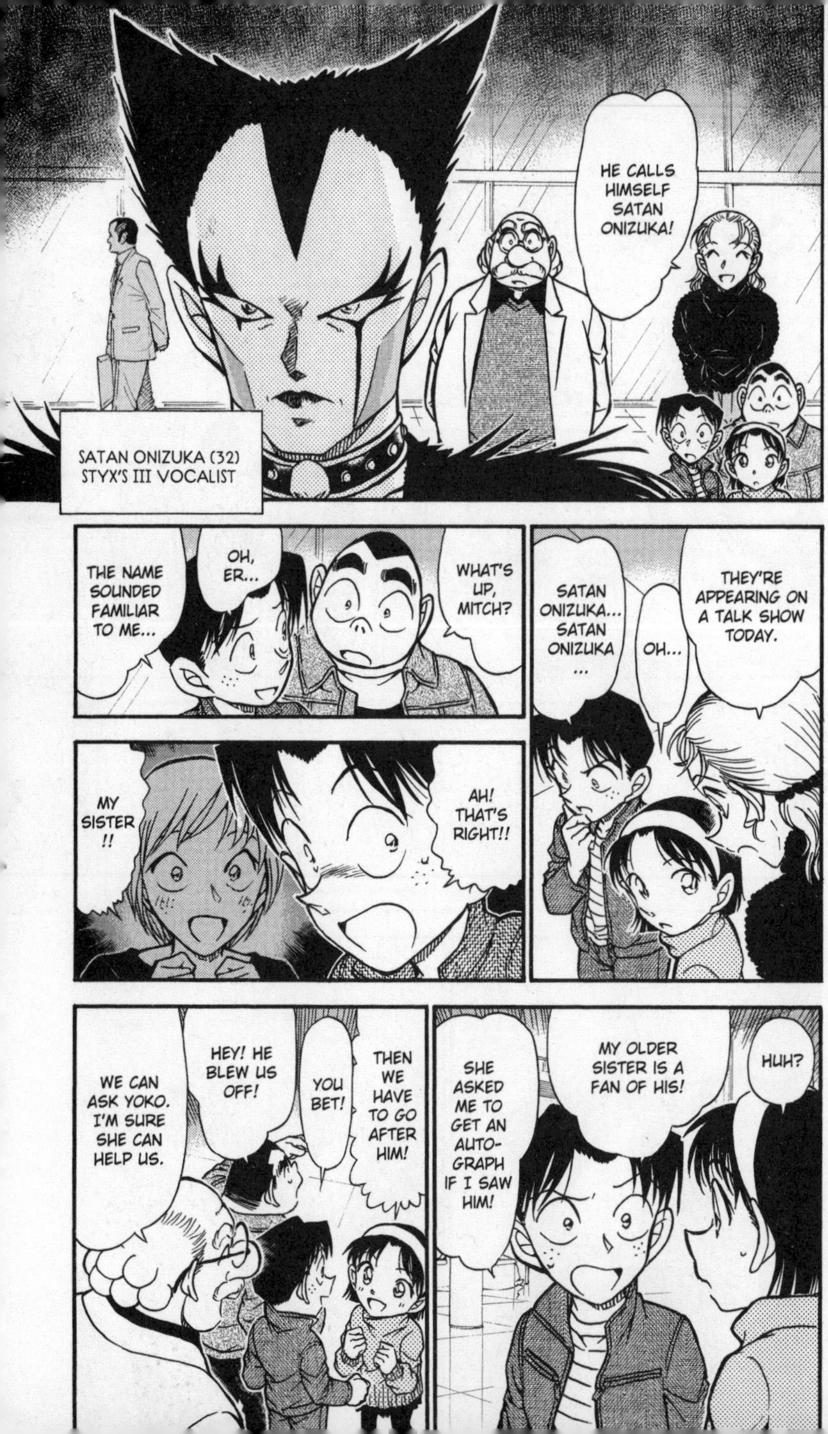
HE CALLS HIMSELF SATAN ONIZUKA!
SATAN ONIZUKA (32) STYX'S III VOCALIST
THEY'RE APPEARING ON A TALK SHOW TODAY.
OH...
SATAN ONIZUKA... SATAN ONIZUKA ...
WHAT'S UP, MITCH?
OH, ER...
THE NAME SOUNDED FAMILIAR TO ME...
AH! THAT'S RIGHT!!
MY SISTER !!
HUH?
MY OLDER SISTER IS A FAN OF HIS!
SHE ASKED ME TO GET AN AUTO-GRAPH IF I SAW HIM!
THEN WE HAVE TO GO AFTER HIM!
YOU BET!
HEY! HE BLEW US OFF!
WE CAN ASK YOKO. I'M SURE SHE CAN HELP US.

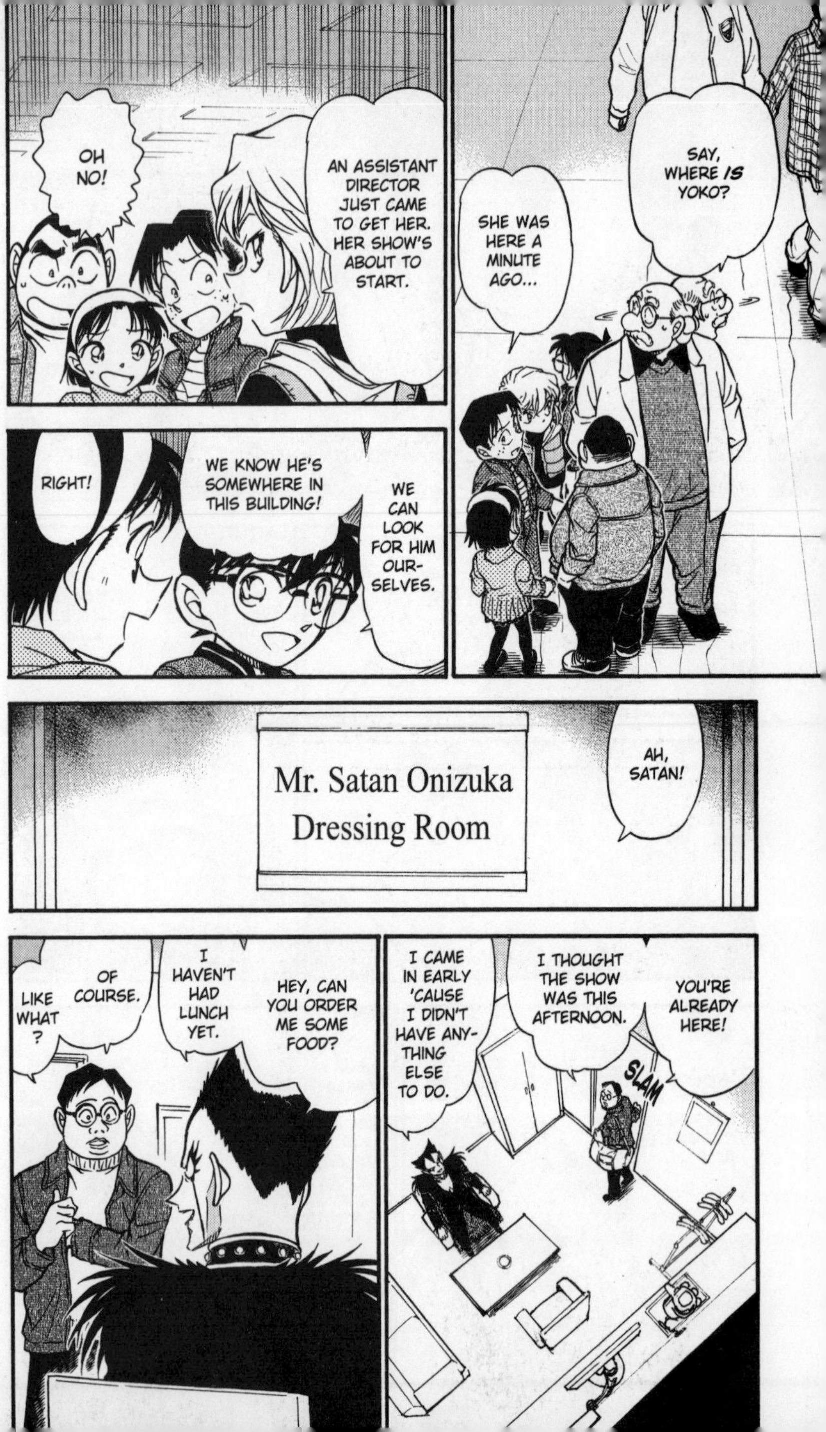
SAY, WHERE *IS* YOKO?
SHE WAS HERE A MINUTE AGO...
AN ASSISTANT DIRECTOR JUST CAME TO GET HER. HER SHOW'S ABOUT TO START.
OH NO!
WE CAN LOOK FOR HIM OURSELVES.
WE KNOW HE'S SOMEWHERE IN THIS BUILDING!
RIGHT!
AH, SATAN!
Mr. Satan Onizuka
Dressing Room
YOU'RE ALREADY HERE!
I THOUGHT THE SHOW WAS THIS AFTERNOON.
SLAM
I CAME IN EARLY 'CAUSE I DIDN'T HAVE ANYTHING ELSE TO DO.
HEY, CAN YOU ORDER ME SOME FOOD?
I HAVEN'T HAD LUNCH YET.
OF COURSE.
LIKE WHAT?

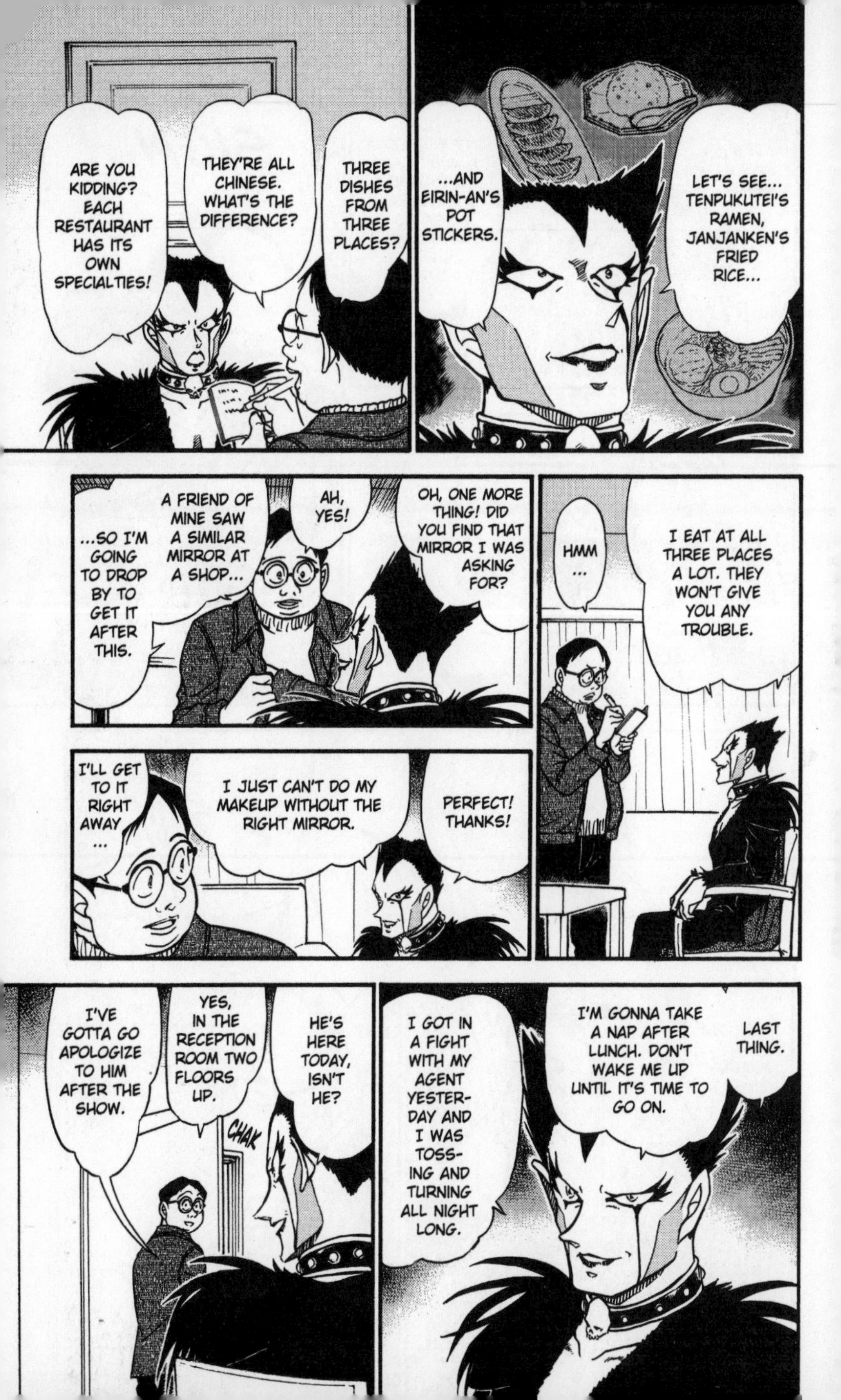
LET'S SEE... TENPUKUTEI'S RAMEN, JANJANKEN'S FRIED RICE...
...AND EIRIN-AN'S POT STICKERS.
THREE DISHES FROM THREE PLACES?
THEY'RE ALL CHINESE. WHAT'S THE DIFFERENCE?
ARE YOU KIDDING? EACH RESTAURANT HAS ITS OWN SPECIALTIES!
I EAT AT ALL THREE PLACES A LOT. THEY WON'T GIVE YOU ANY TROUBLE.
HMM...
OH, ONE MORE THING! DID YOU FIND THAT MIRROR I WAS ASKING FOR?
AH, YES!
A FRIEND OF MINE SAW A SIMILAR MIRROR AT A SHOP...
...SO I'M GOING TO DROP BY TO GET IT AFTER THIS.
PERFECT! THANKS!
I JUST CAN'T DO MY MAKEUP WITHOUT THE RIGHT MIRROR.
I'LL GET TO IT RIGHT AWAY...
LAST THING.
I'M GONNA TAKE A NAP AFTER LUNCH. DON'T WAKE ME UP UNTIL IT'S TIME TO GO ON.
I GOT IN A FIGHT WITH MY AGENT YESTER-DAY AND I WAS TOSS-ING AND TURNING ALL NIGHT LONG.
HE'S HERE TODAY, ISN'T HE?
YES, IN THE RECEPTION ROOM TWO FLOORS UP.
CHAK
I'VE GOTTA GO APOLOGIZE TO HIM AFTER THE SHOW.

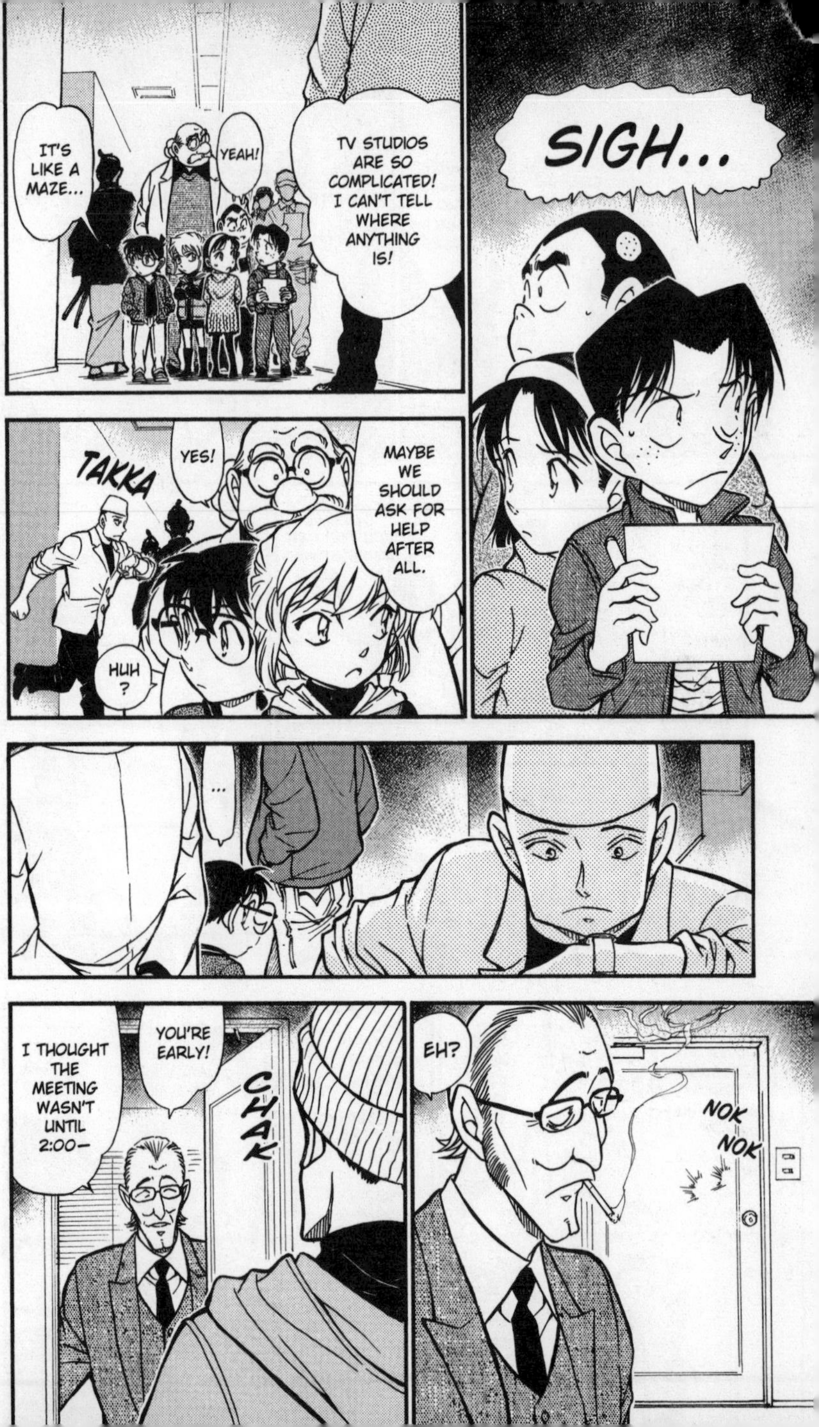
SIGH...
TV STUDIOS ARE SO COMPLICATED! I CAN'T TELL WHERE ANYTHING IS!
YEAH!
IT'S LIKE A MAZE...
MAYBE WE SHOULD ASK FOR HELP AFTER ALL.
YES!
TAKKA
HUH?
...
EH?
NOK NOK
CHAK
YOU'RE EARLY!
I THOUGHT THE MEETING WASN'T UNTIL 2:00—

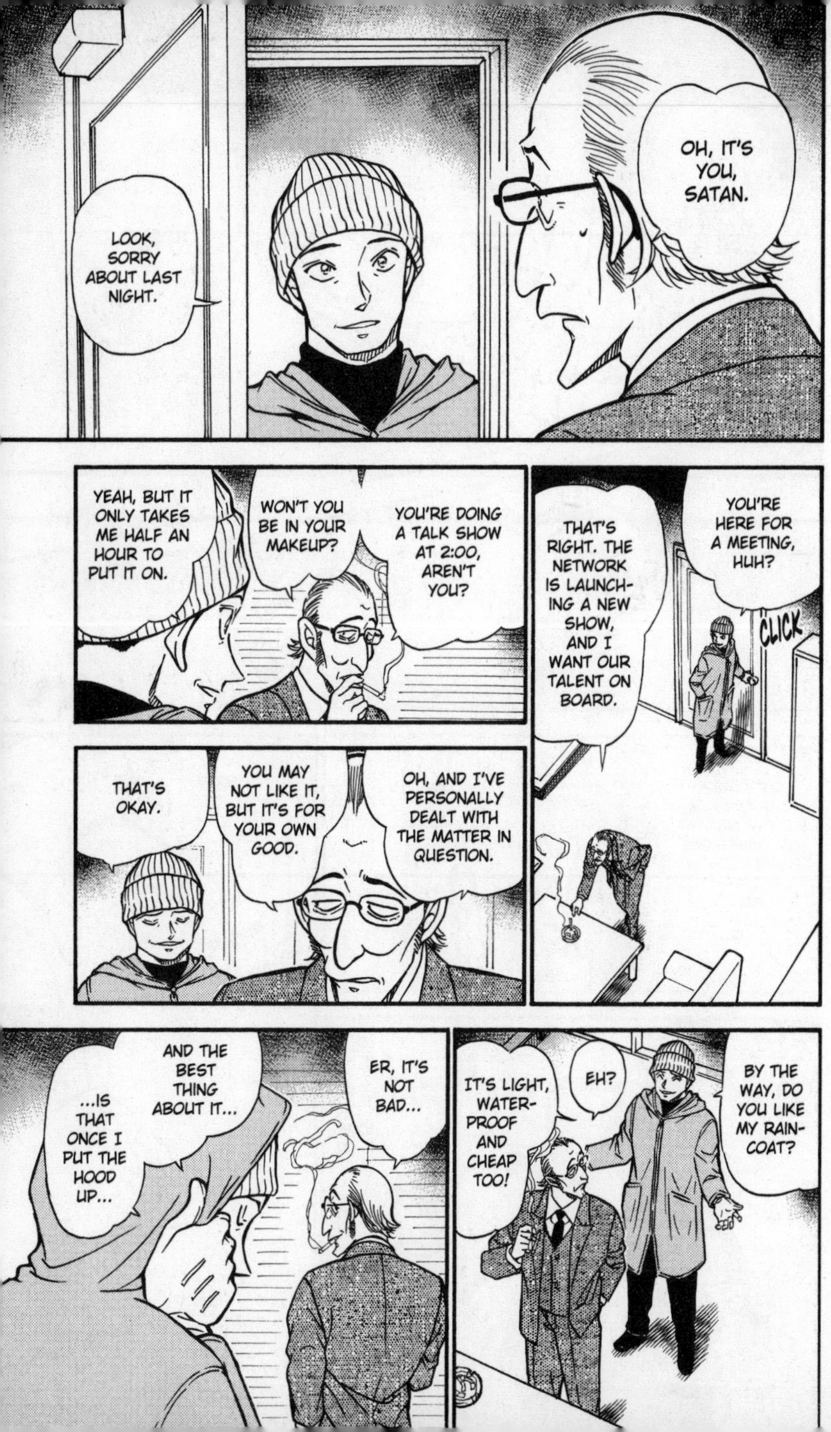
OH, IT'S YOU, SATAN.
LOOK, SORRY ABOUT LAST NIGHT.
YOU'RE HERE FOR A MEETING, HUH?
CLICK
THAT'S RIGHT. THE NETWORK IS LAUNCHING A NEW SHOW, AND I WANT OUR TALENT ON BOARD.
YOU'RE DOING A TALK SHOW AT 2:00, AREN'T YOU?
WON'T YOU BE IN YOUR MAKEUP?
YEAH, BUT IT ONLY TAKES ME HALF AN HOUR TO PUT IT ON.
OH, AND I'VE PERSONALLY DEALT WITH THE MATTER IN QUESTION.
YOU MAY NOT LIKE IT, BUT IT'S FOR YOUR OWN GOOD.
THAT'S OKAY.
BY THE WAY, DO YOU LIKE MY RAIN-COAT?
EH?
IT'S LIGHT, WATER-PROOF AND CHEAP TOO!
ER, IT'S NOT BAD...
AND THE BEST THING ABOUT IT...
...IS THAT ONCE I PUT THE HOOD UP...

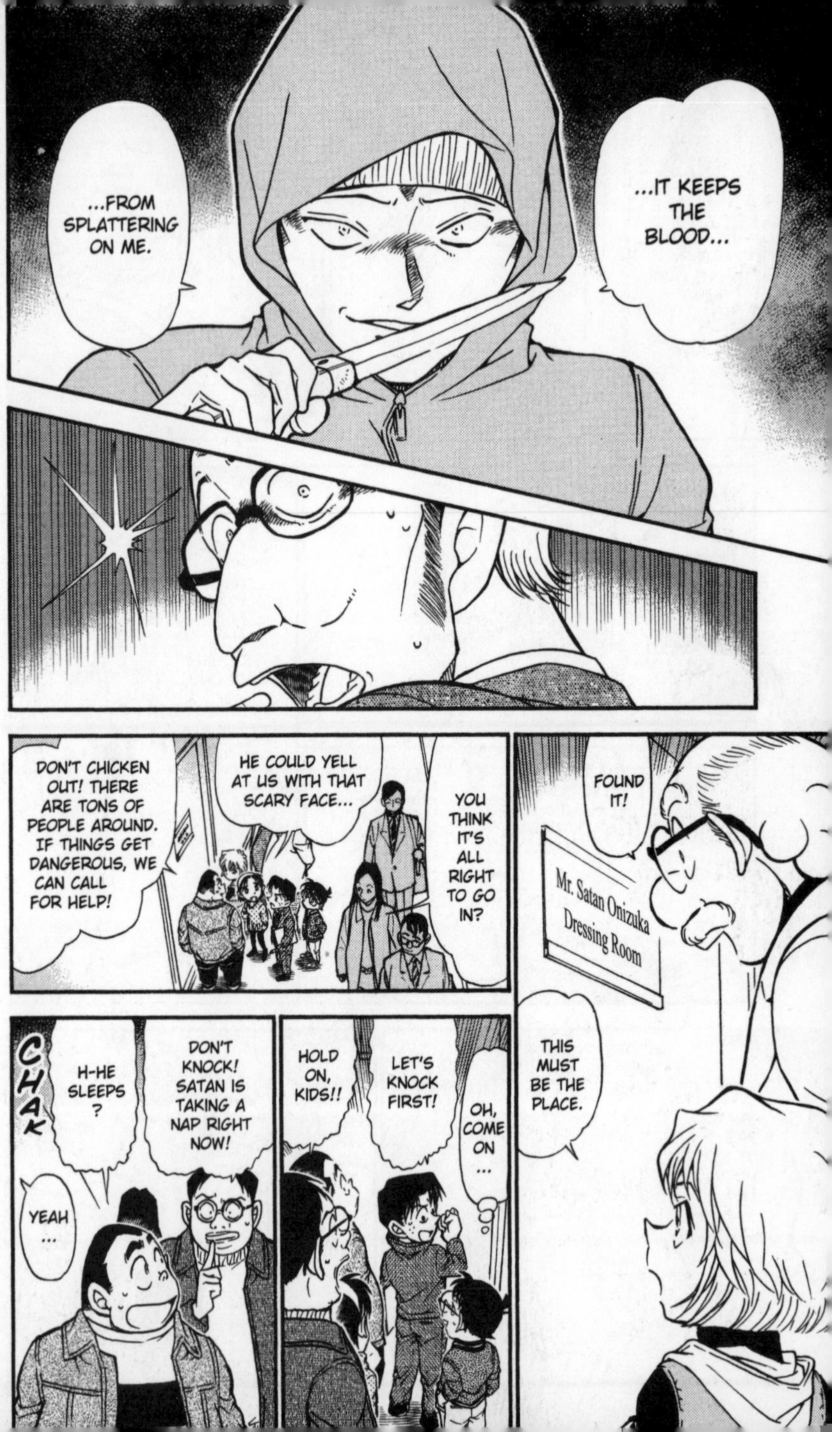
...IT KEEPS THE BLOOD...
...FROM SPLATTERING ON ME.
FOUND IT!
Mr. Satan Onizuka Dressing Room
THIS MUST BE THE PLACE.
YOU THINK IT'S ALL RIGHT TO GO IN?
HE COULD YELL AT US WITH THAT SCARY FACE...
DON'T CHICKEN OUT! THERE ARE TONS OF PEOPLE AROUND. IF THINGS GET DANGEROUS, WE CAN CALL FOR HELP!
OH, COME ON ...
LET'S KNOCK FIRST!
HOLD ON, KIDS!!
DON'T KNOCK! SATAN IS TAKING A NAP RIGHT NOW!
H-HE SLEEPS?
YEAH ...
CHAK

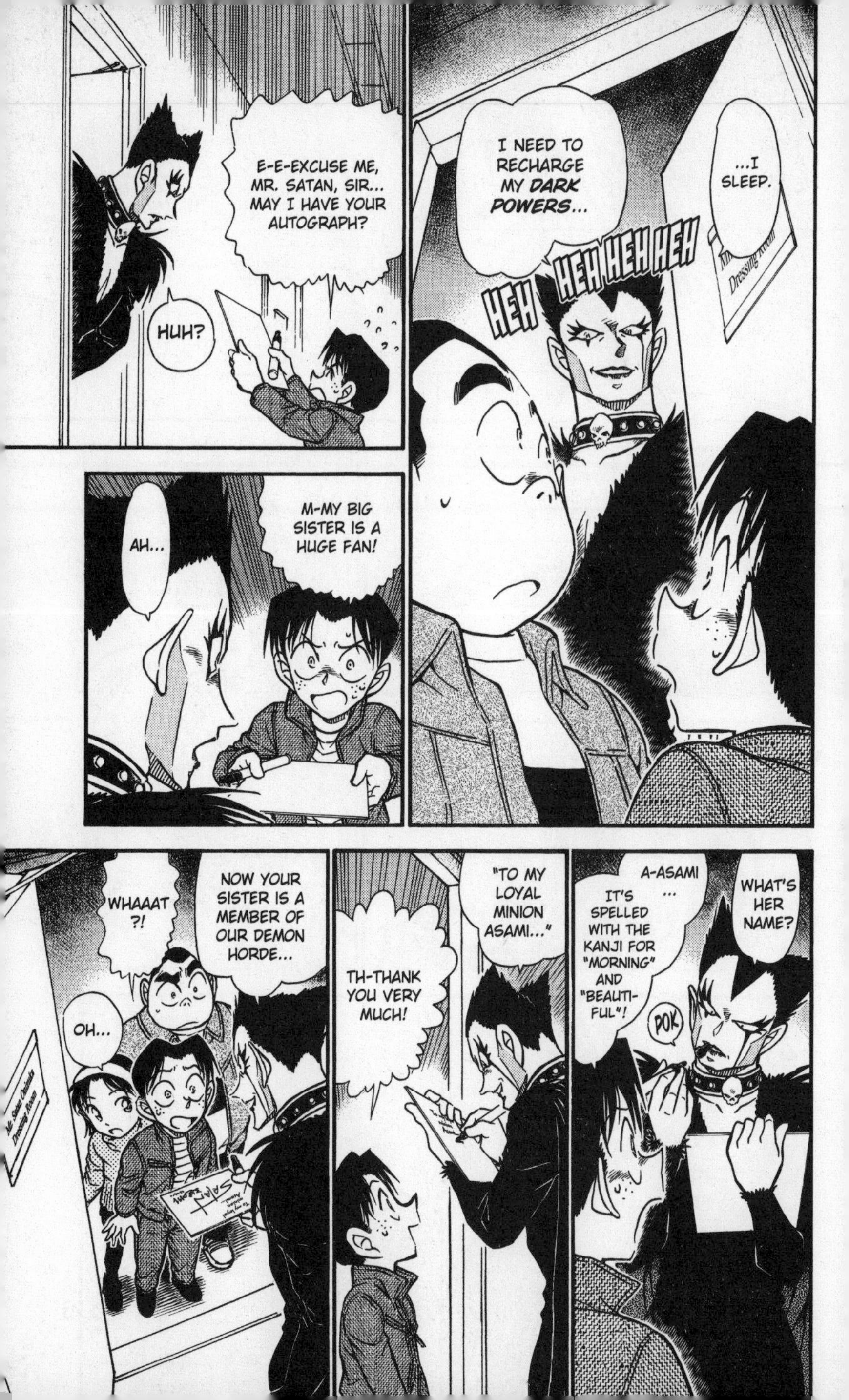
...I SLEEP.
I NEED TO RECHARGE MY *DARK POWERS*...
HEH HEH HEH HEH
Dressing Room
E-E-EXCUSE ME, MR. SATAN, SIR... MAY I HAVE YOUR AUTOGRAPH?
HUH?
M-MY BIG SISTER IS A HUGE FAN!
AH...
WHAT'S HER NAME?
A-ASAMI...
IT'S SPELLED WITH THE KANJI FOR "MORNING" AND "BEAUTIFUL"!
POK
"TO MY LOYAL MINION ASAMI..."
TH-THANK YOU VERY MUCH!
NOW YOUR SISTER IS A MEMBER OF OUR DEMON HORDE...
WHAAAT?!
OH...

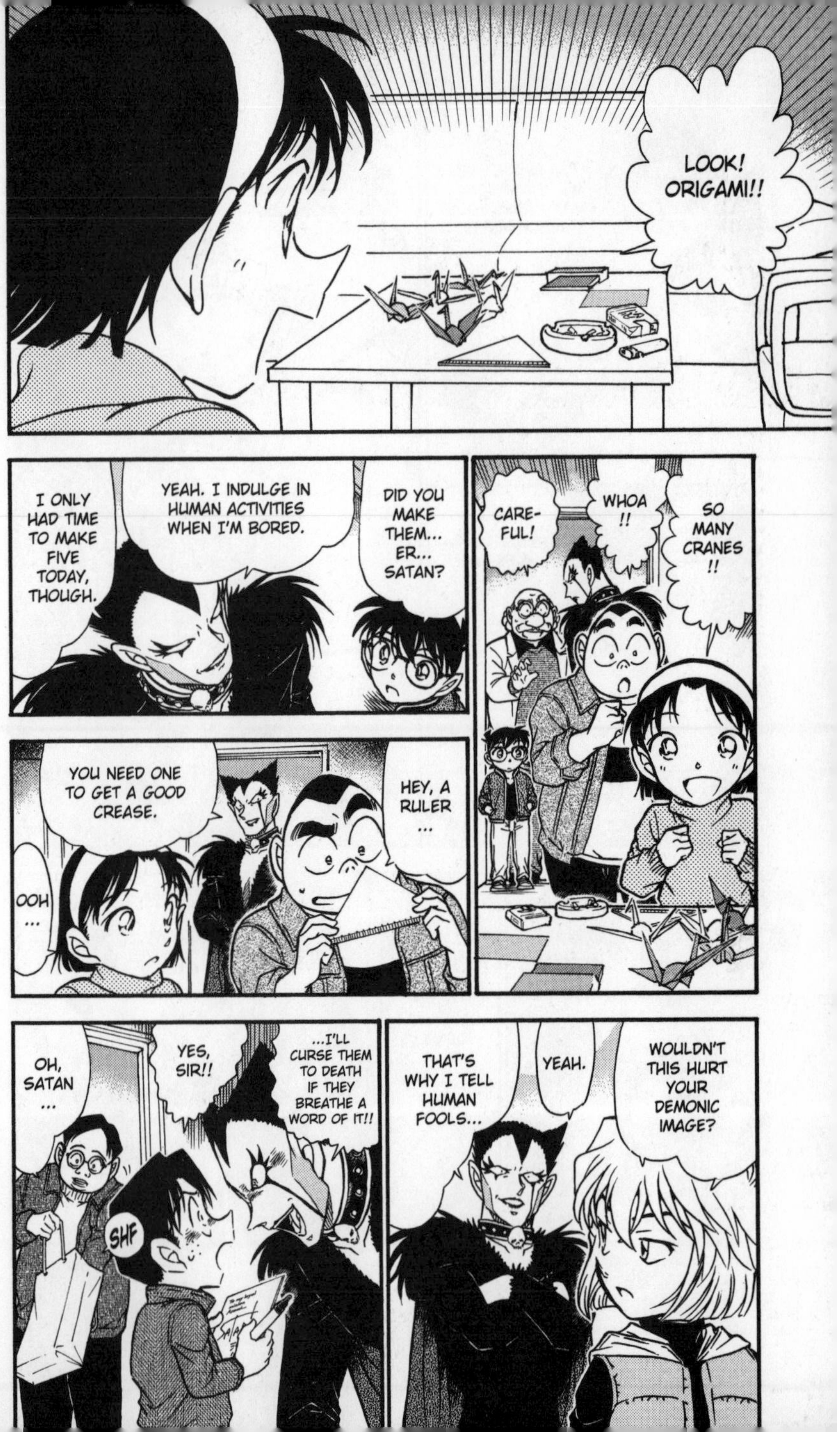
LOOK! ORIGAMI!!
SO MANY CRANES!!
WHOA!!
CARE-FUL!
DID YOU MAKE THEM... ER... SATAN?
YEAH. I INDULGE IN HUMAN ACTIVITIES WHEN I'M BORED.
I ONLY HAD TIME TO MAKE FIVE TODAY, THOUGH.
HEY, A RULER...
YOU NEED ONE TO GET A GOOD CREASE.
OOH...
WOULDN'T THIS HURT YOUR DEMONIC IMAGE?
YEAH.
THAT'S WHY I TELL HUMAN FOOLS...
...I'LL CURSE THEM TO DEATH IF THEY BREATHE A WORD OF IT!!
YES, SIR!!
OH, SATAN...
SHF

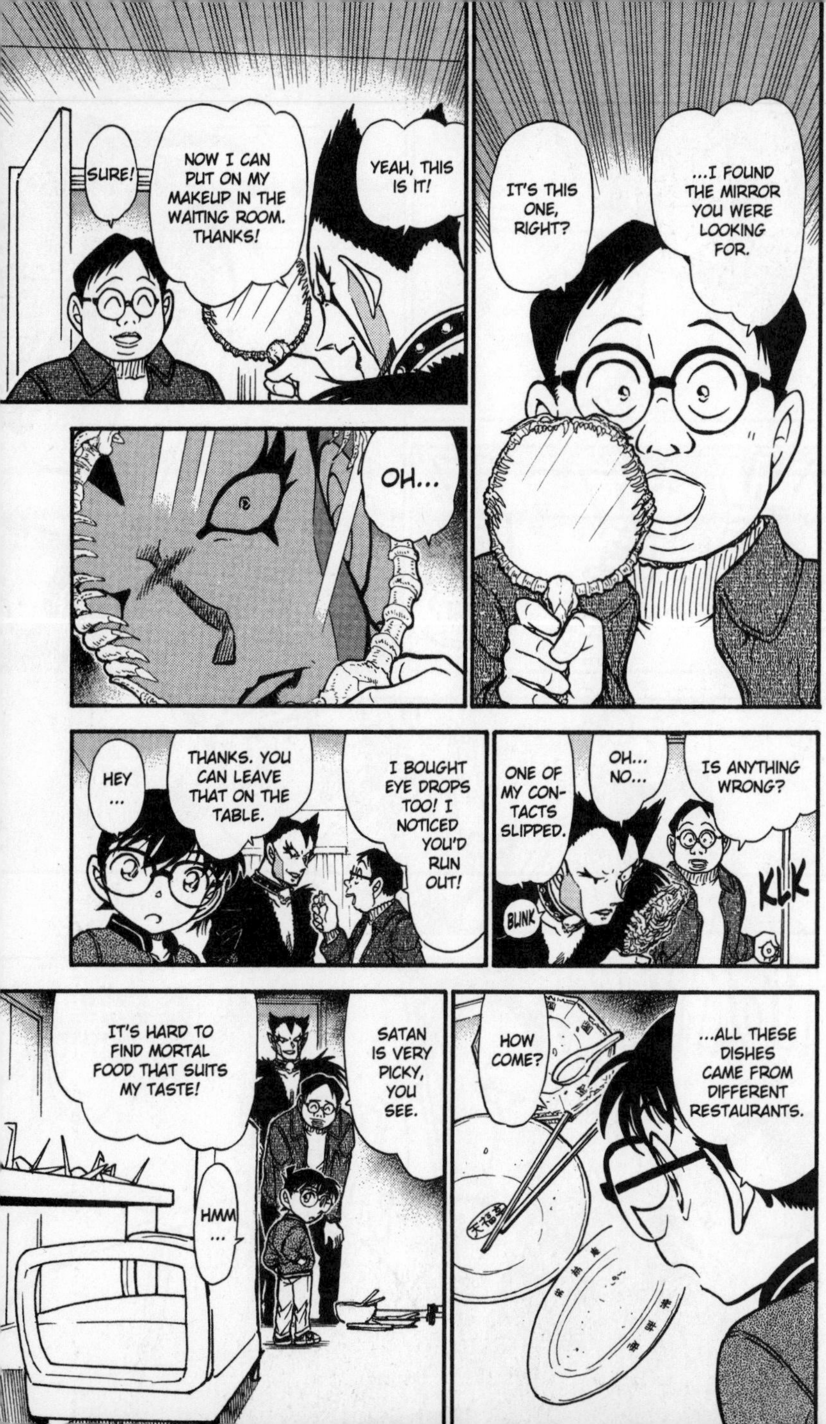
...I FOUND THE MIRROR YOU WERE LOOKING FOR.
IT'S THIS ONE, RIGHT?
YEAH, THIS IS IT!
NOW I CAN PUT ON MY MAKEUP IN THE WAITING ROOM. THANKS!
SURE!
OH...
IS ANYTHING WRONG?
KLK
OH... NO...
ONE OF MY CONTACTS SLIPPED.
BLINK
I BOUGHT EYE DROPS TOO! I NOTICED YOU'D RUN OUT!
THANKS. YOU CAN LEAVE THAT ON THE TABLE.
HEY ...
...ALL THESE DISHES CAME FROM DIFFERENT RESTAURANTS.
HOW COME?
SATAN IS VERY PICKY, YOU SEE.
IT'S HARD TO FIND MORTAL FOOD THAT SUITS MY TASTE!
HMM ...

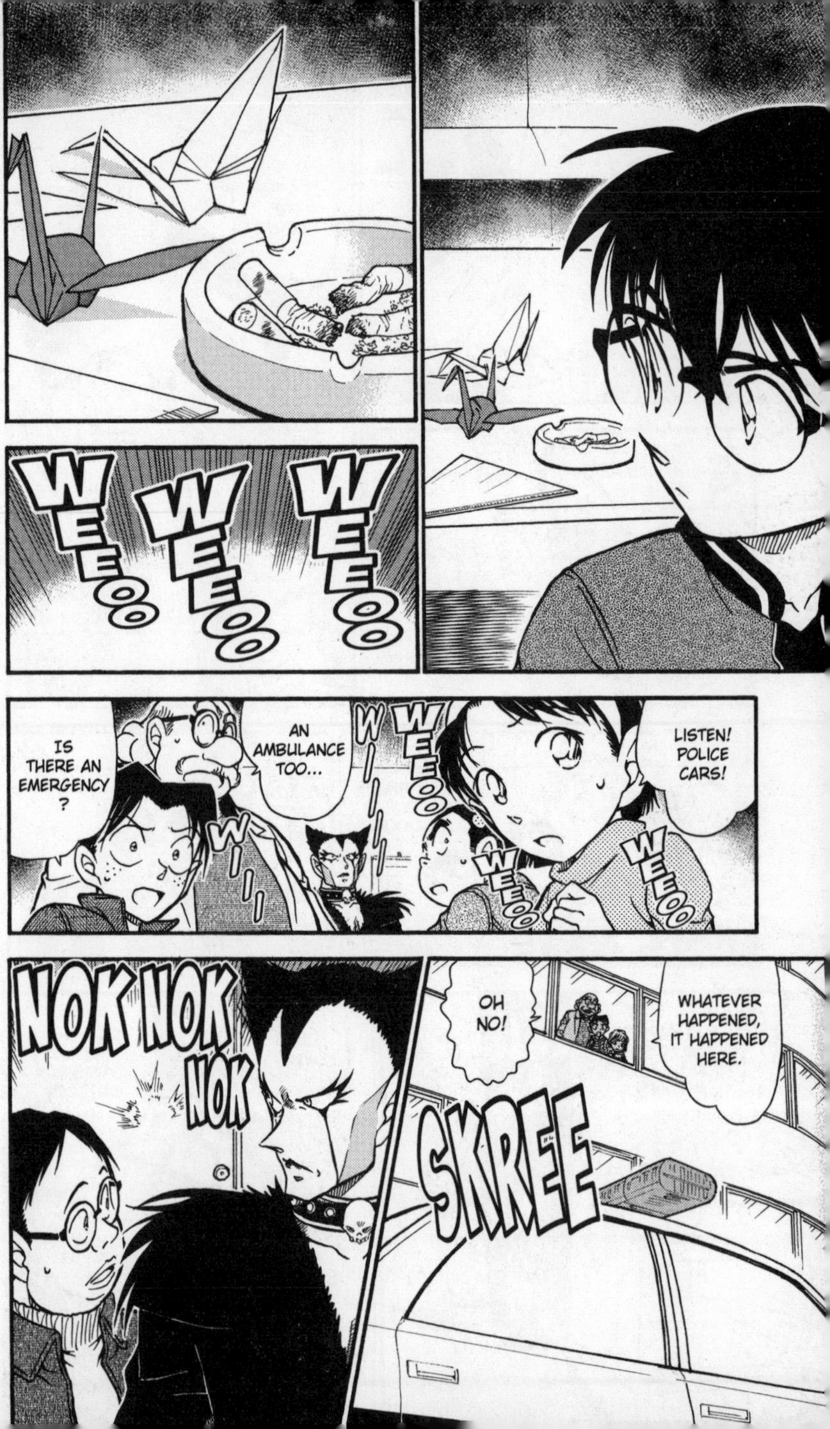
WEEOO
WEEOO
WEEOO
LISTEN! POLICE CARS!
WEEOO
WEEOO
WEEOO
AN AMBULANCE TOO...
WIIII
WIIII
IS THERE AN EMERGENCY?
WHATEVER HAPPENED, IT HAPPENED HERE.
OH NO!
SKREE
NOK NOK NOK

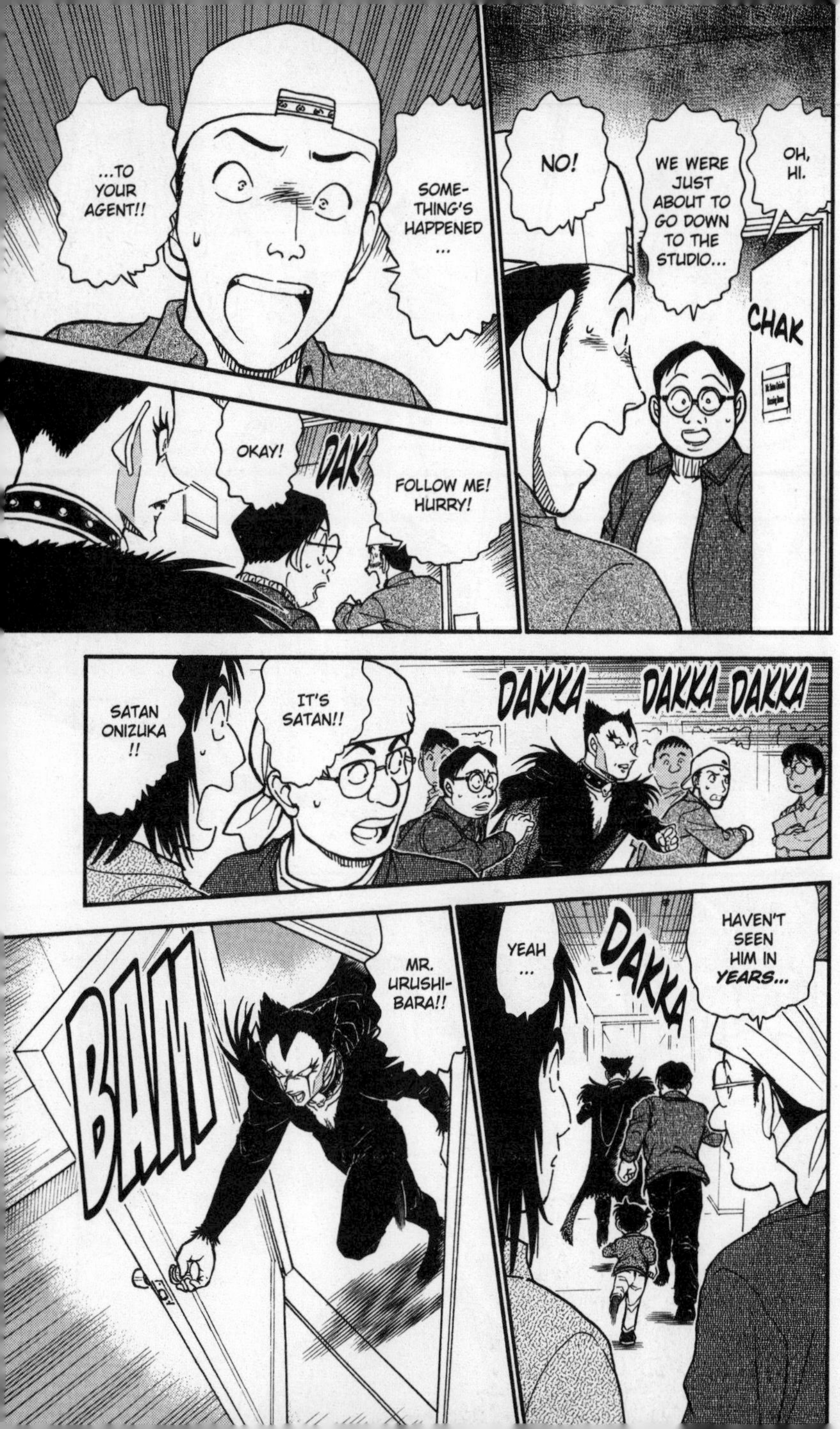
OH, HI.
WE WERE JUST ABOUT TO GO DOWN TO THE STUDIO...
NO!
CHAK
SOME-THING'S HAPPENED ...
...TO YOUR AGENT!!
FOLLOW ME! HURRY!
DAK
OKAY!
DAKKA DAKKA DAKKA
IT'S SATAN!!
SATAN ONIZUKA !!
HAVEN'T SEEN HIM IN *YEARS*...
DAKKA
YEAH ...
MR. URUSHI-BARA!!
BAM

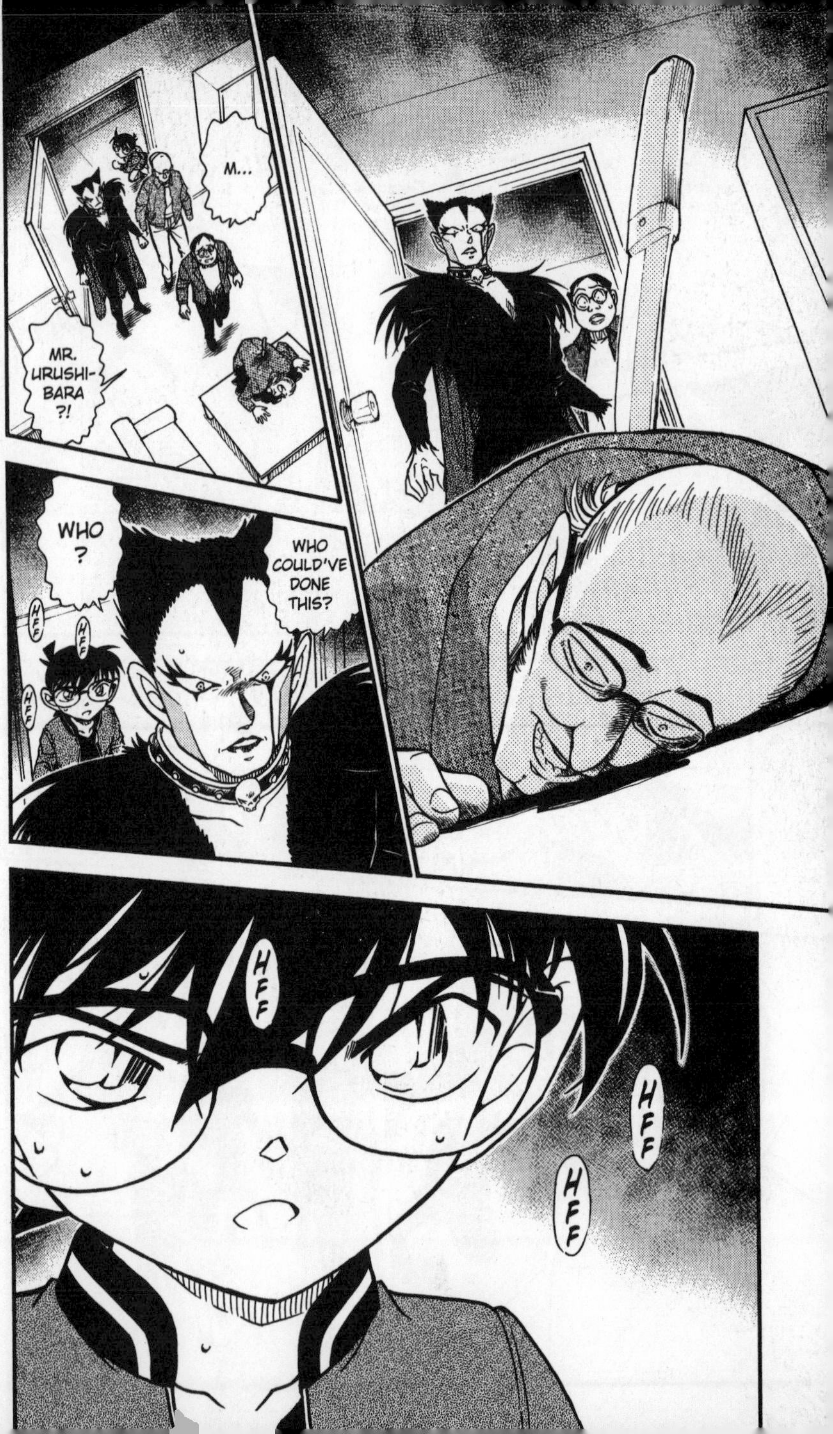
M...
MR. URUSHI-BARA ?!
WHO COULD'VE DONE THIS?
WHO ?
HFF
HFF
HFF
HFF
HFF
HFF

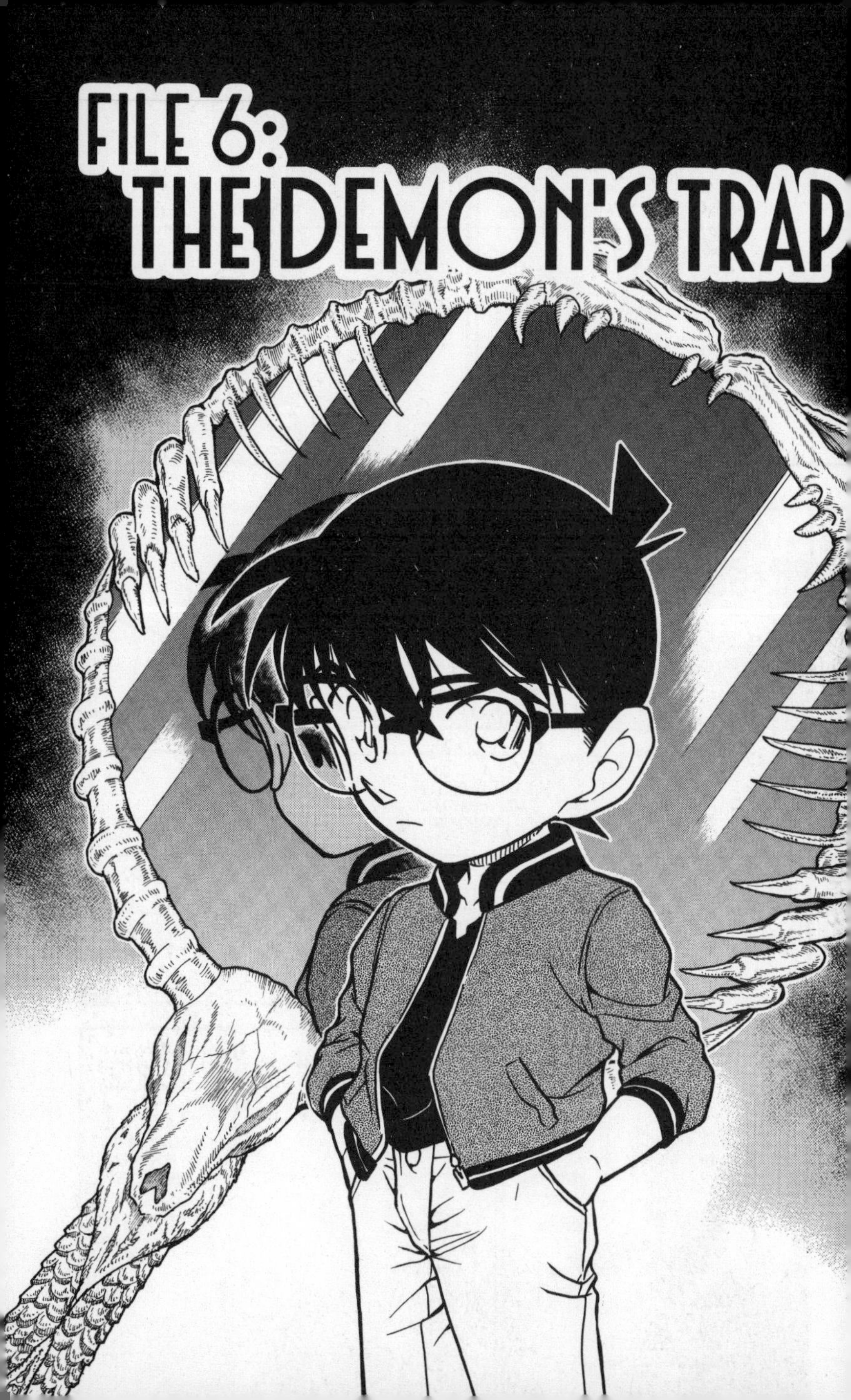
FILE 6:
THE DEMON'S TRAP

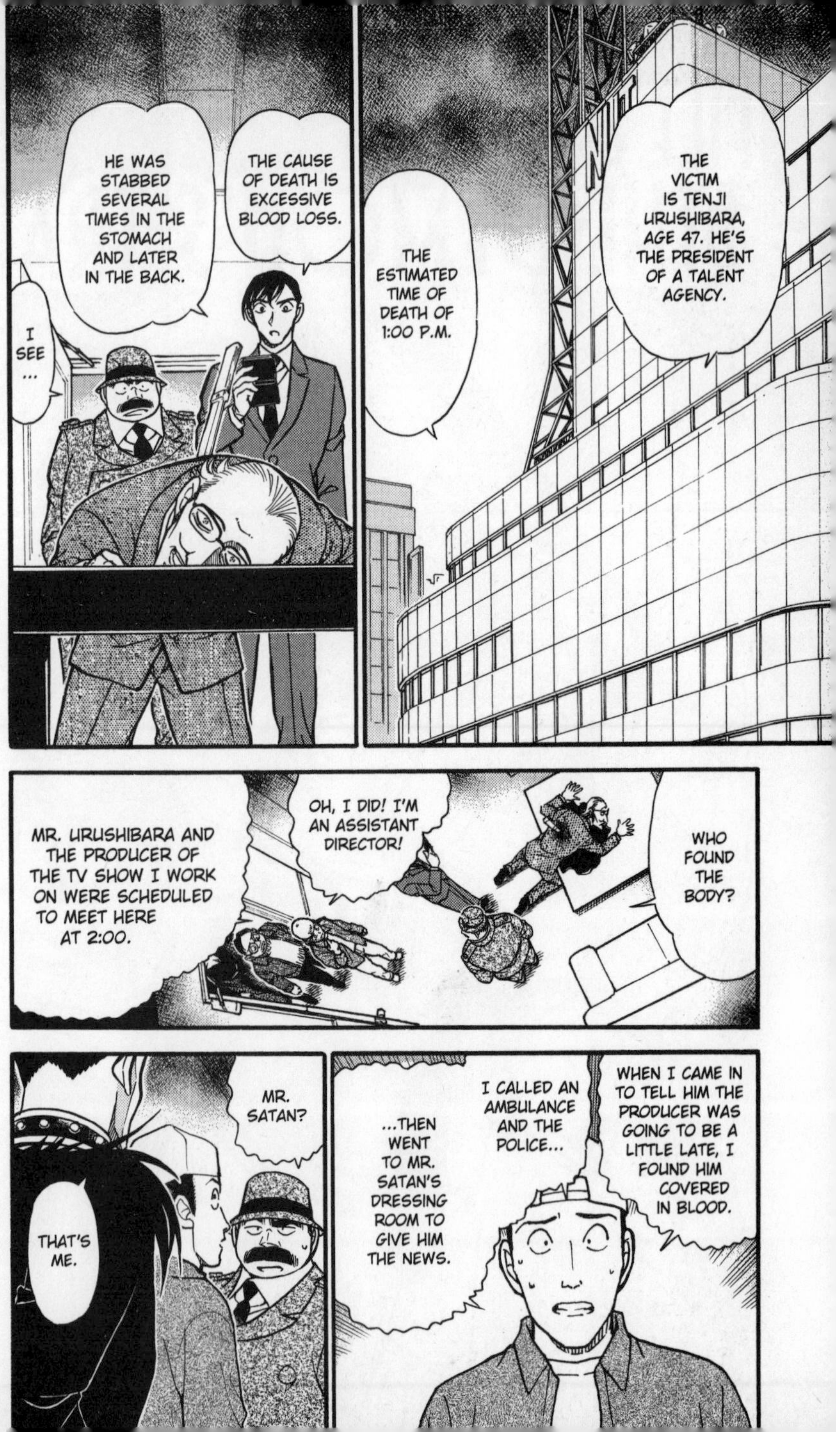
THE VICTIM IS TENJI URUSHIBARA, AGE 47. HE'S THE PRESIDENT OF A TALENT AGENCY.
THE ESTIMATED TIME OF DEATH OF 1:00 P.M.
THE CAUSE OF DEATH IS EXCESSIVE BLOOD LOSS.
HE WAS STABBED SEVERAL TIMES IN THE STOMACH AND LATER IN THE BACK.
I SEE ...
WHO FOUND THE BODY?
OH, I DID! I'M AN ASSISTANT DIRECTOR!
MR. URUSHIBARA AND THE PRODUCER OF THE TV SHOW I WORK ON WERE SCHEDULED TO MEET HERE AT 2:00.
WHEN I CAME IN TO TELL HIM THE PRODUCER WAS GOING TO BE A LITTLE LATE, I FOUND HIM COVERED IN BLOOD.
I CALLED AN AMBULANCE AND THE POLICE...
...THEN WENT TO MR. SATAN'S DRESSING ROOM TO GIVE HIM THE NEWS.
MR. SATAN?
THAT'S ME.

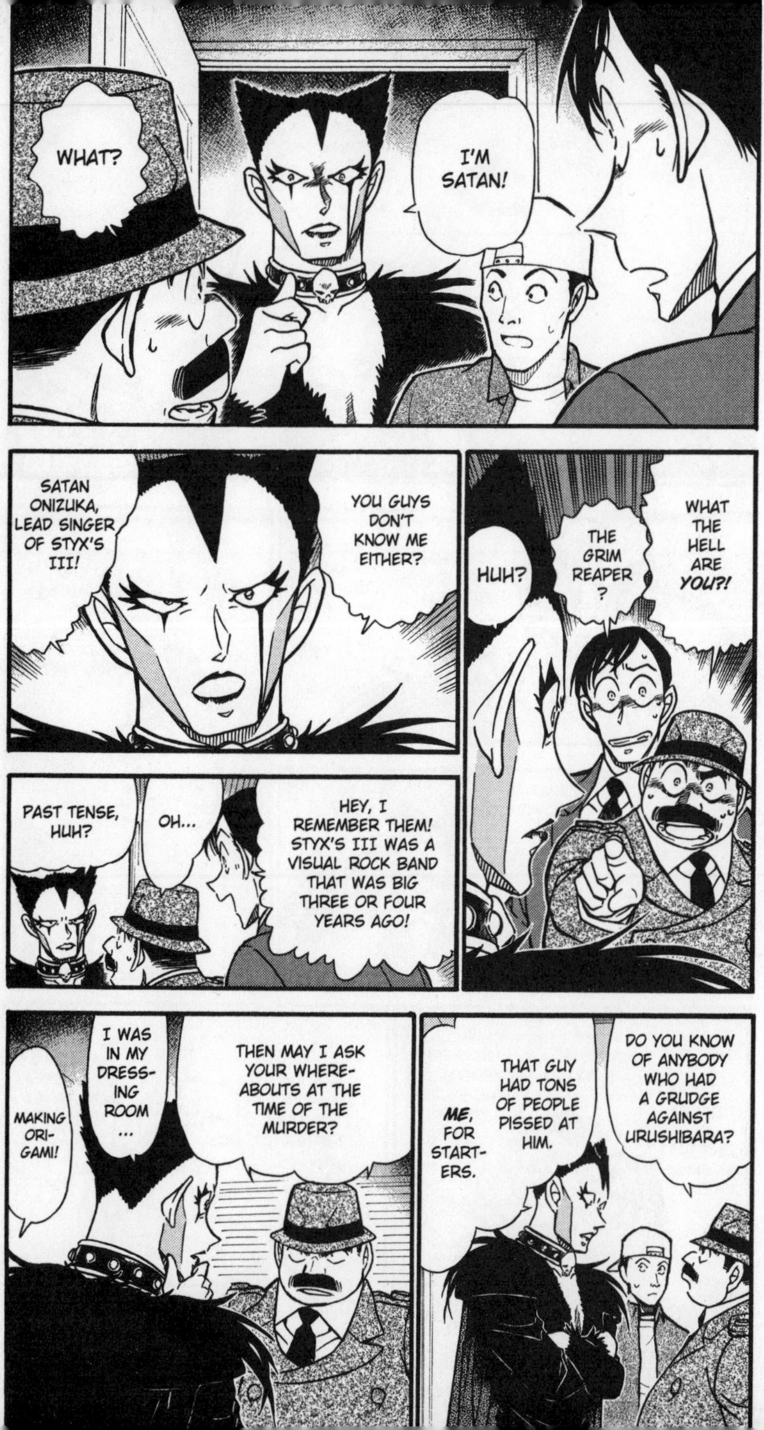

I'M SATAN!
WHAT?
WHAT THE HELL ARE *YOU?!*
THE GRIM REAPER?
HUH?
YOU GUYS DON'T KNOW ME EITHER?
SATAN ONIZUKA, LEAD SINGER OF STYX'S III!
HEY, I REMEMBER THEM! STYX'S III WAS A VISUAL ROCK BAND THAT WAS BIG THREE OR FOUR YEARS AGO!
OH...
PAST TENSE, HUH?
DO YOU KNOW OF ANYBODY WHO HAD A GRUDGE AGAINST URUSHIBARA?
THAT GUY HAD TONS OF PEOPLE PISSED AT HIM.
ME, FOR STARTERS.
THEN MAY I ASK YOUR WHEREABOUTS AT THE TIME OF THE MURDER?
I WAS IN MY DRESSING ROOM...
MAKING ORIGAMI!

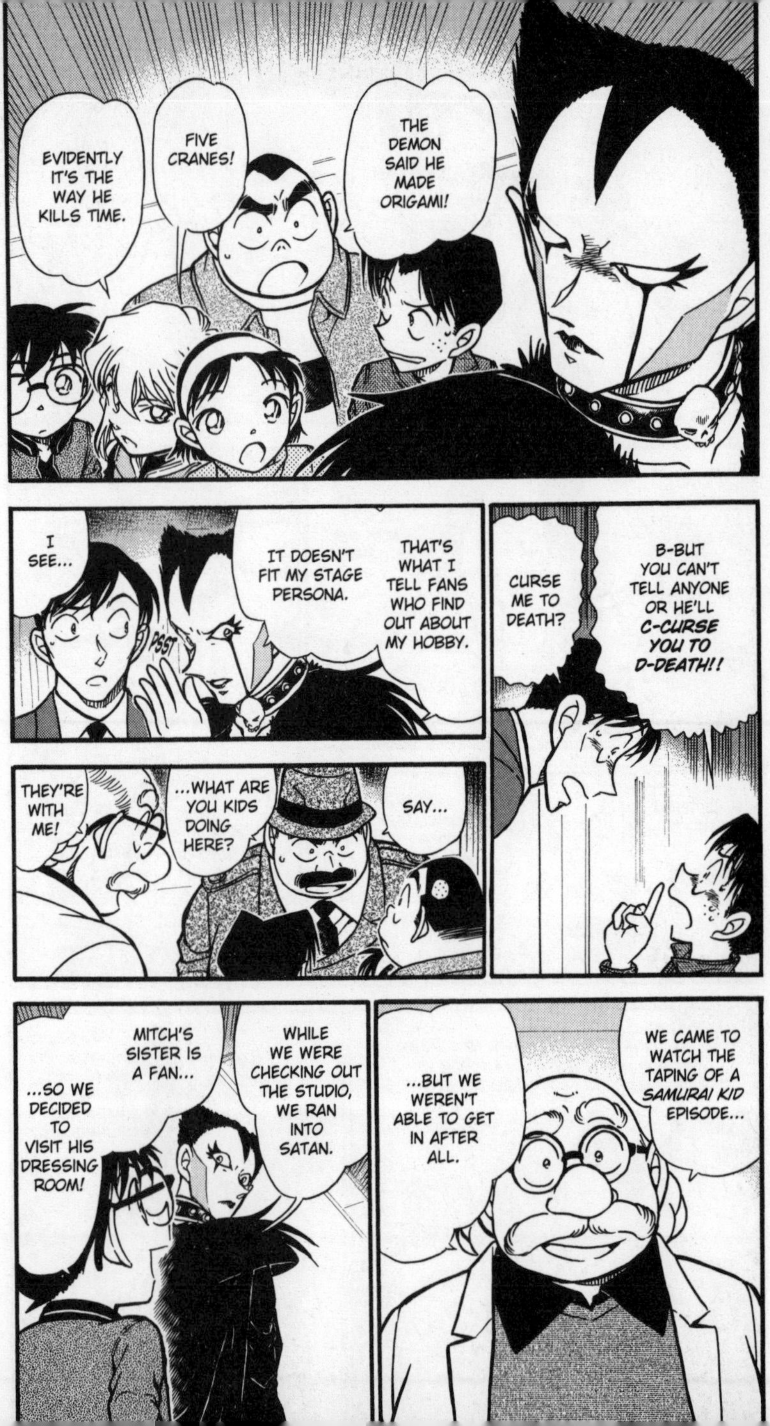
THE DEMON SAID HE MADE ORIGAMI!
FIVE CRANES!
EVIDENTLY IT'S THE WAY HE KILLS TIME.
B-BUT YOU CAN'T TELL ANYONE OR HE'LL *C-CURSE YOU TO D-DEATH!!*
CURSE ME TO DEATH?
THAT'S WHAT I TELL FANS WHO FIND OUT ABOUT MY HOBBY.
IT DOESN'T FIT MY STAGE PERSONA.
I SEE...
PSST
SAY...
...WHAT ARE YOU KIDS DOING HERE?
THEY'RE WITH ME!
WE CAME TO WATCH THE TAPING OF A *SAMURAI KID* EPISODE...
...BUT WE WEREN'T ABLE TO GET IN AFTER ALL.
WHILE WE WERE CHECKING OUT THE STUDIO, WE RAN INTO SATAN.
MITCH'S SISTER IS A FAN...
...SO WE DECIDED TO VISIT HIS DRESSING ROOM!

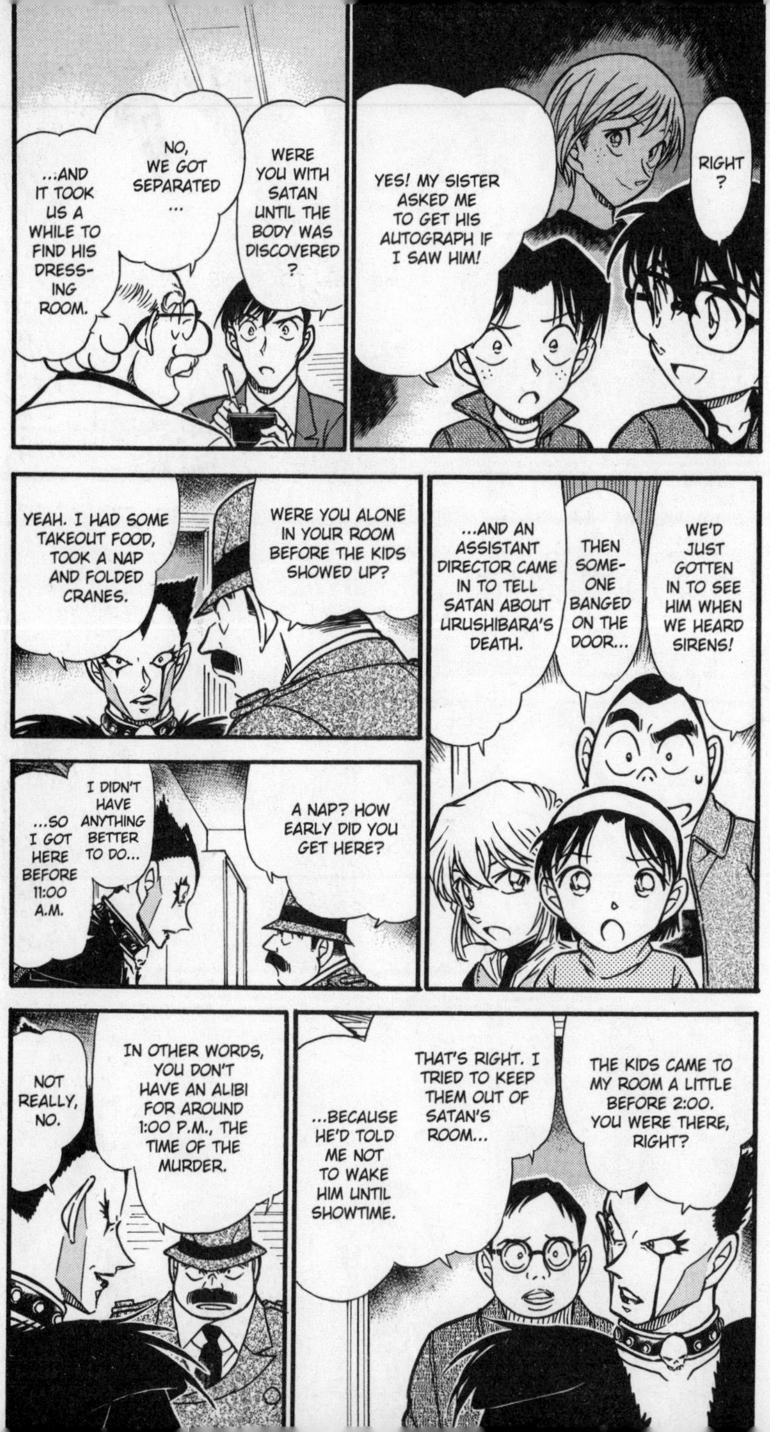
RIGHT?
YES! MY SISTER ASKED ME TO GET HIS AUTOGRAPH IF I SAW HIM!
WERE YOU WITH SATAN UNTIL THE BODY WAS DISCOVERED?
NO, WE GOT SEPARATED...
...AND IT TOOK US A WHILE TO FIND HIS DRESSING ROOM.
WE'D JUST GOTTEN IN TO SEE HIM WHEN WE HEARD SIRENS!
THEN SOMEONE BANGED ON THE DOOR...
...AND AN ASSISTANT DIRECTOR CAME IN TO TELL SATAN ABOUT URUSHIBARA'S DEATH.
WERE YOU ALONE IN YOUR ROOM BEFORE THE KIDS SHOWED UP?
YEAH. I HAD SOME TAKEOUT FOOD, TOOK A NAP AND FOLDED CRANES.
A NAP? HOW EARLY DID YOU GET HERE?
I DIDN'T HAVE ANYTHING BETTER TO DO...
...SO I GOT HERE BEFORE 11:00 A.M.
THE KIDS CAME TO MY ROOM A LITTLE BEFORE 2:00. YOU WERE THERE, RIGHT?
THAT'S RIGHT. I TRIED TO KEEP THEM OUT OF SATAN'S ROOM...
...BECAUSE HE'D TOLD ME NOT TO WAKE HIM UNTIL SHOWTIME.
IN OTHER WORDS, YOU DON'T HAVE AN ALIBI FOR AROUND 1:00 P.M., THE TIME OF THE MURDER.
NOT REALLY, NO.

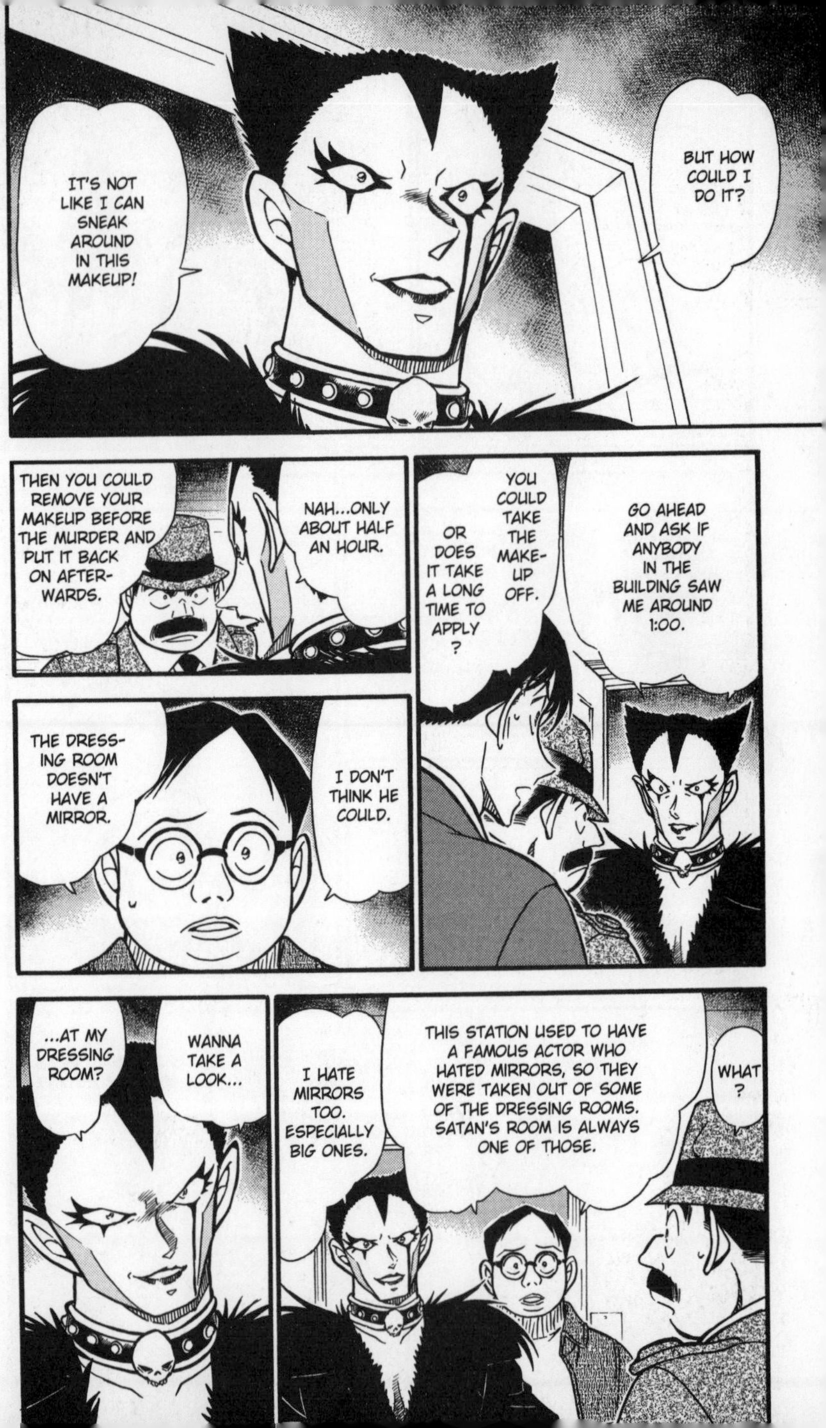
BUT HOW COULD I DO IT?
IT'S NOT LIKE I CAN SNEAK AROUND IN THIS MAKEUP!
GO AHEAD AND ASK IF ANYBODY IN THE BUILDING SAW ME AROUND 1:00.
YOU COULD TAKE THE MAKE-UP OFF.
OR DOES IT TAKE A LONG TIME TO APPLY?
NAH...ONLY ABOUT HALF AN HOUR.
THEN YOU COULD REMOVE YOUR MAKEUP BEFORE THE MURDER AND PUT IT BACK ON AFTER-WARDS.
I DON'T THINK HE COULD.
THE DRESS-ING ROOM DOESN'T HAVE A MIRROR.
WHAT?
THIS STATION USED TO HAVE A FAMOUS ACTOR WHO HATED MIRRORS, SO THEY WERE TAKEN OUT OF SOME OF THE DRESSING ROOMS. SATAN'S ROOM IS ALWAYS ONE OF THOSE.
I HATE MIRRORS TOO. ESPECIALLY BIG ONES.
WANNA TAKE A LOOK...
...AT MY DRESSING ROOM?

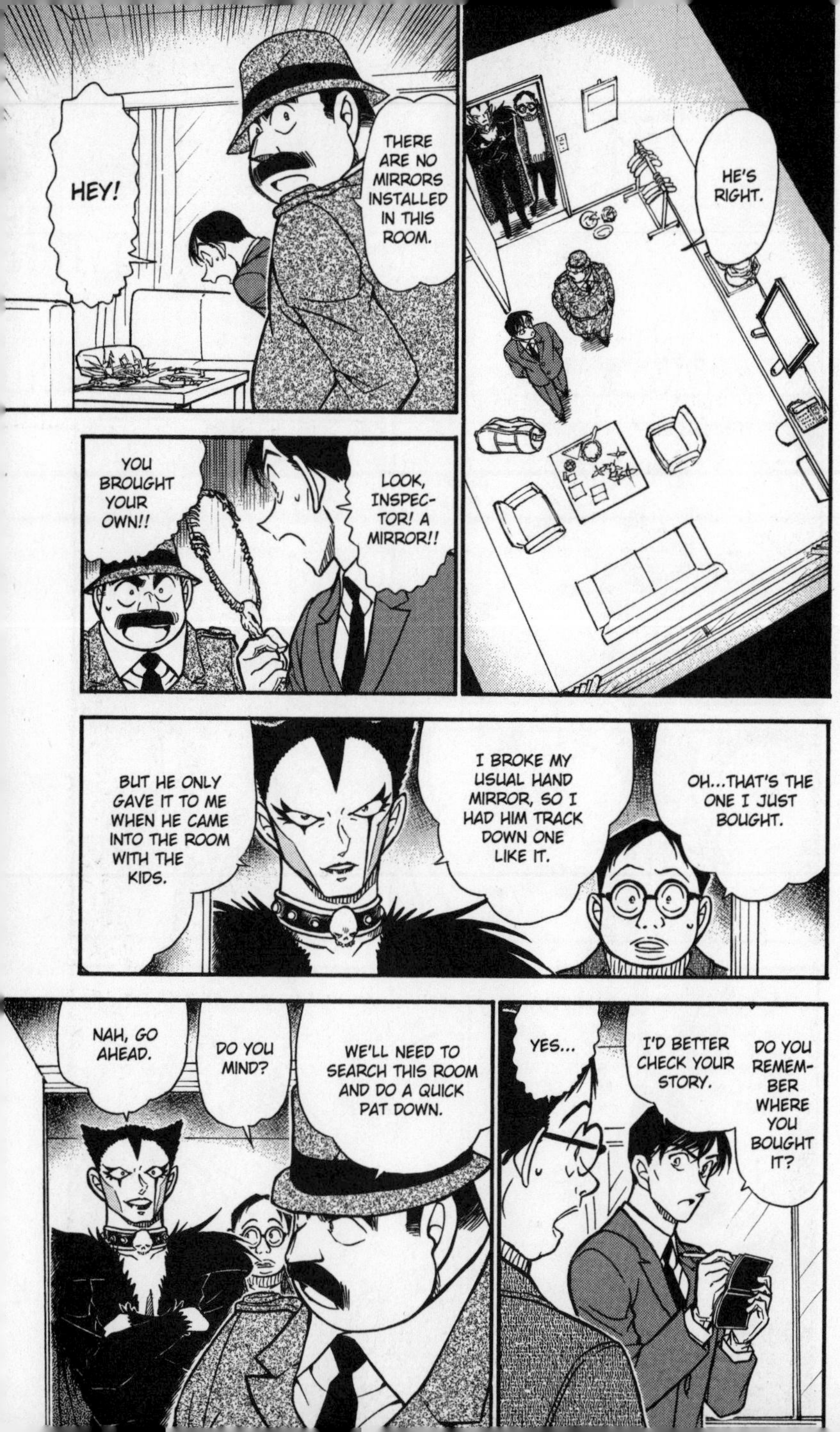
HE'S RIGHT.
THERE ARE NO MIRRORS INSTALLED IN THIS ROOM.
HEY!
LOOK, INSPECTOR! A MIRROR!!
YOU BROUGHT YOUR OWN!!
OH...THAT'S THE ONE I JUST BOUGHT.
I BROKE MY USUAL HAND MIRROR, SO I HAD HIM TRACK DOWN ONE LIKE IT.
BUT HE ONLY GAVE IT TO ME WHEN HE CAME INTO THE ROOM WITH THE KIDS.
DO YOU REMEMBER WHERE YOU BOUGHT IT?
I'D BETTER CHECK YOUR STORY.
YES...
WE'LL NEED TO SEARCH THIS ROOM AND DO A QUICK PAT DOWN.
DO YOU MIND?
NAH, GO AHEAD.

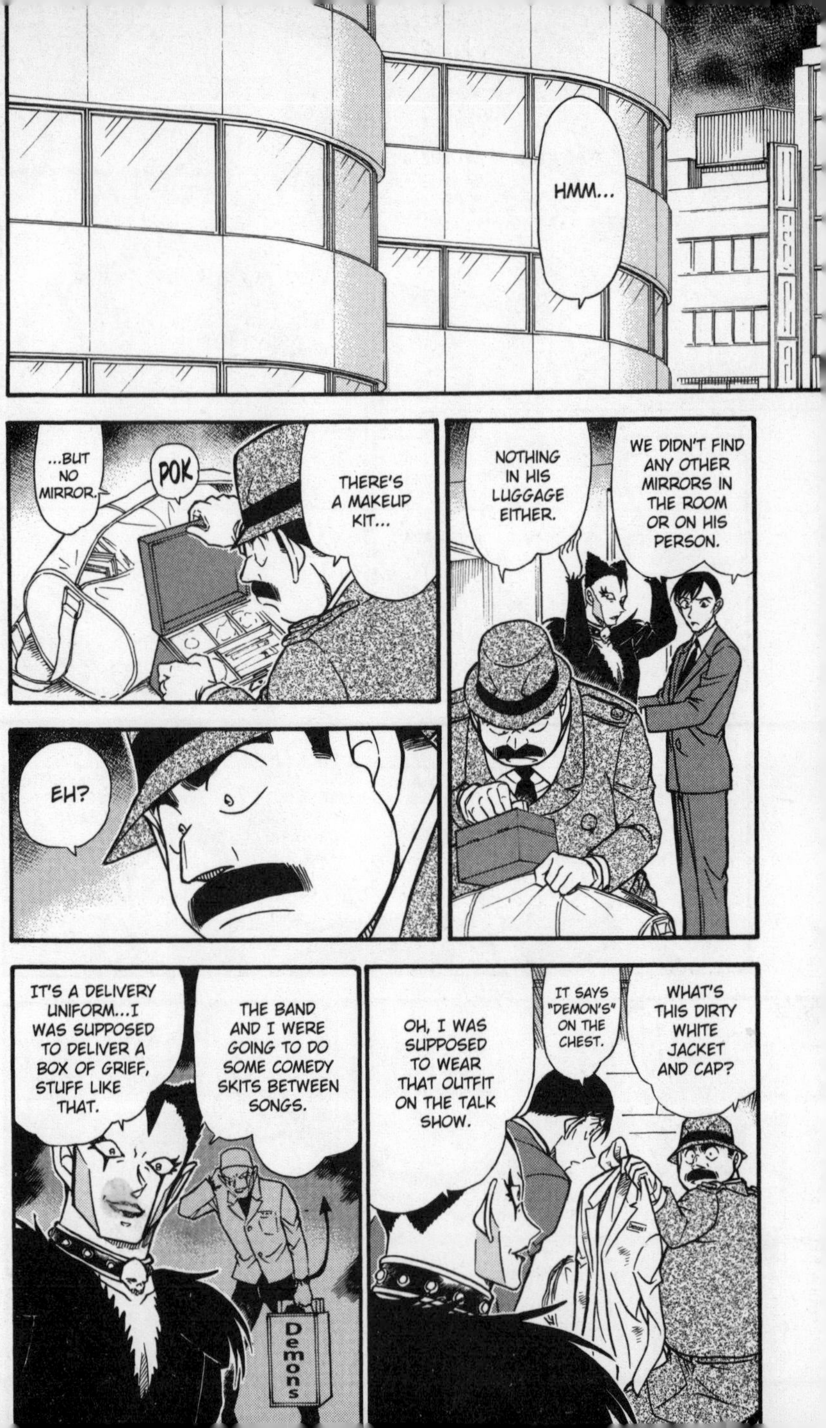
HMM...
WE DIDN'T FIND ANY OTHER MIRRORS IN THE ROOM OR ON HIS PERSON.
NOTHING IN HIS LUGGAGE EITHER.
THERE'S A MAKEUP KIT...
POK
...BUT NO MIRROR.
EH?
WHAT'S THIS DIRTY WHITE JACKET AND CAP?
IT SAYS "DEMON'S" ON THE CHEST.
OH, I WAS SUPPOSED TO WEAR THAT OUTFIT ON THE TALK SHOW.
THE BAND AND I WERE GOING TO DO SOME COMEDY SKITS BETWEEN SONGS.
IT'S A DELIVERY UNIFORM...I WAS SUPPOSED TO DELIVER A BOX OF GRIEF, STUFF LIKE THAT.
Demons

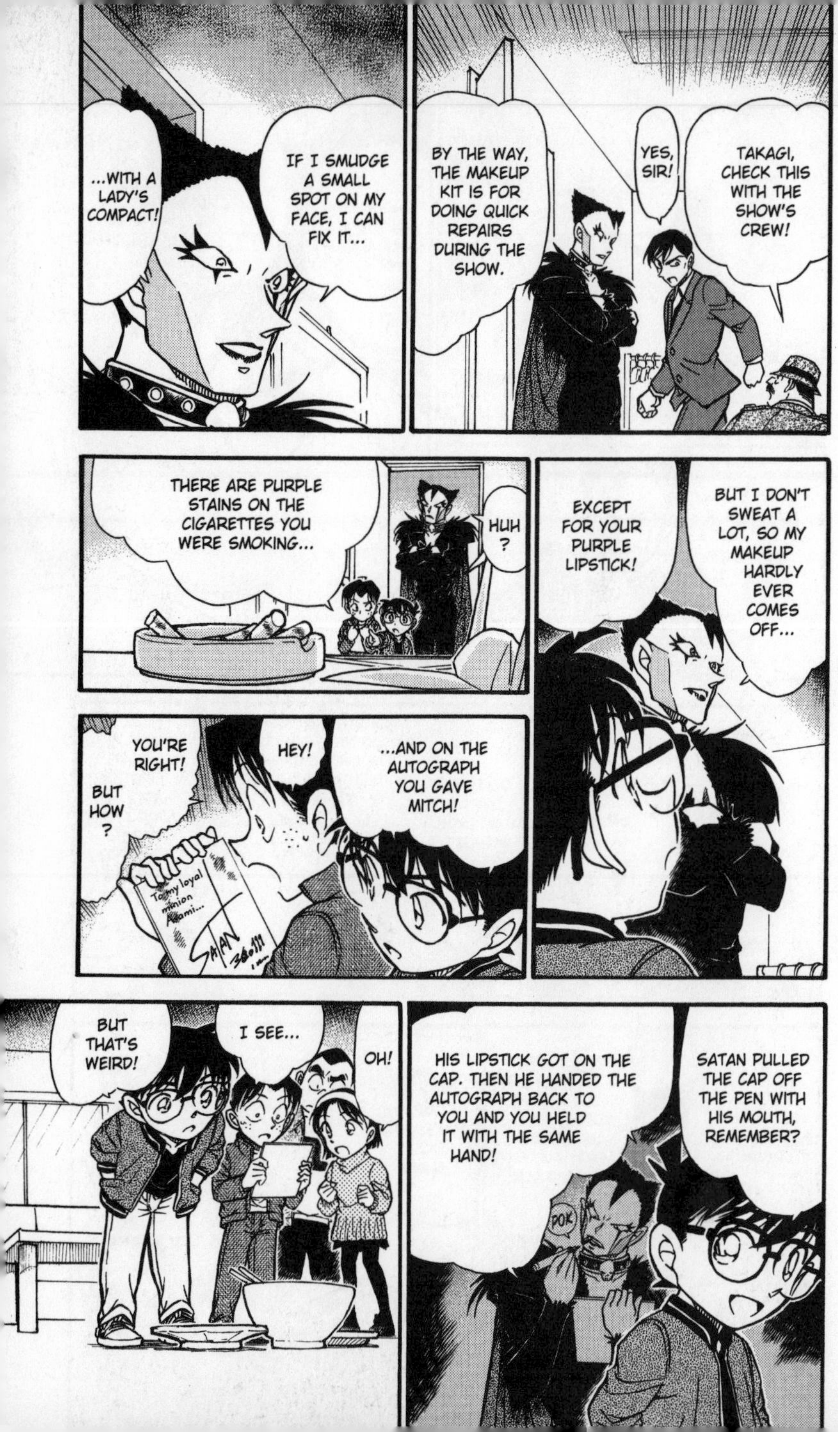
TAKAGI, CHECK THIS WITH THE SHOW'S CREW!
YES, SIR!
BY THE WAY, THE MAKEUP KIT IS FOR DOING QUICK REPAIRS DURING THE SHOW.
IF I SMUDGE A SMALL SPOT ON MY FACE, I CAN FIX IT...
...WITH A LADY'S COMPACT!
BUT I DON'T SWEAT A LOT, SO MY MAKEUP HARDLY EVER COMES OFF...
EXCEPT FOR YOUR PURPLE LIPSTICK!
HUH?
THERE ARE PURPLE STAINS ON THE CIGARETTES YOU WERE SMOKING...
...AND ON THE AUTOGRAPH YOU GAVE MITCH!
HEY!
YOU'RE RIGHT!
BUT HOW?
To my loyal minion Asami...
SATAN
SATAN PULLED THE CAP OFF THE PEN WITH HIS MOUTH, REMEMBER?
HIS LIPSTICK GOT ON THE CAP. THEN HE HANDED THE AUTOGRAPH BACK TO YOU AND YOU HELD IT WITH THE SAME HAND!
POK
OH!
I SEE...
BUT THAT'S WEIRD!

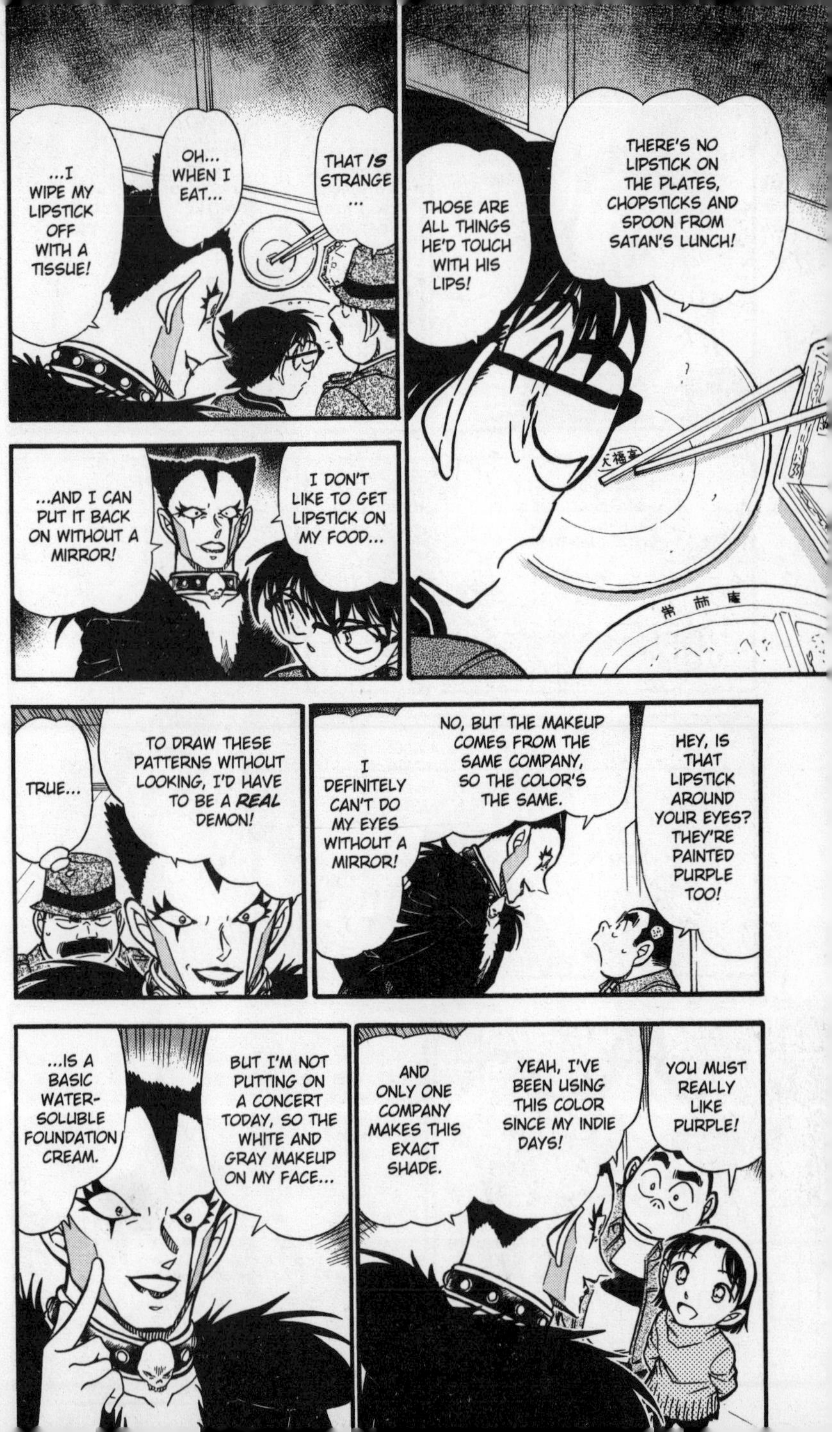
THERE'S NO LIPSTICK ON THE PLATES, CHOPSTICKS AND SPOON FROM SATAN'S LUNCH!
THOSE ARE ALL THINGS HE'D TOUCH WITH HIS LIPS!
THAT *IS* STRANGE...
OH... WHEN I EAT...
...I WIPE MY LIPSTICK OFF WITH A TISSUE!
I DON'T LIKE TO GET LIPSTICK ON MY FOOD...
...AND I CAN PUT IT BACK ON WITHOUT A MIRROR!
HEY, IS THAT LIPSTICK AROUND YOUR EYES? THEY'RE PAINTED PURPLE TOO!
NO, BUT THE MAKEUP COMES FROM THE SAME COMPANY, SO THE COLOR'S THE SAME.
I DEFINITELY CAN'T DO MY EYES WITHOUT A MIRROR!
TO DRAW THESE PATTERNS WITHOUT LOOKING, I'D HAVE TO BE A *REAL* DEMON!
TRUE...
YOU MUST REALLY LIKE PURPLE!
YEAH, I'VE BEEN USING THIS COLOR SINCE MY INDIE DAYS!
AND ONLY ONE COMPANY MAKES THIS EXACT SHADE.
BUT I'M NOT PUTTING ON A CONCERT TODAY, SO THE WHITE AND GRAY MAKEUP ON MY FACE...
...IS A BASIC WATER-SOLUBLE FOUNDATION CREAM.

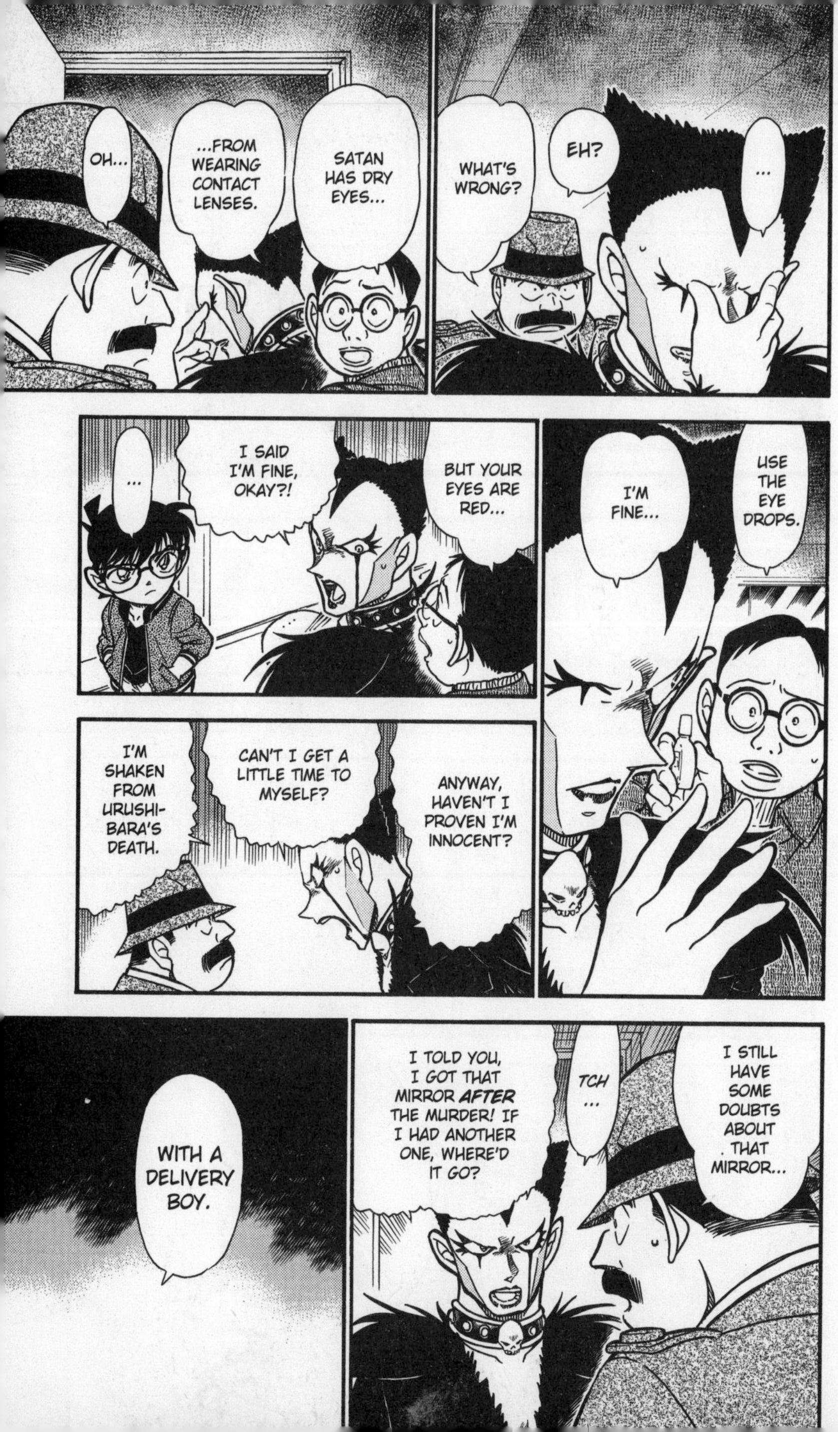
...
EH?
WHAT'S WRONG?
SATAN HAS DRY EYES...
...FROM WEARING CONTACT LENSES.
OH...
USE THE EYE DROPS.
I'M FINE...
BUT YOUR EYES ARE RED...
I SAID I'M FINE, OKAY?!
...
ANYWAY, HAVEN'T I PROVEN I'M INNOCENT?
CAN'T I GET A LITTLE TIME TO MYSELF?
I'M SHAKEN FROM URUSHI-BARA'S DEATH.
I STILL HAVE SOME DOUBTS ABOUT THAT MIRROR...
TCH...
I TOLD YOU, I GOT THAT MIRROR *AFTER* THE MURDER! IF I HAD ANOTHER ONE, WHERE'D IT GO?
WITH A DELIVERY BOY.

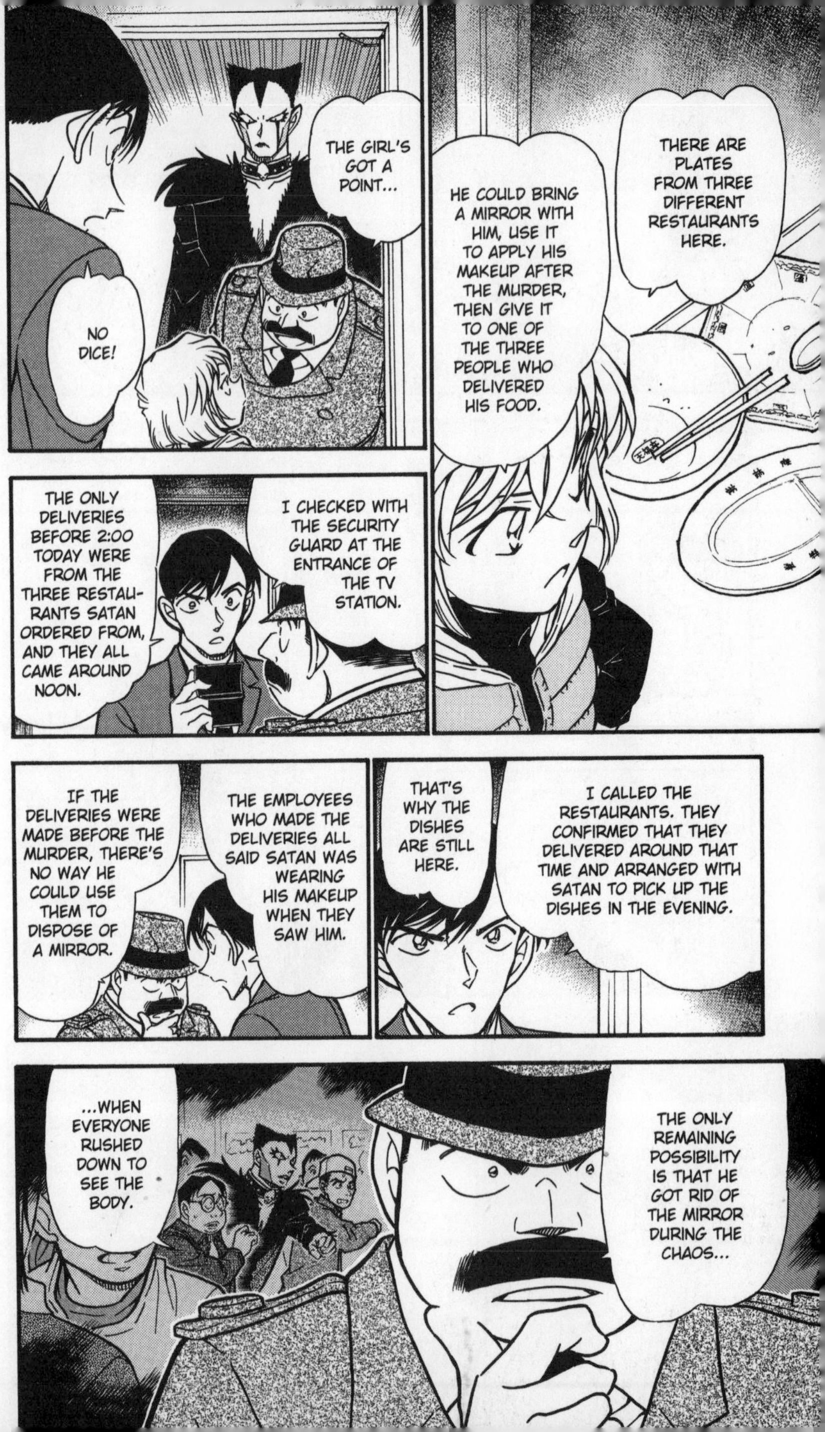
THERE ARE PLATES FROM THREE DIFFERENT RESTAURANTS HERE.
HE COULD BRING A MIRROR WITH HIM, USE IT TO APPLY HIS MAKEUP AFTER THE MURDER, THEN GIVE IT TO ONE OF THE THREE PEOPLE WHO DELIVERED HIS FOOD.
THE GIRL'S GOT A POINT...
NO DICE!
I CHECKED WITH THE SECURITY GUARD AT THE ENTRANCE OF THE TV STATION.
THE ONLY DELIVERIES BEFORE 2:00 TODAY WERE FROM THE THREE RESTAU-RANTS SATAN ORDERED FROM, AND THEY ALL CAME AROUND NOON.
I CALLED THE RESTAURANTS. THEY CONFIRMED THAT THEY DELIVERED AROUND THAT TIME AND ARRANGED WITH SATAN TO PICK UP THE DISHES IN THE EVENING.
THAT'S WHY THE DISHES ARE STILL HERE.
THE EMPLOYEES WHO MADE THE DELIVERIES ALL SAID SATAN WAS WEARING HIS MAKEUP WHEN THEY SAW HIM.
IF THE DELIVERIES WERE MADE BEFORE THE MURDER, THERE'S NO WAY HE COULD USE THEM TO DISPOSE OF A MIRROR.
THE ONLY REMAINING POSSIBILITY IS THAT HE GOT RID OF THE MIRROR DURING THE CHAOS...
...WHEN EVERYONE RUSHED DOWN TO SEE THE BODY.

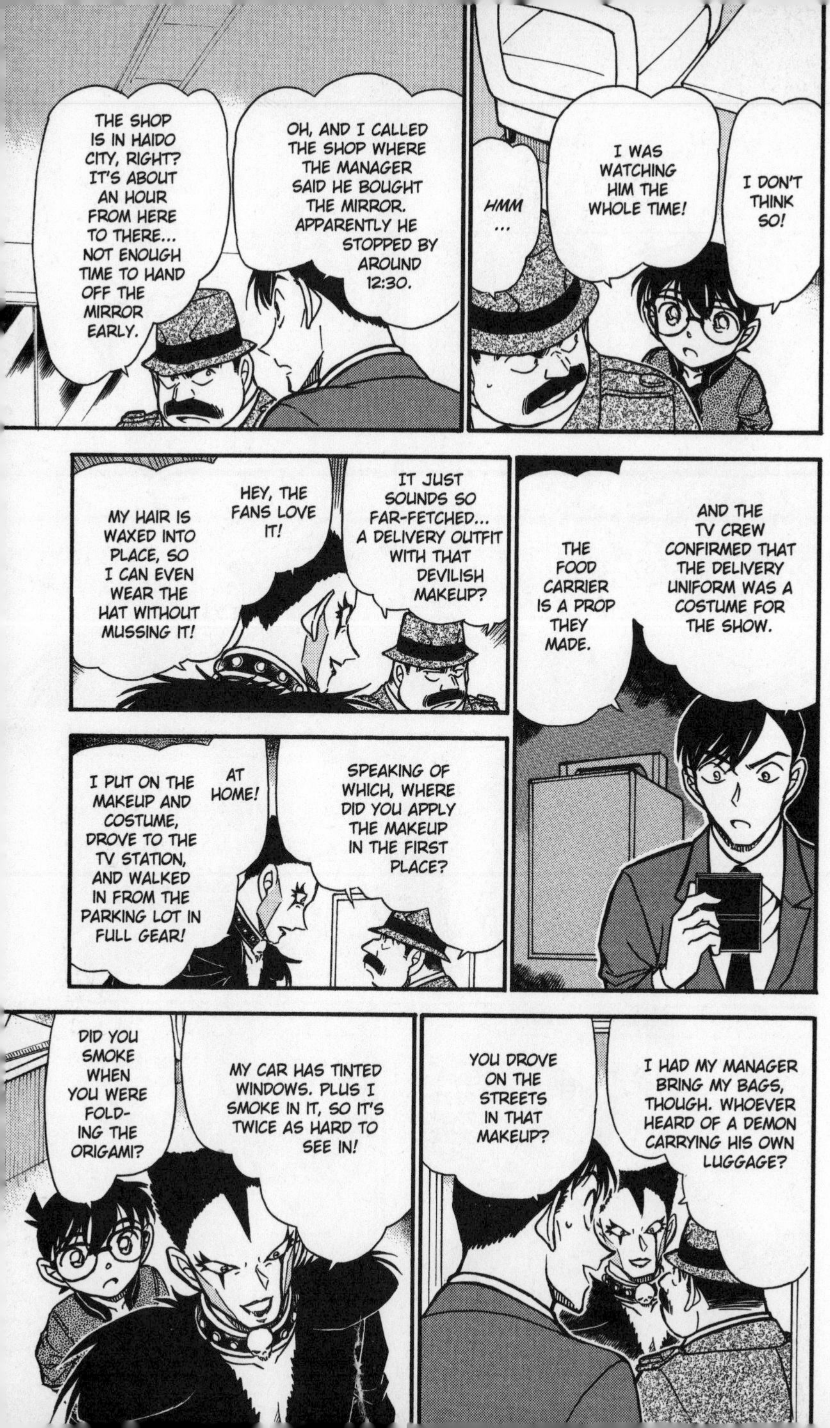
I DON'T THINK SO!
I WAS WATCHING HIM THE WHOLE TIME!
HMM...
OH, AND I CALLED THE SHOP WHERE THE MANAGER SAID HE BOUGHT THE MIRROR. APPARENTLY HE STOPPED BY AROUND 12:30.
THE SHOP IS IN HAIDO CITY, RIGHT? IT'S ABOUT AN HOUR FROM HERE TO THERE... NOT ENOUGH TIME TO HAND OFF THE MIRROR EARLY.
AND THE TV CREW CONFIRMED THAT THE DELIVERY UNIFORM WAS A COSTUME FOR THE SHOW.
THE FOOD CARRIER IS A PROP THEY MADE.
IT JUST SOUNDS SO FAR-FETCHED... A DELIVERY OUTFIT WITH THAT DEVILISH MAKEUP?
HEY, THE FANS LOVE IT!
MY HAIR IS WAXED INTO PLACE, SO I CAN EVEN WEAR THE HAT WITHOUT MUSSING IT!
SPEAKING OF WHICH, WHERE DID YOU APPLY THE MAKEUP IN THE FIRST PLACE?
AT HOME!
I PUT ON THE MAKEUP AND COSTUME, DROVE TO THE TV STATION, AND WALKED IN FROM THE PARKING LOT IN FULL GEAR!
I HAD MY MANAGER BRING MY BAGS, THOUGH. WHOEVER HEARD OF A DEMON CARRYING HIS OWN LUGGAGE?
YOU DROVE ON THE STREETS IN THAT MAKEUP?
MY CAR HAS TINTED WINDOWS. PLUS I SMOKE IN IT, SO IT'S TWICE AS HARD TO SEE IN!
DID YOU SMOKE WHEN YOU WERE FOLD-ING THE ORIGAMI?

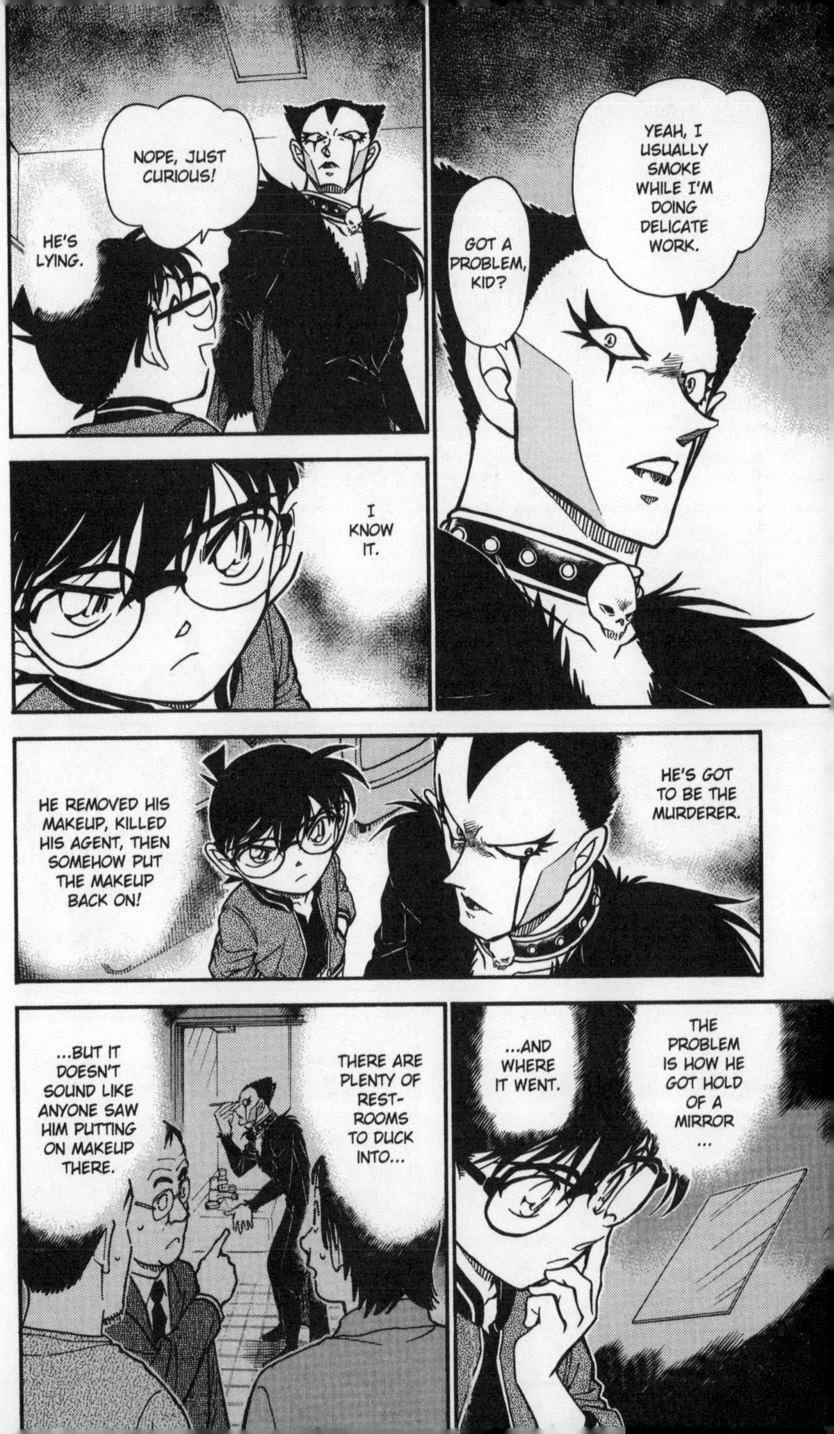
YEAH, I USUALLY SMOKE WHILE I'M DOING DELICATE WORK.
GOT A PROBLEM, KID?
NOPE, JUST CURIOUS!
HE'S LYING.
I KNOW IT.
HE'S GOT TO BE THE MURDERER.
HE REMOVED HIS MAKEUP, KILLED HIS AGENT, THEN SOMEHOW PUT THE MAKEUP BACK ON!
THE PROBLEM IS HOW HE GOT HOLD OF A MIRROR ...
...AND WHERE IT WENT.
THERE ARE PLENTY OF REST-ROOMS TO DUCK INTO...
...BUT IT DOESN'T SOUND LIKE ANYONE SAW HIM PUTTING ON MAKEUP THERE.

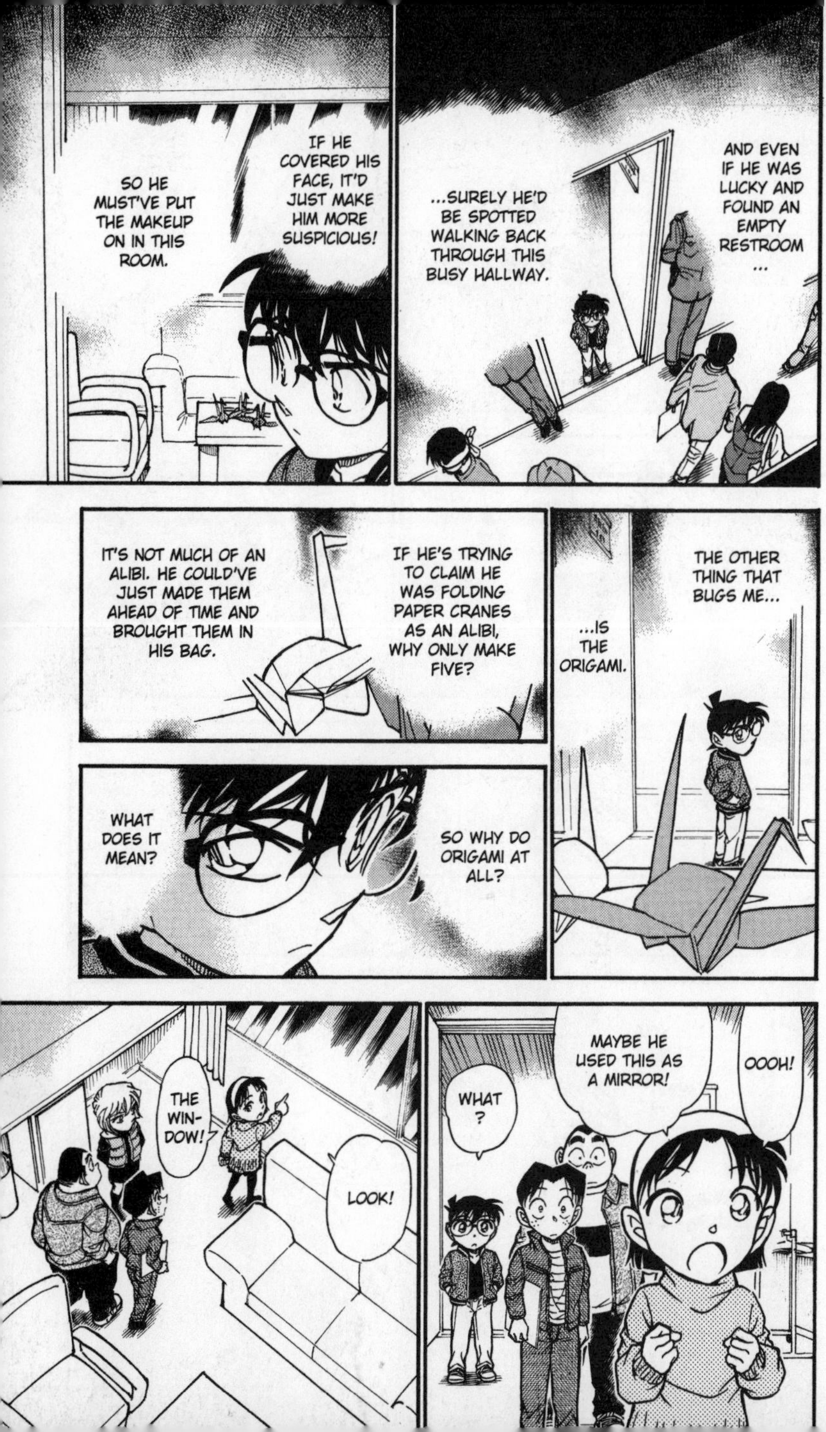
AND EVEN IF HE WAS LUCKY AND FOUND AN EMPTY RESTROOM ...
...SURELY HE'D BE SPOTTED WALKING BACK THROUGH THIS BUSY HALLWAY.
IF HE COVERED HIS FACE, IT'D JUST MAKE HIM MORE SUSPICIOUS!
SO HE MUST'VE PUT THE MAKEUP ON IN THIS ROOM.
THE OTHER THING THAT BUGS ME...
...IS THE ORIGAMI.
IF HE'S TRYING TO CLAIM HE WAS FOLDING PAPER CRANES AS AN ALIBI, WHY ONLY MAKE FIVE?
IT'S NOT MUCH OF AN ALIBI. HE COULD'VE JUST MADE THEM AHEAD OF TIME AND BROUGHT THEM IN HIS BAG.
SO WHY DO ORIGAMI AT ALL?
WHAT DOES IT MEAN?
OOOH!
MAYBE HE USED THIS AS A MIRROR!
WHAT?
THE WIN-DOW!
LOOK!

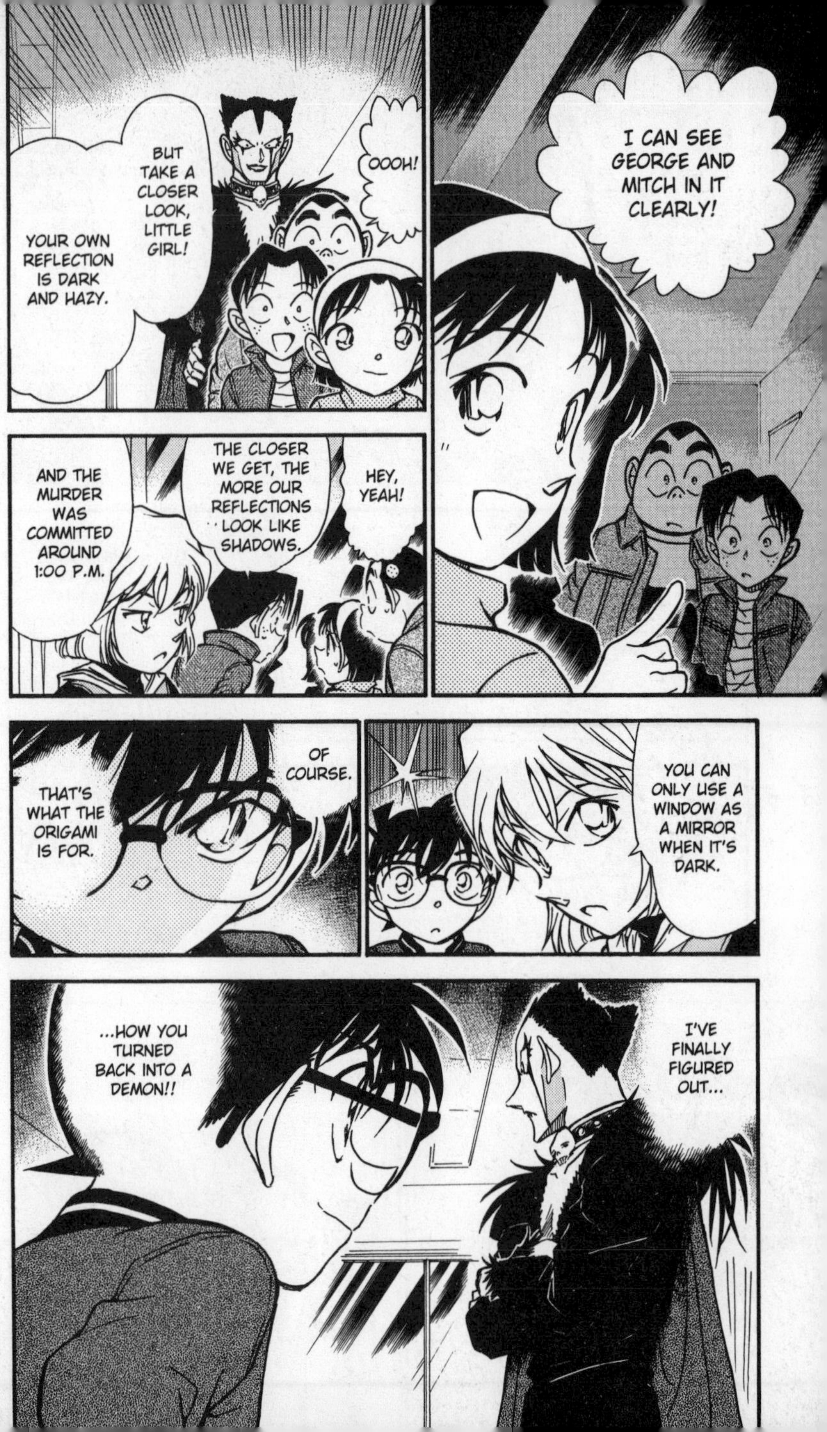
I CAN SEE GEORGE AND MITCH IN IT CLEARLY!
OOOH!
BUT TAKE A CLOSER LOOK, LITTLE GIRL!
YOUR OWN REFLECTION IS DARK AND HAZY.
HEY, YEAH!
THE CLOSER WE GET, THE MORE OUR REFLECTIONS LOOK LIKE SHADOWS.
AND THE MURDER WAS COMMITTED AROUND 1:00 P.M.
YOU CAN ONLY USE A WINDOW AS A MIRROR WHEN IT'S DARK.
OF COURSE.
THAT'S WHAT THE ORIGAMI IS FOR.
I'VE FINALLY FIGURED OUT...
...HOW YOU TURNED BACK INTO A DEMON!!

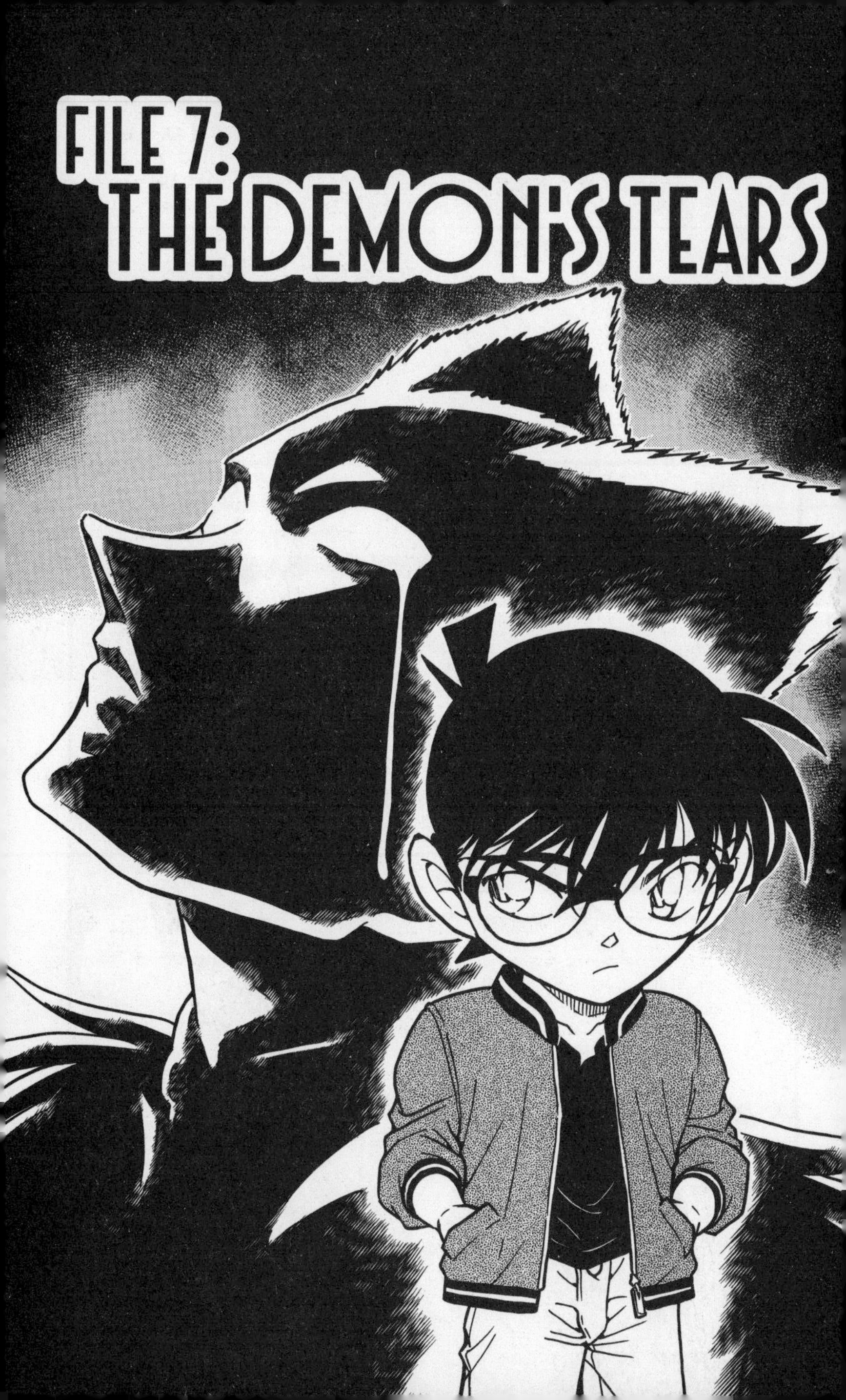
FILE 7:
THE DEMON'S TEARS

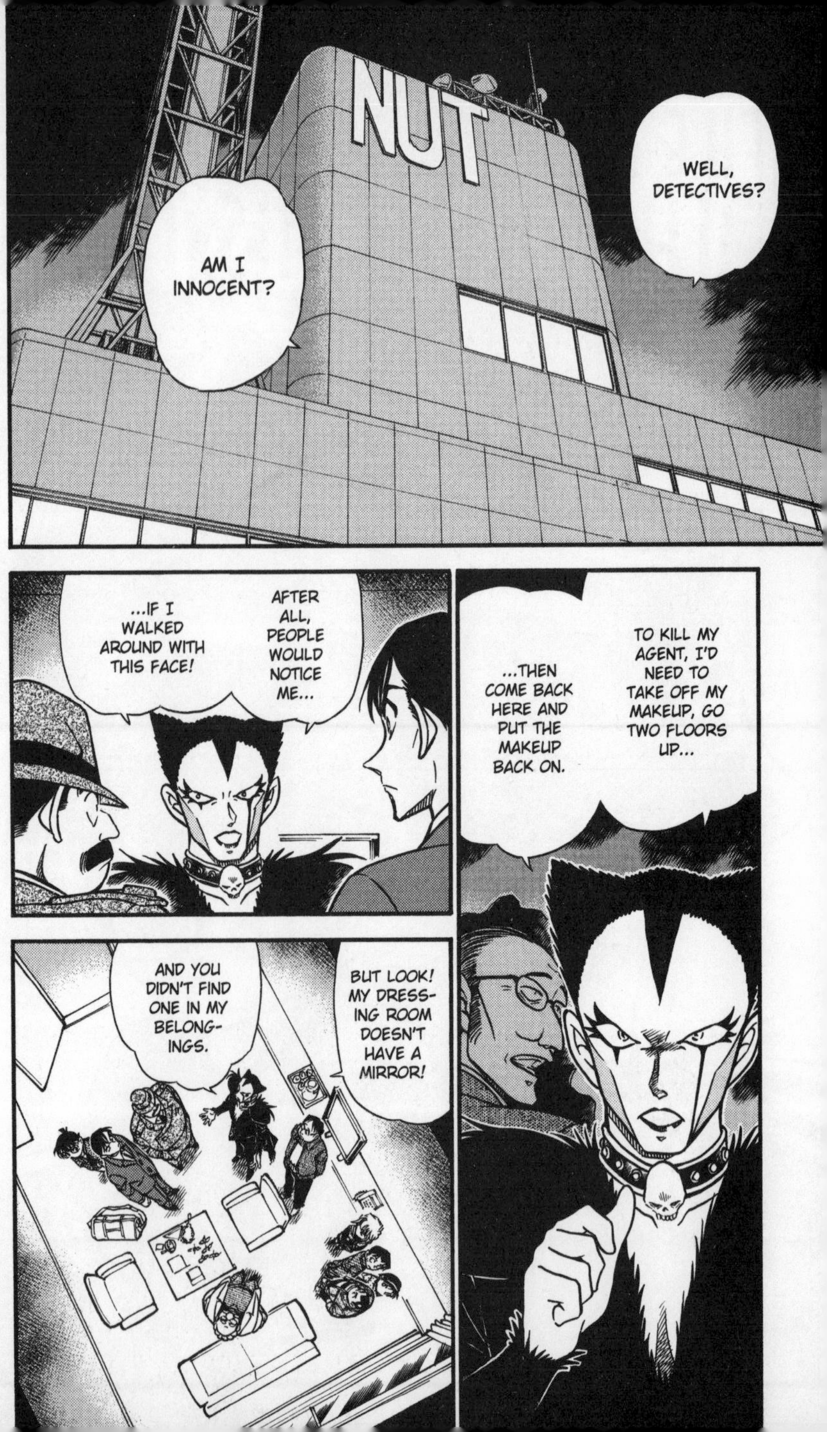

NUT
WELL, DETECTIVES?
AM I INNOCENT?
TO KILL MY AGENT, I'D NEED TO TAKE OFF MY MAKEUP, GO TWO FLOORS UP...
...THEN COME BACK HERE AND PUT THE MAKEUP BACK ON.
AFTER ALL, PEOPLE WOULD NOTICE ME...
...IF I WALKED AROUND WITH THIS FACE!
BUT LOOK! MY DRESSING ROOM DOESN'T HAVE A MIRROR!
AND YOU DIDN'T FIND ONE IN MY BELONGINGS.

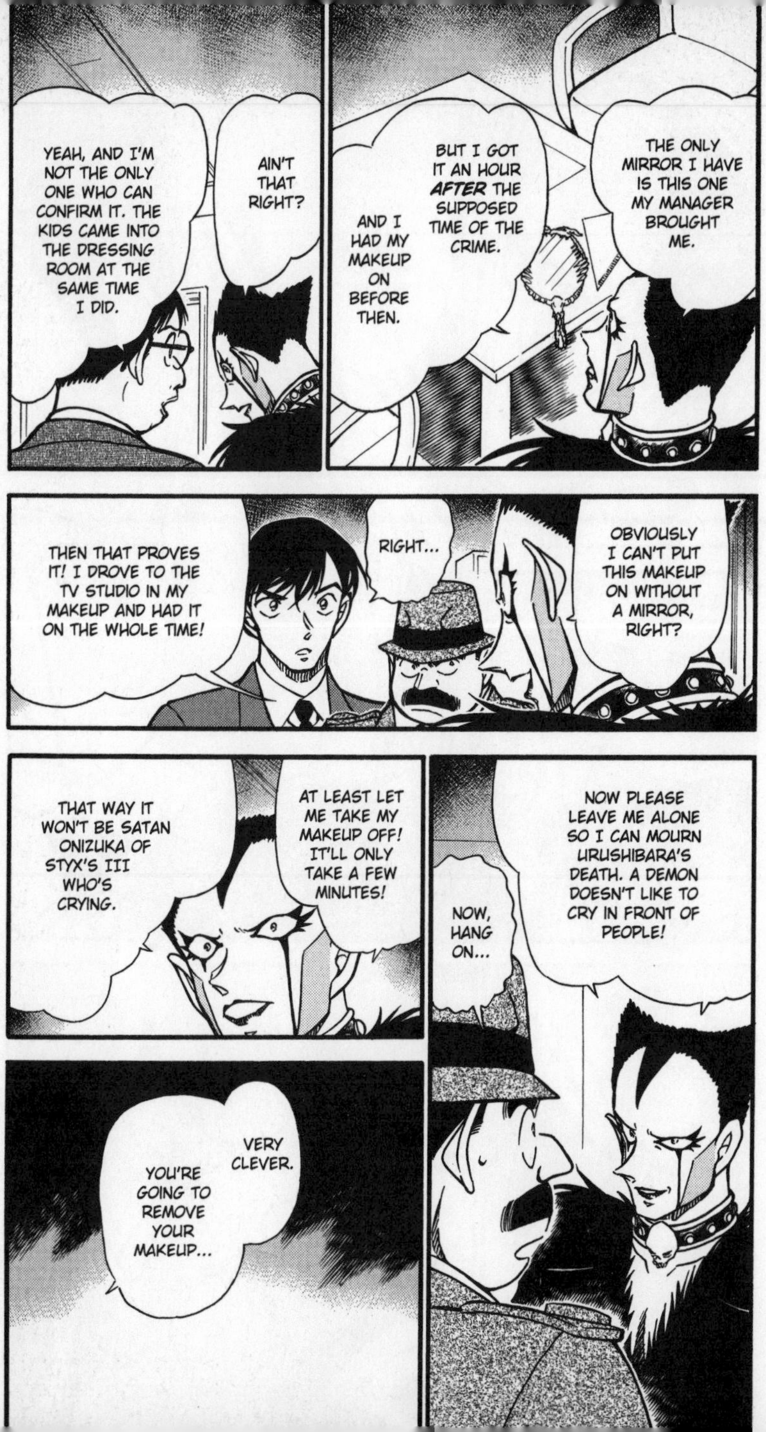
THE ONLY MIRROR I HAVE IS THIS ONE MY MANAGER BROUGHT ME.
BUT I GOT IT AN HOUR **AFTER** THE SUPPOSED TIME OF THE CRIME.
AND I HAD MY MAKEUP ON BEFORE THEN.
AIN'T THAT RIGHT?
YEAH, AND I'M NOT THE ONLY ONE WHO CAN CONFIRM IT. THE KIDS CAME INTO THE DRESSING ROOM AT THE SAME TIME I DID.
OBVIOUSLY I CAN'T PUT THIS MAKEUP ON WITHOUT A MIRROR, RIGHT?
RIGHT...
THEN THAT PROVES IT! I DROVE TO THE TV STUDIO IN MY MAKEUP AND HAD IT ON THE WHOLE TIME!
NOW PLEASE LEAVE ME ALONE SO I CAN MOURN URUSHIBARA'S DEATH. A DEMON DOESN'T LIKE TO CRY IN FRONT OF PEOPLE!
NOW, HANG ON...
AT LEAST LET ME TAKE MY MAKEUP OFF! IT'LL ONLY TAKE A FEW MINUTES!
THAT WAY IT WON'T BE SATAN ONIZUKA OF STYX'S III WHO'S CRYING.
VERY CLEVER.
YOU'RE GOING TO REMOVE YOUR MAKEUP...

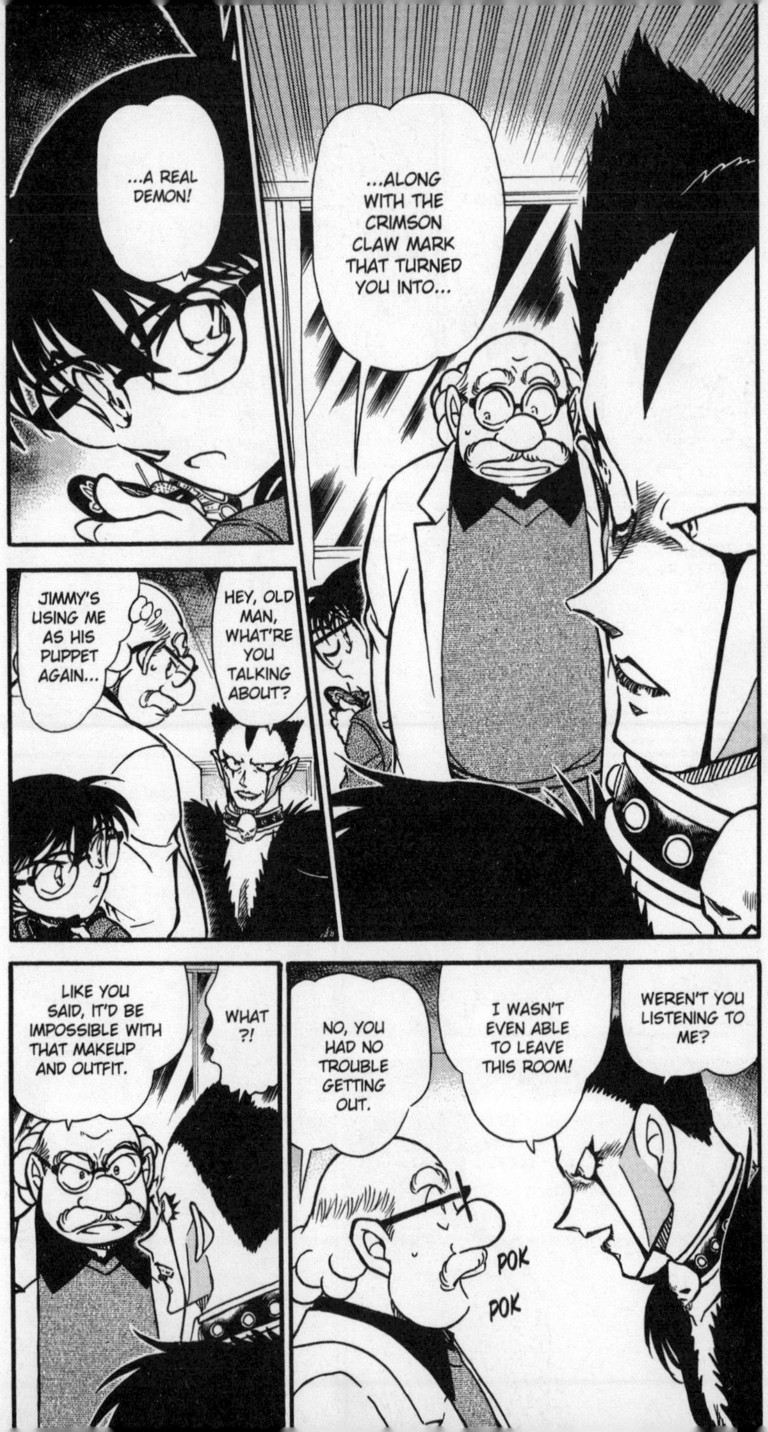
...ALONG WITH THE CRIMSON CLAW MARK THAT TURNED YOU INTO...
...A REAL DEMON!
HEY, OLD MAN, WHAT'RE YOU TALKING ABOUT?
JIMMY'S USING ME AS HIS PUPPET AGAIN...
WEREN'T YOU LISTENING TO ME?
I WASN'T EVEN ABLE TO LEAVE THIS ROOM!
NO, YOU HAD NO TROUBLE GETTING OUT.
POK
POK
WHAT?!
LIKE YOU SAID, IT'D BE IMPOSSIBLE WITH THAT MAKEUP AND OUTFIT.

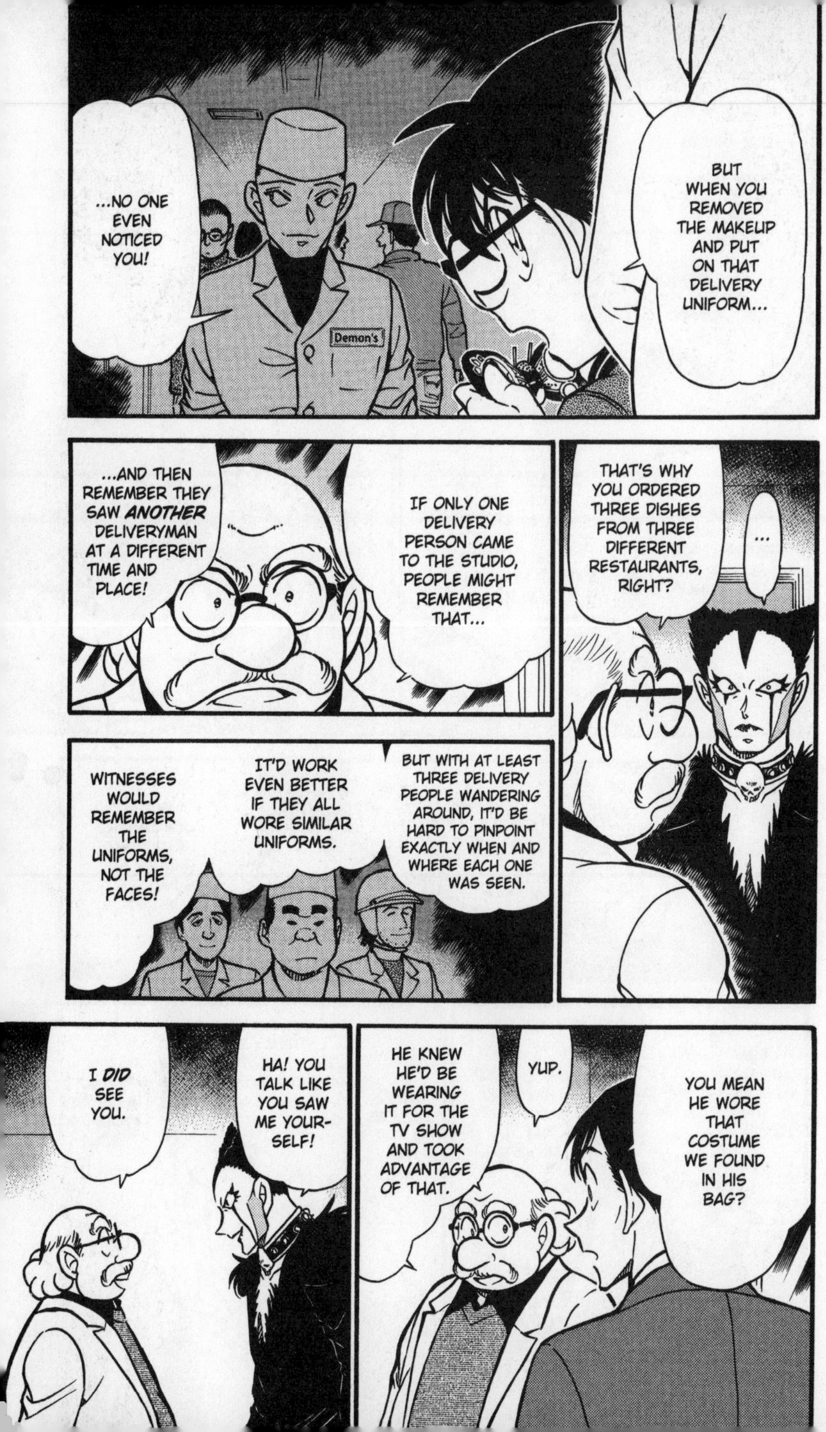
BUT WHEN YOU REMOVED THE MAKEUP AND PUT ON THAT DELIVERY UNIFORM...
Demon's
...NO ONE EVEN NOTICED YOU!
THAT'S WHY YOU ORDERED THREE DISHES FROM THREE DIFFERENT RESTAURANTS, RIGHT?
...
IF ONLY ONE DELIVERY PERSON CAME TO THE STUDIO, PEOPLE MIGHT REMEMBER THAT...
...AND THEN REMEMBER THEY SAW *ANOTHER* DELIVERYMAN AT A DIFFERENT TIME AND PLACE!
BUT WITH AT LEAST THREE DELIVERY PEOPLE WANDERING AROUND, IT'D BE HARD TO PINPOINT EXACTLY WHEN AND WHERE EACH ONE WAS SEEN.
IT'D WORK EVEN BETTER IF THEY ALL WORE SIMILAR UNIFORMS.
WITNESSES WOULD REMEMBER THE UNIFORMS, NOT THE FACES!
YOU MEAN HE WORE THAT COSTUME WE FOUND IN HIS BAG?
YUP.
HE KNEW HE'D BE WEARING IT FOR THE TV SHOW AND TOOK ADVANTAGE OF THAT.
HA! YOU TALK LIKE YOU SAW ME YOURSELF!
I *DID* SEE YOU.

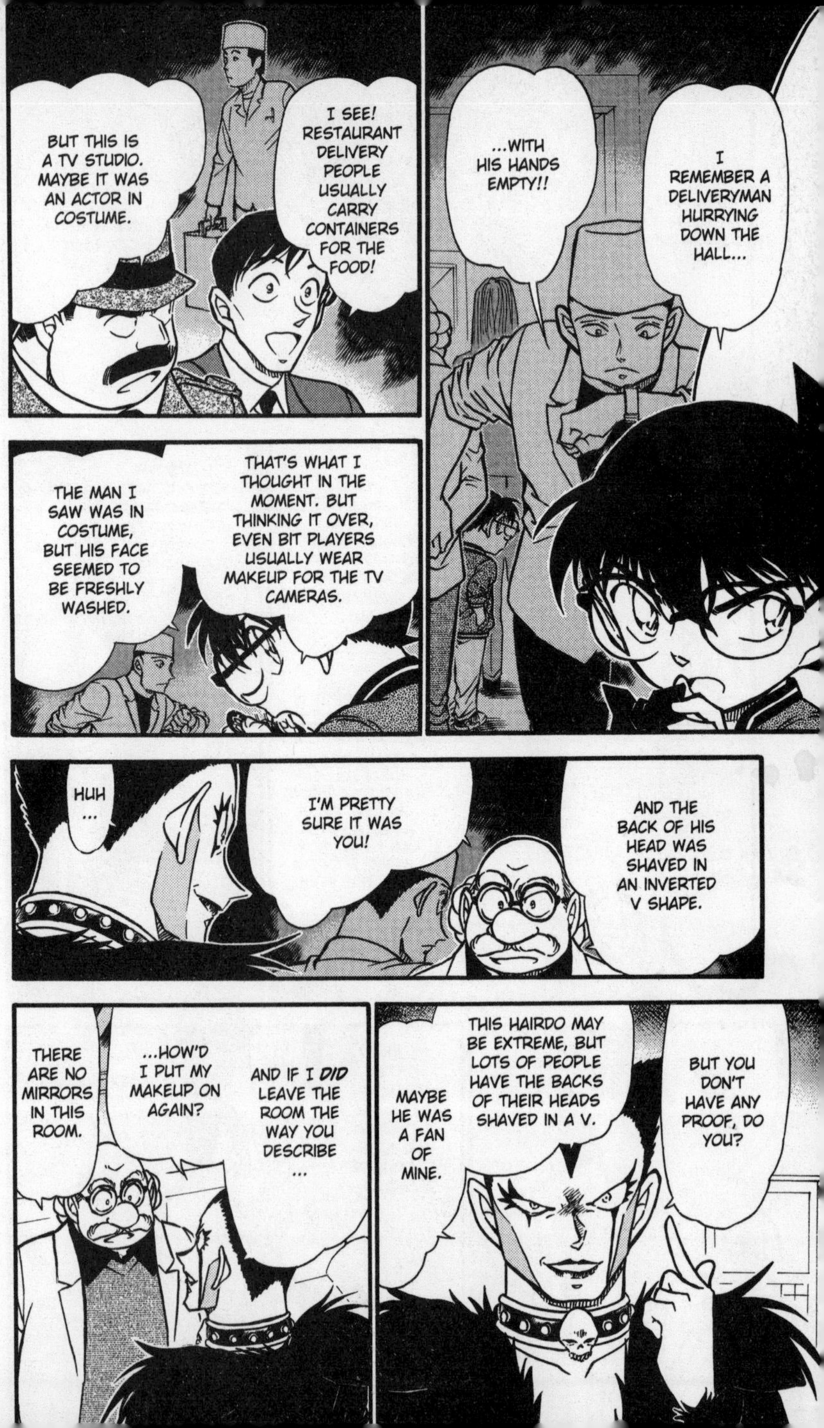
I REMEMBER A DELIVERYMAN HURRYING DOWN THE HALL...
...WITH HIS HANDS EMPTY!!
I SEE! RESTAURANT DELIVERY PEOPLE USUALLY CARRY CONTAINERS FOR THE FOOD!
BUT THIS IS A TV STUDIO. MAYBE IT WAS AN ACTOR IN COSTUME.
THAT'S WHAT I THOUGHT IN THE MOMENT. BUT THINKING IT OVER, EVEN BIT PLAYERS USUALLY WEAR MAKEUP FOR THE TV CAMERAS.
THE MAN I SAW WAS IN COSTUME, BUT HIS FACE SEEMED TO BE FRESHLY WASHED.
AND THE BACK OF HIS HEAD WAS SHAVED IN AN INVERTED V SHAPE.
I'M PRETTY SURE IT WAS YOU!
HUH ...
BUT YOU DON'T HAVE ANY PROOF, DO YOU?
THIS HAIRDO MAY BE EXTREME, BUT LOTS OF PEOPLE HAVE THE BACKS OF THEIR HEADS SHAVED IN A V.
MAYBE HE WAS A FAN OF MINE.
AND IF I *DID* LEAVE THE ROOM THE WAY YOU DESCRIBE ...
...HOW'D I PUT MY MAKEUP ON AGAIN?
THERE ARE NO MIRRORS IN THIS ROOM.

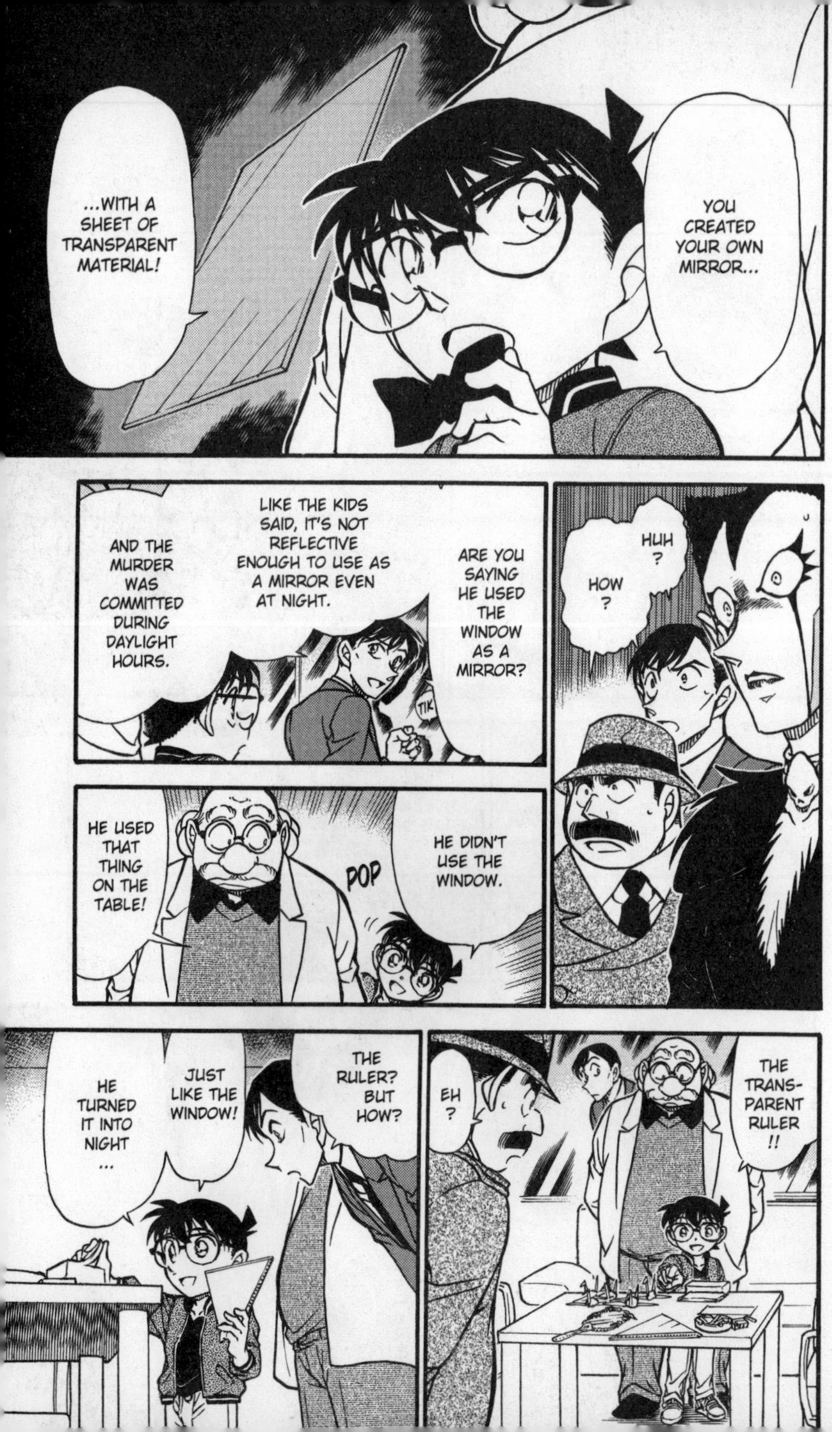
YOU CREATED YOUR OWN MIRROR...
...WITH A SHEET OF TRANSPARENT MATERIAL!
HUH?
HOW?
ARE YOU SAYING HE USED THE WINDOW AS A MIRROR?
TIK
LIKE THE KIDS SAID, IT'S NOT REFLECTIVE ENOUGH TO USE AS A MIRROR EVEN AT NIGHT.
AND THE MURDER WAS COMMITTED DURING DAYLIGHT HOURS.
HE DIDN'T USE THE WINDOW.
POP
HE USED THAT THING ON THE TABLE!
THE TRANS-PARENT RULER!!
EH?
THE RULER? BUT HOW?
JUST LIKE THE WINDOW!
HE TURNED IT INTO NIGHT...

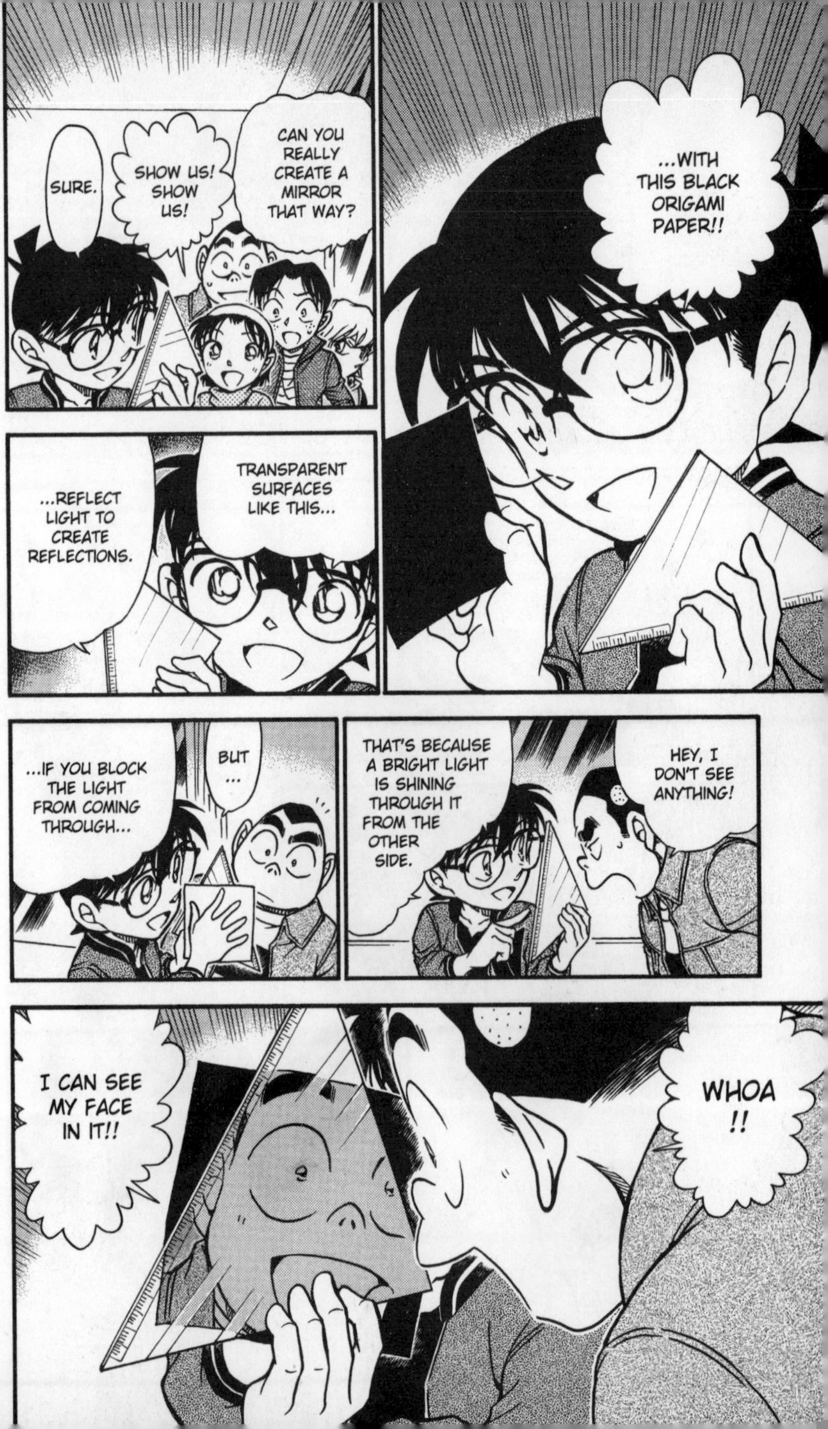
...WITH THIS BLACK ORIGAMI PAPER!!
CAN YOU REALLY CREATE A MIRROR THAT WAY?
SHOW US! SHOW US!
SURE.
TRANSPARENT SURFACES LIKE THIS...
...REFLECT LIGHT TO CREATE REFLECTIONS.
HEY, I DON'T SEE ANYTHING!
THAT'S BECAUSE A BRIGHT LIGHT IS SHINING THROUGH IT FROM THE OTHER SIDE.
BUT ...
...IF YOU BLOCK THE LIGHT FROM COMING THROUGH...
WHOA !!
I CAN SEE MY FACE IN IT!!

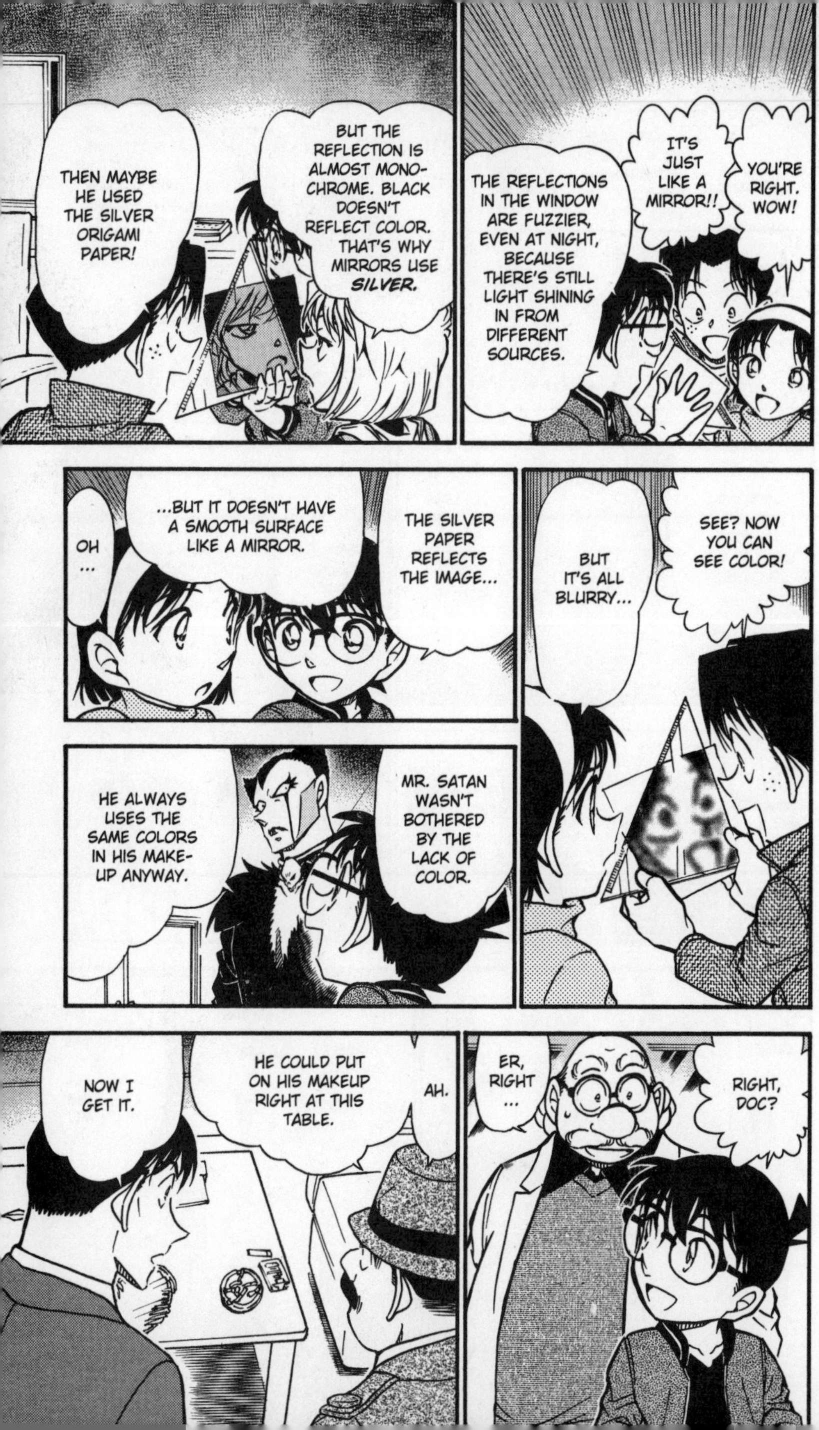
YOU'RE RIGHT. WOW!
IT'S JUST LIKE A MIRROR!!
THE REFLECTIONS IN THE WINDOW ARE FUZZIER, EVEN AT NIGHT, BECAUSE THERE'S STILL LIGHT SHINING IN FROM DIFFERENT SOURCES.
BUT THE REFLECTION IS ALMOST MONO-CHROME. BLACK DOESN'T REFLECT COLOR. THAT'S WHY MIRRORS USE *SILVER.*
THEN MAYBE HE USED THE SILVER ORIGAMI PAPER!
SEE? NOW YOU CAN SEE COLOR!
BUT IT'S ALL BLURRY...
THE SILVER PAPER REFLECTS THE IMAGE...
...BUT IT DOESN'T HAVE A SMOOTH SURFACE LIKE A MIRROR.
OH ...
MR. SATAN WASN'T BOTHERED BY THE LACK OF COLOR.
HE ALWAYS USES THE SAME COLORS IN HIS MAKE-UP ANYWAY.
RIGHT, DOC?
ER, RIGHT ...
AH.
HE COULD PUT ON HIS MAKEUP RIGHT AT THIS TABLE.
NOW I GET IT.

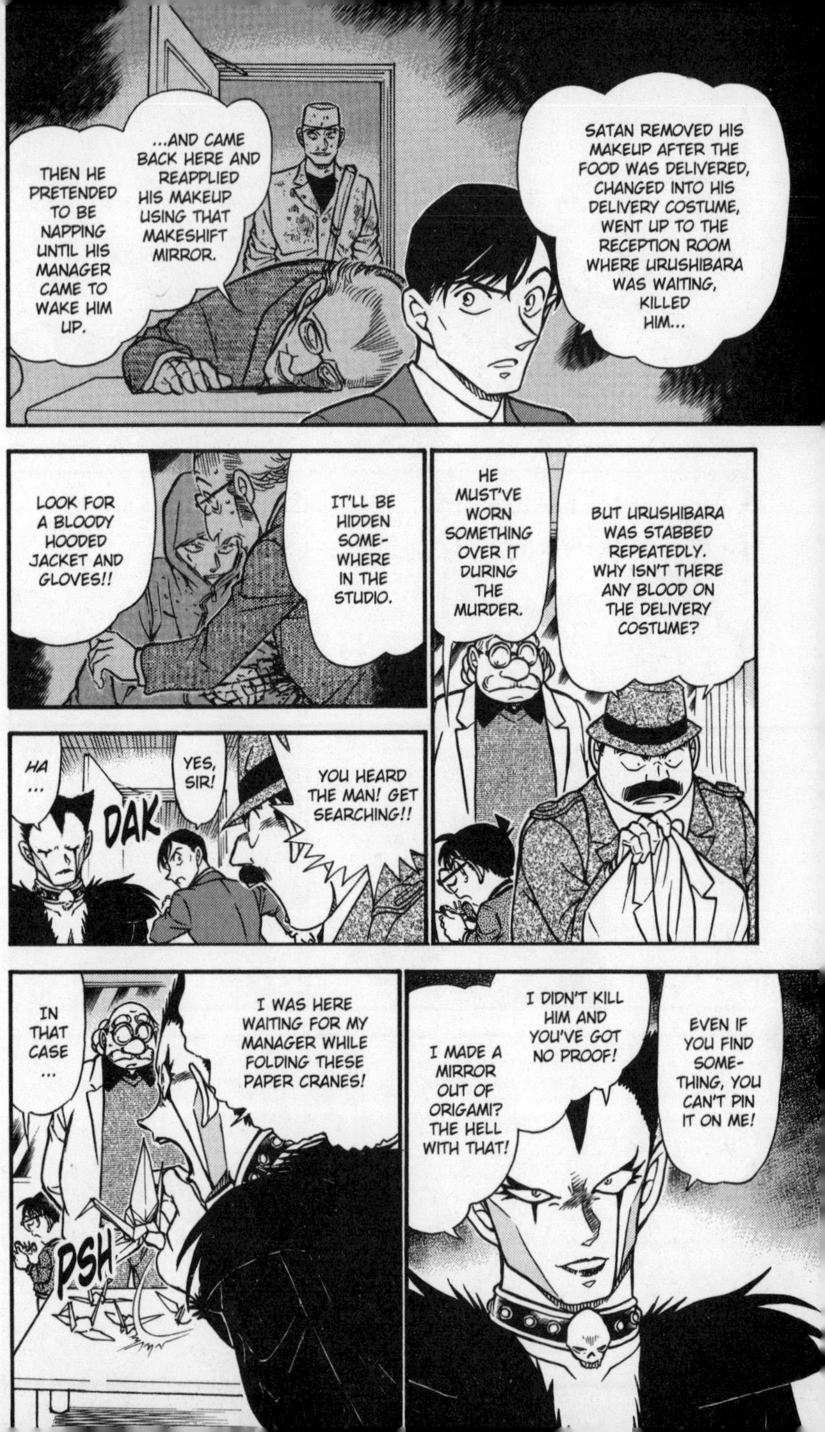
SATAN REMOVED HIS MAKEUP AFTER THE FOOD WAS DELIVERED, CHANGED INTO HIS DELIVERY COSTUME, WENT UP TO THE RECEPTION ROOM WHERE URUSHIBARA WAS WAITING, KILLED HIM...
...AND CAME BACK HERE AND REAPPLIED HIS MAKEUP USING THAT MAKESHIFT MIRROR.
THEN HE PRETENDED TO BE NAPPING UNTIL HIS MANAGER CAME TO WAKE HIM UP.
BUT URUSHIBARA WAS STABBED REPEATEDLY. WHY ISN'T THERE ANY BLOOD ON THE DELIVERY COSTUME?
HE MUST'VE WORN SOMETHING OVER IT DURING THE MURDER.
IT'LL BE HIDDEN SOMEWHERE IN THE STUDIO.
LOOK FOR A BLOODY HOODED JACKET AND GLOVES!!
YOU HEARD THE MAN! GET SEARCHING!!
YES, SIR!
DAK
HA...
EVEN IF YOU FIND SOMETHING, YOU CAN'T PIN IT ON ME!
I DIDN'T KILL HIM AND YOU'VE GOT NO PROOF!
I MADE A MIRROR OUT OF ORIGAMI? THE HELL WITH THAT!
I WAS HERE WAITING FOR MY MANAGER WHILE FOLDING THESE PAPER CRANES!
IN THAT CASE...
PSH

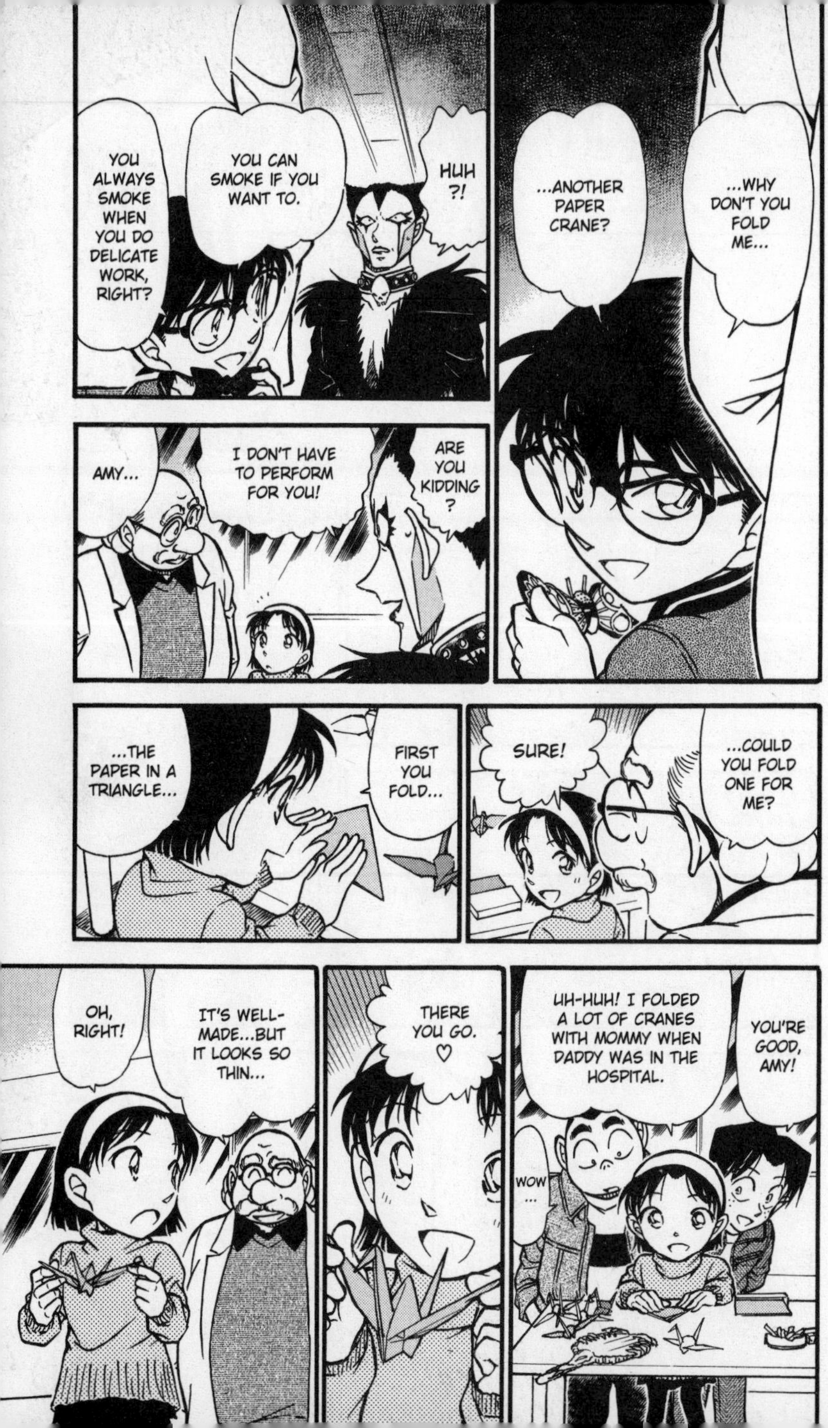
...WHY DON'T YOU FOLD ME...
...ANOTHER PAPER CRANE?
HUH ?!
YOU CAN SMOKE IF YOU WANT TO.
YOU ALWAYS SMOKE WHEN YOU DO DELICATE WORK, RIGHT?
ARE YOU KIDDING ?
I DON'T HAVE TO PERFORM FOR YOU!
AMY...
...COULD YOU FOLD ONE FOR ME?
SURE!
FIRST YOU FOLD...
...THE PAPER IN A TRIANGLE...
YOU'RE GOOD, AMY!
UH-HUH! I FOLDED A LOT OF CRANES WITH MOMMY WHEN DADDY WAS IN THE HOSPITAL.
WOW ...
THERE YOU GO. ♡
IT'S WELL-MADE...BUT IT LOOKS SO THIN...
OH, RIGHT!

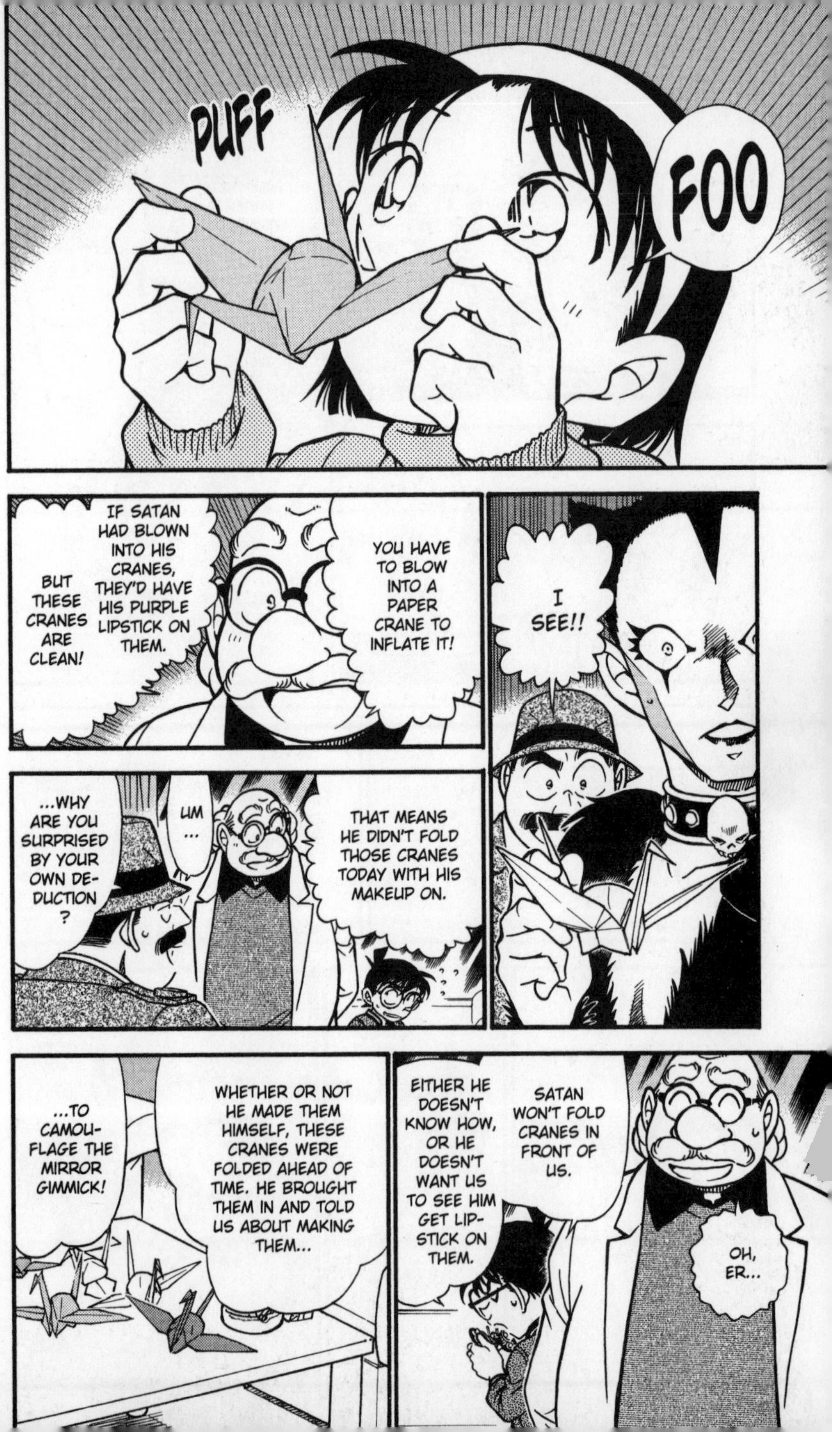
FOO
PUFF
I SEE!!
YOU HAVE TO BLOW INTO A PAPER CRANE TO INFLATE IT!
IF SATAN HAD BLOWN INTO HIS CRANES, THEY'D HAVE HIS PURPLE LIPSTICK ON THEM.
BUT THESE CRANES ARE CLEAN!
THAT MEANS HE DIDN'T FOLD THOSE CRANES TODAY WITH HIS MAKEUP ON.
UM ...
...WHY ARE YOU SURPRISED BY YOUR OWN DE-DUCTION ?
SATAN WON'T FOLD CRANES IN FRONT OF US.
EITHER HE DOESN'T KNOW HOW, OR HE DOESN'T WANT US TO SEE HIM GET LIP-STICK ON THEM.
OH, ER...
WHETHER OR NOT HE MADE THEM HIMSELF, THESE CRANES WERE FOLDED AHEAD OF TIME. HE BROUGHT THEM IN AND TOLD US ABOUT MAKING THEM...
...TO CAMOU-FLAGE THE MIRROR GIMMICK!

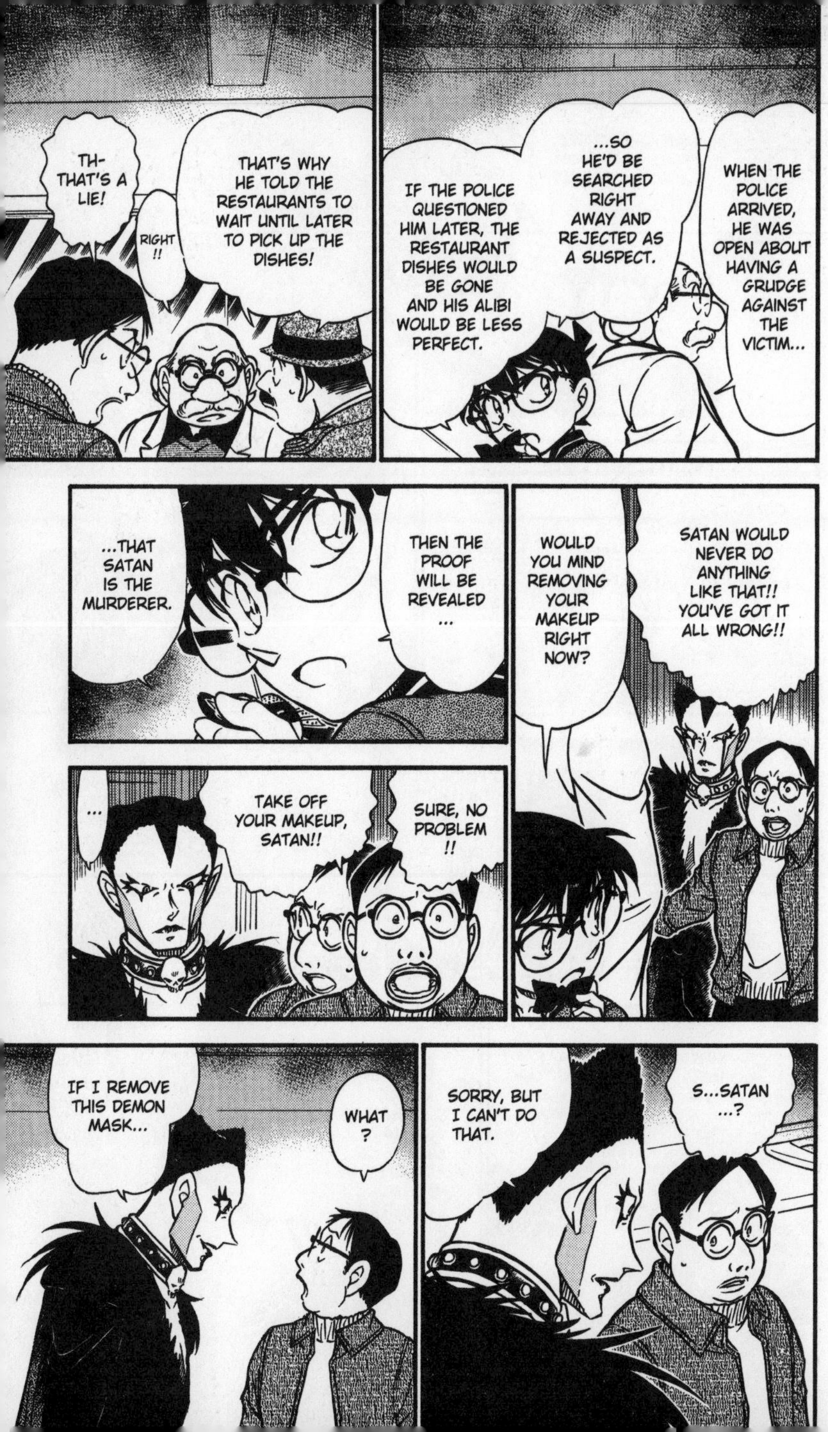

WHEN THE POLICE ARRIVED, HE WAS OPEN ABOUT HAVING A GRUDGE AGAINST THE VICTIM...
...SO HE'D BE SEARCHED RIGHT AWAY AND REJECTED AS A SUSPECT.
IF THE POLICE QUESTIONED HIM LATER, THE RESTAURANT DISHES WOULD BE GONE AND HIS ALIBI WOULD BE LESS PERFECT.
THAT'S WHY HE TOLD THE RESTAURANTS TO WAIT UNTIL LATER TO PICK UP THE DISHES!
RIGHT !!
TH- THAT'S A LIE!
SATAN WOULD NEVER DO ANYTHING LIKE THAT!! YOU'VE GOT IT ALL WRONG!!
WOULD YOU MIND REMOVING YOUR MAKEUP RIGHT NOW?
THEN THE PROOF WILL BE REVEALED ...
...THAT SATAN IS THE MURDERER.
SURE, NO PROBLEM !!
TAKE OFF YOUR MAKEUP, SATAN!!
...
S...SATAN ...?
SORRY, BUT I CAN'T DO THAT.
WHAT ?
IF I REMOVE THIS DEMON MASK...

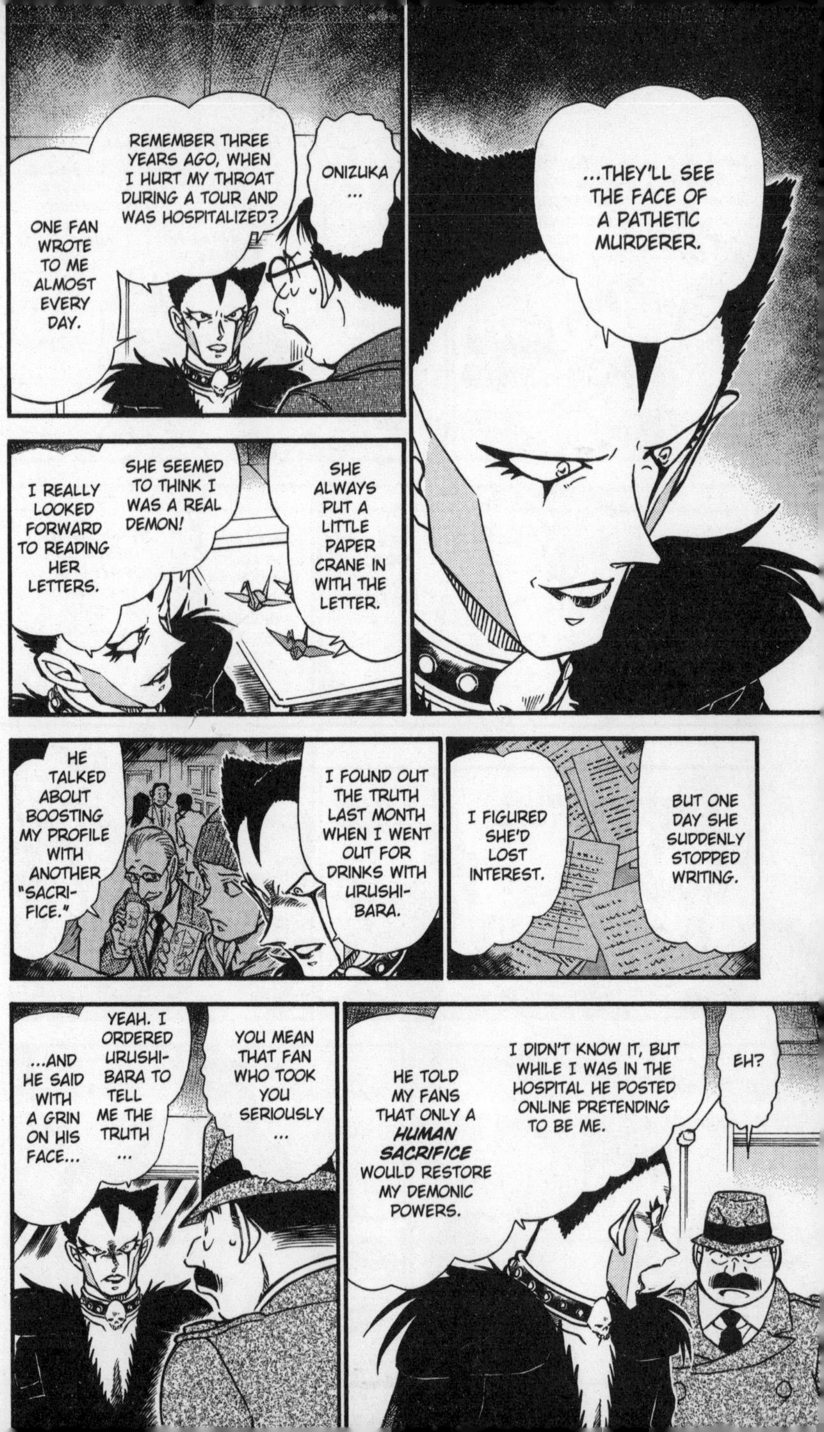
...THEY'LL SEE THE FACE OF A PATHETIC MURDERER.
ONIZUKA ...
REMEMBER THREE YEARS AGO, WHEN I HURT MY THROAT DURING A TOUR AND WAS HOSPITALIZED?
ONE FAN WROTE TO ME ALMOST EVERY DAY.
SHE ALWAYS PUT A LITTLE PAPER CRANE IN WITH THE LETTER.
SHE SEEMED TO THINK I WAS A REAL DEMON!
I REALLY LOOKED FORWARD TO READING HER LETTERS.
BUT ONE DAY SHE SUDDENLY STOPPED WRITING.
I FIGURED SHE'D LOST INTEREST.
I FOUND OUT THE TRUTH LAST MONTH WHEN I WENT OUT FOR DRINKS WITH URUSHIBARA.
HE TALKED ABOUT BOOSTING MY PROFILE WITH ANOTHER "SACRIFICE."
EH?
I DIDN'T KNOW IT, BUT WHILE I WAS IN THE HOSPITAL HE POSTED ONLINE PRETENDING TO BE ME.
HE TOLD MY FANS THAT ONLY A ***HUMAN SACRIFICE*** WOULD RESTORE MY DEMONIC POWERS.
YOU MEAN THAT FAN WHO TOOK YOU SERIOUSLY ...
YEAH. I ORDERED URUSHIBARA TO TELL ME THE TRUTH ...
...AND HE SAID WITH A GRIN ON HIS FACE...

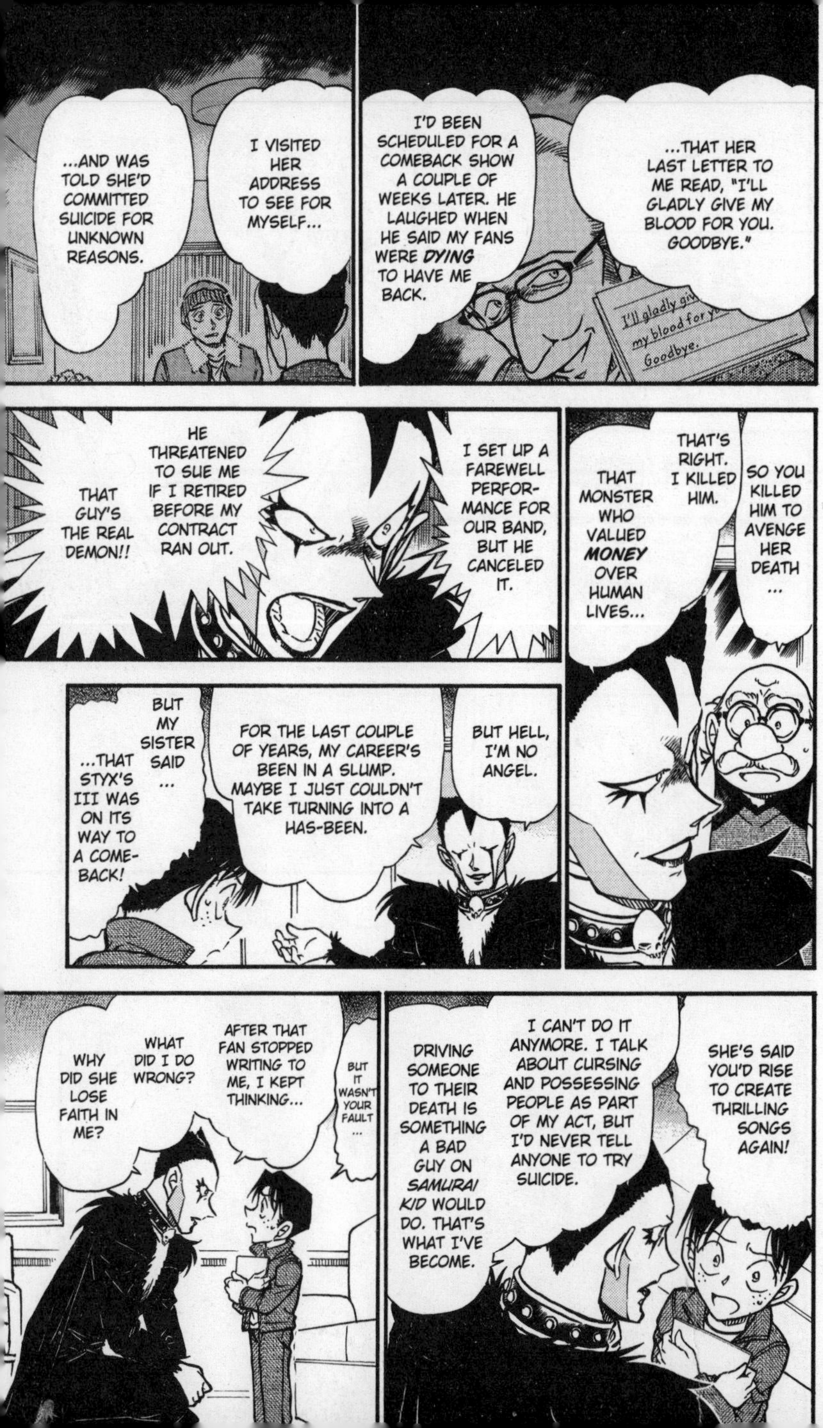

...THAT HER LAST LETTER TO ME READ, "I'LL GLADLY GIVE MY BLOOD FOR YOU. GOODBYE."
I'D BEEN SCHEDULED FOR A COMEBACK SHOW A COUPLE OF WEEKS LATER. HE LAUGHED WHEN HE SAID MY FANS WERE *DYING* TO HAVE ME BACK.
Goodbye.
I VISITED HER ADDRESS TO SEE FOR MYSELF...
...AND WAS TOLD SHE'D COMMITTED SUICIDE FOR UNKNOWN REASONS.
SO YOU KILLED HIM TO AVENGE HER DEATH ...
THAT'S RIGHT. I KILLED HIM.
THAT MONSTER WHO VALUED ***MONEY*** OVER HUMAN LIVES...
I SET UP A FAREWELL PERFOR-MANCE FOR OUR BAND, BUT HE CANCELED IT.
HE THREATENED TO SUE ME IF I RETIRED BEFORE MY CONTRACT RAN OUT.
THAT GUY'S THE REAL DEMON!!
BUT HELL, I'M NO ANGEL.
FOR THE LAST COUPLE OF YEARS, MY CAREER'S BEEN IN A SLUMP. MAYBE I JUST COULDN'T TAKE TURNING INTO A HAS-BEEN.
BUT MY SISTER SAID ...
...THAT STYX'S III WAS ON ITS WAY TO A COME-BACK!
SHE'S SAID YOU'D RISE TO CREATE THRILLING SONGS AGAIN!
I CAN'T DO IT ANYMORE. I TALK ABOUT CURSING AND POSSESSING PEOPLE AS PART OF MY ACT, BUT I'D NEVER TELL ANYONE TO TRY SUICIDE.
DRIVING SOMEONE TO THEIR DEATH IS SOMETHING A BAD GUY ON *SAMURAI KID* WOULD DO. THAT'S WHAT I'VE BECOME.
BUT IT WASN'T YOUR FAULT ...
AFTER THAT FAN STOPPED WRITING TO ME, I KEPT THINKING...
WHAT DID I DO WRONG?
WHY DID SHE LOSE FAITH IN ME?

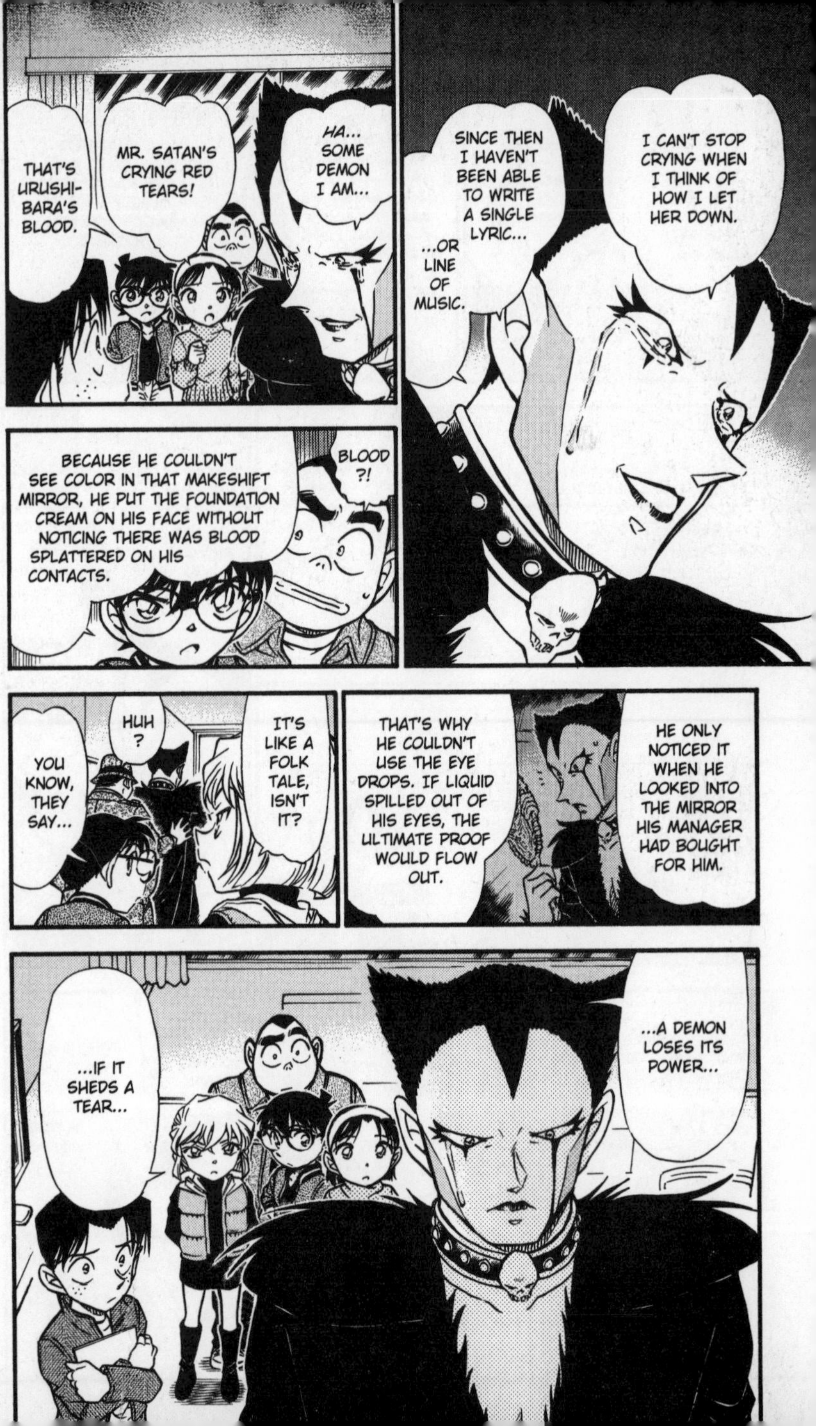
I CAN'T STOP CRYING WHEN I THINK OF HOW I LET HER DOWN.
SINCE THEN I HAVEN'T BEEN ABLE TO WRITE A SINGLE LYRIC...
...OR LINE OF MUSIC.
HA... SOME DEMON I AM...
MR. SATAN'S CRYING RED TEARS!
THAT'S URUSHIBARA'S BLOOD.
BLOOD ?!
BECAUSE HE COULDN'T SEE COLOR IN THAT MAKESHIFT MIRROR, HE PUT THE FOUNDATION CREAM ON HIS FACE WITHOUT NOTICING THERE WAS BLOOD SPLATTERED ON HIS CONTACTS.
HE ONLY NOTICED IT WHEN HE LOOKED INTO THE MIRROR HIS MANAGER HAD BOUGHT FOR HIM.
THAT'S WHY HE COULDN'T USE THE EYE DROPS. IF LIQUID SPILLED OUT OF HIS EYES, THE ULTIMATE PROOF WOULD FLOW OUT.
IT'S LIKE A FOLK TALE, ISN'T IT?
HUH ?
YOU KNOW, THEY SAY...
...A DEMON LOSES ITS POWER...
...IF IT SHEDS A TEAR...

FILE 8: FUGITIVE

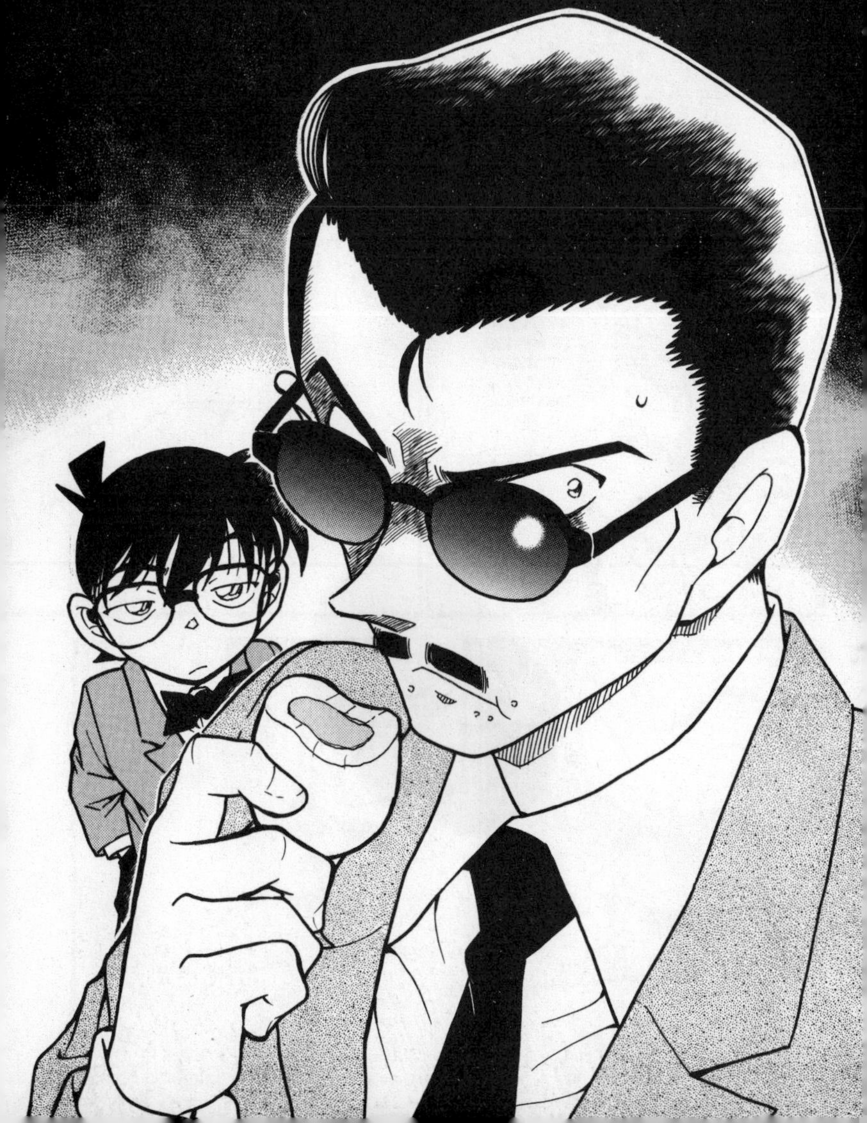

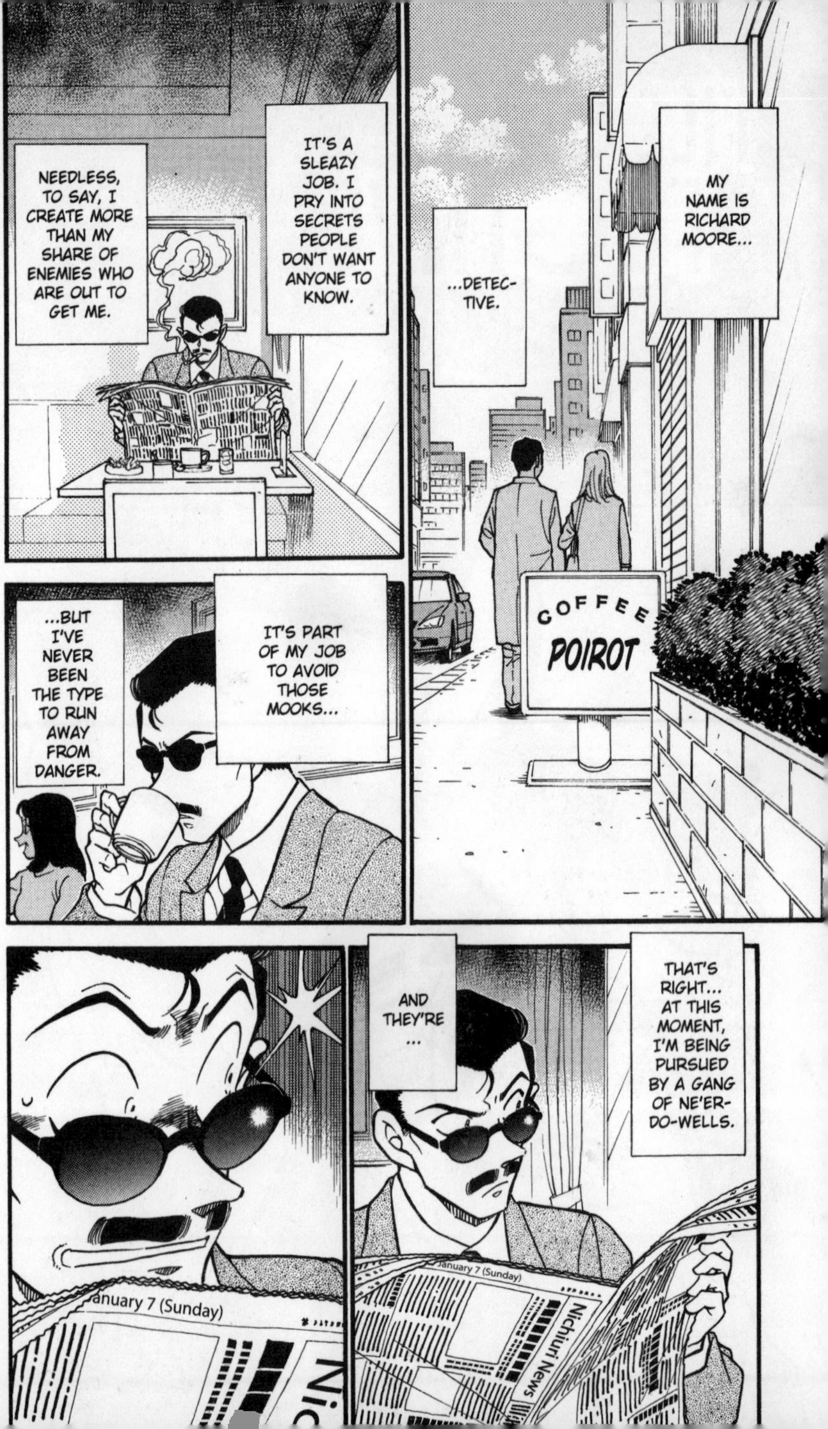
MY NAME IS RICHARD MOORE...
...DETEC-TIVE.
COFFEE
POIROT
IT'S A SLEAZY JOB. I PRY INTO SECRETS PEOPLE DON'T WANT ANYONE TO KNOW.
NEEDLESS, TO SAY, I CREATE MORE THAN MY SHARE OF ENEMIES WHO ARE OUT TO GET ME.
IT'S PART OF MY JOB TO AVOID THOSE MOOKS...
...BUT I'VE NEVER BEEN THE TYPE TO RUN AWAY FROM DANGER.
THAT'S RIGHT... AT THIS MOMENT, I'M BEING PURSUED BY A GANG OF NE'ER-DO-WELLS.
AND THEY'RE ...
January 7 (Sunday)
Nichiuri News
January 7 (Sunday)

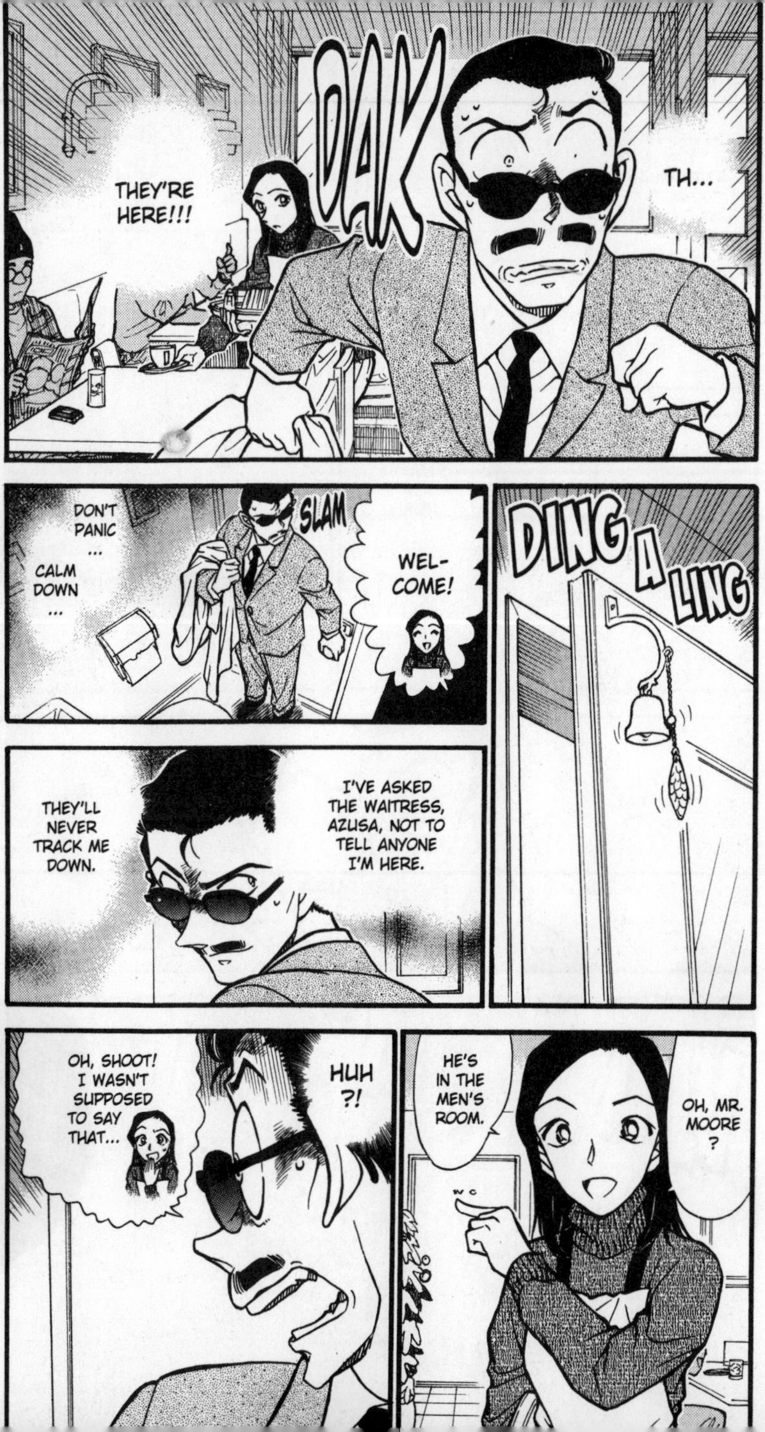
TH...
DAK
THEY'RE HERE!!!
DING A LING
WEL-COME!
SLAM
DON'T PANIC ... CALM DOWN ...
I'VE ASKED THE WAITRESS, AZUSA, NOT TO TELL ANYONE I'M HERE.
THEY'LL NEVER TRACK ME DOWN.
OH, MR. MOORE?
HE'S IN THE MEN'S ROOM.
HUH?!
OH, SHOOT! I WASN'T SUPPOSED TO SAY THAT...

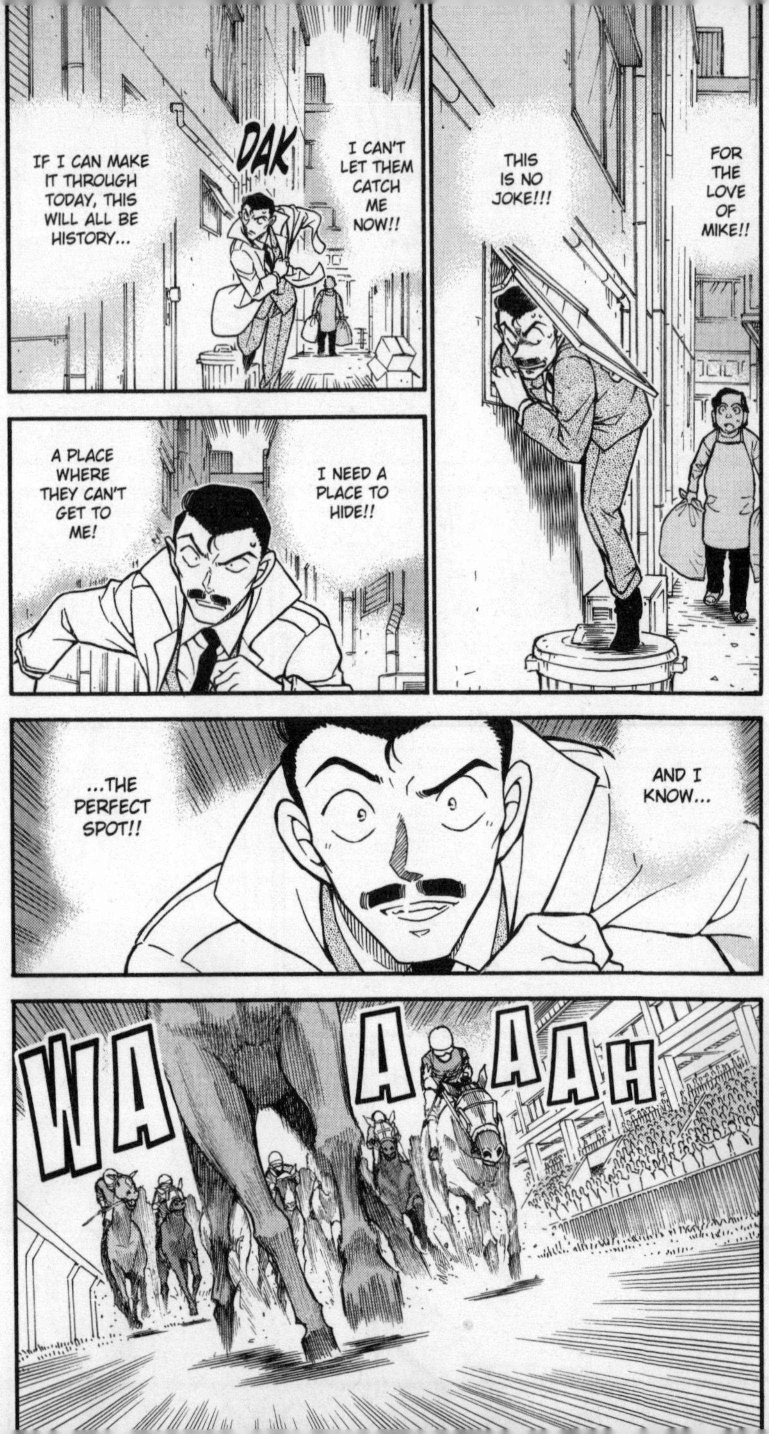
FOR THE LOVE OF MIKE!!
THIS IS NO JOKE!!!
I CAN'T LET THEM CATCH ME NOW!!
DAK
IF I CAN MAKE IT THROUGH TODAY, THIS WILL ALL BE HISTORY...
I NEED A PLACE TO HIDE!!
A PLACE WHERE THEY CAN'T GET TO ME!
AND I KNOW...
...THE PERFECT SPOT!!
WA A A AH

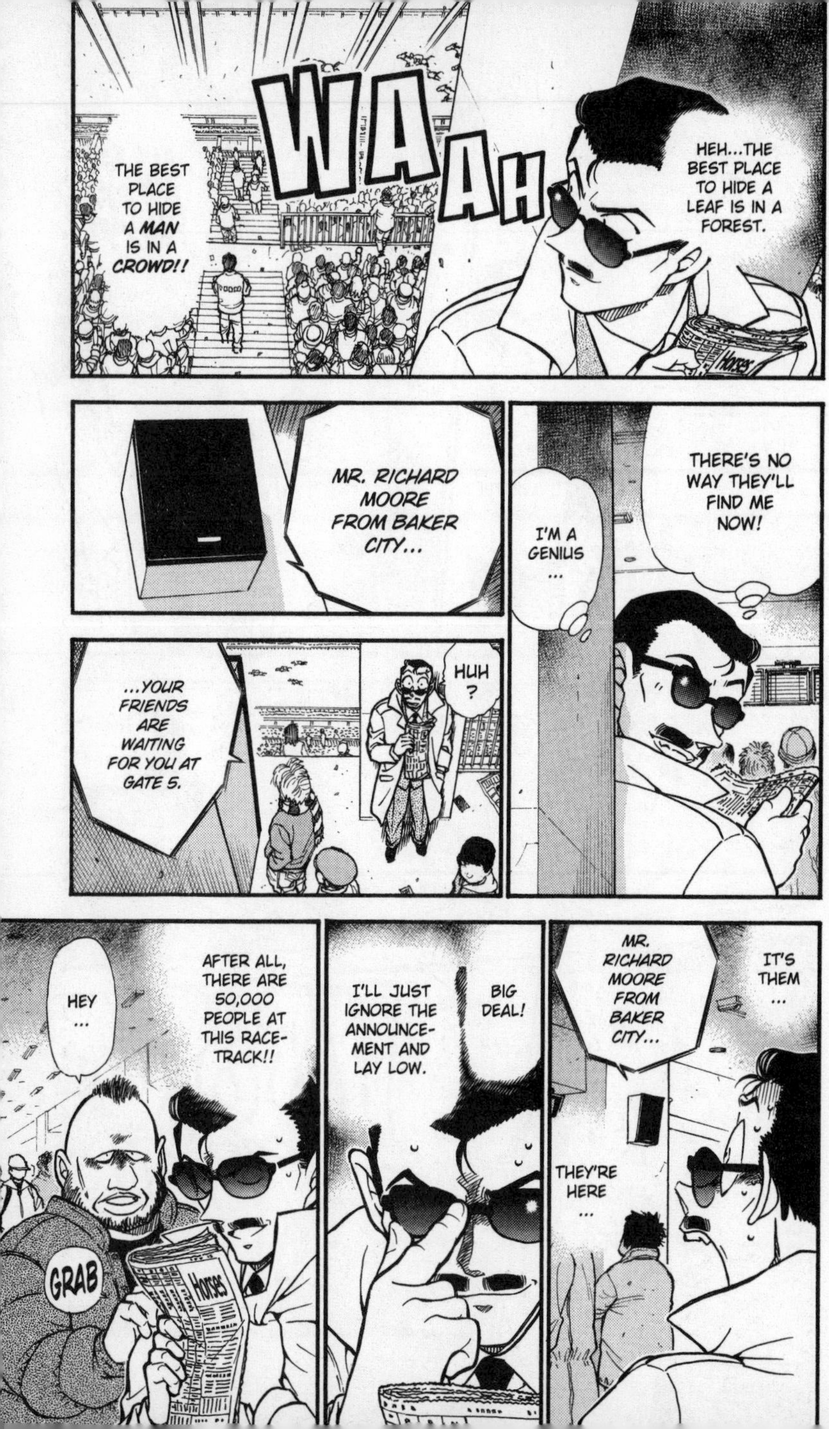
HEH...THE BEST PLACE TO HIDE A LEAF IS IN A FOREST.
Horses
WAAH
THE BEST PLACE TO HIDE A *MAN* IS IN A *CROWD!!*
THERE'S NO WAY THEY'LL FIND ME NOW!
I'M A GENIUS ...
MR. RICHARD MOORE FROM BAKER CITY...
HUH ?
...YOUR FRIENDS ARE WAITING FOR YOU AT GATE 5.
IT'S THEM ...
MR. RICHARD MOORE FROM BAKER CITY...
THEY'RE HERE ...
BIG DEAL!
I'LL JUST IGNORE THE ANNOUNCEMENT AND LAY LOW.
AFTER ALL, THERE ARE 50,000 PEOPLE AT THIS RACE-TRACK!!
HEY ...
GRAB
Horses

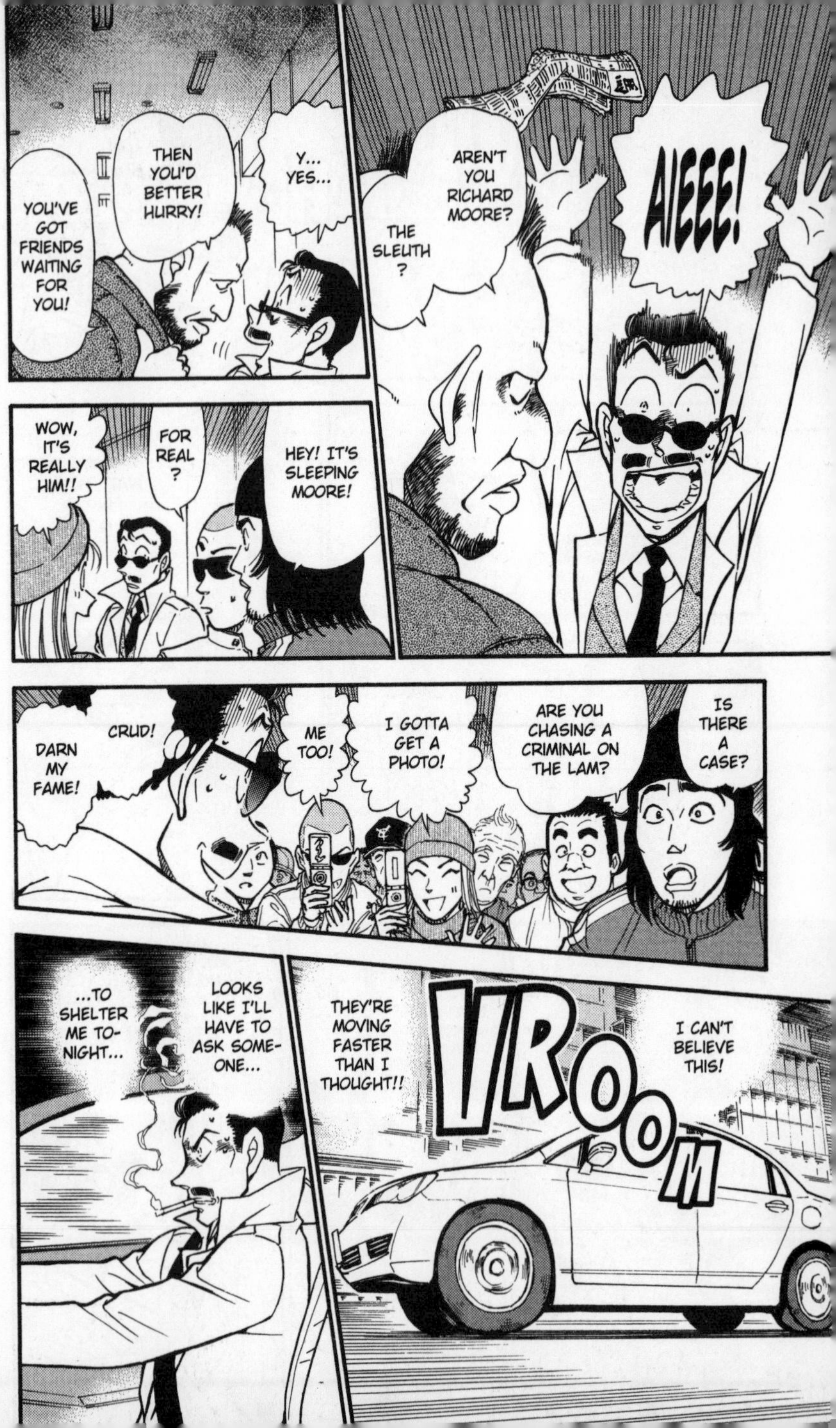
AIEEE!
AREN'T YOU RICHARD MOORE?
THE SLEUTH?
Y... YES...
THEN YOU'D BETTER HURRY!
YOU'VE GOT FRIENDS WAITING FOR YOU!
HEY! IT'S SLEEPING MOORE!
FOR REAL?
WOW, IT'S REALLY HIM!!
IS THERE A CASE?
ARE YOU CHASING A CRIMINAL ON THE LAM?
I GOTTA GET A PHOTO!
ME TOO!
CRUD!
DARN MY FAME!
I CAN'T BELIEVE THIS!
VROOM
THEY'RE MOVING FASTER THAN I THOUGHT!!
LOOKS LIKE I'LL HAVE TO ASK SOME-ONE...
...TO SHELTER ME TO-NIGHT...

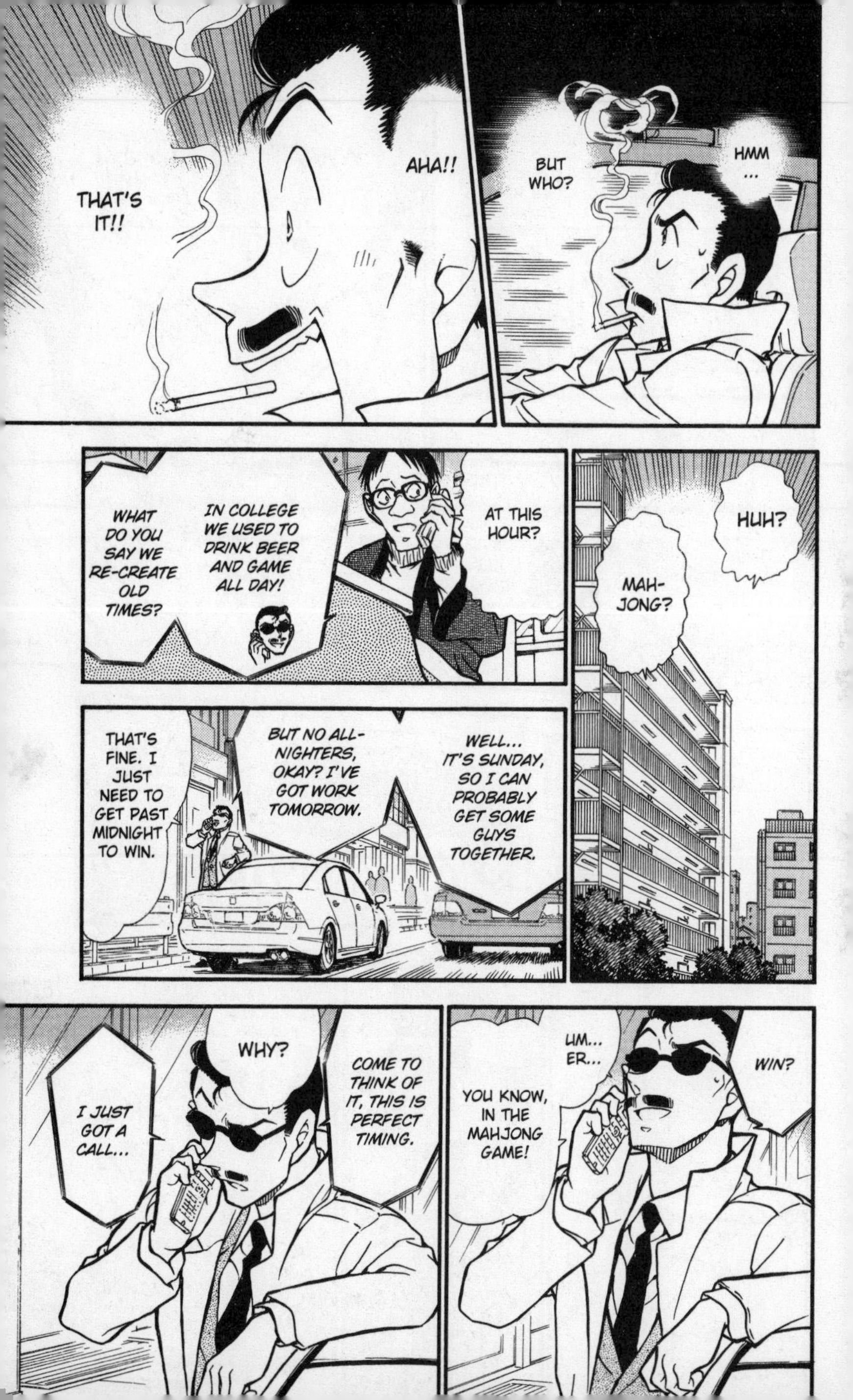
HMM ...
BUT WHO?
AHA!!
THAT'S IT!!
HUH?
MAH-JONG?
AT THIS HOUR?
IN COLLEGE WE USED TO DRINK BEER AND GAME ALL DAY!
WHAT DO YOU SAY WE RE-CREATE OLD TIMES?
WELL... IT'S SUNDAY, SO I CAN PROBABLY GET SOME GUYS TOGETHER.
BUT NO ALL-NIGHTERS, OKAY? I'VE GOT WORK TOMORROW.
THAT'S FINE. I JUST NEED TO GET PAST MIDNIGHT TO WIN.
WIN?
UM... ER...
YOU KNOW, IN THE MAHJONG GAME!
COME TO THINK OF IT, THIS IS PERFECT TIMING.
WHY?
I JUST GOT A CALL...

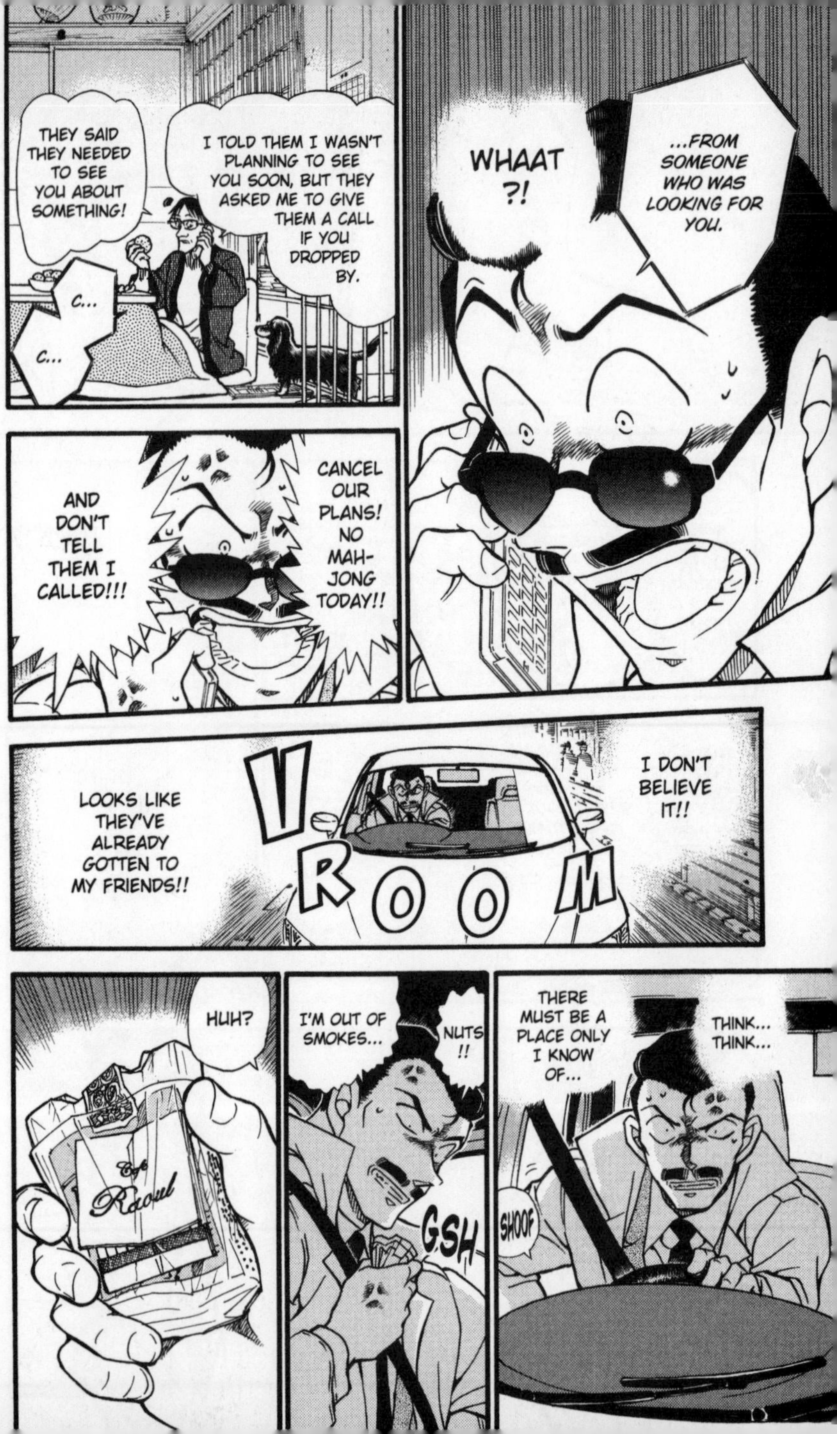
...FROM SOMEONE WHO WAS LOOKING FOR YOU.
WHAAT ?!
I TOLD THEM I WASN'T PLANNING TO SEE YOU SOON, BUT THEY ASKED ME TO GIVE THEM A CALL IF YOU DROPPED BY.
THEY SAID THEY NEEDED TO SEE YOU ABOUT SOMETHING!
C...
C...
CANCEL OUR PLANS! NO MAH-JONG TODAY!!
AND DON'T TELL THEM I CALLED!!!
I DON'T BELIEVE IT!!
VROOM
LOOKS LIKE THEY'VE ALREADY GOTTEN TO MY FRIENDS!!
THINK... THINK...
THERE MUST BE A PLACE ONLY I KNOW OF...
SHOOF
NUTS!!
I'M OUT OF SMOKES...
GSH
HUH?
Café Raoul

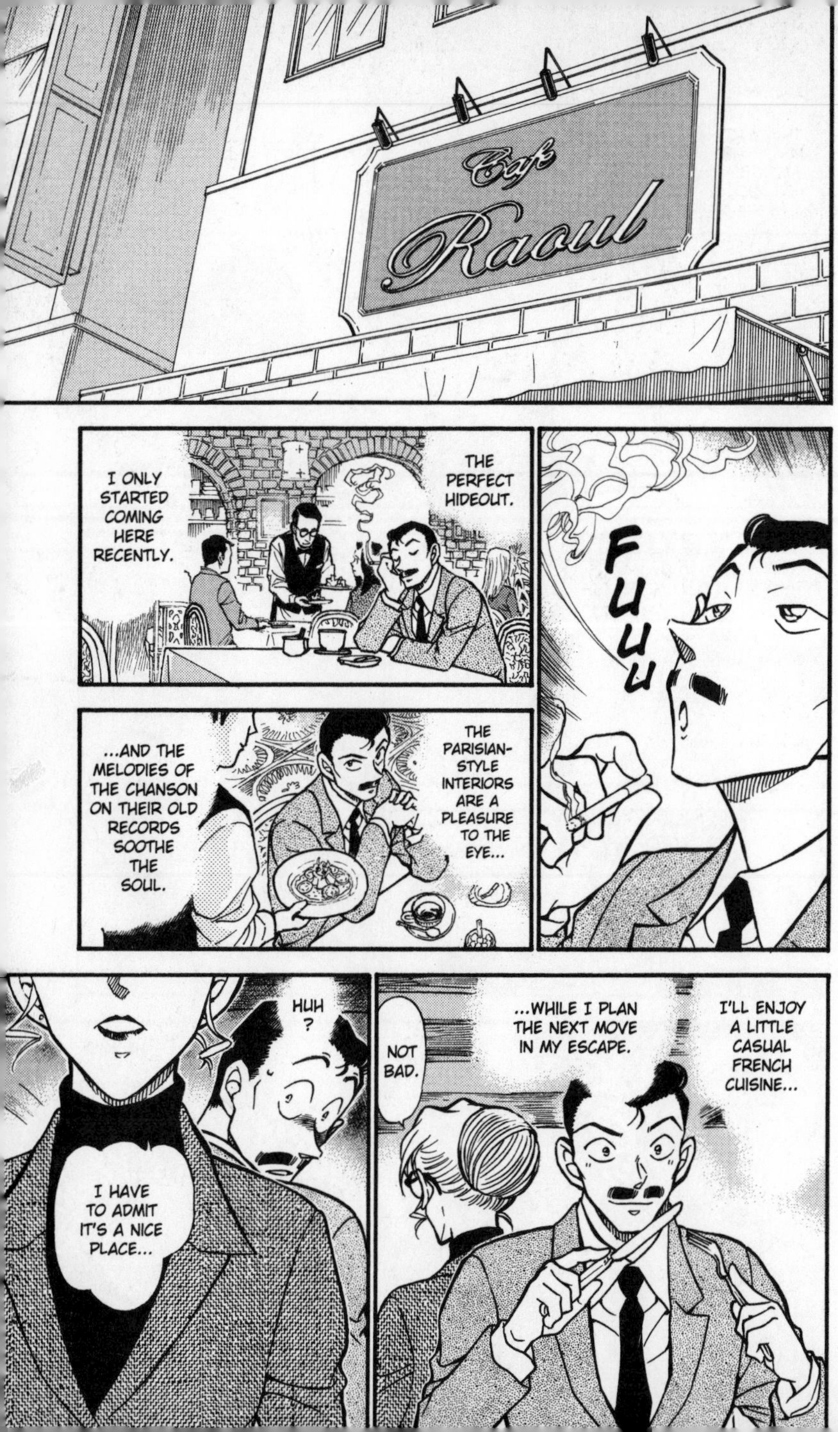
Café Raoul
FUUU
THE PERFECT HIDEOUT.
I ONLY STARTED COMING HERE RECENTLY.
THE PARISIAN-STYLE INTERIORS ARE A PLEASURE TO THE EYE...
...AND THE MELODIES OF THE CHANSON ON THEIR OLD RECORDS SOOTHE THE SOUL.
I'LL ENJOY A LITTLE CASUAL FRENCH CUISINE...
...WHILE I PLAN THE NEXT MOVE IN MY ESCAPE.
NOT BAD.
HUH?
I HAVE TO ADMIT IT'S A NICE PLACE...

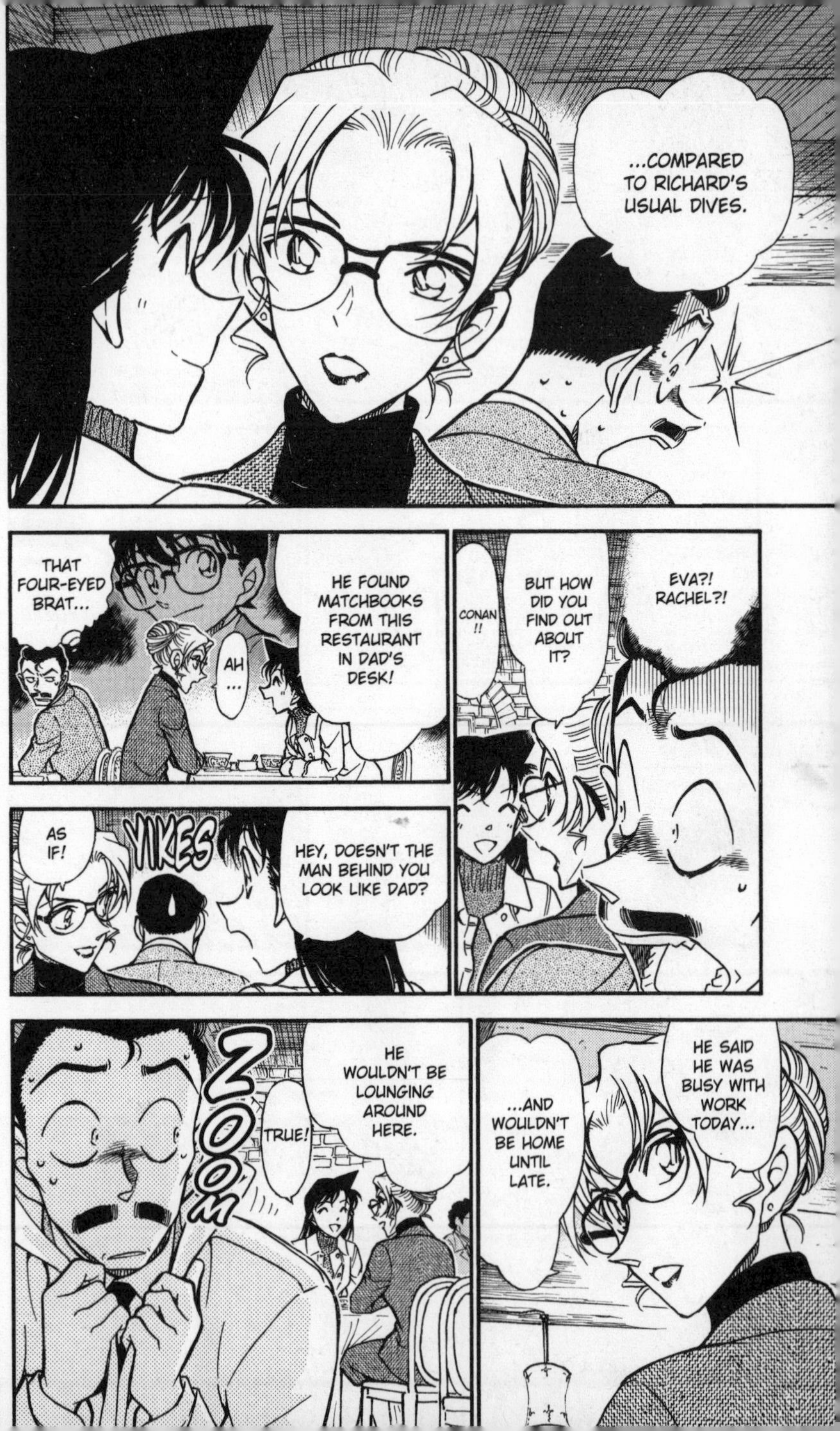
...COMPARED TO RICHARD'S USUAL DIVES.
EVA?! RACHEL?!
BUT HOW DID YOU FIND OUT ABOUT IT?
CONAN !!
HE FOUND MATCHBOOKS FROM THIS RESTAURANT IN DAD'S DESK!
AH ...
THAT FOUR-EYED BRAT...
HEY, DOESN'T THE MAN BEHIND YOU LOOK LIKE DAD?
YIKES
AS IF!
HE SAID HE WAS BUSY WITH WORK TODAY...
...AND WOULDN'T BE HOME UNTIL LATE.
HE WOULDN'T BE LOUNGING AROUND HERE.
TRUE!
ZOOM

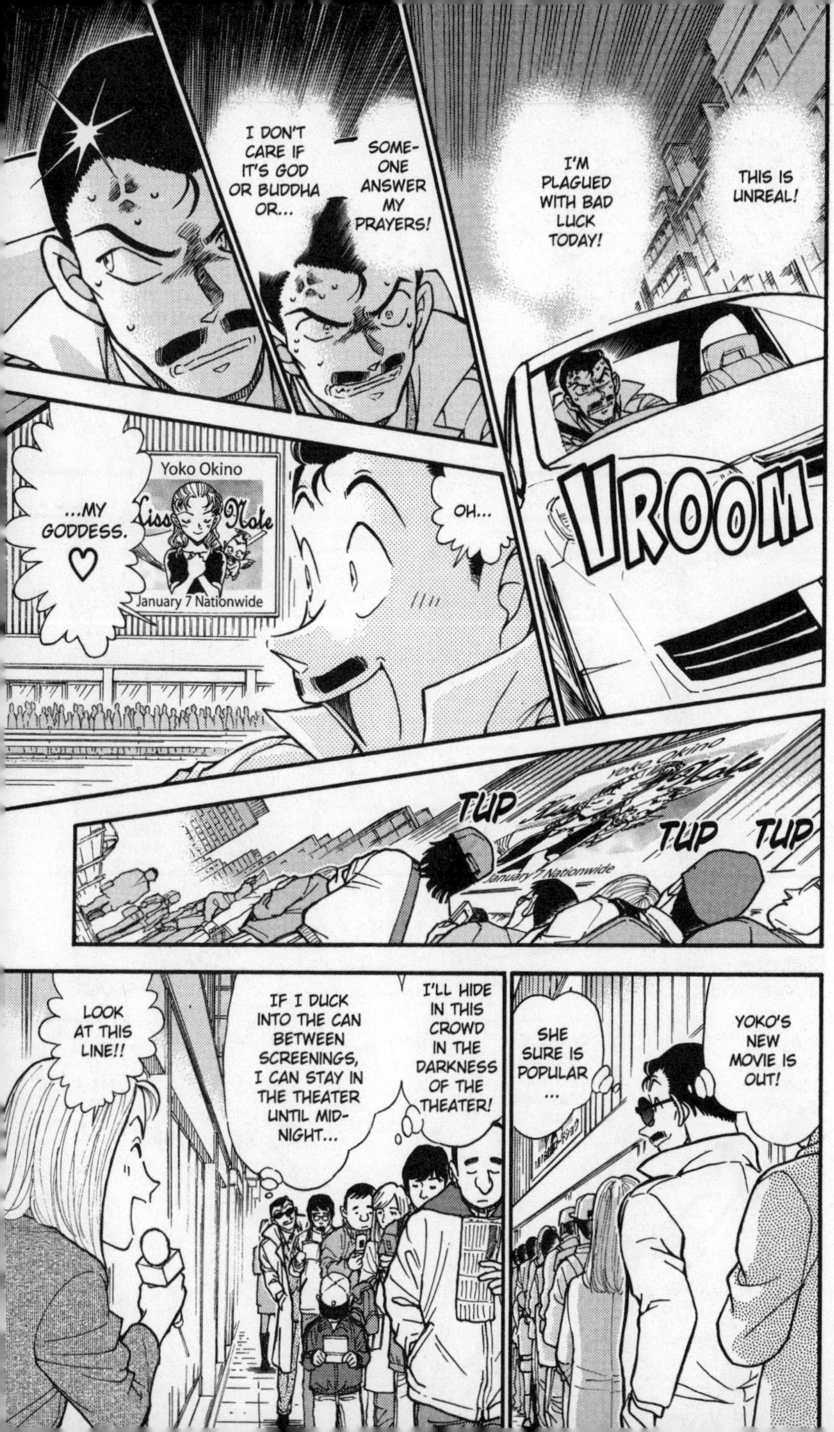
THIS IS UNREAL!
I'M PLAGUED WITH BAD LUCK TODAY!
SOME-ONE ANSWER MY PRAYERS!
I DON'T CARE IF IT'S GOD OR BUDDHA OR...
VROOM
OH...
Yoko Okino
Kiss Note
January 7 Nationwide
...MY GODDESS. ♡
Yoko Okino
January 7 Nationwide
TUP
TUP
TUP
YOKO'S NEW MOVIE IS OUT!
SHE SURE IS POPULAR...
I'LL HIDE IN THIS CROWD IN THE DARKNESS OF THE THEATER!
IF I DUCK INTO THE CAN BETWEEN SCREENINGS, I CAN STAY IN THE THEATER UNTIL MID-NIGHT...
LOOK AT THIS LINE!!

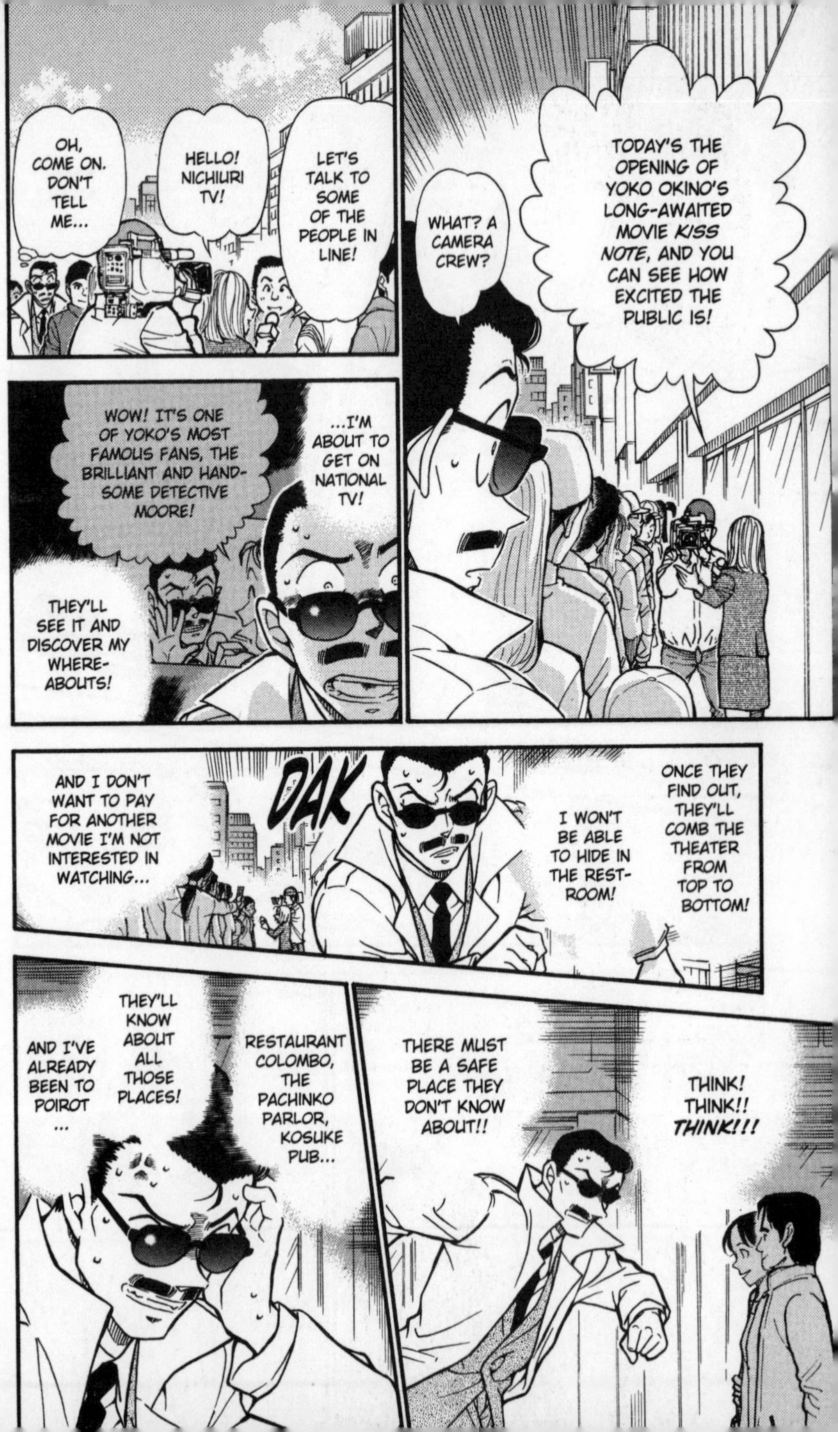
TODAY'S THE OPENING OF YOKO OKINO'S LONG-AWAITED MOVIE *KISS NOTE*, AND YOU CAN SEE HOW EXCITED THE PUBLIC IS!
WHAT? A CAMERA CREW?
LET'S TALK TO SOME OF THE PEOPLE IN LINE!
HELLO! NICHIURI TV!
OH, COME ON. DON'T TELL ME...
...I'M ABOUT TO GET ON NATIONAL TV!
WOW! IT'S ONE OF YOKO'S MOST FAMOUS FANS, THE BRILLIANT AND HANDSOME DETECTIVE MOORE!
THEY'LL SEE IT AND DISCOVER MY WHEREABOUTS!
ONCE THEY FIND OUT, THEY'LL COMB THE THEATER FROM TOP TO BOTTOM!
I WON'T BE ABLE TO HIDE IN THE RESTROOM!
DAK
AND I DON'T WANT TO PAY FOR ANOTHER MOVIE I'M NOT INTERESTED IN WATCHING...
THINK! THINK!! *THINK!!!*
THERE MUST BE A SAFE PLACE THEY DON'T KNOW ABOUT!!
RESTAURANT COLOMBO, THE PACHINKO PARLOR, KOSUKE PUB...
THEY'LL KNOW ABOUT ALL THOSE PLACES!
AND I'VE ALREADY BEEN TO POIROT ...

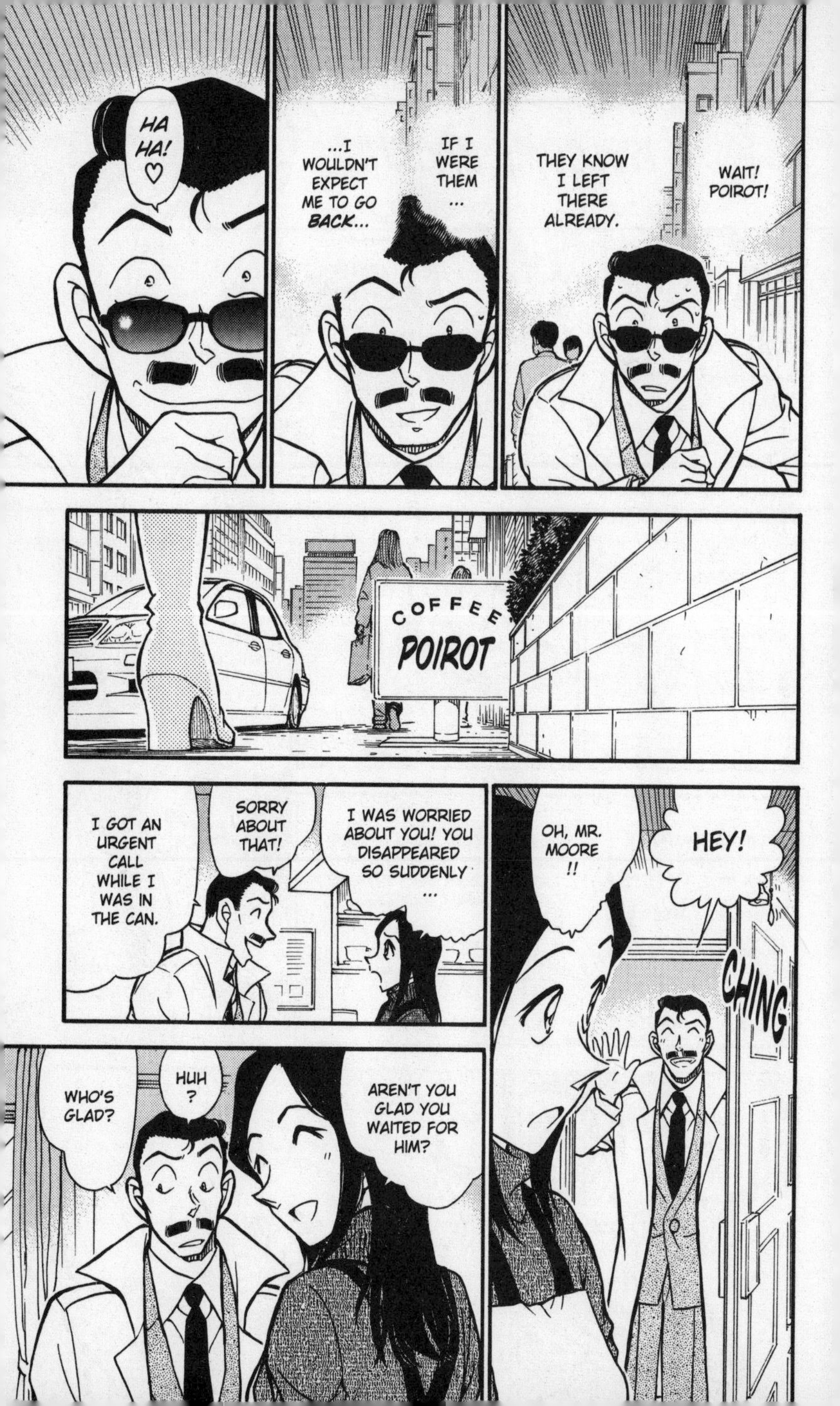
WAIT! POIROT!
THEY KNOW I LEFT THERE ALREADY.
IF I WERE THEM ...
...I WOULDN'T EXPECT ME TO GO BACK...
HA HA! ♡
COFFEE
POIROT
HEY!
CHING
OH, MR. MOORE !!
I WAS WORRIED ABOUT YOU! YOU DISAPPEARED SO SUDDENLY ...
SORRY ABOUT THAT!
I GOT AN URGENT CALL WHILE I WAS IN THE CAN.
AREN'T YOU GLAD YOU WAITED FOR HIM?
HUH ?
WHO'S GLAD?

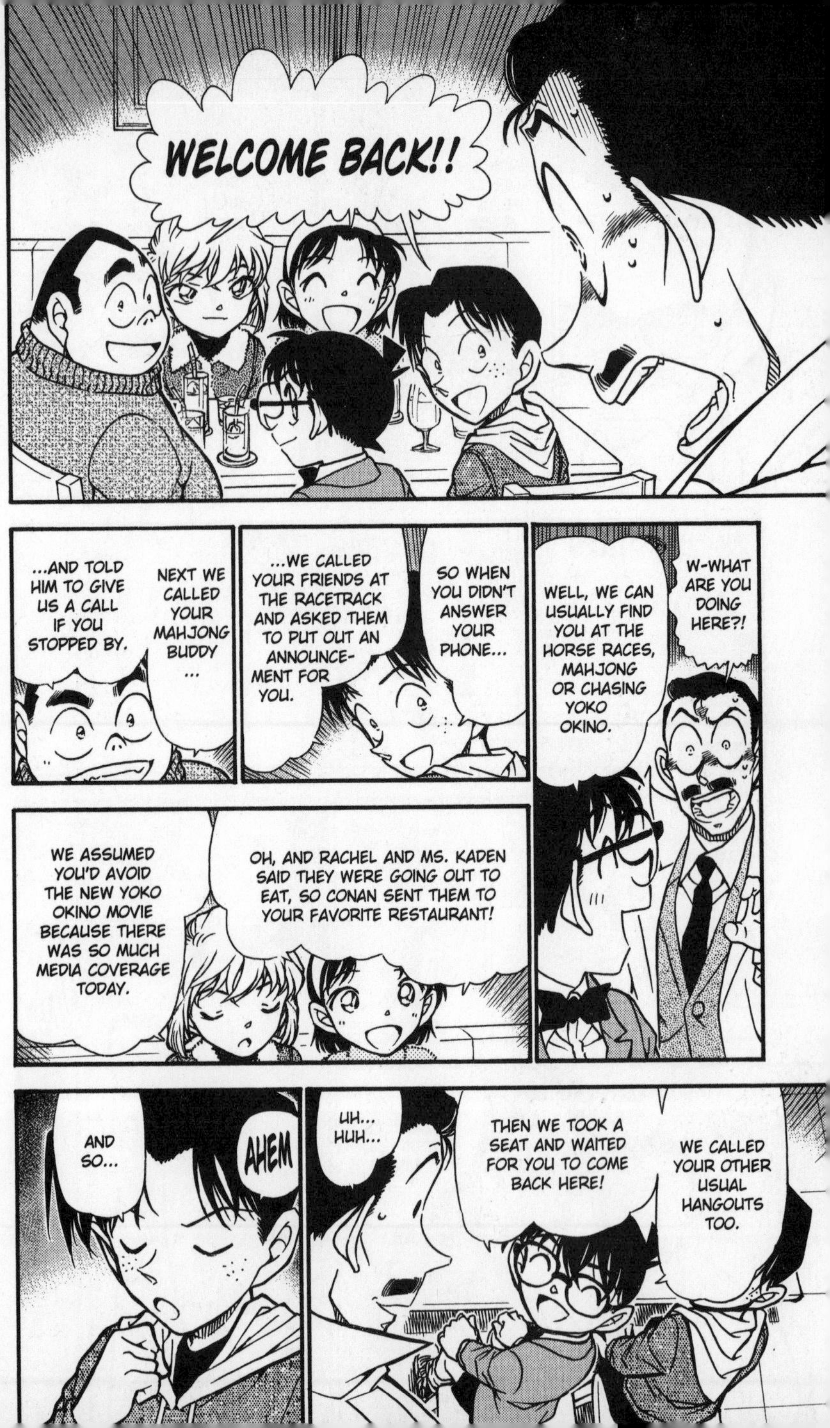
WELCOME BACK!!
W-WHAT ARE YOU DOING HERE?!
WELL, WE CAN USUALLY FIND YOU AT THE HORSE RACES, MAHJONG OR CHASING YOKO OKINO.
SO WHEN YOU DIDN'T ANSWER YOUR PHONE...
...WE CALLED YOUR FRIENDS AT THE RACETRACK AND ASKED THEM TO PUT OUT AN ANNOUNCE-MENT FOR YOU.
NEXT WE CALLED YOUR MAHJONG BUDDY ...
...AND TOLD HIM TO GIVE US A CALL IF YOU STOPPED BY.
OH, AND RACHEL AND MS. KADEN SAID THEY WERE GOING OUT TO EAT, SO CONAN SENT THEM TO YOUR FAVORITE RESTAURANT!
WE ASSUMED YOU'D AVOID THE NEW YOKO OKINO MOVIE BECAUSE THERE WAS SO MUCH MEDIA COVERAGE TODAY.
WE CALLED YOUR OTHER USUAL HANGOUTS TOO.
THEN WE TOOK A SEAT AND WAITED FOR YOU TO COME BACK HERE!
UH... HUH...
AHEM
AND SO...

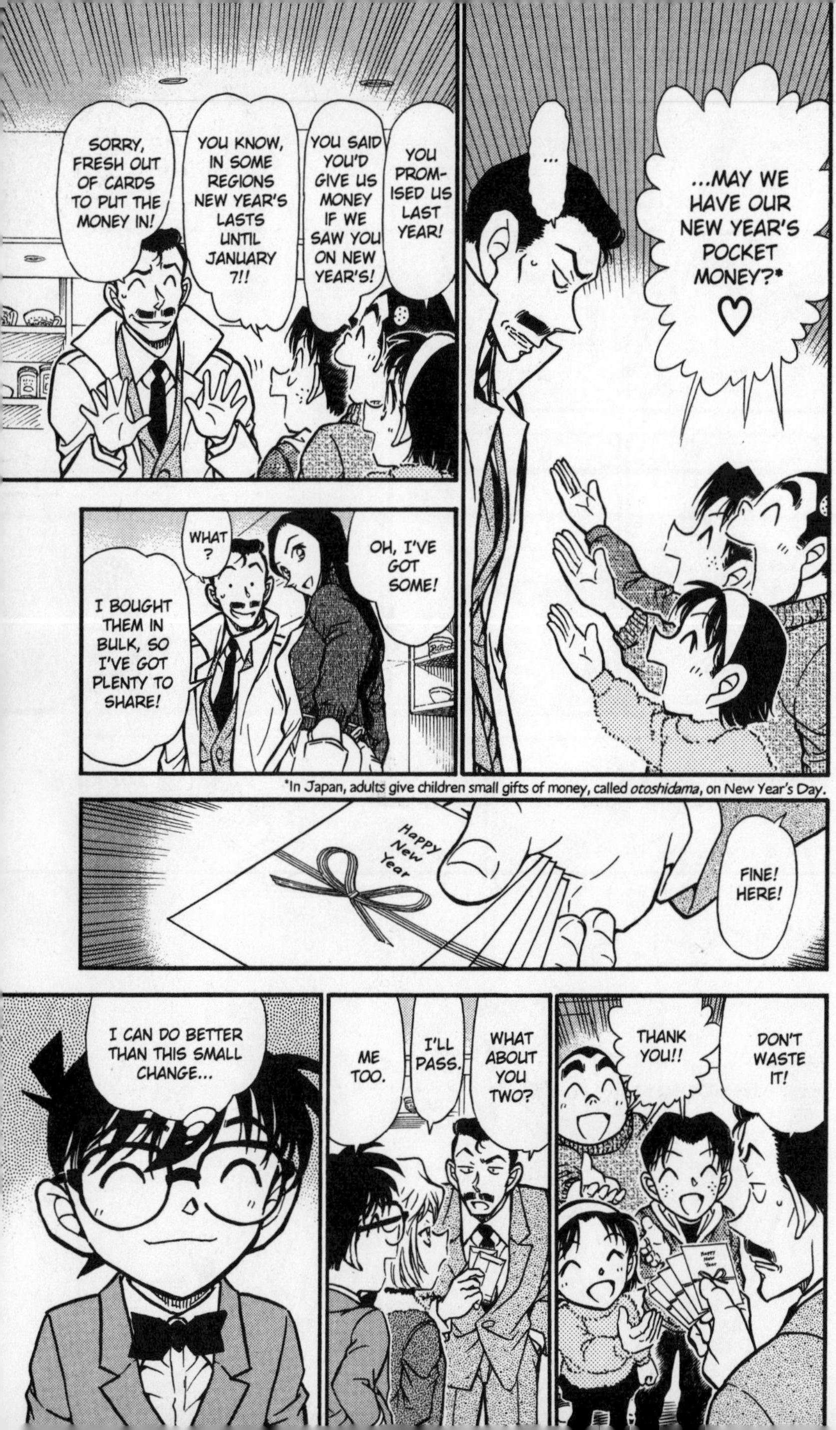
...MAY WE HAVE OUR NEW YEAR'S POCKET MONEY?* ♡
...
YOU PROMISED US LAST YEAR!
YOU SAID YOU'D GIVE US MONEY IF WE SAW YOU ON NEW YEAR'S!
YOU KNOW, IN SOME REGIONS NEW YEAR'S LASTS UNTIL JANUARY 7!!
SORRY, FRESH OUT OF CARDS TO PUT THE MONEY IN!
OH, I'VE GOT SOME!
WHAT?
I BOUGHT THEM IN BULK, SO I'VE GOT PLENTY TO SHARE!
FINE! HERE!
Happy New Year
DON'T WASTE IT!
THANK YOU!!
WHAT ABOUT YOU TWO?
I'LL PASS.
ME TOO.
I CAN DO BETTER THAN THIS SMALL CHANGE...

*In Japan, adults give children small gifts of money, called *otoshidama*, on New Year's Day.

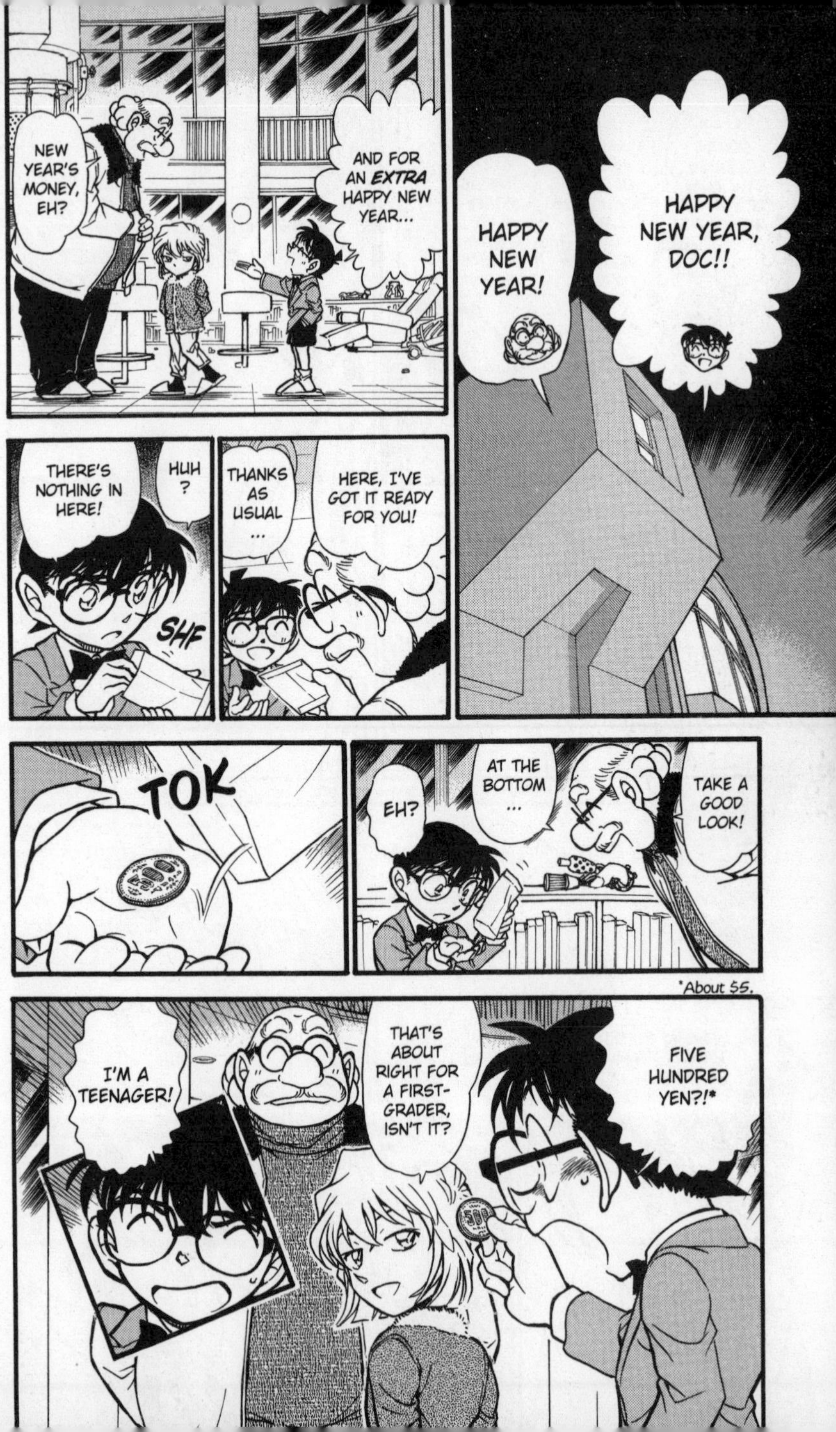
HAPPY NEW YEAR, DOC!!
HAPPY NEW YEAR!
AND FOR AN *EXTRA* HAPPY NEW YEAR...
NEW YEAR'S MONEY, EH?
HERE, I'VE GOT IT READY FOR YOU!
THANKS AS USUAL ...
HUH?
THERE'S NOTHING IN HERE!
SHF
TAKE A GOOD LOOK!
AT THE BOTTOM ...
EH?
TOK
FIVE HUNDRED YEN?!*
THAT'S ABOUT RIGHT FOR A FIRST-GRADER, ISN'T IT?
I'M A TEENAGER!

*About $5.

FILE 9: THE CROW'S SONG

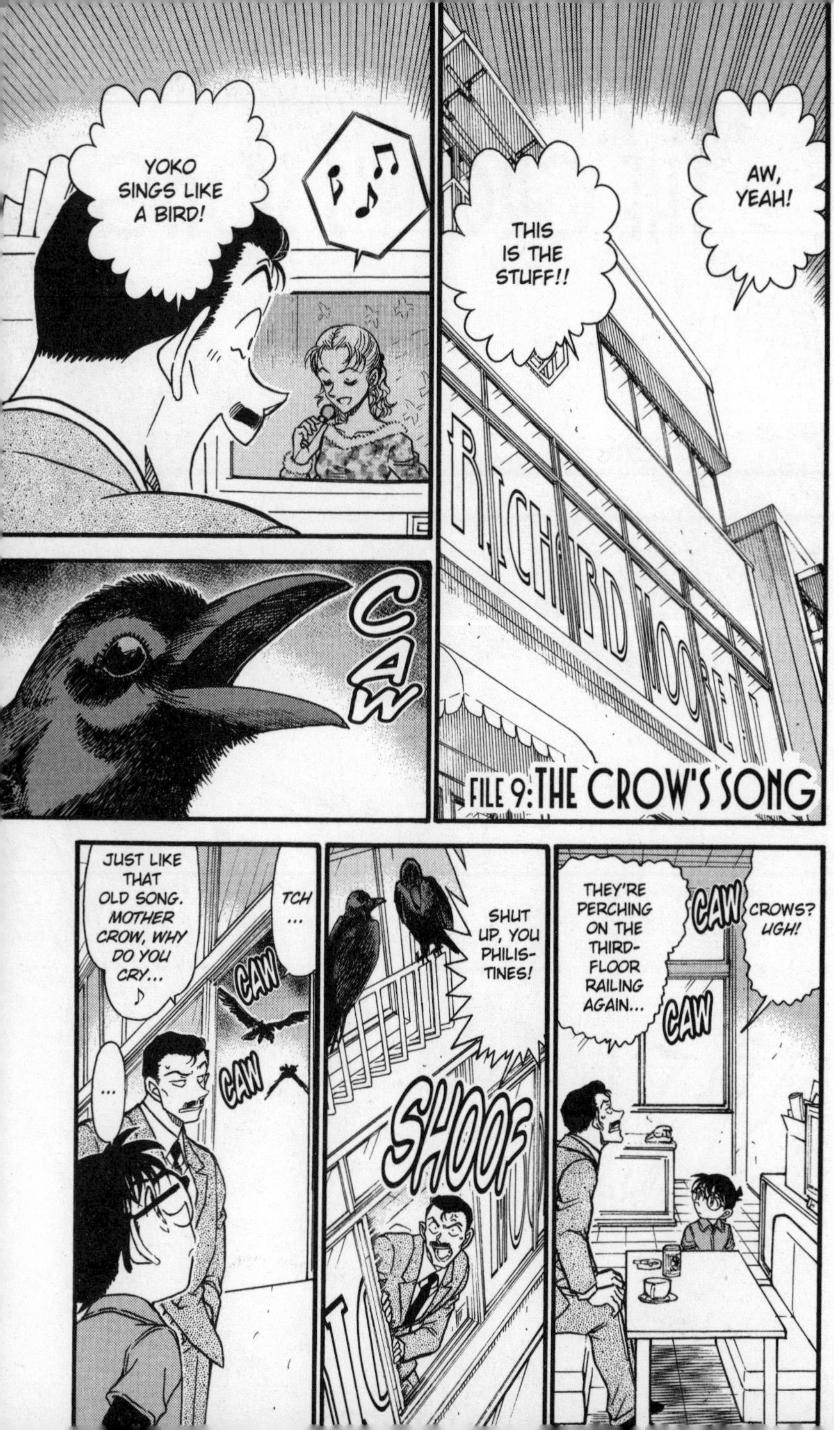
AW, YEAH!
THIS IS THE STUFF!!
RICHARD MOORE
YOKO SINGS LIKE A BIRD!
CAW CAW
CROWS? UGH!
CAW
THEY'RE PERCHING ON THE THIRD-FLOOR RAILING AGAIN...
CAW
SHUT UP, YOU PHILISTINES!
SHOOF
TCH...
JUST LIKE THAT OLD SONG. MOTHER CROW, WHY DO YOU CRY... ♪
CAW
CAW
...

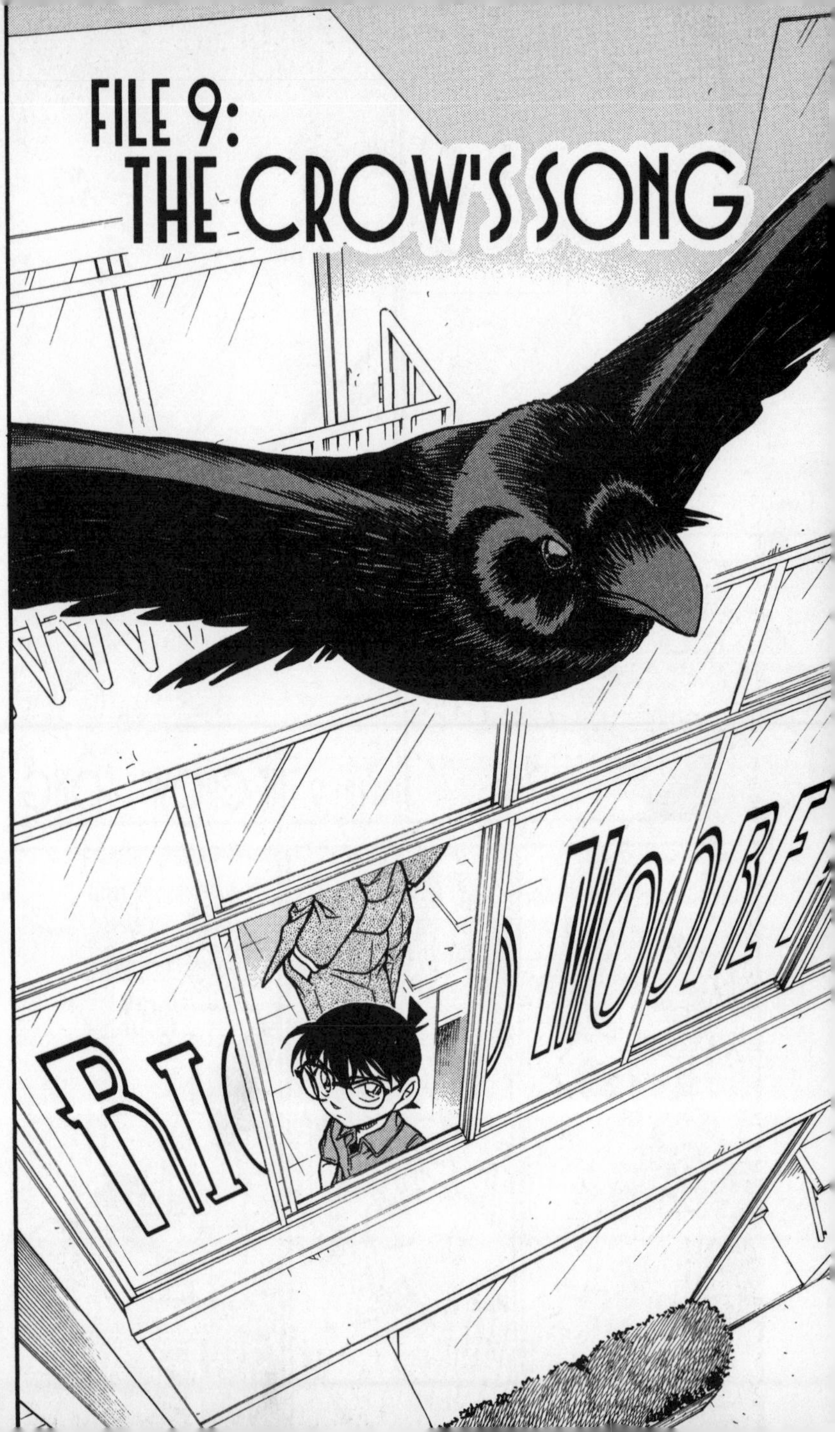
FILE 9:
THE CROW'S SONG

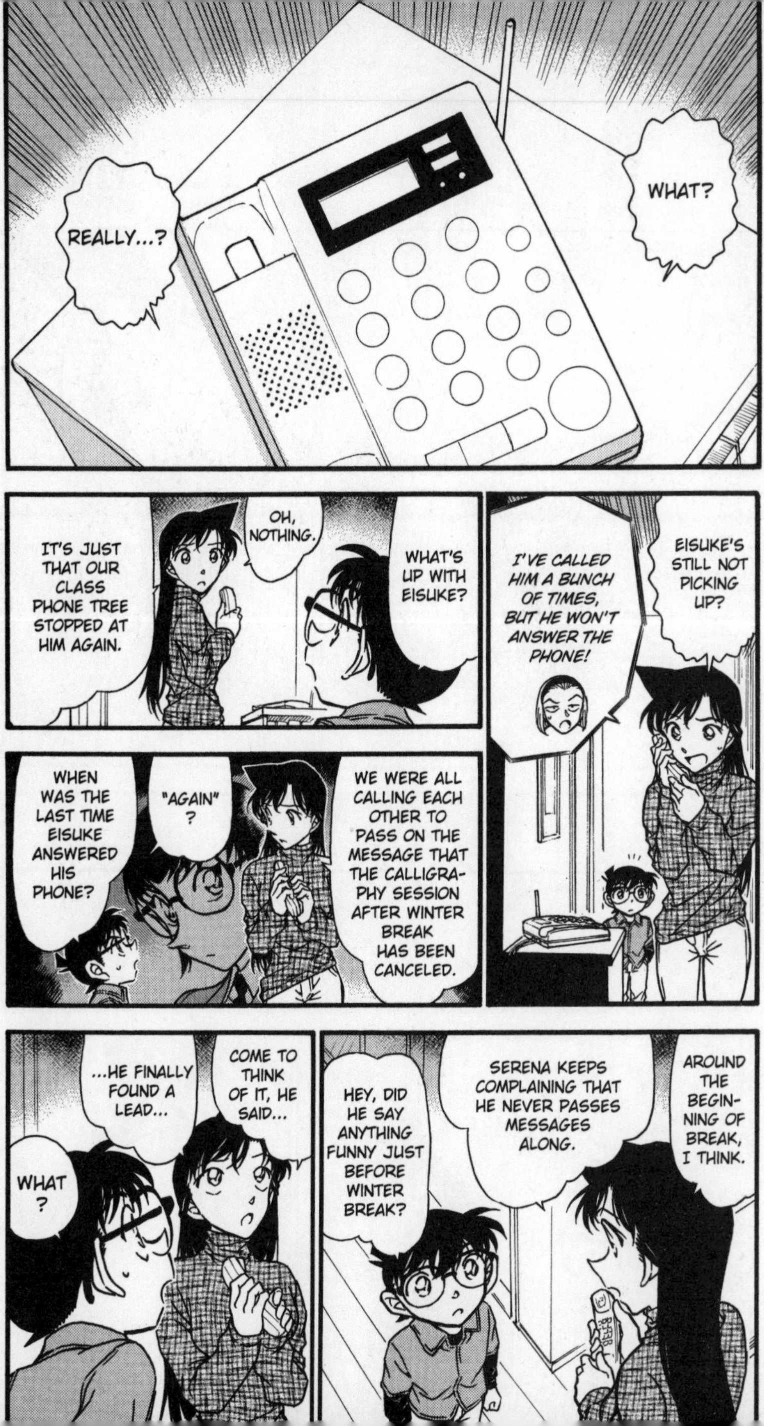
WHAT?
REALLY...?
EISUKE'S STILL NOT PICKING UP?
I'VE CALLED HIM A BUNCH OF TIMES, BUT HE WON'T ANSWER THE PHONE!
WHAT'S UP WITH EISUKE?
OH, NOTHING.
IT'S JUST THAT OUR CLASS PHONE TREE STOPPED AT HIM AGAIN.
WE WERE ALL CALLING EACH OTHER TO PASS ON THE MESSAGE THAT THE CALLIGRAPHY SESSION AFTER WINTER BREAK HAS BEEN CANCELED.
"AGAIN"?
WHEN WAS THE LAST TIME EISUKE ANSWERED HIS PHONE?
AROUND THE BEGINNING OF BREAK, I THINK.
SERENA KEEPS COMPLAINING THAT HE NEVER PASSES MESSAGES ALONG.
HEY, DID HE SAY ANYTHING FUNNY JUST BEFORE WINTER BREAK?
COME TO THINK OF IT, HE SAID...
...HE FINALLY FOUND A LEAD...
WHAT?

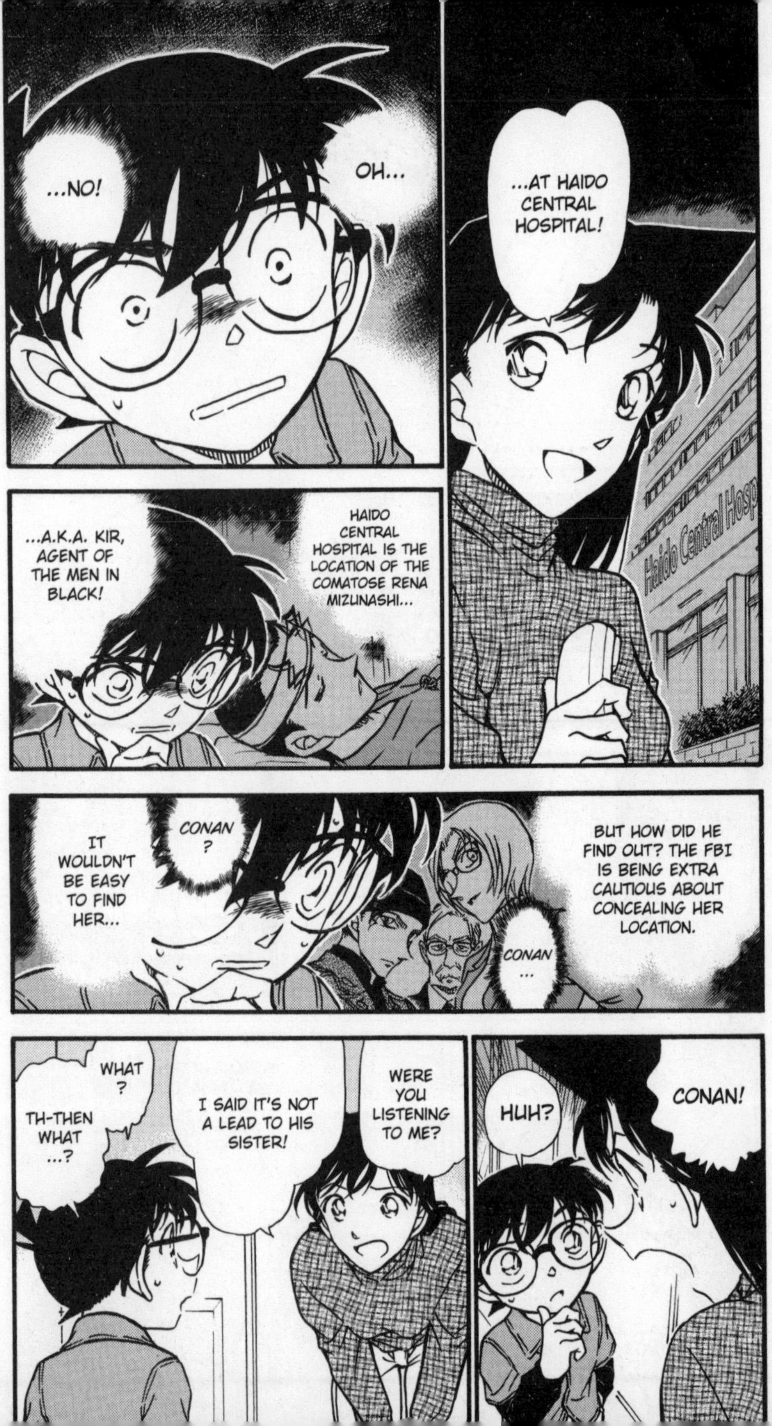
...AT HAIDO CENTRAL HOSPITAL!
OH...
...NO!
HAIDO CENTRAL HOSPITAL IS THE LOCATION OF THE COMATOSE RENA MIZUNASHI...
...A.K.A. KIR, AGENT OF THE MEN IN BLACK!
BUT HOW DID HE FIND OUT? THE FBI IS BEING EXTRA CAUTIOUS ABOUT CONCEALING HER LOCATION.
CONAN ?
IT WOULDN'T BE EASY TO FIND HER...
CONAN ...
CONAN!
HUH?
WERE YOU LISTENING TO ME?
I SAID IT'S NOT A LEAD TO HIS SISTER!
WHAT ?
TH-THEN WHAT ...?

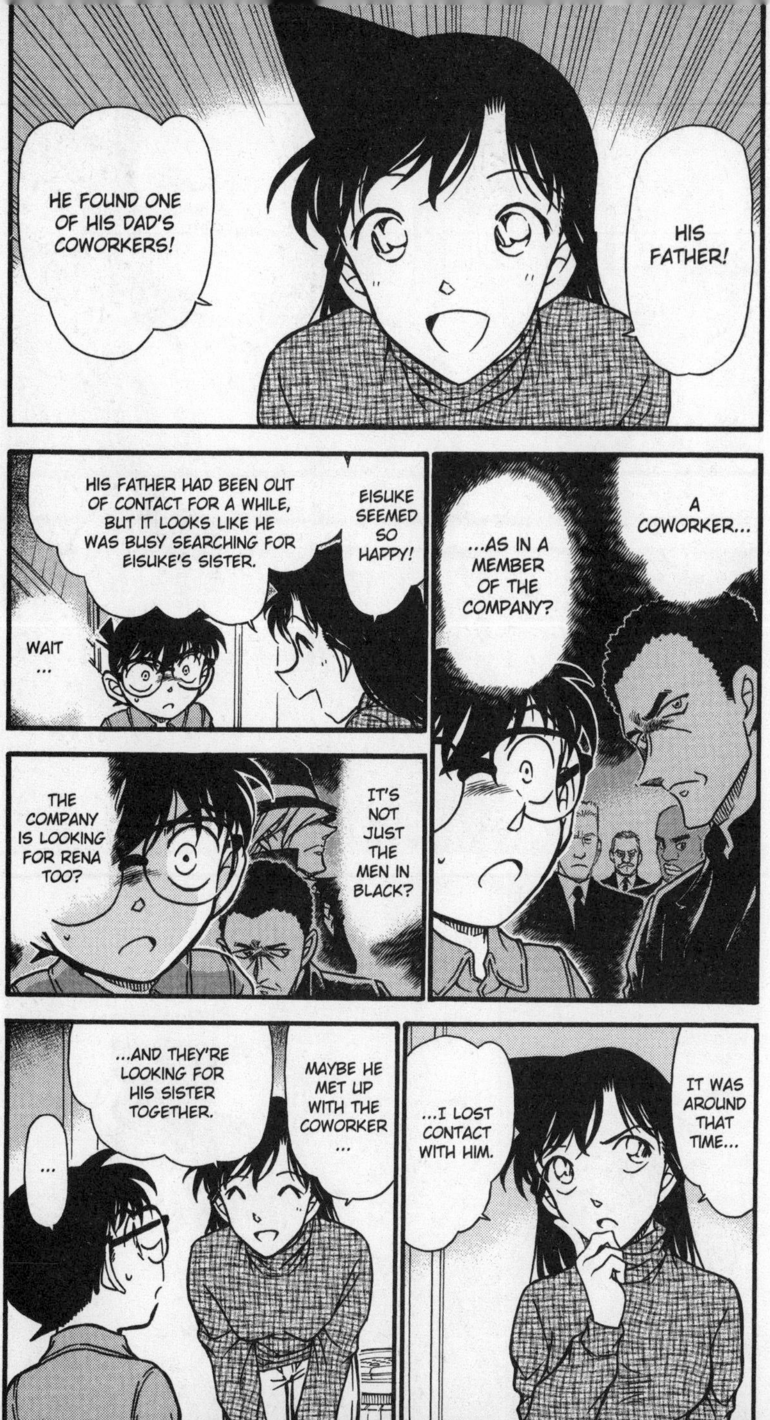
HIS FATHER!
HE FOUND ONE OF HIS DAD'S COWORKERS!
A COWORKER...
...AS IN A MEMBER OF THE COMPANY?
EISUKE SEEMED SO HAPPY!
HIS FATHER HAD BEEN OUT OF CONTACT FOR A WHILE, BUT IT LOOKS LIKE HE WAS BUSY SEARCHING FOR EISUKE'S SISTER.
WAIT ...
IT'S NOT JUST THE MEN IN BLACK?
THE COMPANY IS LOOKING FOR RENA TOO?
IT WAS AROUND THAT TIME...
...I LOST CONTACT WITH HIM.
MAYBE HE MET UP WITH THE COWORKER ...
...AND THEY'RE LOOKING FOR HIS SISTER TOGETHER.
...

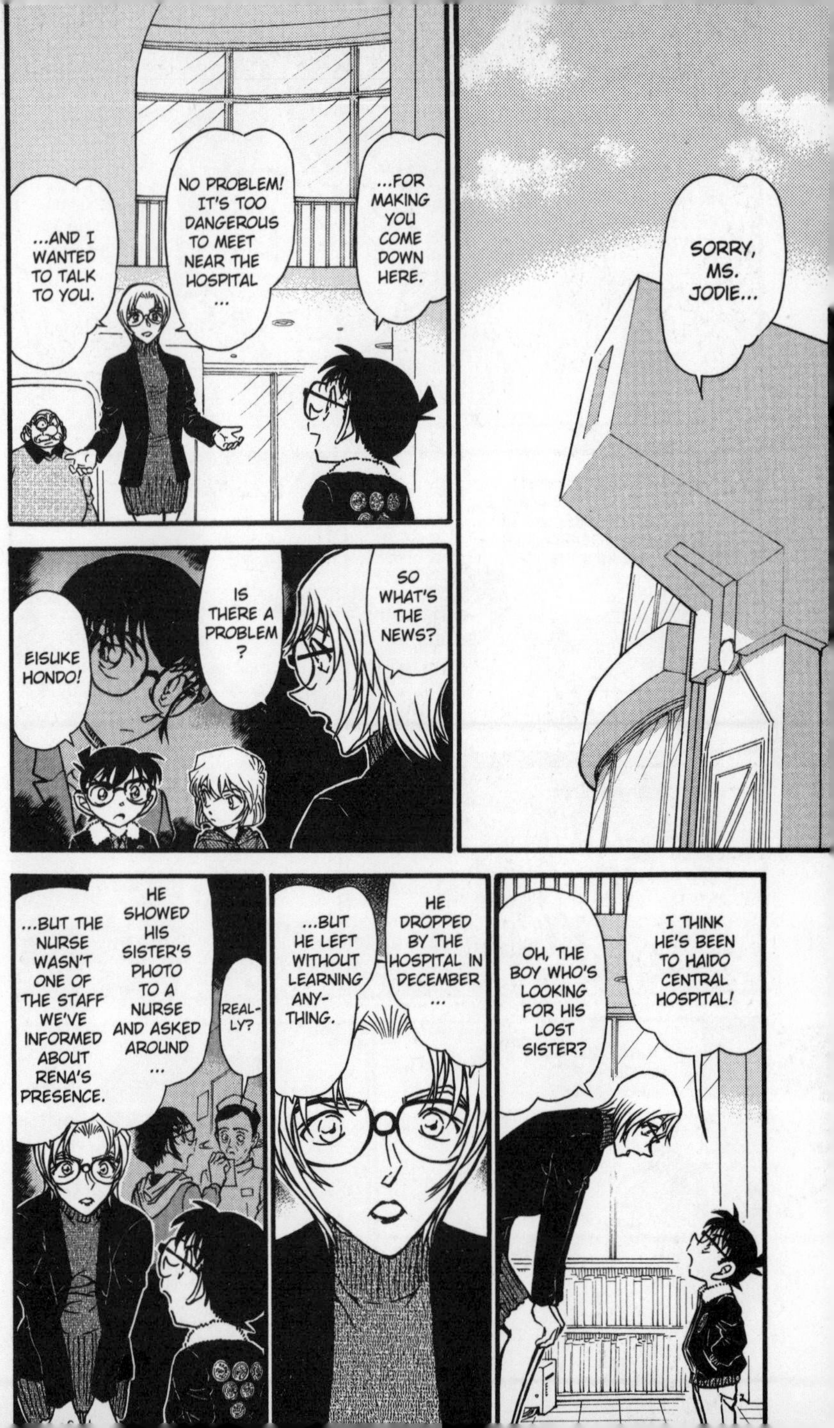
SORRY, MS. JODIE...
...FOR MAKING YOU COME DOWN HERE.
NO PROBLEM! IT'S TOO DANGEROUS TO MEET NEAR THE HOSPITAL ...
...AND I WANTED TO TALK TO YOU.
SO WHAT'S THE NEWS?
IS THERE A PROBLEM ?
EISUKE HONDO!
I THINK HE'S BEEN TO HAIDO CENTRAL HOSPITAL!
OH, THE BOY WHO'S LOOKING FOR HIS LOST SISTER?
HE DROPPED BY THE HOSPITAL IN DECEMBER ...
...BUT HE LEFT WITHOUT LEARNING ANY-THING.
HE SHOWED HIS SISTER'S PHOTO TO A NURSE AND ASKED AROUND ...
REAL-LY?
...BUT THE NURSE WASN'T ONE OF THE STAFF WE'VE INFORMED ABOUT RENA'S PRESENCE.

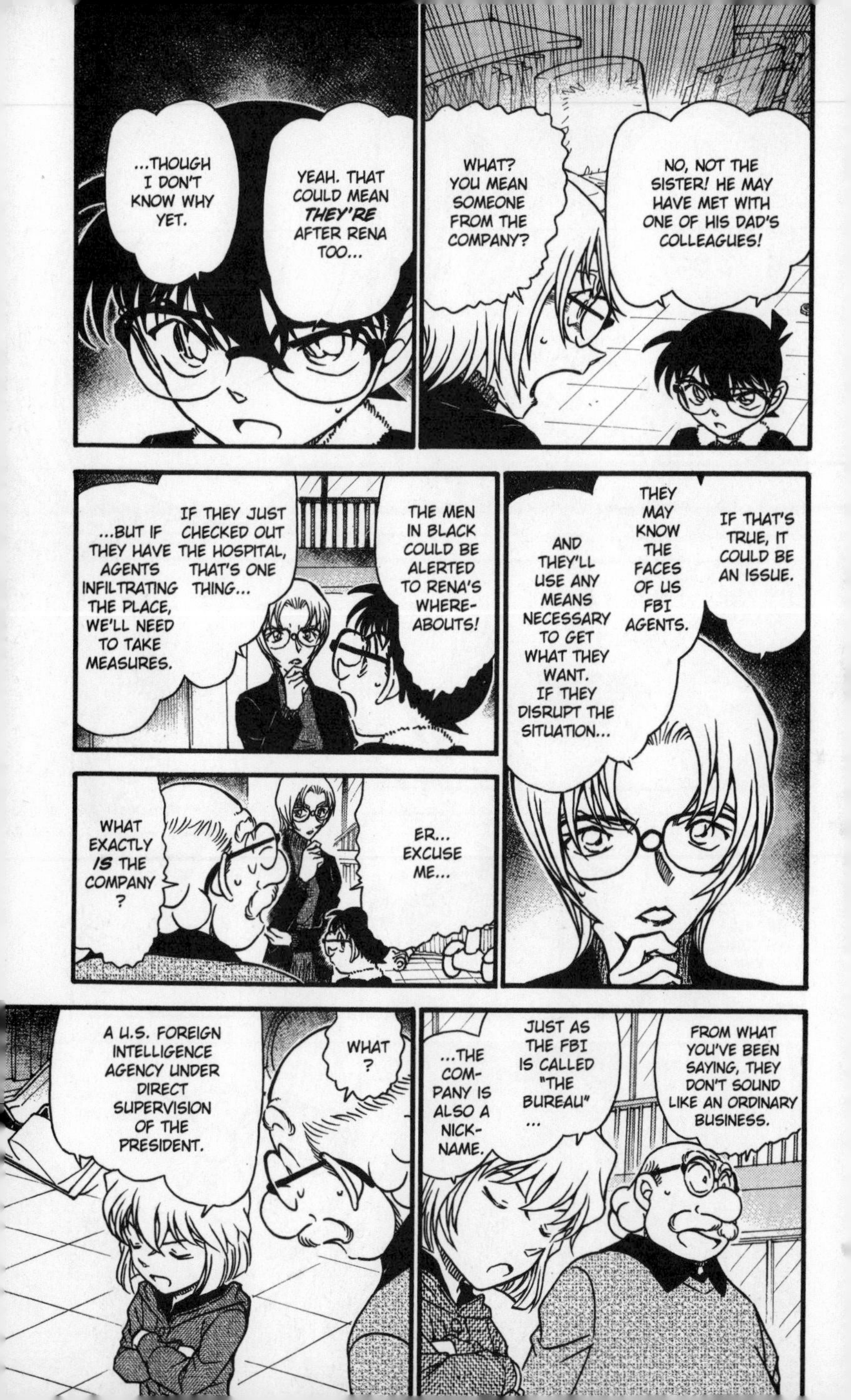
NO, NOT THE SISTER! HE MAY HAVE MET WITH ONE OF HIS DAD'S COLLEAGUES!
WHAT? YOU MEAN SOMEONE FROM THE COMPANY?
YEAH. THAT COULD MEAN *THEY'RE* AFTER RENA TOO...
...THOUGH I DON'T KNOW WHY YET.
IF THAT'S TRUE, IT COULD BE AN ISSUE.
THEY MAY KNOW THE FACES OF US FBI AGENTS.
AND THEY'LL USE ANY MEANS NECESSARY TO GET WHAT THEY WANT. IF THEY DISRUPT THE SITUATION...
THE MEN IN BLACK COULD BE ALERTED TO RENA'S WHERE-ABOUTS!
IF THEY JUST CHECKED OUT THE HOSPITAL, THAT'S ONE THING...
...BUT IF THEY HAVE AGENTS INFILTRATING THE PLACE, WE'LL NEED TO TAKE MEASURES.
ER... EXCUSE ME...
WHAT EXACTLY *IS* THE COMPANY?
FROM WHAT YOU'VE BEEN SAYING, THEY DON'T SOUND LIKE AN ORDINARY BUSINESS.
JUST AS THE FBI IS CALLED "THE BUREAU"...
...THE COM-PANY IS ALSO A NICK-NAME.
WHAT?
A U.S. FOREIGN INTELLIGENCE AGENCY UNDER DIRECT SUPERVISION OF THE PRESIDENT.

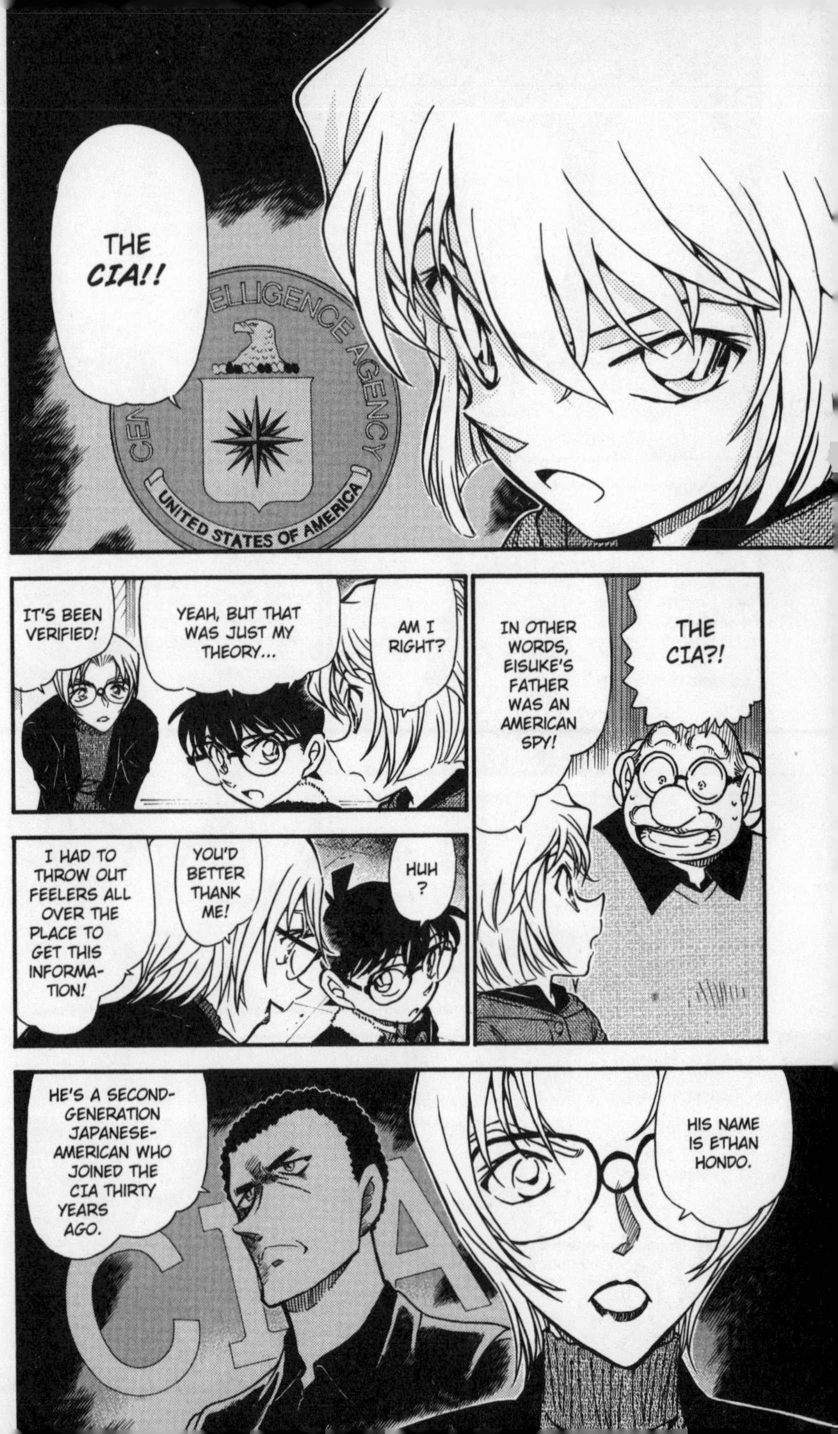
THE CIA!!
UNITED STATES OF AMERICA
THE CIA?!
IN OTHER WORDS, EISUKE'S FATHER WAS AN AMERICAN SPY!
AM I RIGHT?
YEAH, BUT THAT WAS JUST MY THEORY...
IT'S BEEN VERIFIED!
HUH?
YOU'D BETTER THANK ME!
I HAD TO THROW OUT FEELERS ALL OVER THE PLACE TO GET THIS INFORMATION!
HIS NAME IS ETHAN HONDO.
HE'S A SECOND-GENERATION JAPANESE-AMERICAN WHO JOINED THE CIA THIRTY YEARS AGO.

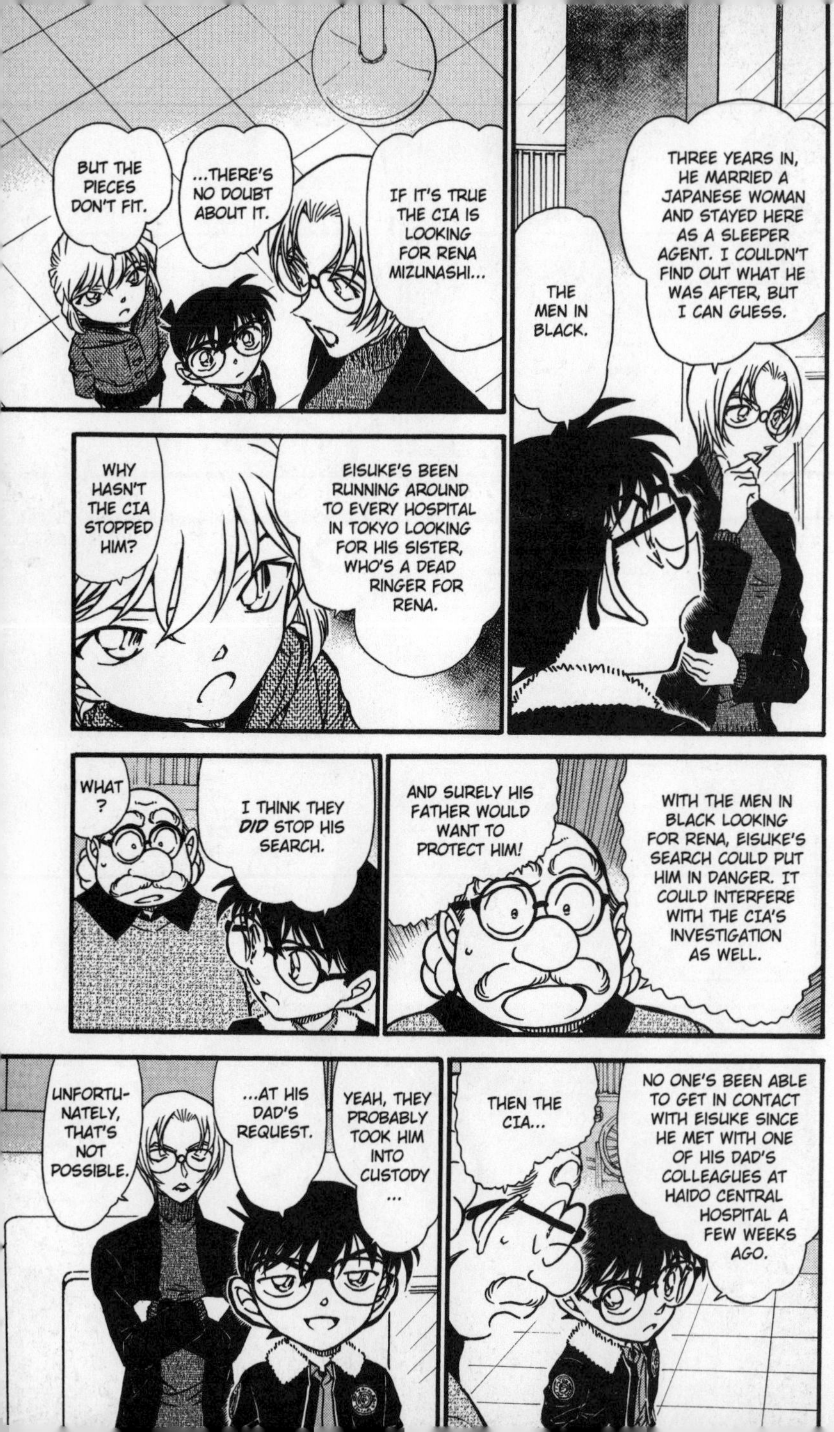
THREE YEARS IN, HE MARRIED A JAPANESE WOMAN AND STAYED HERE AS A SLEEPER AGENT. I COULDN'T FIND OUT WHAT HE WAS AFTER, BUT I CAN GUESS.
THE MEN IN BLACK.
IF IT'S TRUE THE CIA IS LOOKING FOR RENA MIZUNASHI...
...THERE'S NO DOUBT ABOUT IT.
BUT THE PIECES DON'T FIT.
EISUKE'S BEEN RUNNING AROUND TO EVERY HOSPITAL IN TOKYO LOOKING FOR HIS SISTER, WHO'S A DEAD RINGER FOR RENA.
WHY HASN'T THE CIA STOPPED HIM?
WITH THE MEN IN BLACK LOOKING FOR RENA, EISUKE'S SEARCH COULD PUT HIM IN DANGER. IT COULD INTERFERE WITH THE CIA'S INVESTIGATION AS WELL.
AND SURELY HIS FATHER WOULD WANT TO PROTECT HIM!
I THINK THEY *DID* STOP HIS SEARCH.
WHAT?
NO ONE'S BEEN ABLE TO GET IN CONTACT WITH EISUKE SINCE HE MET WITH ONE OF HIS DAD'S COLLEAGUES AT HAIDO CENTRAL HOSPITAL A FEW WEEKS AGO.
THEN THE CIA...
YEAH, THEY PROBABLY TOOK HIM INTO CUSTODY...
...AT HIS DAD'S REQUEST.
UNFORTUNATELY, THAT'S NOT POSSIBLE.

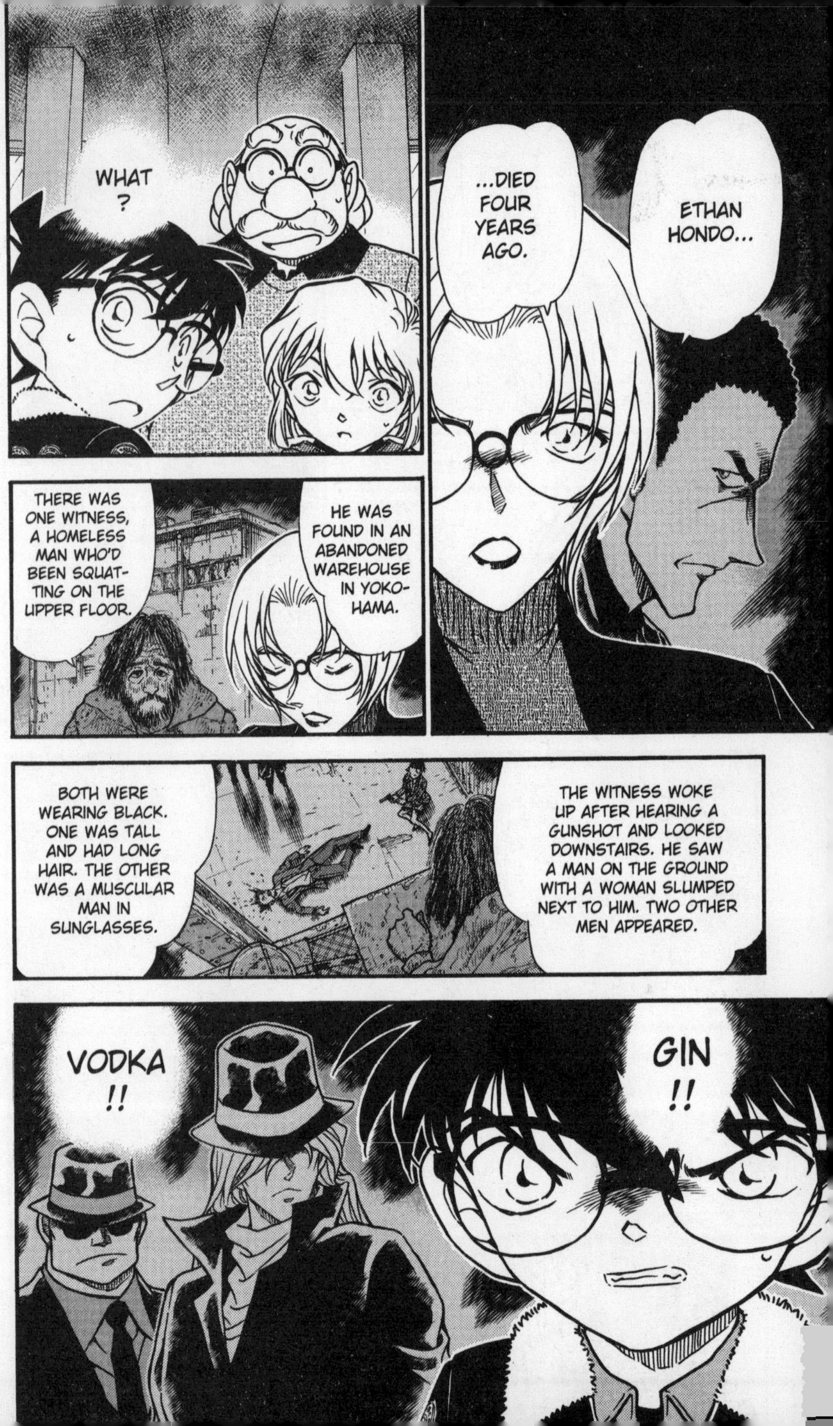
ETHAN HONDO...
...DIED FOUR YEARS AGO.
WHAT ?
HE WAS FOUND IN AN ABANDONED WAREHOUSE IN YOKO-HAMA.
THERE WAS ONE WITNESS, A HOMELESS MAN WHO'D BEEN SQUAT-TING ON THE UPPER FLOOR.
THE WITNESS WOKE UP AFTER HEARING A GUNSHOT AND LOOKED DOWNSTAIRS. HE SAW A MAN ON THE GROUND WITH A WOMAN SLUMPED NEXT TO HIM. TWO OTHER MEN APPEARED.
BOTH WERE WEARING BLACK. ONE WAS TALL AND HAD LONG HAIR. THE OTHER WAS A MUSCULAR MAN IN SUNGLASSES.
GIN !!
VODKA !!

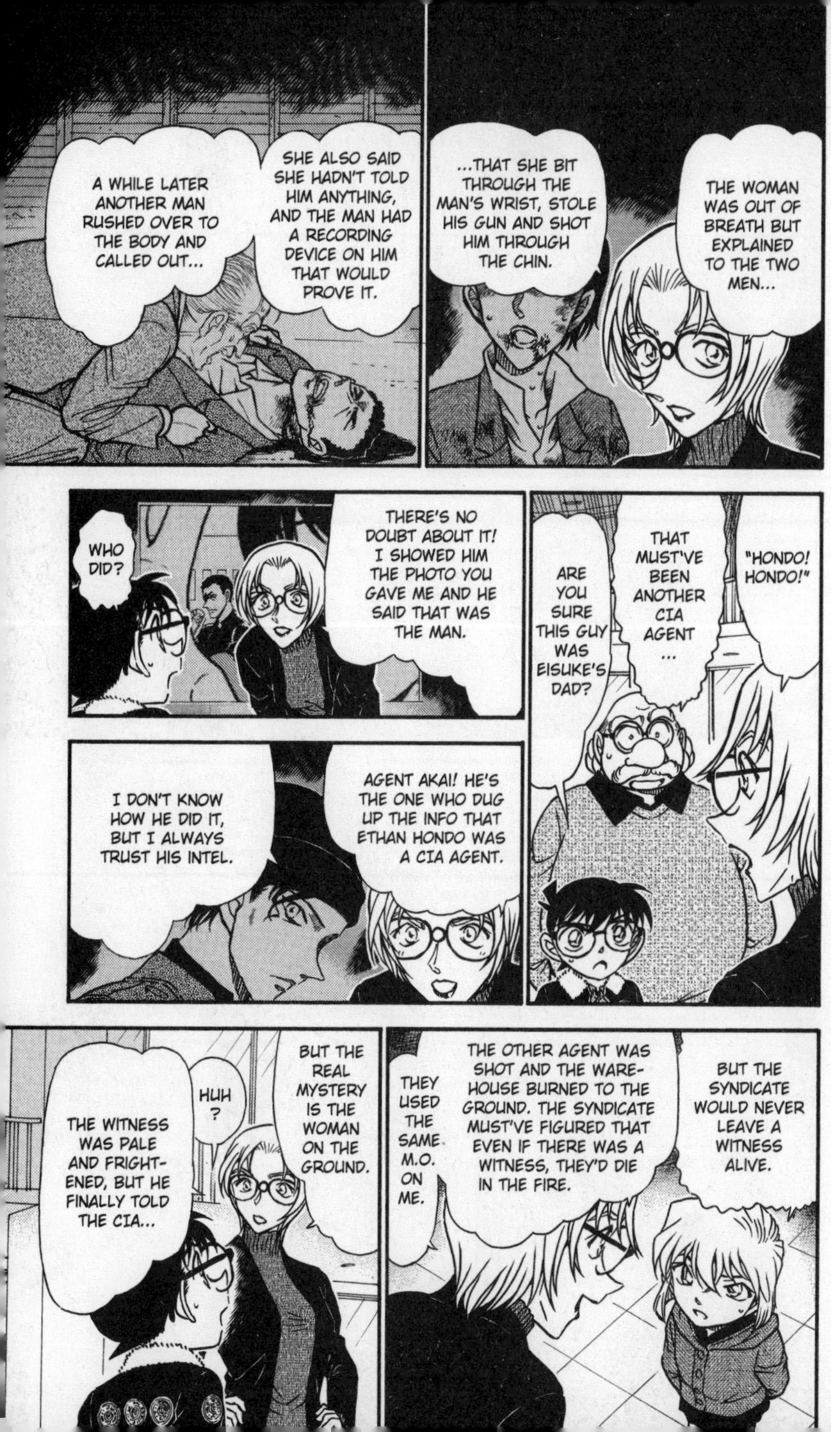
THE WOMAN WAS OUT OF BREATH BUT EXPLAINED TO THE TWO MEN...
...THAT SHE BIT THROUGH THE MAN'S WRIST, STOLE HIS GUN AND SHOT HIM THROUGH THE CHIN.
SHE ALSO SAID SHE HADN'T TOLD HIM ANYTHING, AND THE MAN HAD A RECORDING DEVICE ON HIM THAT WOULD PROVE IT.
A WHILE LATER ANOTHER MAN RUSHED OVER TO THE BODY AND CALLED OUT...
"HONDO! HONDO!"
THAT MUST'VE BEEN ANOTHER CIA AGENT...
ARE YOU SURE THIS GUY WAS EISUKE'S DAD?
THERE'S NO DOUBT ABOUT IT! I SHOWED HIM THE PHOTO YOU GAVE ME AND HE SAID THAT WAS THE MAN.
WHO DID?
AGENT AKAI! HE'S THE ONE WHO DUG UP THE INFO THAT ETHAN HONDO WAS A CIA AGENT.
I DON'T KNOW HOW HE DID IT, BUT I ALWAYS TRUST HIS INTEL.
BUT THE SYNDICATE WOULD NEVER LEAVE A WITNESS ALIVE.
THE OTHER AGENT WAS SHOT AND THE WARE-HOUSE BURNED TO THE GROUND. THE SYNDICATE MUST'VE FIGURED THAT EVEN IF THERE WAS A WITNESS, THEY'D DIE IN THE FIRE.
THEY USED THE SAME M.O. ON ME.
BUT THE REAL MYSTERY IS THE WOMAN ON THE GROUND.
HUH?
THE WITNESS WAS PALE AND FRIGHT-ENED, BUT HE FINALLY TOLD THE CIA...

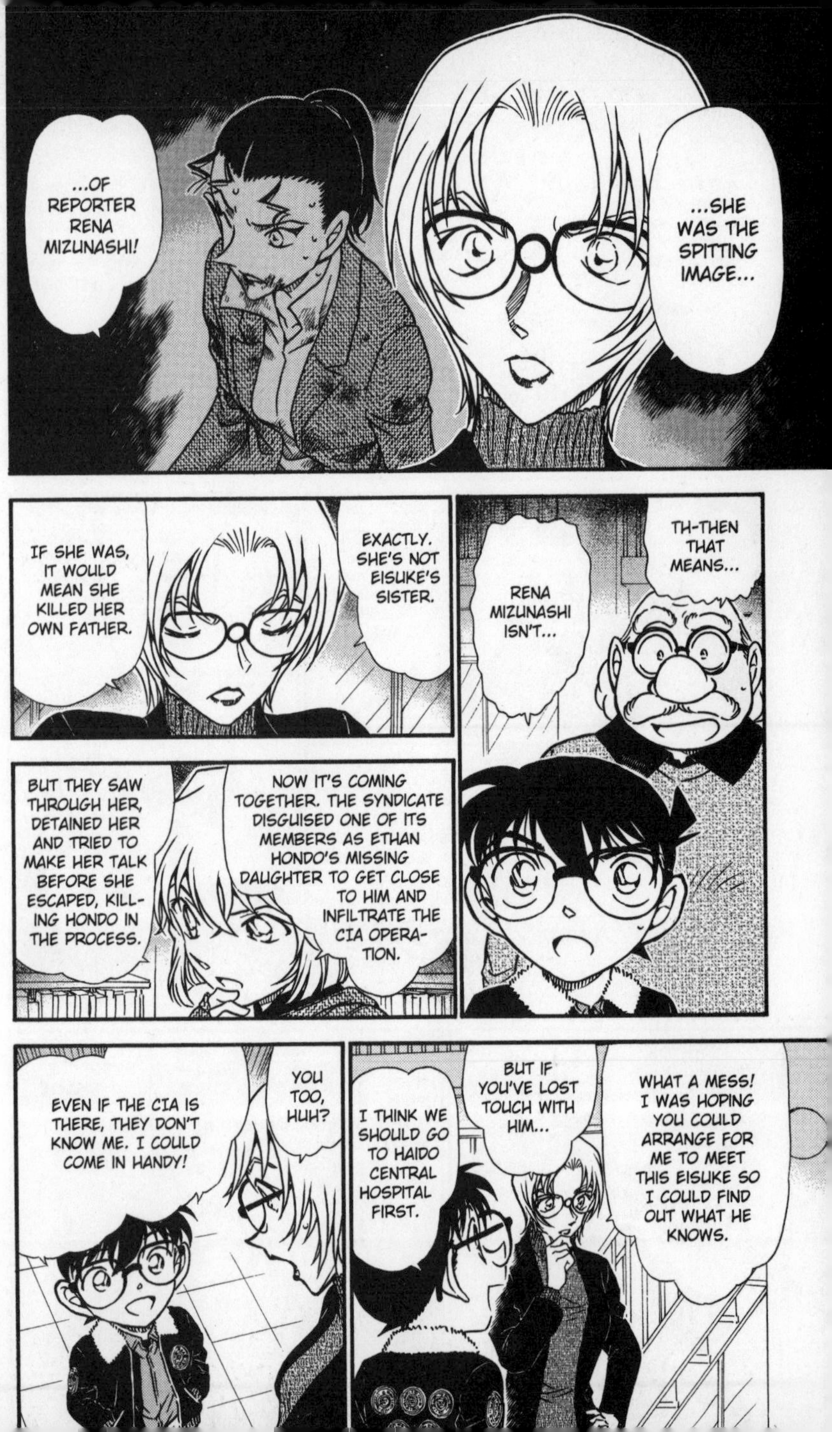
...SHE WAS THE SPITTING IMAGE...
...OF REPORTER RENA MIZUNASHI!
TH-THEN THAT MEANS...
RENA MIZUNASHI ISN'T...
EXACTLY. SHE'S NOT EISUKE'S SISTER.
IF SHE WAS, IT WOULD MEAN SHE KILLED HER OWN FATHER.
NOW IT'S COMING TOGETHER. THE SYNDICATE DISGUISED ONE OF ITS MEMBERS AS ETHAN HONDO'S MISSING DAUGHTER TO GET CLOSE TO HIM AND INFILTRATE THE CIA OPERATION.
BUT THEY SAW THROUGH HER, DETAINED HER AND TRIED TO MAKE HER TALK BEFORE SHE ESCAPED, KILLING HONDO IN THE PROCESS.
WHAT A MESS! I WAS HOPING YOU COULD ARRANGE FOR ME TO MEET THIS EISUKE SO I COULD FIND OUT WHAT HE KNOWS.
BUT IF YOU'VE LOST TOUCH WITH HIM...
I THINK WE SHOULD GO TO HAIDO CENTRAL HOSPITAL FIRST.
YOU TOO, HUH?
EVEN IF THE CIA IS THERE, THEY DON'T KNOW ME. I COULD COME IN HANDY!

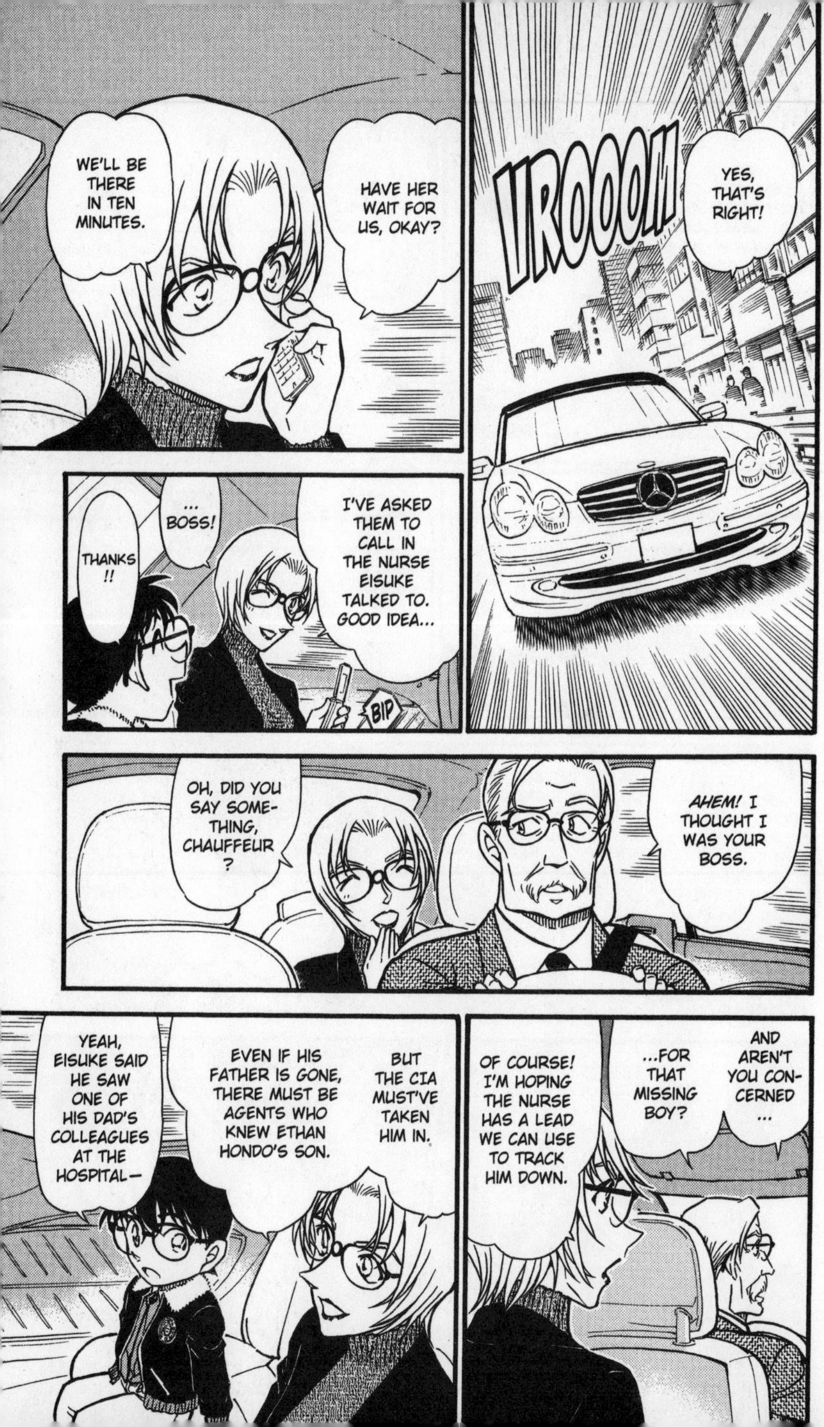
YES, THAT'S RIGHT!
VROOOM
HAVE HER WAIT FOR US, OKAY?
WE'LL BE THERE IN TEN MINUTES.
I'VE ASKED THEM TO CALL IN THE NURSE EISUKE TALKED TO. GOOD IDEA...
...BOSS!
THANKS!!
BIP
AHEM! I THOUGHT I WAS YOUR BOSS.
OH, DID YOU SAY SOME-THING, CHAUFFEUR?
AND AREN'T YOU CON-CERNED...
...FOR THAT MISSING BOY?
OF COURSE! I'M HOPING THE NURSE HAS A LEAD WE CAN USE TO TRACK HIM DOWN.
BUT THE CIA MUST'VE TAKEN HIM IN.
EVEN IF HIS FATHER IS GONE, THERE MUST BE AGENTS WHO KNEW ETHAN HONDO'S SON.
YEAH, EISUKE SAID HE SAW ONE OF HIS DAD'S COLLEAGUES AT THE HOSPITAL—

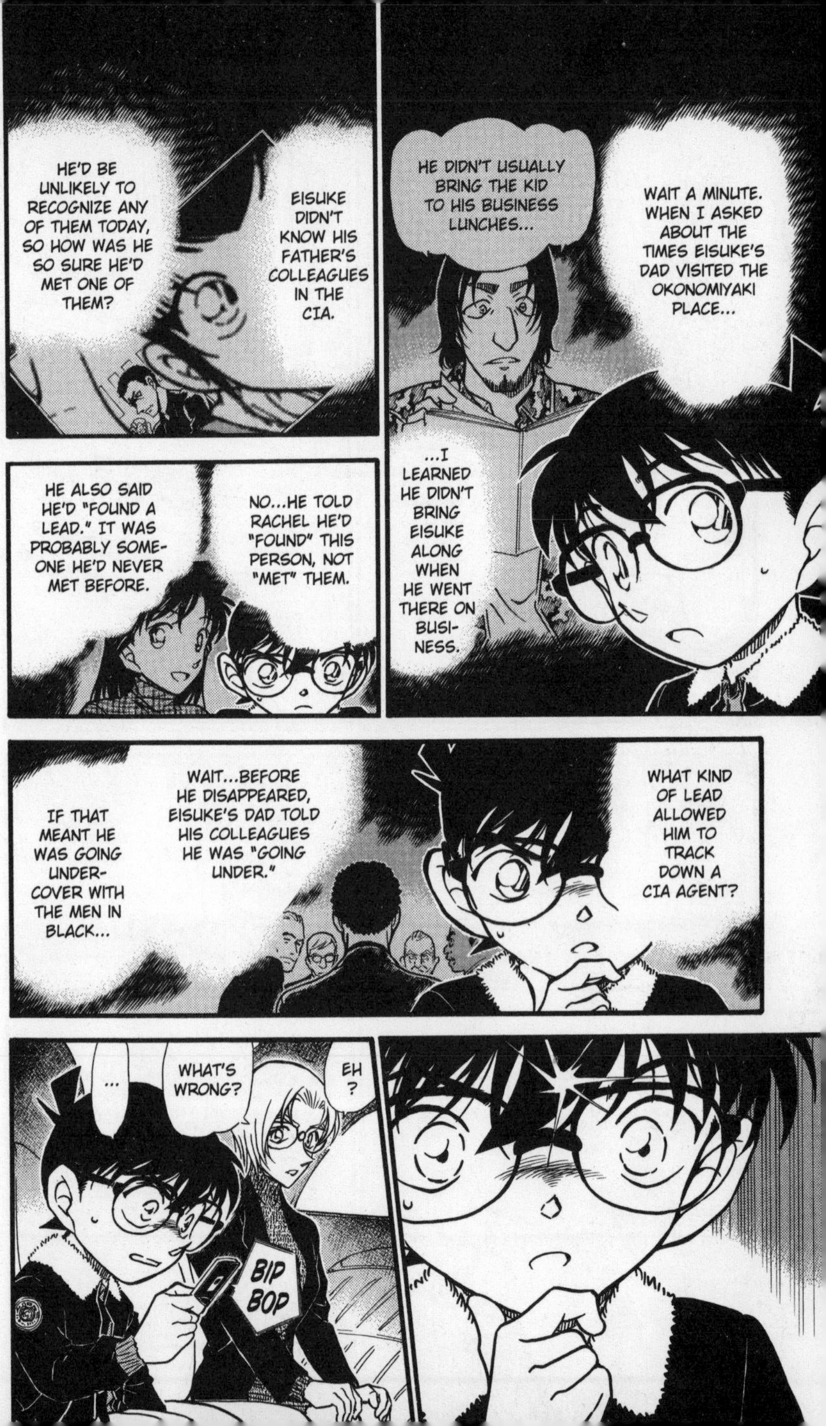
WAIT A MINUTE. WHEN I ASKED ABOUT THE TIMES EISUKE'S DAD VISITED THE OKONOMIYAKI PLACE...
...I LEARNED HE DIDN'T BRING EISUKE ALONG WHEN HE WENT THERE ON BUSI- NESS.
HE DIDN'T USUALLY BRING THE KID TO HIS BUSINESS LUNCHES...
EISUKE DIDN'T KNOW HIS FATHER'S COLLEAGUES IN THE CIA.
HE'D BE UNLIKELY TO RECOGNIZE ANY OF THEM TODAY, SO HOW WAS HE SO SURE HE'D MET ONE OF THEM?
NO...HE TOLD RACHEL HE'D "FOUND" THIS PERSON, NOT "MET" THEM.
HE ALSO SAID HE'D "FOUND A LEAD." IT WAS PROBABLY SOME- ONE HE'D NEVER MET BEFORE.
WHAT KIND OF LEAD ALLOWED HIM TO TRACK DOWN A CIA AGENT?
WAIT...BEFORE HE DISAPPEARED, EISUKE'S DAD TOLD HIS COLLEAGUES HE WAS "GOING UNDER."
IF THAT MEANT HE WAS GOING UNDER- COVER WITH THE MEN IN BLACK...
EH ?
WHAT'S WRONG?
...
BIP BOP

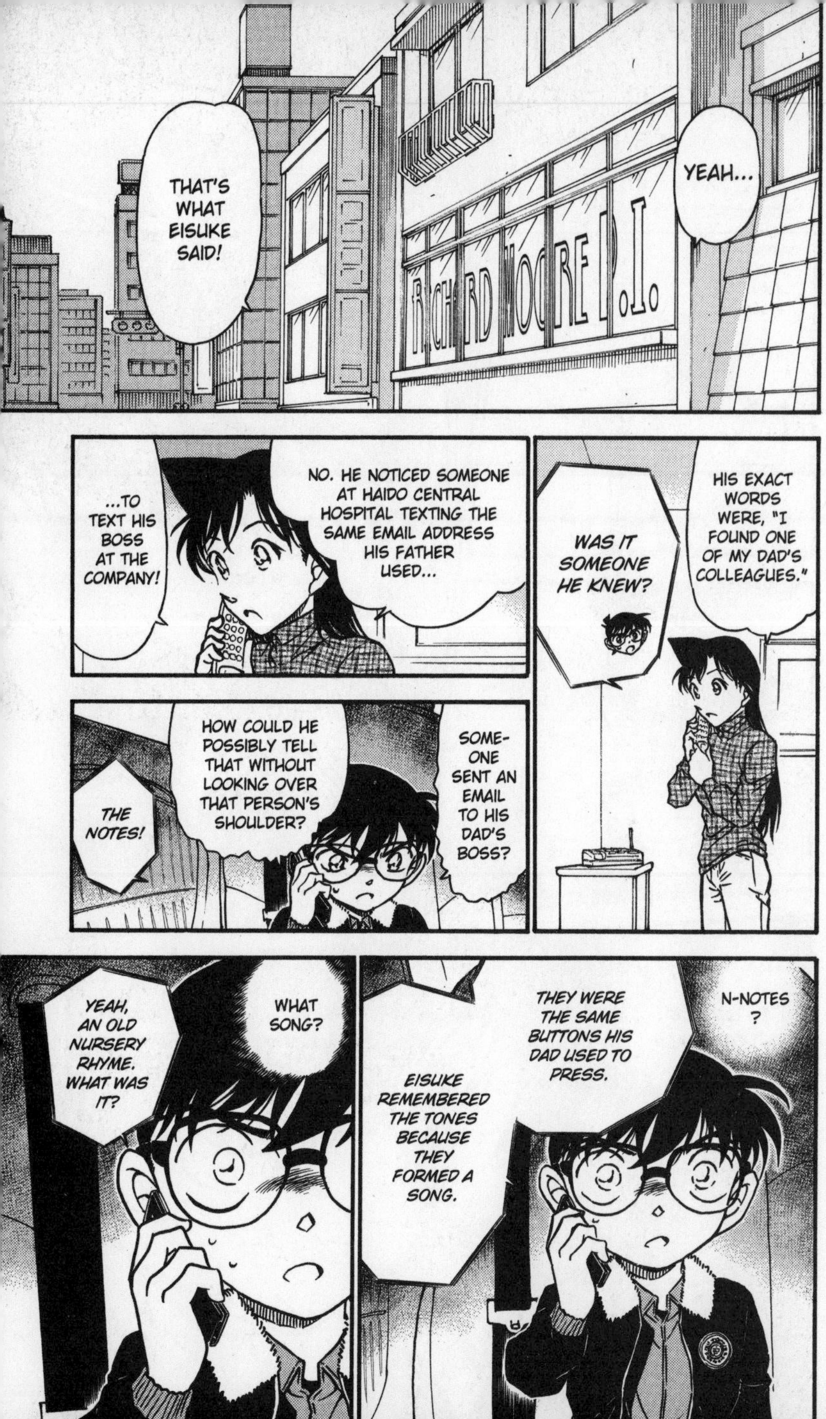
YEAH...
THAT'S WHAT EISUKE SAID!
RICHARD MOORE P.I.
HIS EXACT WORDS WERE, "I FOUND ONE OF MY DAD'S COLLEAGUES."
WAS IT SOMEONE HE KNEW?
NO. HE NOTICED SOMEONE AT HAIDO CENTRAL HOSPITAL TEXTING THE SAME EMAIL ADDRESS HIS FATHER USED...
...TO TEXT HIS BOSS AT THE COMPANY!
SOME-ONE SENT AN EMAIL TO HIS DAD'S BOSS?
HOW COULD HE POSSIBLY TELL THAT WITHOUT LOOKING OVER THAT PERSON'S SHOULDER?
THE NOTES!
N-NOTES?
THEY WERE THE SAME BUTTONS HIS DAD USED TO PRESS.
EISUKE REMEMBERED THE TONES BECAUSE THEY FORMED A SONG.
WHAT SONG?
YEAH, AN OLD NURSERY RHYME. WHAT WAS IT?

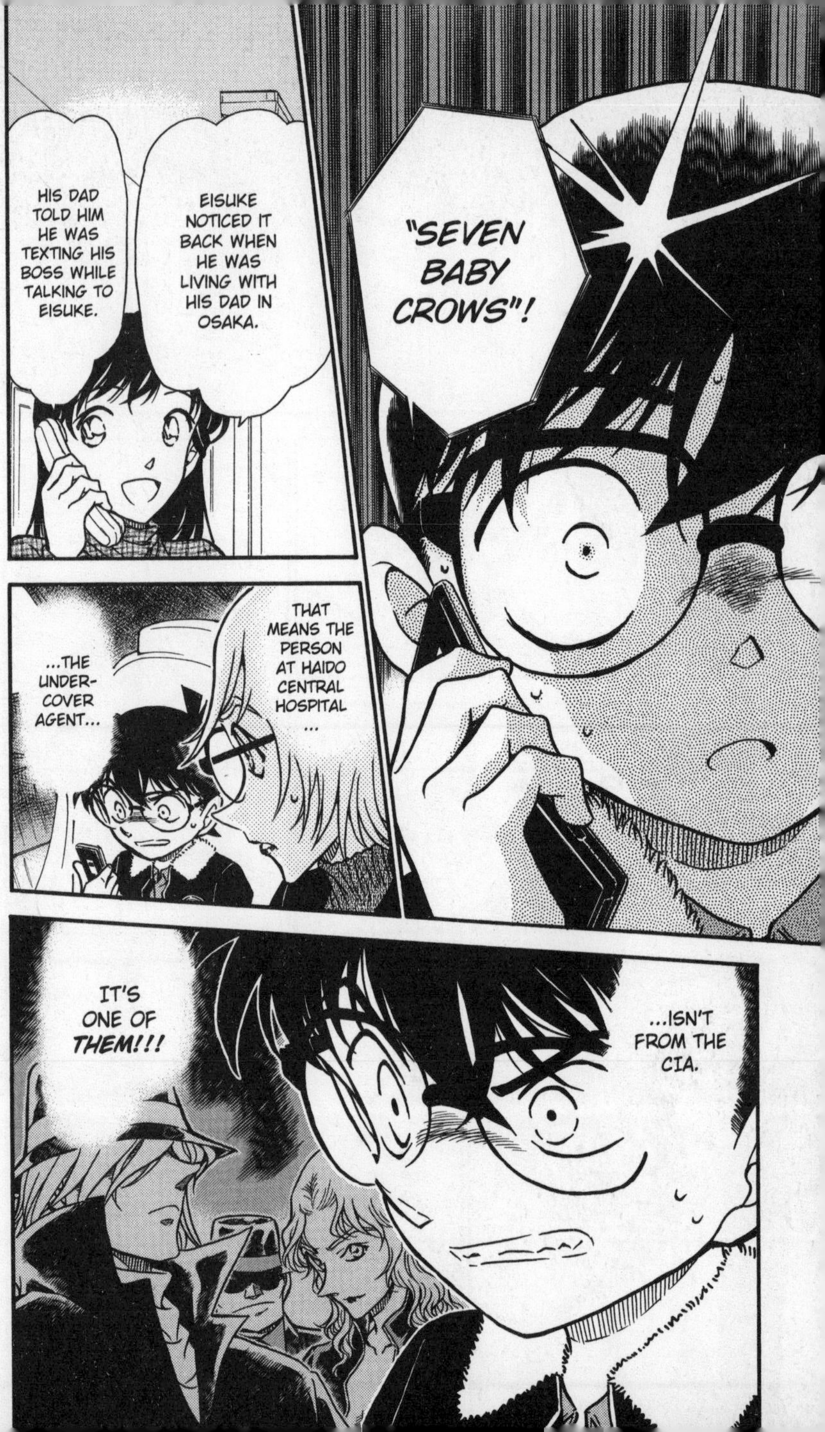
"SEVEN BABY CROWS"!
EISUKE NOTICED IT BACK WHEN HE WAS LIVING WITH HIS DAD IN OSAKA.
HIS DAD TOLD HIM HE WAS TEXTING HIS BOSS WHILE TALKING TO EISUKE.
THAT MEANS THE PERSON AT HAIDO CENTRAL HOSPITAL ...
...THE UNDER-COVER AGENT...
...ISN'T FROM THE CIA.
IT'S ONE OF *THEM!!!*

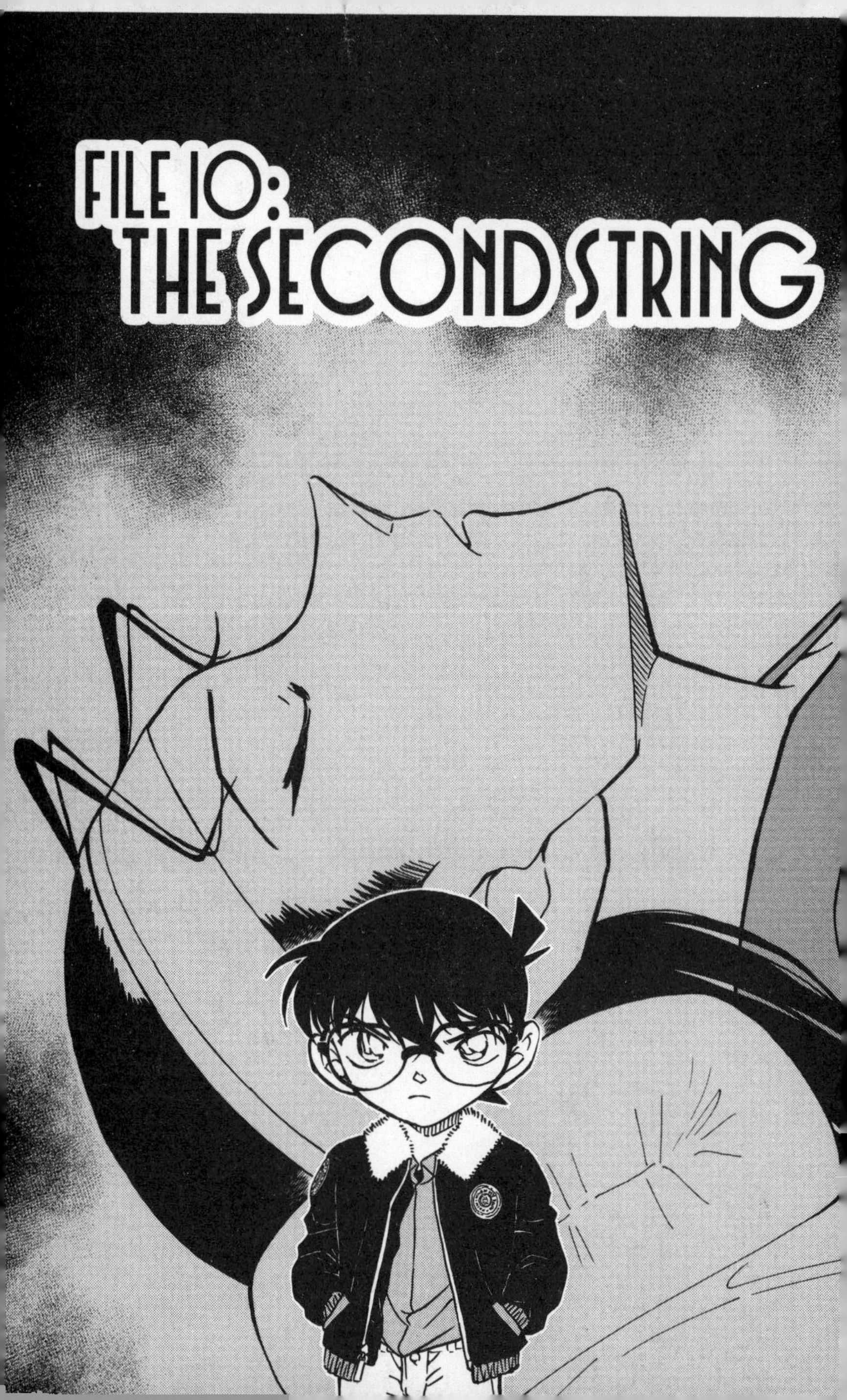
FILE 10:
THE SECOND STRING

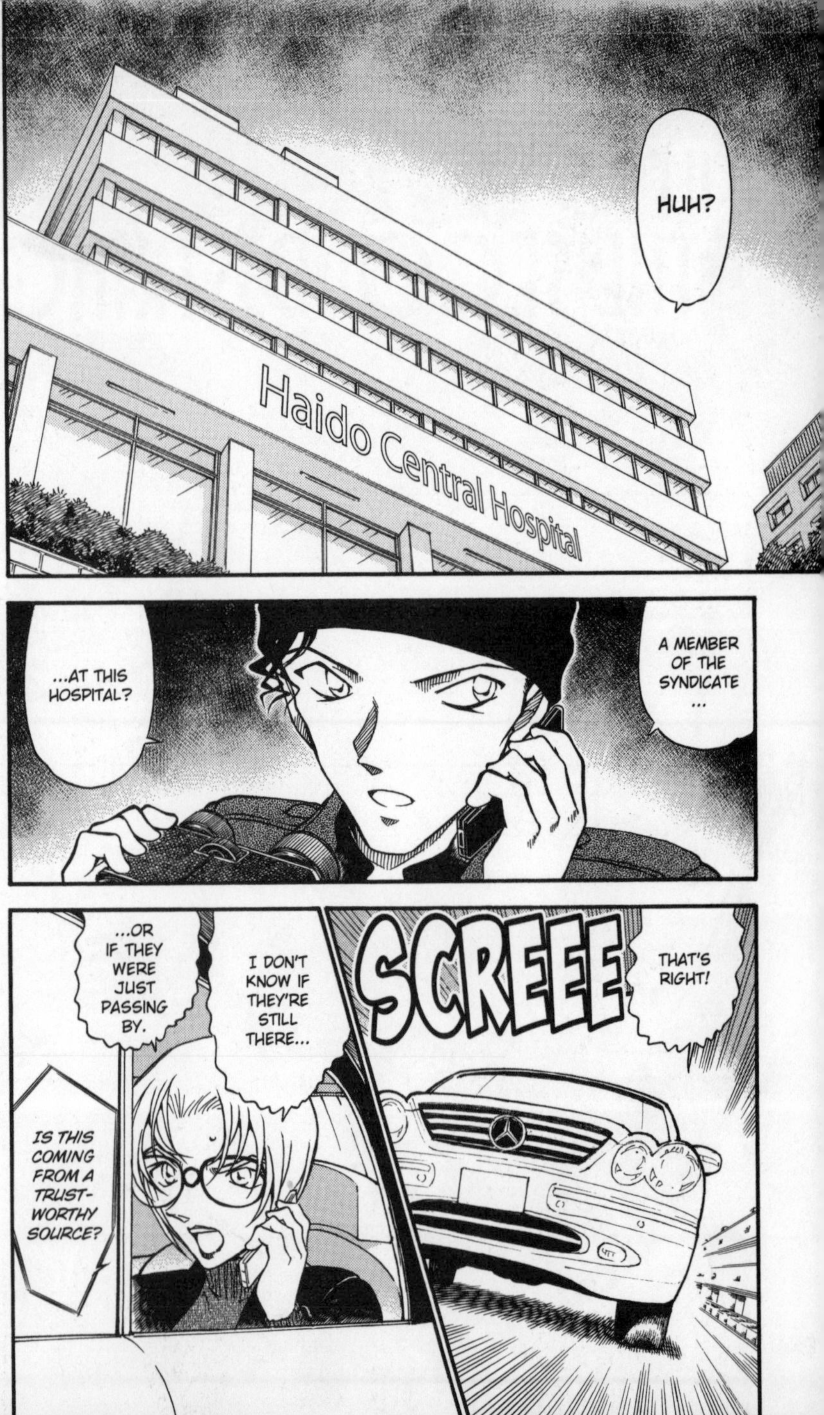
HUH?
Haido Central Hospital
A MEMBER OF THE SYNDICATE ...
...AT THIS HOSPITAL?
THAT'S RIGHT!
SCREEE
I DON'T KNOW IF THEY'RE STILL THERE...
...OR IF THEY WERE JUST PASSING BY.
IS THIS COMING FROM A TRUST-WORTHY SOURCE?

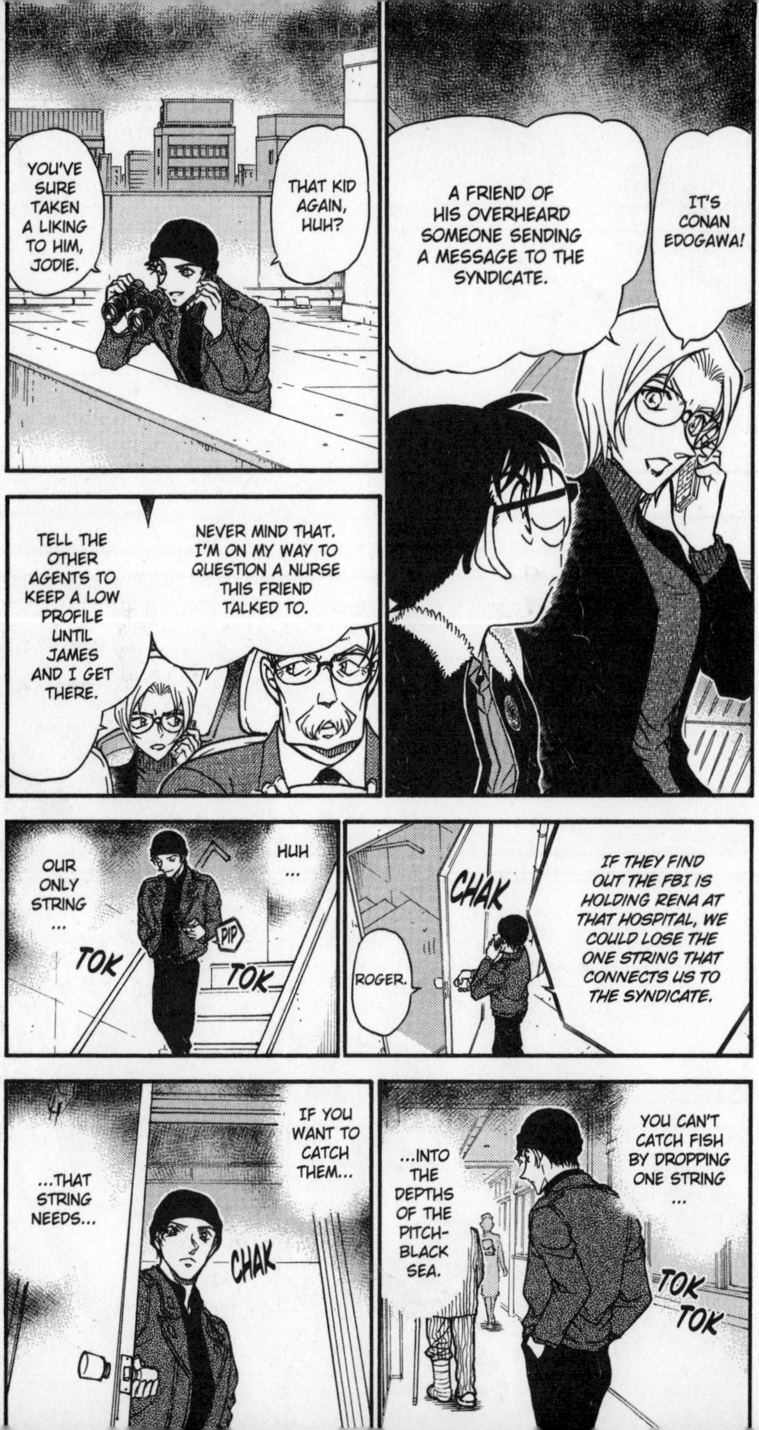
IT'S CONAN EDOGAWA!
A FRIEND OF HIS OVERHEARD SOMEONE SENDING A MESSAGE TO THE SYNDICATE.
THAT KID AGAIN, HUH?
YOU'VE SURE TAKEN A LIKING TO HIM, JODIE.
NEVER MIND THAT. I'M ON MY WAY TO QUESTION A NURSE THIS FRIEND TALKED TO.
TELL THE OTHER AGENTS TO KEEP A LOW PROFILE UNTIL JAMES AND I GET THERE.
IF THEY FIND OUT THE FBI IS HOLDING RENA AT THAT HOSPITAL, WE COULD LOSE THE ONE STRING THAT CONNECTS US TO THE SYNDICATE.
CHAK
ROGER.
HUH ...
PIP
OUR ONLY STRING ...
TOK
TOK
YOU CAN'T CATCH FISH BY DROPPING ONE STRING ...
...INTO THE DEPTHS OF THE PITCH-BLACK SEA.
TOK
TOK
IF YOU WANT TO CATCH THEM...
...THAT STRING NEEDS...
CHAK

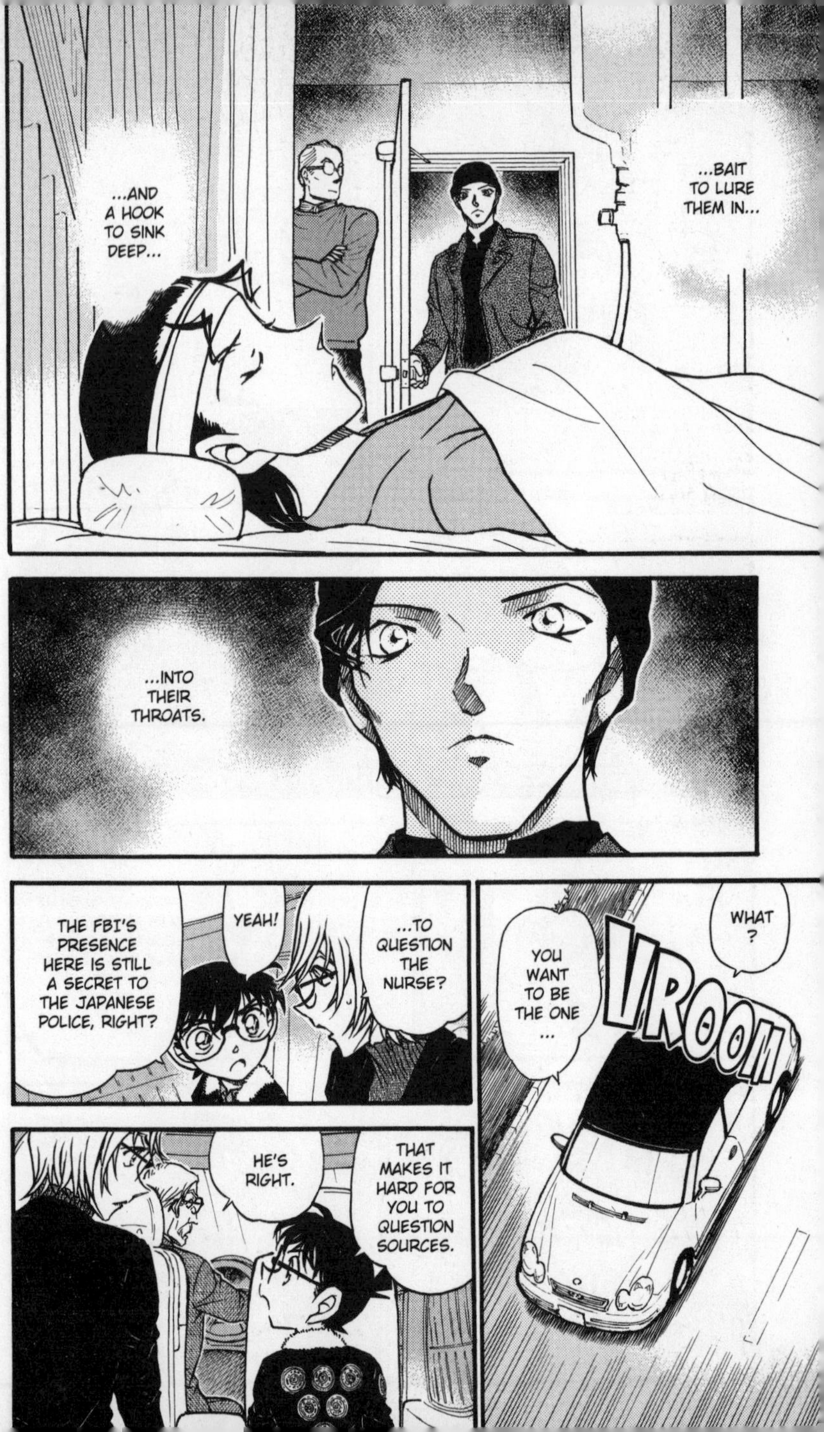
...BAIT TO LURE THEM IN...
...AND A HOOK TO SINK DEEP...
...INTO THEIR THROATS.
WHAT?
VROOM
YOU WANT TO BE THE ONE...
...TO QUESTION THE NURSE?
YEAH!
THE FBI'S PRESENCE HERE IS STILL A SECRET TO THE JAPANESE POLICE, RIGHT?
THAT MAKES IT HARD FOR YOU TO QUESTION SOURCES.
HE'S RIGHT.

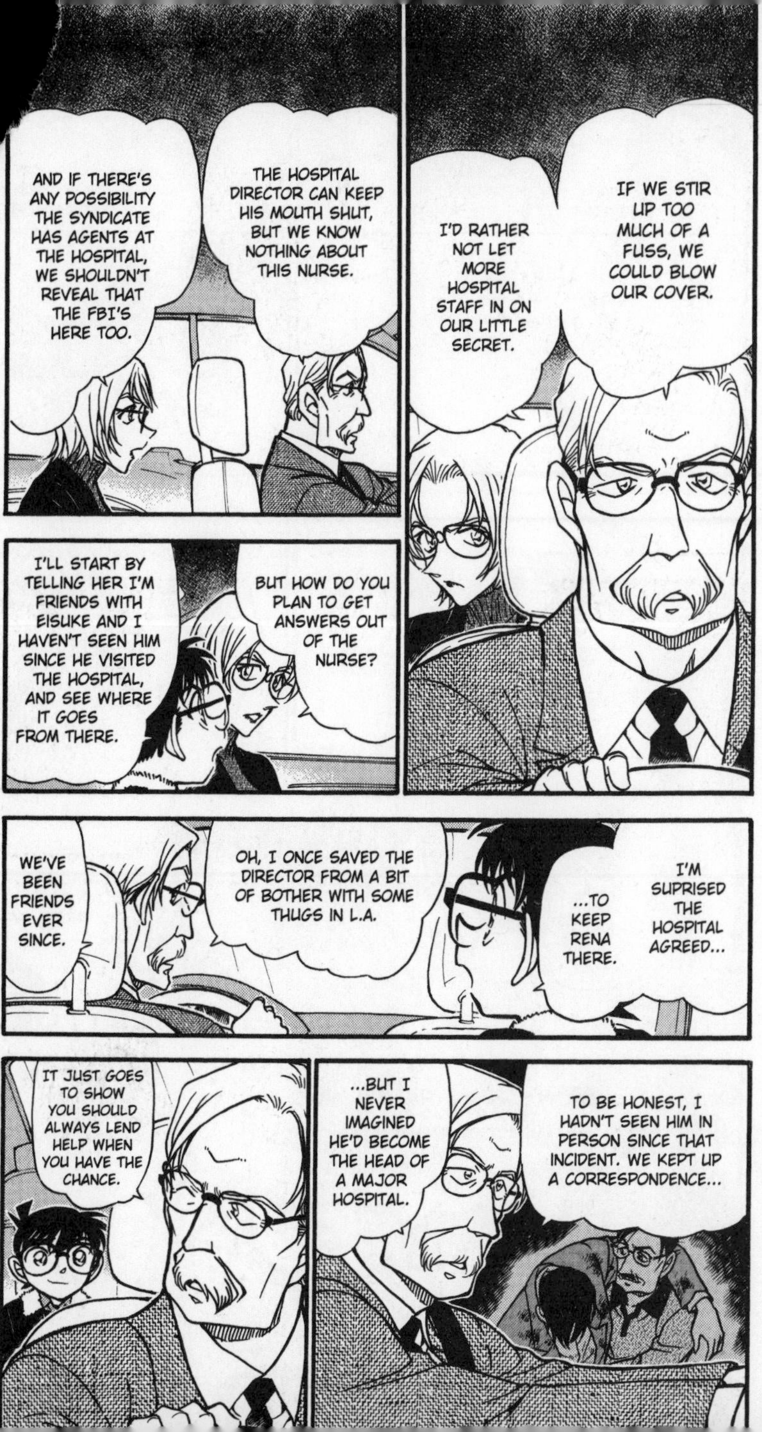
IF WE STIR UP TOO MUCH OF A FUSS, WE COULD BLOW OUR COVER.
I'D RATHER NOT LET MORE HOSPITAL STAFF IN ON OUR LITTLE SECRET.
THE HOSPITAL DIRECTOR CAN KEEP HIS MOUTH SHUT, BUT WE KNOW NOTHING ABOUT THIS NURSE.
AND IF THERE'S ANY POSSIBILITY THE SYNDICATE HAS AGENTS AT THE HOSPITAL, WE SHOULDN'T REVEAL THAT THE FBI'S HERE TOO.
BUT HOW DO YOU PLAN TO GET ANSWERS OUT OF THE NURSE?
I'LL START BY TELLING HER I'M FRIENDS WITH EISUKE AND I HAVEN'T SEEN HIM SINCE HE VISITED THE HOSPITAL, AND SEE WHERE IT GOES FROM THERE.
I'M SUPRISED THE HOSPITAL AGREED...
...TO KEEP RENA THERE.
OH, I ONCE SAVED THE DIRECTOR FROM A BIT OF BOTHER WITH SOME THUGS IN L.A.
WE'VE BEEN FRIENDS EVER SINCE.
TO BE HONEST, I HADN'T SEEN HIM IN PERSON SINCE THAT INCIDENT. WE KEPT UP A CORRESPONDENCE...
...BUT I NEVER IMAGINED HE'D BECOME THE HEAD OF A MAJOR HOSPITAL.
IT JUST GOES TO SHOW YOU SHOULD ALWAYS LEND HELP WHEN YOU HAVE THE CHANCE.

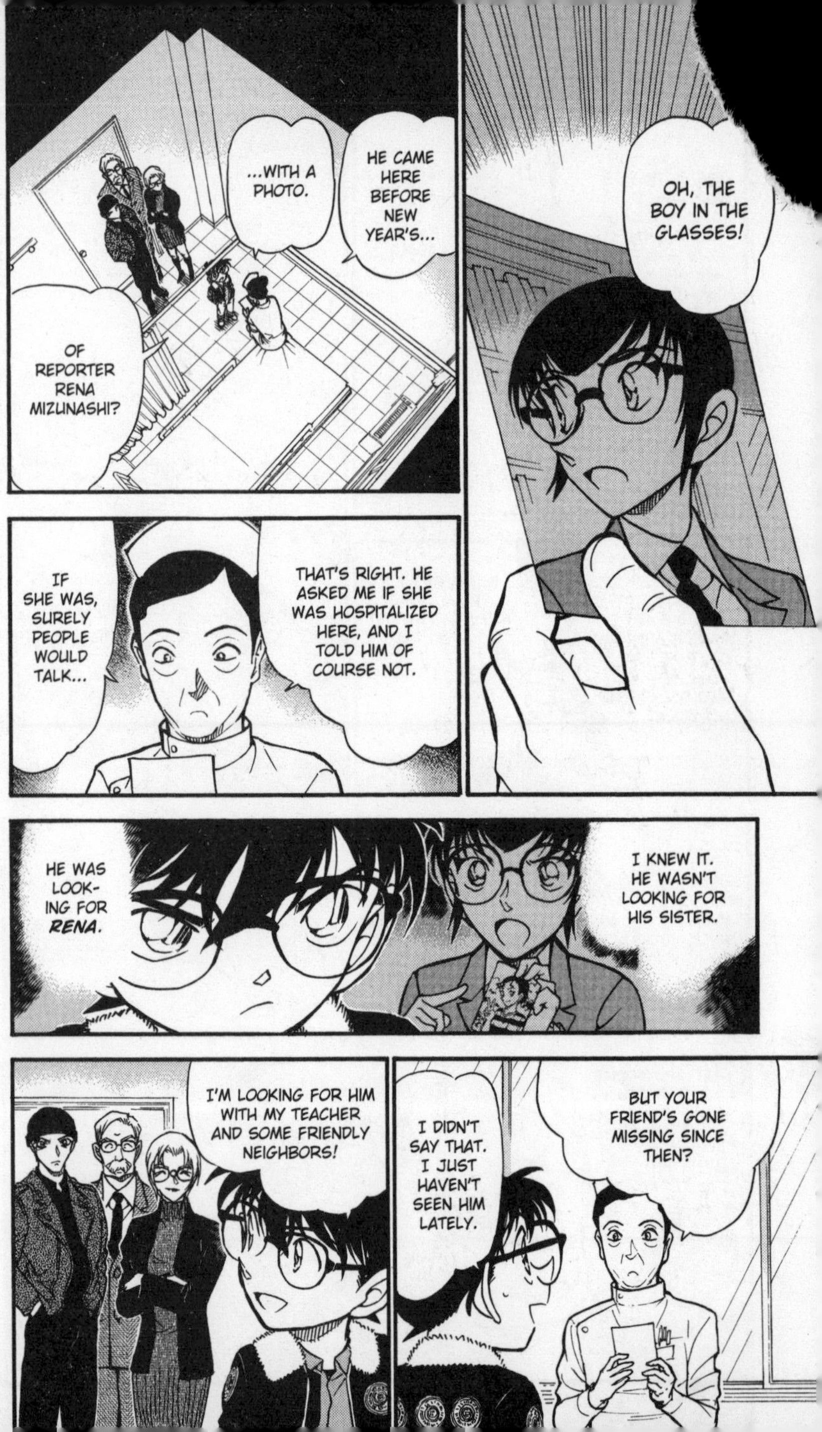
OH, THE BOY IN THE GLASSES!
HE CAME HERE BEFORE NEW YEAR'S...
...WITH A PHOTO.
OF REPORTER RENA MIZUNASHI?
THAT'S RIGHT. HE ASKED ME IF SHE WAS HOSPITALIZED HERE, AND I TOLD HIM OF COURSE NOT.
IF SHE WAS, SURELY PEOPLE WOULD TALK...
I KNEW IT. HE WASN'T LOOKING FOR HIS SISTER.
HE WAS LOOK-ING FOR *RENA*.
BUT YOUR FRIEND'S GONE MISSING SINCE THEN?
I DIDN'T SAY THAT. I JUST HAVEN'T SEEN HIM LATELY.
I'M LOOKING FOR HIM WITH MY TEACHER AND SOME FRIENDLY NEIGHBORS!

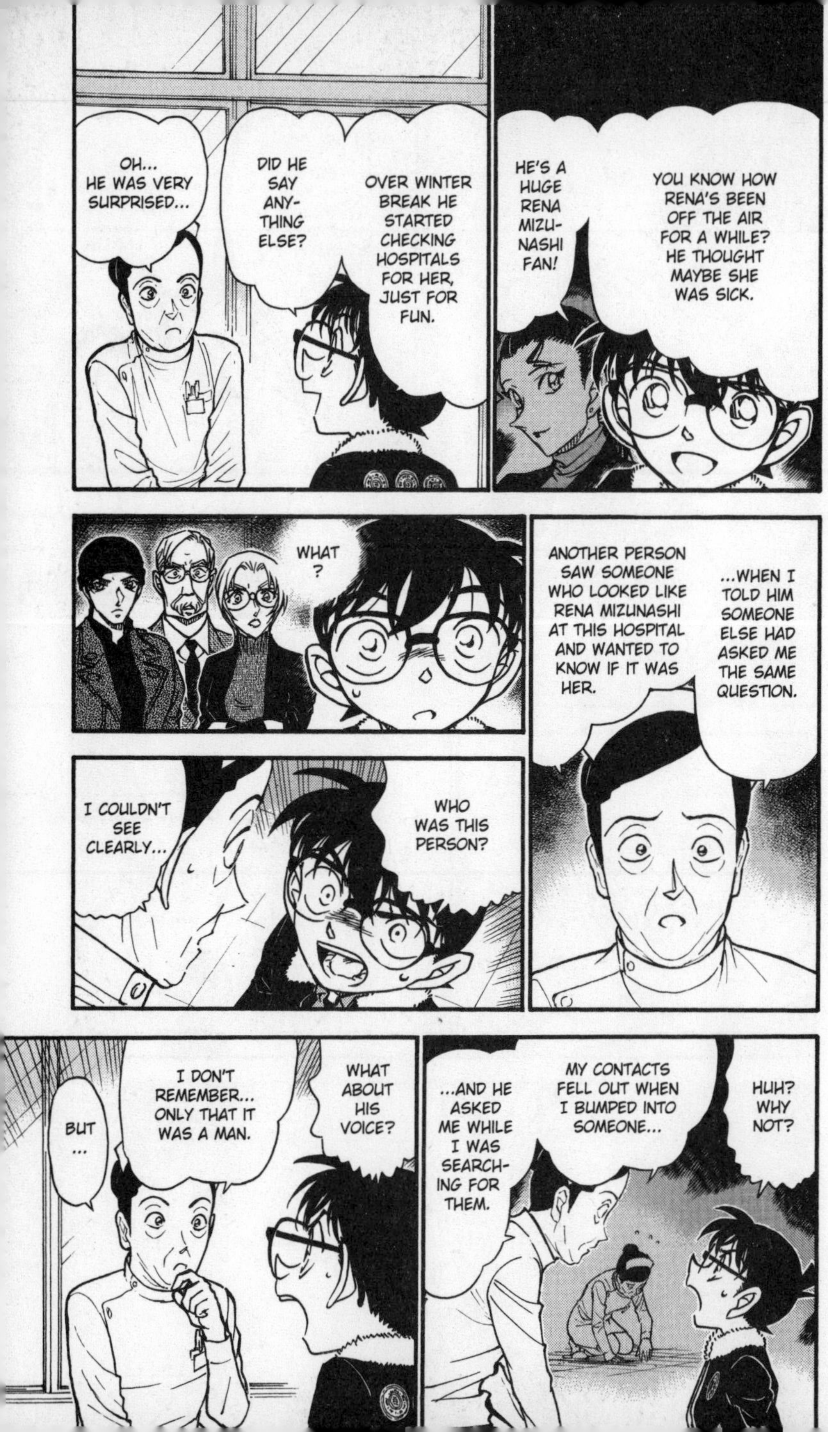
YOU KNOW HOW RENA'S BEEN OFF THE AIR FOR A WHILE? HE THOUGHT MAYBE SHE WAS SICK.
HE'S A HUGE RENA MIZU-NASHI FAN!
OVER WINTER BREAK HE STARTED CHECKING HOSPITALS FOR HER, JUST FOR FUN.
DID HE SAY ANY-THING ELSE?
OH... HE WAS VERY SURPRISED...
...WHEN I TOLD HIM SOMEONE ELSE HAD ASKED ME THE SAME QUESTION.
ANOTHER PERSON SAW SOMEONE WHO LOOKED LIKE RENA MIZUNASHI AT THIS HOSPITAL AND WANTED TO KNOW IF IT WAS HER.
WHAT?
WHO WAS THIS PERSON?
I COULDN'T SEE CLEARLY...
HUH? WHY NOT?
MY CONTACTS FELL OUT WHEN I BUMPED INTO SOMEONE...
...AND HE ASKED ME WHILE I WAS SEARCH-ING FOR THEM.
WHAT ABOUT HIS VOICE?
I DON'T REMEMBER... ONLY THAT IT WAS A MAN.
BUT...

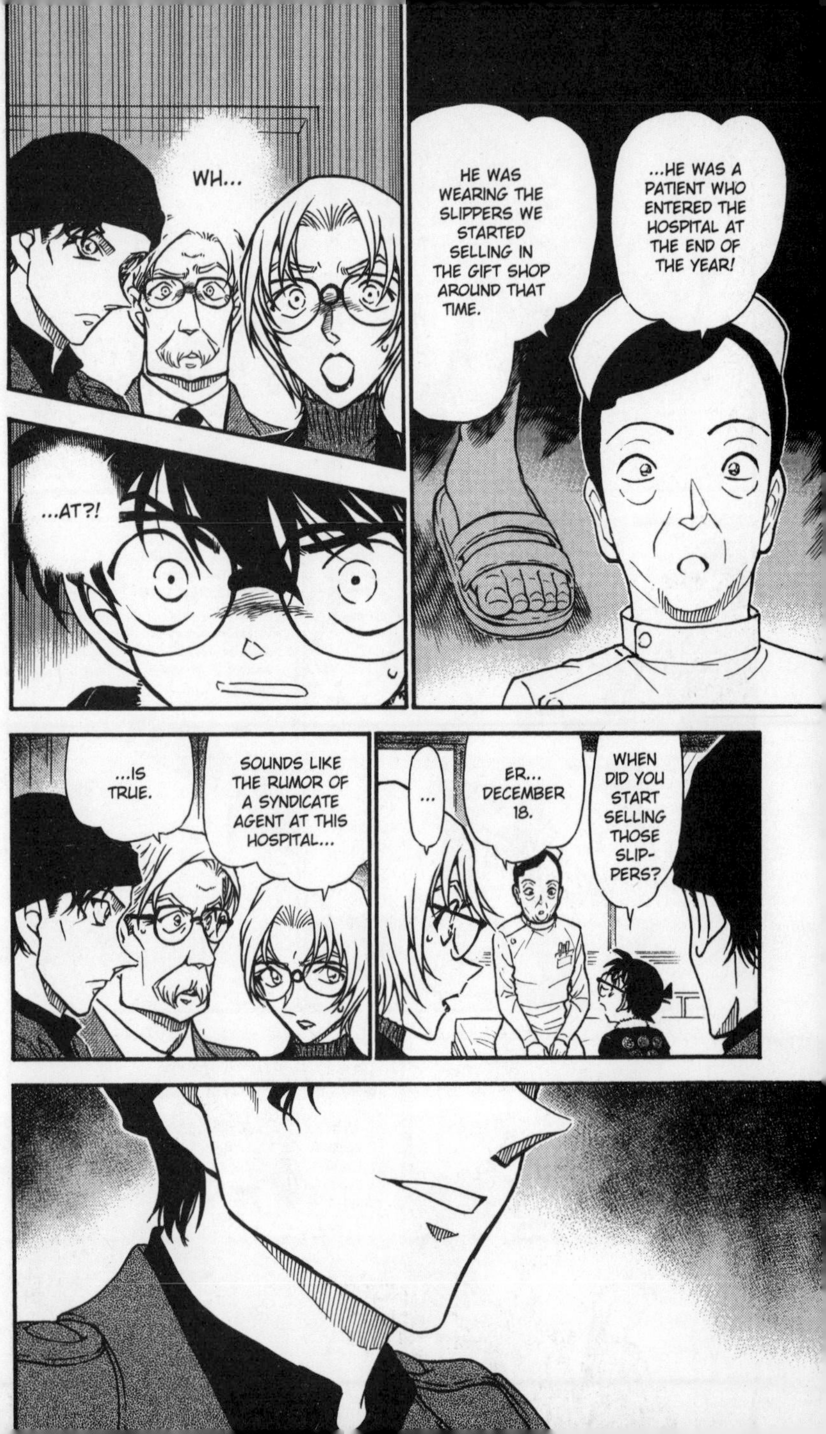
...HE WAS A PATIENT WHO ENTERED THE HOSPITAL AT THE END OF THE YEAR!
HE WAS WEARING THE SLIPPERS WE STARTED SELLING IN THE GIFT SHOP AROUND THAT TIME.
WH...
...AT?!
WHEN DID YOU START SELLING THOSE SLIP-PERS?
ER... DECEMBER 18.
...
SOUNDS LIKE THE RUMOR OF A SYNDICATE AGENT AT THIS HOSPITAL...
...IS TRUE.

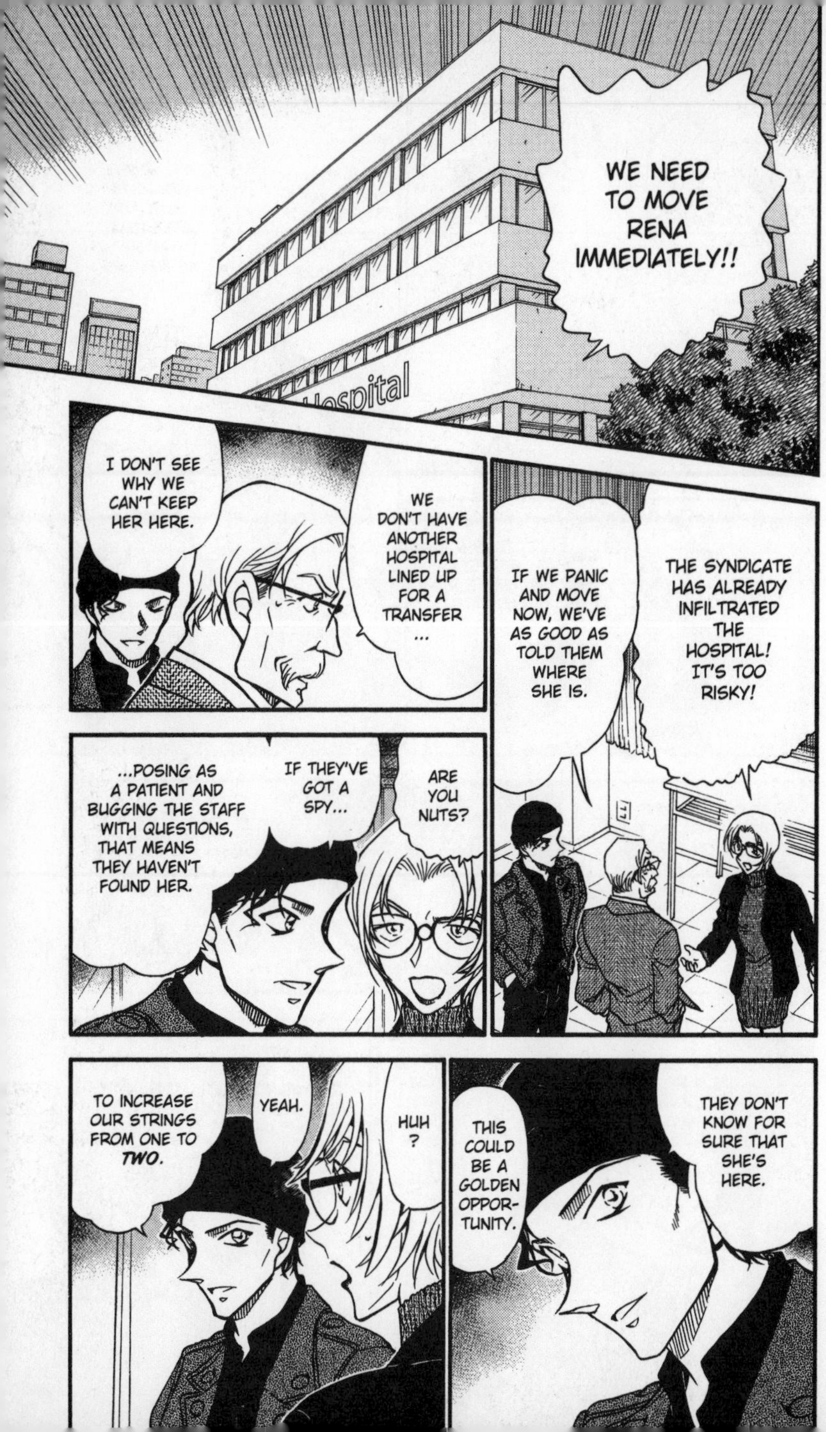
WE NEED TO MOVE RENA IMMEDIATELY!!
Hospital
THE SYNDICATE HAS ALREADY INFILTRATED THE HOSPITAL! IT'S TOO RISKY!
IF WE PANIC AND MOVE NOW, WE'VE AS GOOD AS TOLD THEM WHERE SHE IS.
WE DON'T HAVE ANOTHER HOSPITAL LINED UP FOR A TRANSFER...
I DON'T SEE WHY WE CAN'T KEEP HER HERE.
ARE YOU NUTS?
IF THEY'VE GOT A SPY...
...POSING AS A PATIENT AND BUGGING THE STAFF WITH QUESTIONS, THAT MEANS THEY HAVEN'T FOUND HER.
THEY DON'T KNOW FOR SURE THAT SHE'S HERE.
THIS COULD BE A GOLDEN OPPORTUNITY.
HUH?
YEAH.
TO INCREASE OUR STRINGS FROM ONE TO *TWO*.

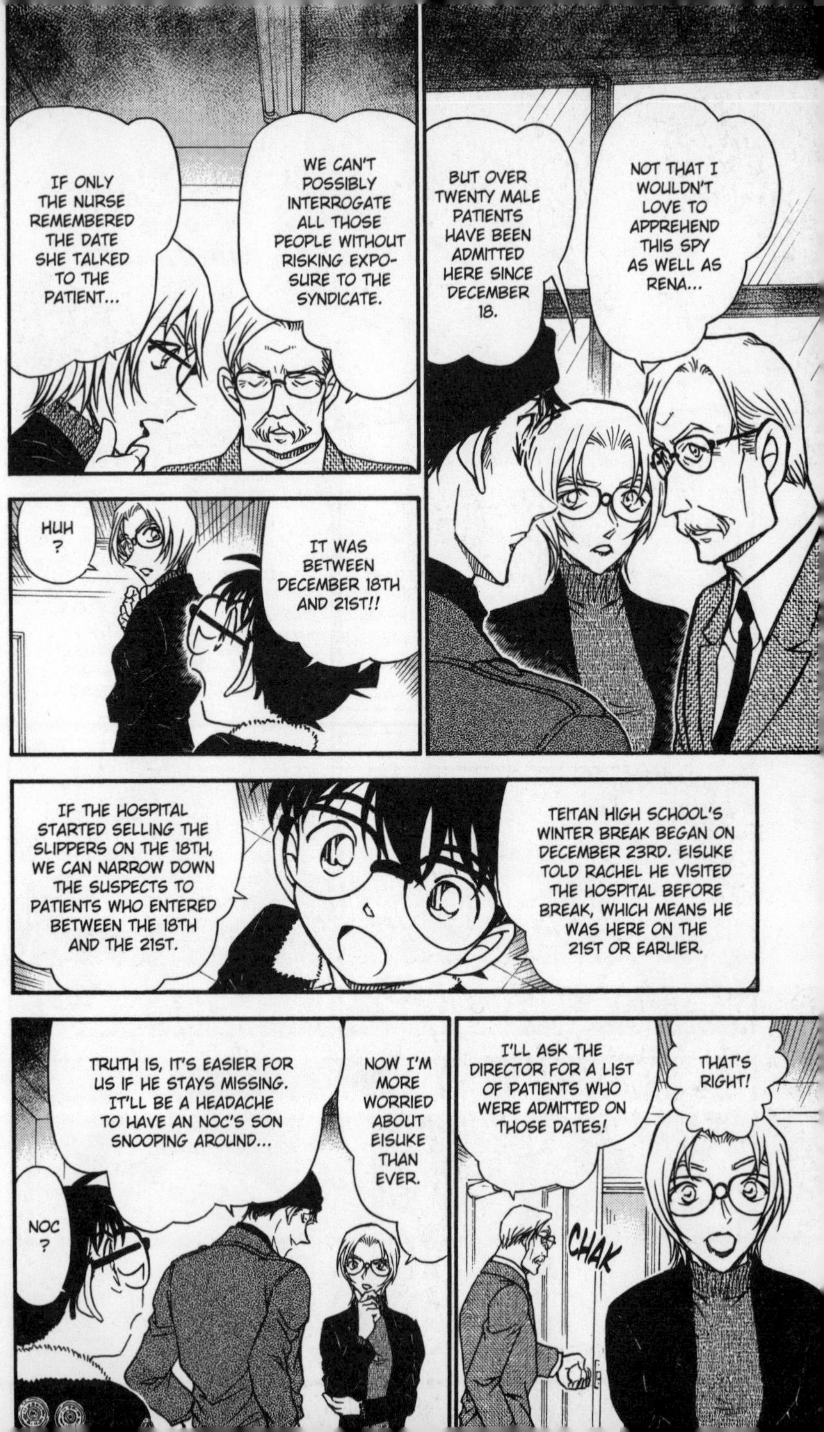
NOT THAT I WOULDN'T LOVE TO APPREHEND THIS SPY AS WELL AS RENA...
BUT OVER TWENTY MALE PATIENTS HAVE BEEN ADMITTED HERE SINCE DECEMBER 18.
WE CAN'T POSSIBLY INTERROGATE ALL THOSE PEOPLE WITHOUT RISKING EXPOSURE TO THE SYNDICATE.
IF ONLY THE NURSE REMEMBERED THE DATE SHE TALKED TO THE PATIENT...
IT WAS BETWEEN DECEMBER 18TH AND 21ST!!
HUH?
TEITAN HIGH SCHOOL'S WINTER BREAK BEGAN ON DECEMBER 23RD. EISUKE TOLD RACHEL HE VISITED THE HOSPITAL BEFORE BREAK, WHICH MEANS HE WAS HERE ON THE 21ST OR EARLIER.
IF THE HOSPITAL STARTED SELLING THE SLIPPERS ON THE 18TH, WE CAN NARROW DOWN THE SUSPECTS TO PATIENTS WHO ENTERED BETWEEN THE 18TH AND THE 21ST.
THAT'S RIGHT!
I'LL ASK THE DIRECTOR FOR A LIST OF PATIENTS WHO WERE ADMITTED ON THOSE DATES!
CHAK
NOW I'M MORE WORRIED ABOUT EISUKE THAN EVER.
TRUTH IS, IT'S EASIER FOR US IF HE STAYS MISSING. IT'LL BE A HEADACHE TO HAVE AN NOC'S SON SNOOPING AROUND...
NOC?

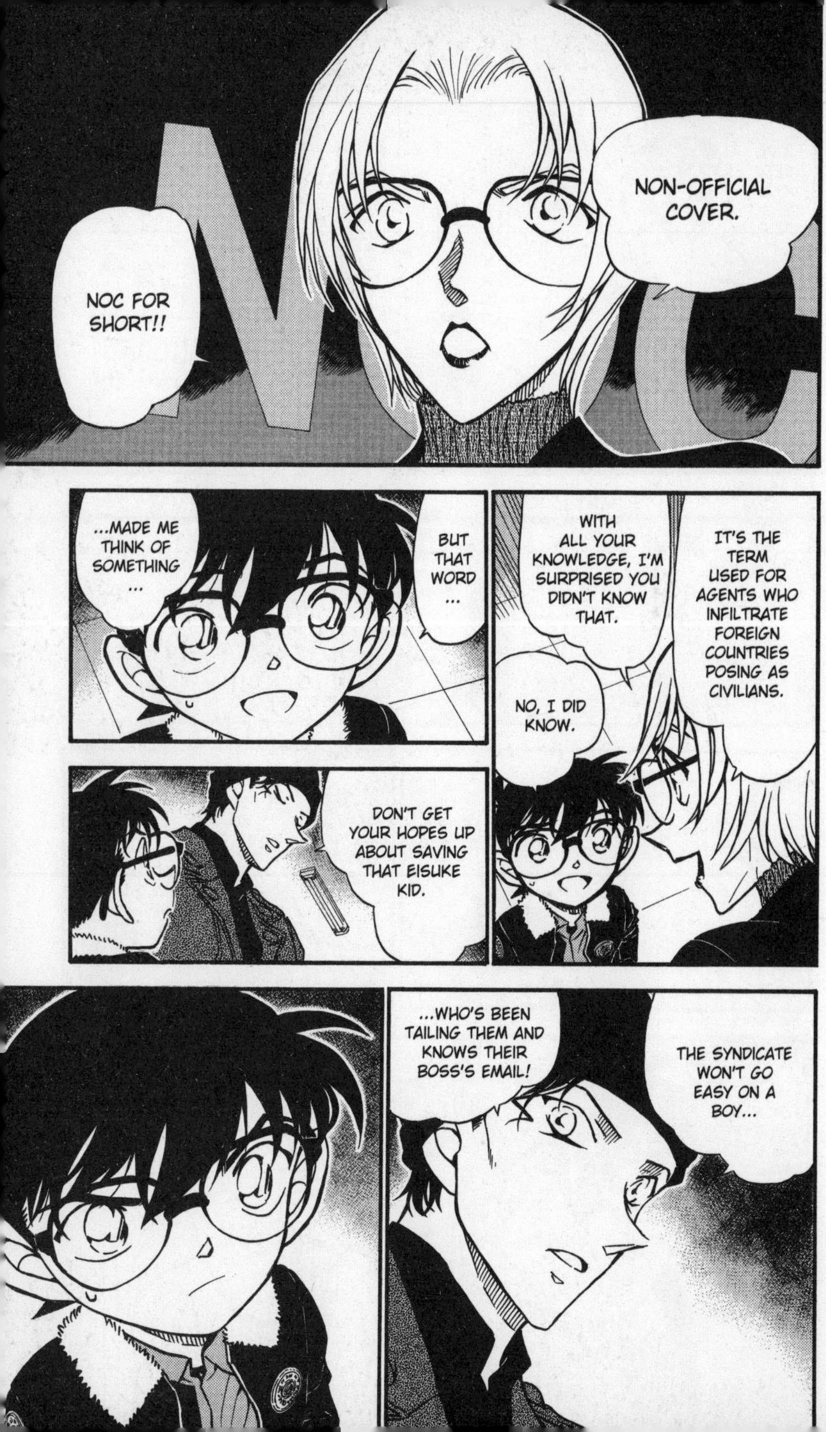
NON-OFFICIAL COVER.
NOC FOR SHORT!!
IT'S THE TERM USED FOR AGENTS WHO INFILTRATE FOREIGN COUNTRIES POSING AS CIVILIANS.
WITH ALL YOUR KNOWLEDGE, I'M SURPRISED YOU DIDN'T KNOW THAT.
NO, I DID KNOW.
BUT THAT WORD ...
...MADE ME THINK OF SOMETHING ...
DON'T GET YOUR HOPES UP ABOUT SAVING THAT EISUKE KID.
THE SYNDICATE WON'T GO EASY ON A BOY...
...WHO'S BEEN TAILING THEM AND KNOWS THEIR BOSS'S EMAIL!

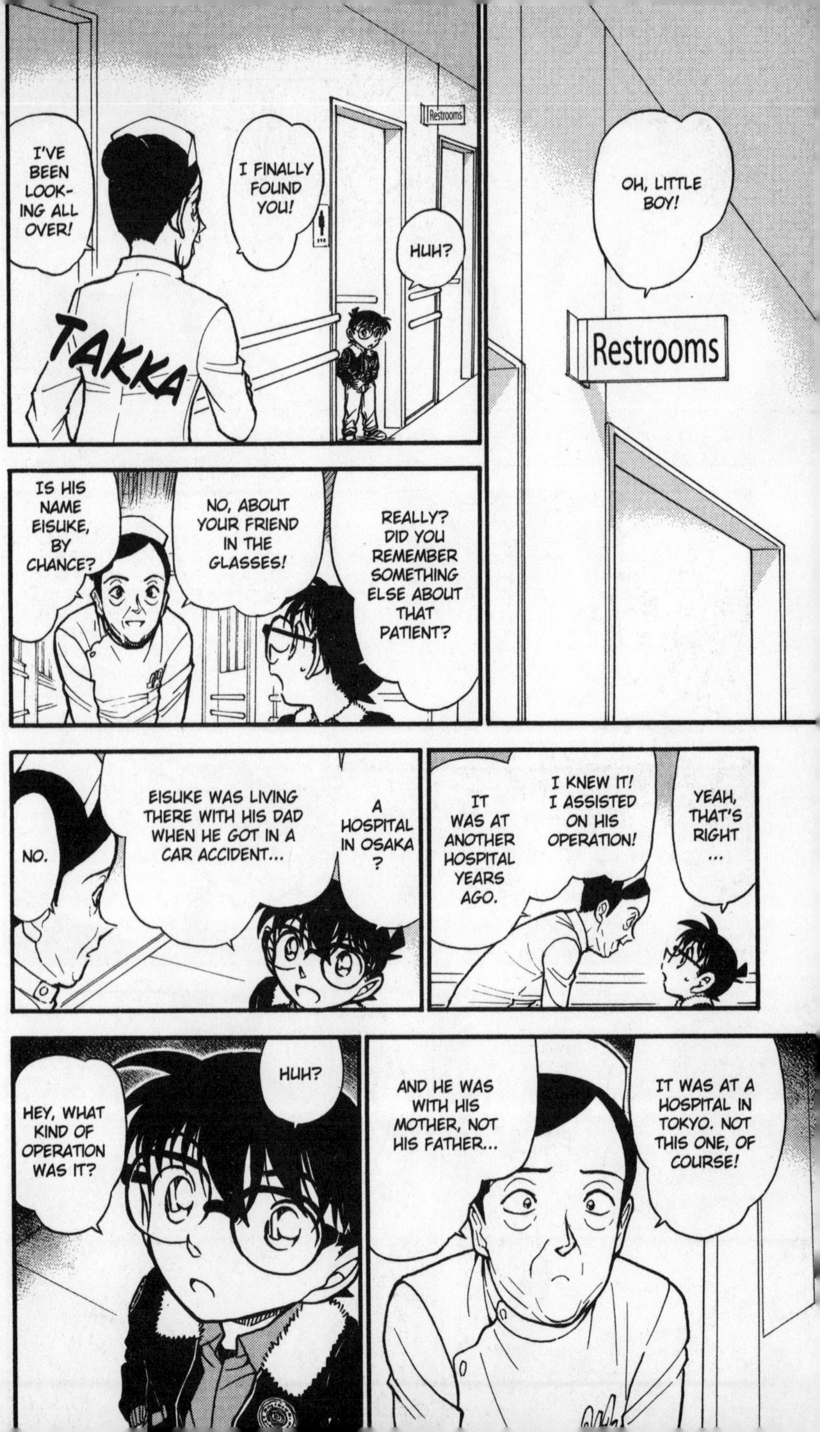
OH, LITTLE BOY!
Restrooms
HUH?
I FINALLY FOUND YOU!
I'VE BEEN LOOK-ING ALL OVER!
TAKKA
Restrooms
REALLY? DID YOU REMEMBER SOMETHING ELSE ABOUT THAT PATIENT?
NO, ABOUT YOUR FRIEND IN THE GLASSES!
IS HIS NAME EISUKE, BY CHANCE?
YEAH, THAT'S RIGHT...
I KNEW IT! I ASSISTED ON HIS OPERATION!
IT WAS AT ANOTHER HOSPITAL YEARS AGO.
A HOSPITAL IN OSAKA?
EISUKE WAS LIVING THERE WITH HIS DAD WHEN HE GOT IN A CAR ACCIDENT...
NO.
IT WAS AT A HOSPITAL IN TOKYO. NOT THIS ONE, OF COURSE!
AND HE WAS WITH HIS MOTHER, NOT HIS FATHER...
HUH?
HEY, WHAT KIND OF OPERATION WAS IT?

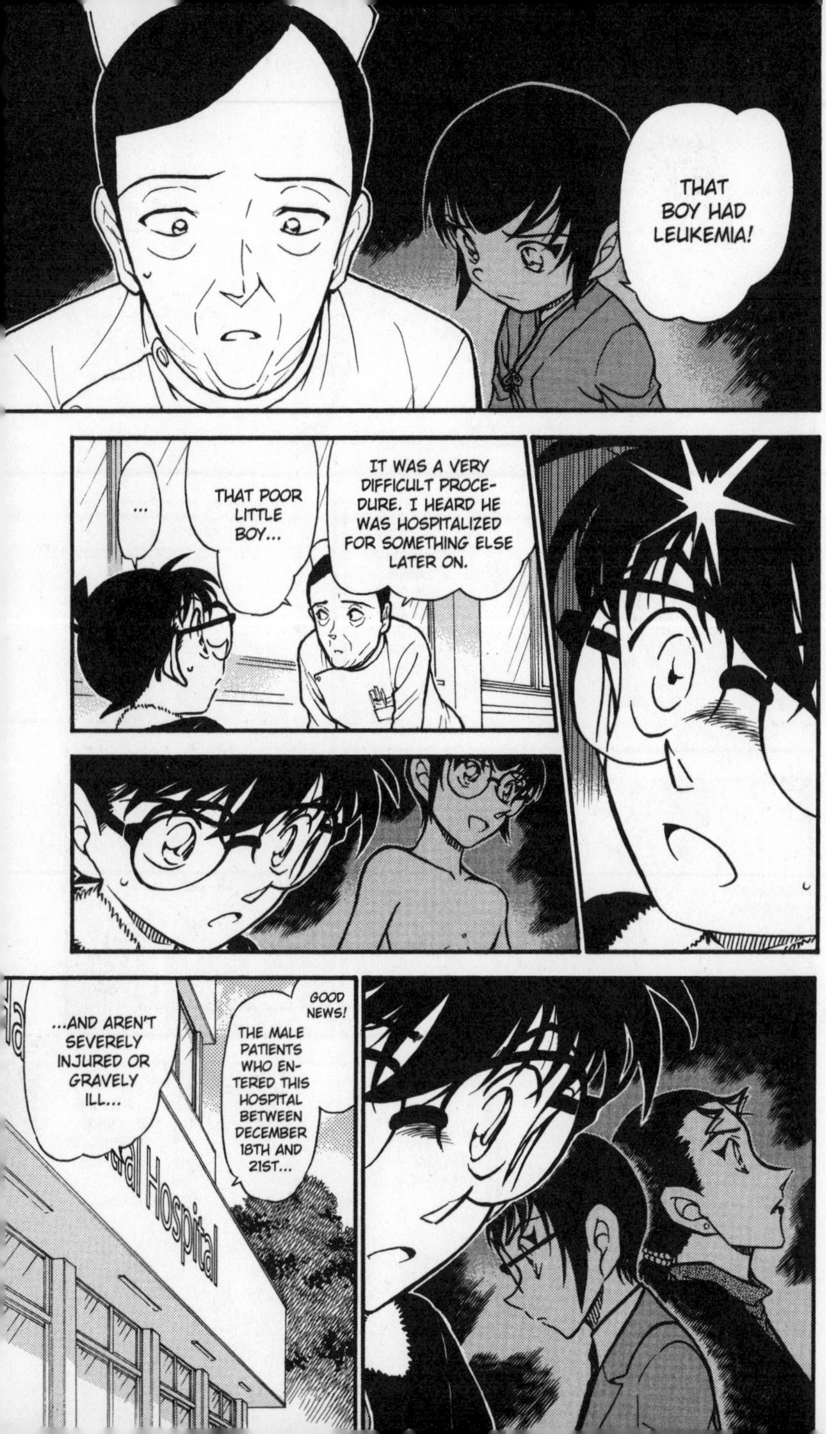
THAT BOY HAD LEUKEMIA!
IT WAS A VERY DIFFICULT PROCEDURE. I HEARD HE WAS HOSPITALIZED FOR SOMETHING ELSE LATER ON.
THAT POOR LITTLE BOY...
...
GOOD NEWS!
THE MALE PATIENTS WHO ENTERED THIS HOSPITAL BETWEEN DECEMBER 18TH AND 21ST...
...AND AREN'T SEVERELY INJURED OR GRAVELY ILL...

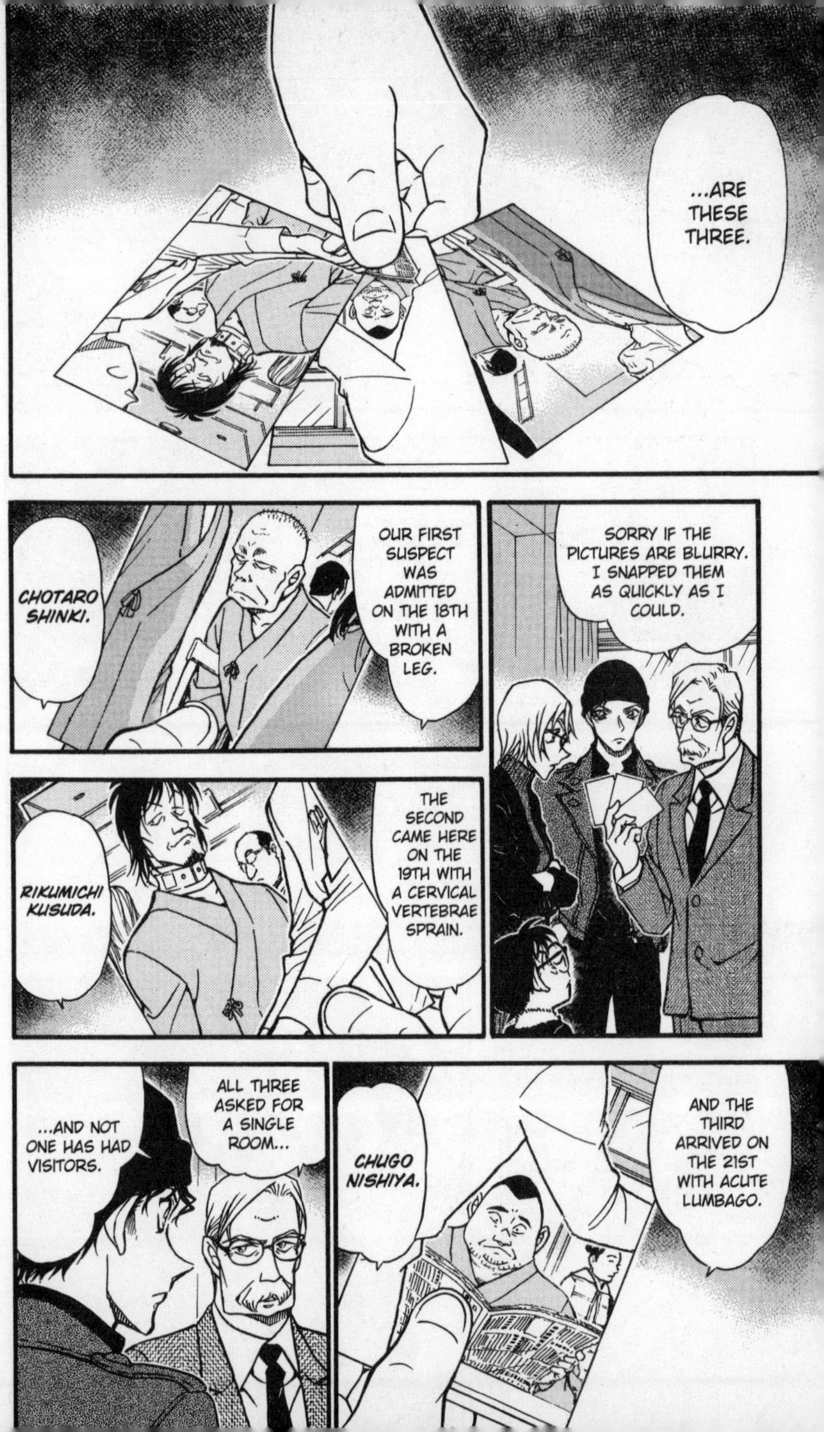
...ARE THESE THREE.
SORRY IF THE PICTURES ARE BLURRY. I SNAPPED THEM AS QUICKLY AS I COULD.
OUR FIRST SUSPECT WAS ADMITTED ON THE 18TH WITH A BROKEN LEG.
CHOTARO SHINKI.
THE SECOND CAME HERE ON THE 19TH WITH A CERVICAL VERTEBRAE SPRAIN.
RIKUMICHI KUSUDA.
AND THE THIRD ARRIVED ON THE 21ST WITH ACUTE LUMBAGO.
CHUGO NISHIYA.
ALL THREE ASKED FOR A SINGLE ROOM...
...AND NOT ONE HAS HAD VISITORS.

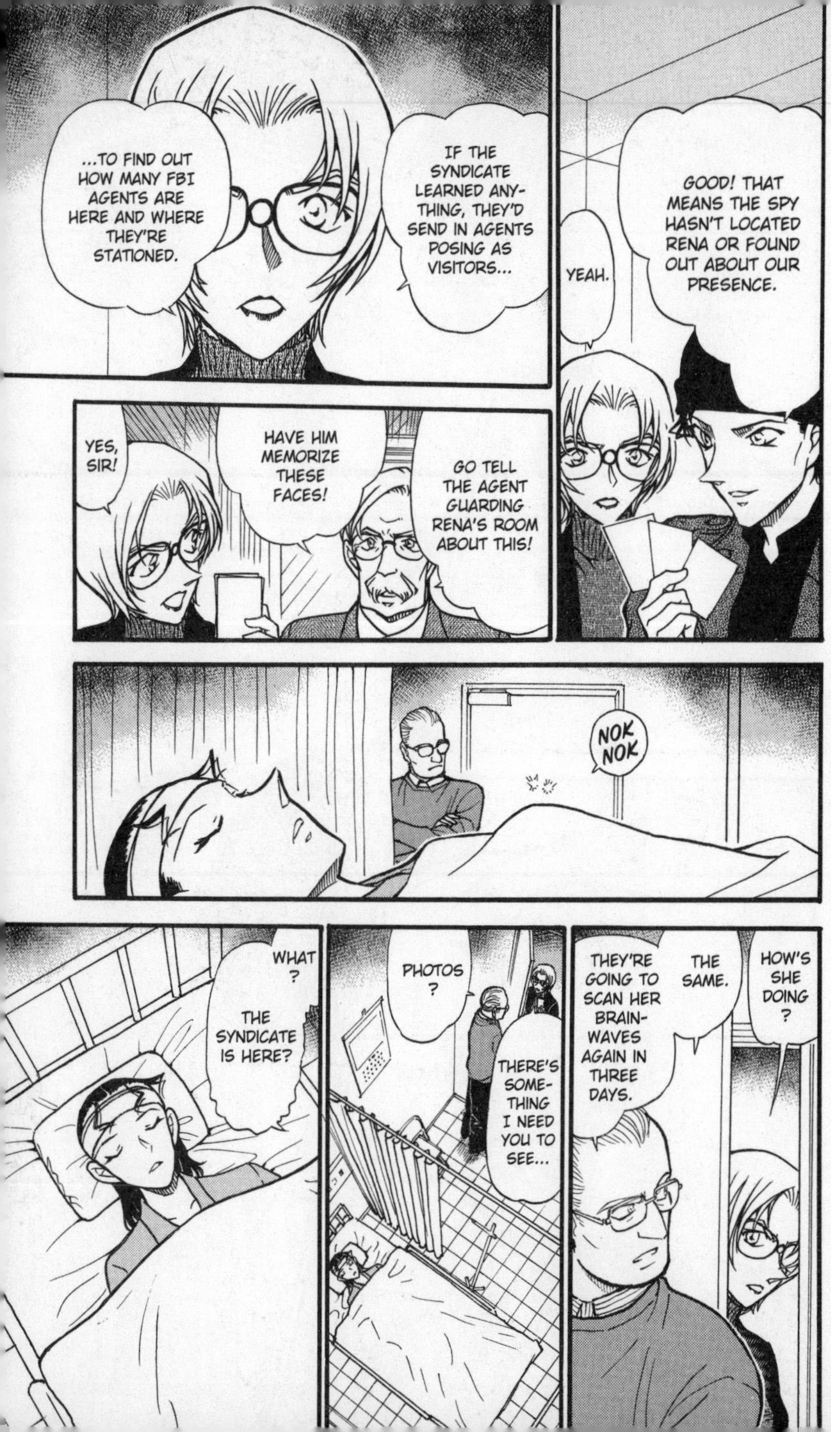
GOOD! THAT MEANS THE SPY HASN'T LOCATED RENA OR FOUND OUT ABOUT OUR PRESENCE.
YEAH.
IF THE SYNDICATE LEARNED ANY-THING, THEY'D SEND IN AGENTS POSING AS VISITORS...
...TO FIND OUT HOW MANY FBI AGENTS ARE HERE AND WHERE THEY'RE STATIONED.
GO TELL THE AGENT GUARDING RENA'S ROOM ABOUT THIS!
HAVE HIM MEMORIZE THESE FACES!
YES, SIR!
NOK NOK
HOW'S SHE DOING?
THE SAME.
THEY'RE GOING TO SCAN HER BRAIN-WAVES AGAIN IN THREE DAYS.
THERE'S SOME-THING I NEED YOU TO SEE...
PHOTOS?
WHAT?
THE SYNDICATE IS HERE?

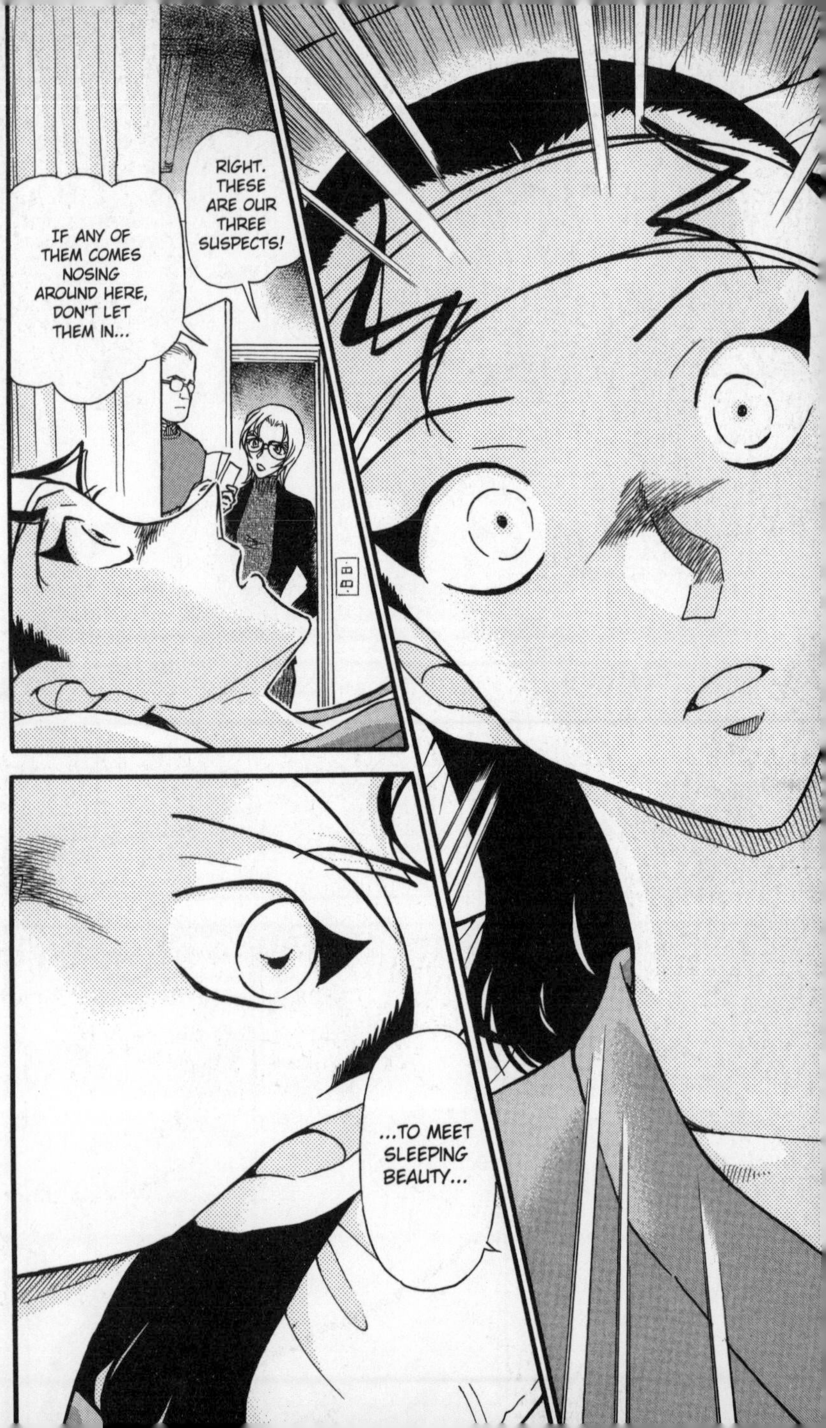
RIGHT. THESE ARE OUR THREE SUSPECTS!
IF ANY OF THEM COMES NOSING AROUND HERE, DON'T LET THEM IN...
...TO MEET SLEEPING BEAUTY...

THE FALSE PATIENT

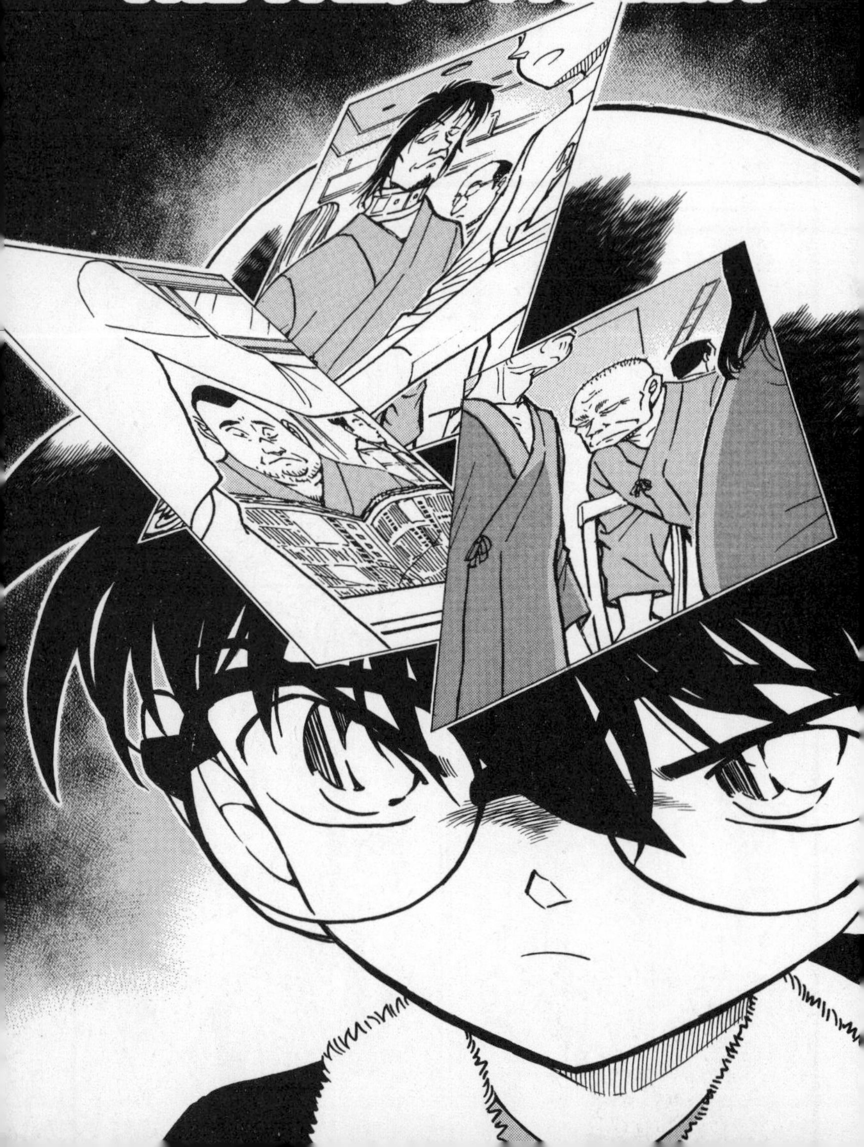

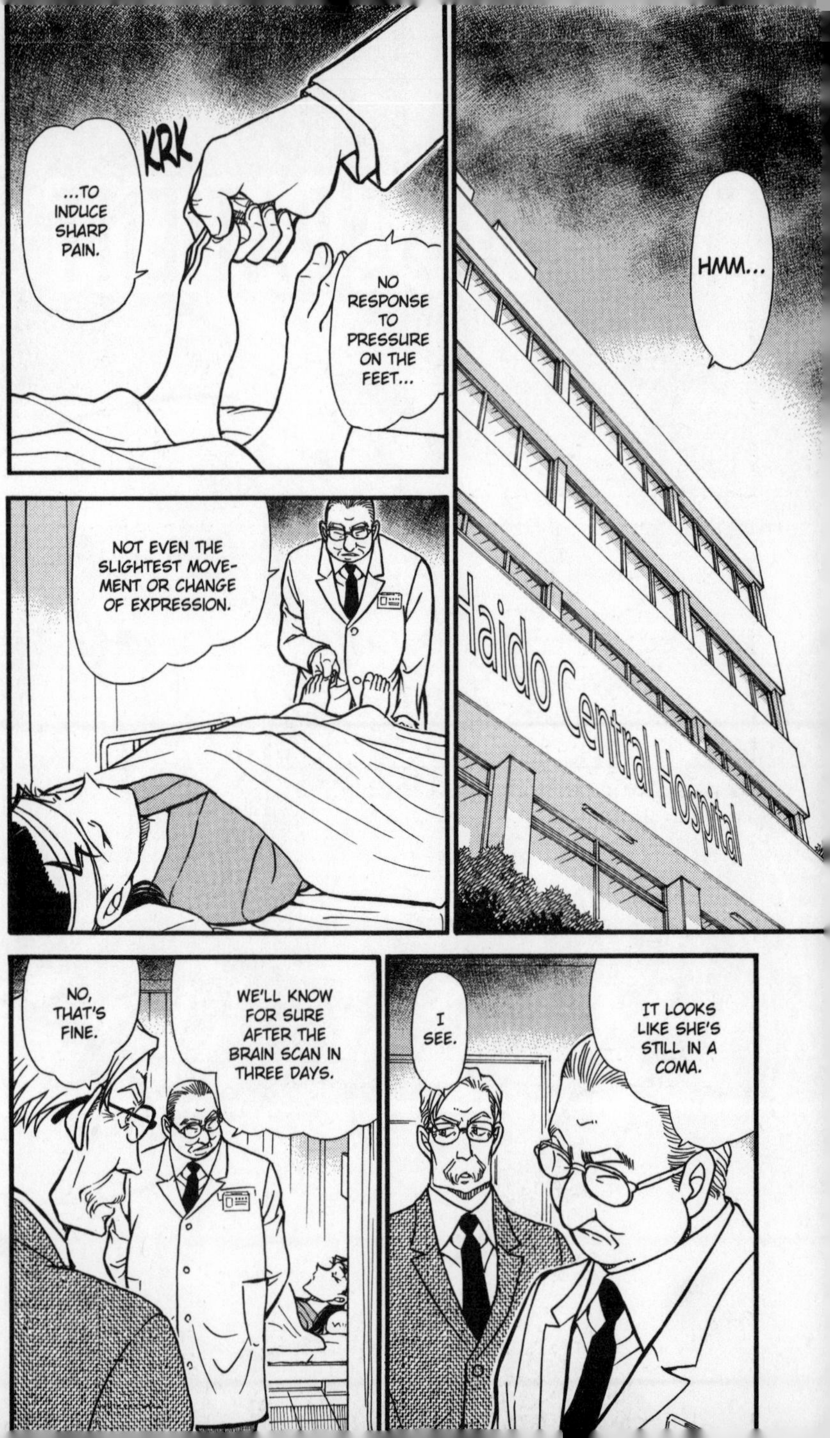
HMM...
Haido Central Hospital
NO RESPONSE TO PRESSURE ON THE FEET...
KRK
...TO INDUCE SHARP PAIN.
NOT EVEN THE SLIGHTEST MOVEMENT OR CHANGE OF EXPRESSION.
IT LOOKS LIKE SHE'S STILL IN A COMA.
I SEE.
WE'LL KNOW FOR SURE AFTER THE BRAIN SCAN IN THREE DAYS.
NO, THAT'S FINE.

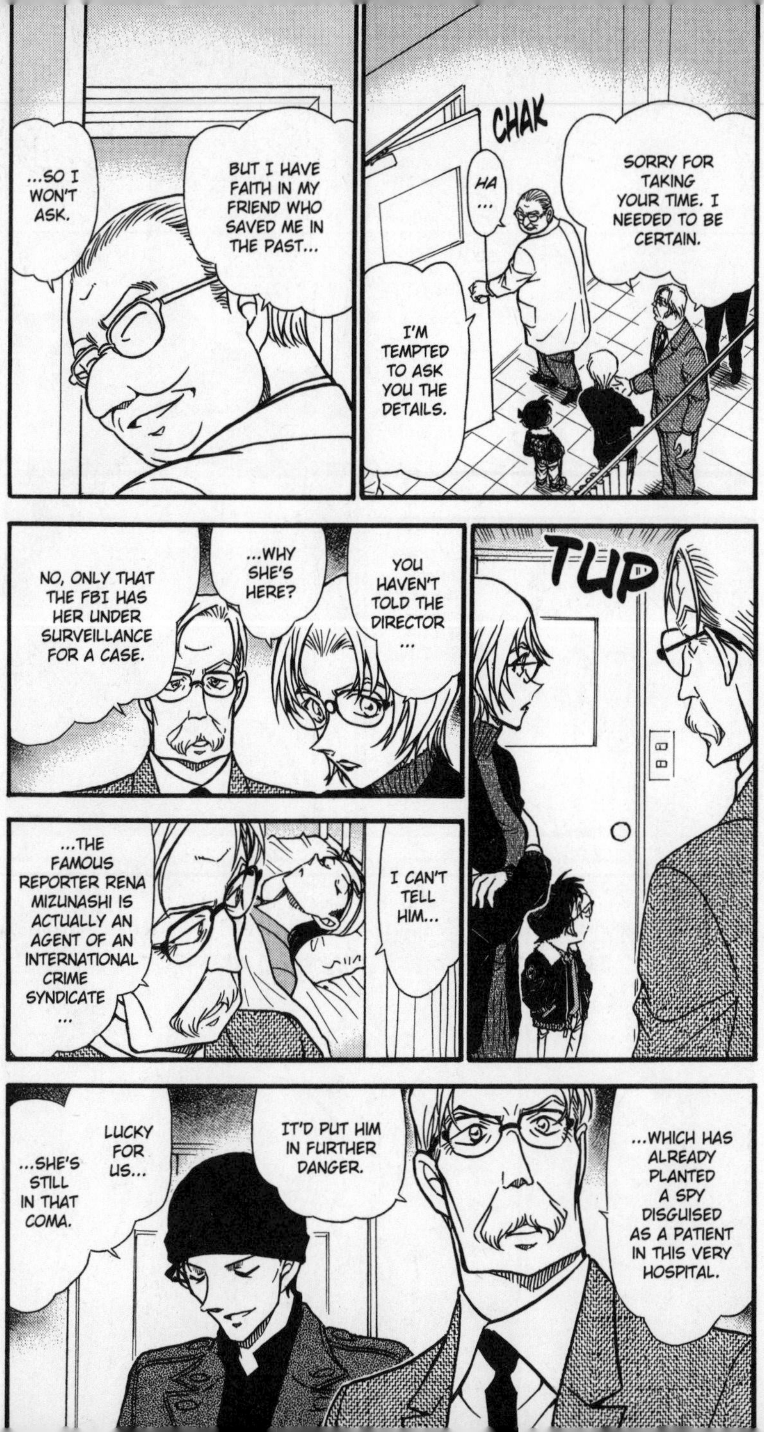
CHAK
SORRY FOR TAKING YOUR TIME. I NEEDED TO BE CERTAIN.
HA ...
I'M TEMPTED TO ASK YOU THE DETAILS.
BUT I HAVE FAITH IN MY FRIEND WHO SAVED ME IN THE PAST...
...SO I WON'T ASK.
TUP
YOU HAVEN'T TOLD THE DIRECTOR ...
...WHY SHE'S HERE?
NO, ONLY THAT THE FBI HAS HER UNDER SURVEILLANCE FOR A CASE.
I CAN'T TELL HIM...
...THE FAMOUS REPORTER RENA MIZUNASHI IS ACTUALLY AN AGENT OF AN INTERNATIONAL CRIME SYNDICATE ...
...WHICH HAS ALREADY PLANTED A SPY DISGUISED AS A PATIENT IN THIS VERY HOSPITAL.
IT'D PUT HIM IN FURTHER DANGER.
LUCKY FOR US...
...SHE'S STILL IN THAT COMA.

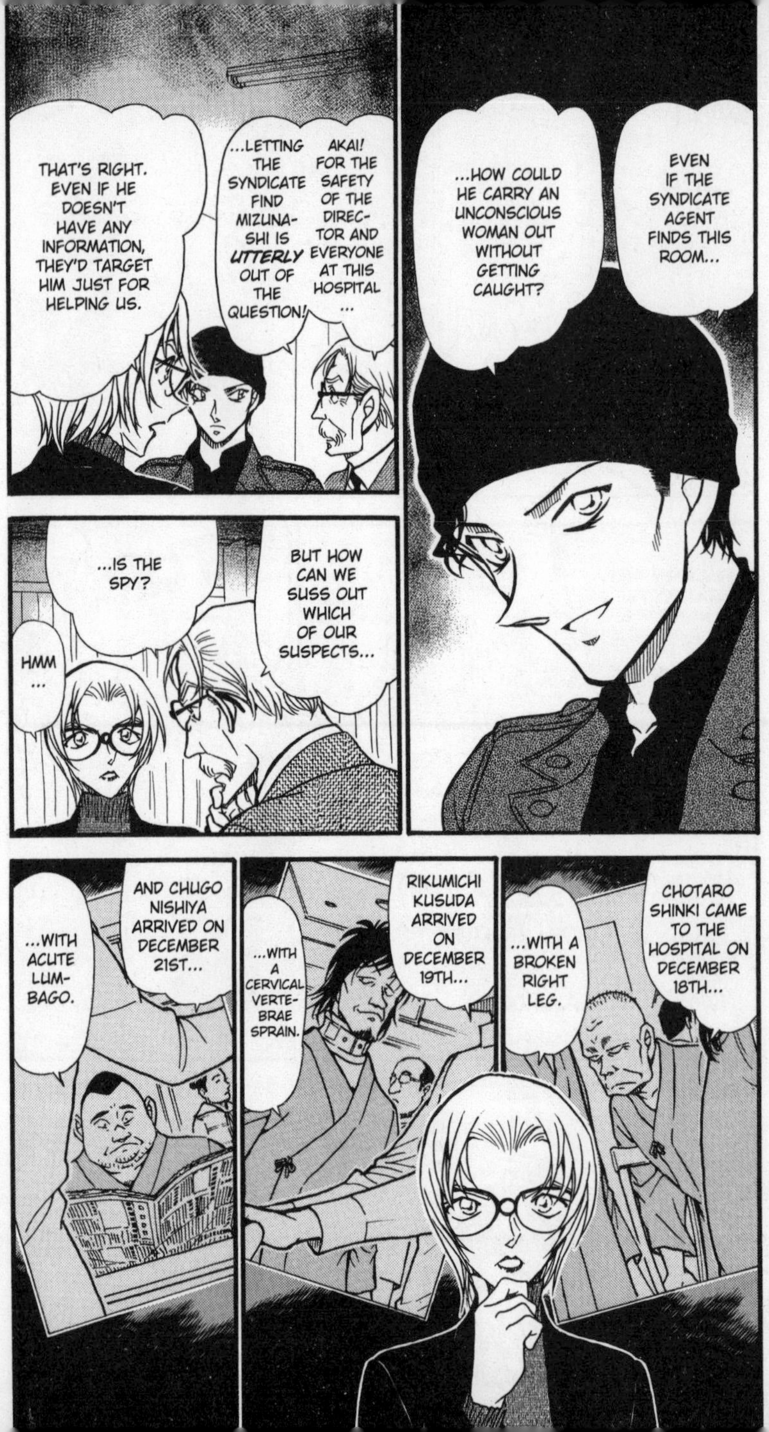
EVEN IF THE SYNDICATE AGENT FINDS THIS ROOM...
...HOW COULD HE CARRY AN UNCONSCIOUS WOMAN OUT WITHOUT GETTING CAUGHT?
AKAI! FOR THE SAFETY OF THE DIREC-TOR AND EVERYONE AT THIS HOSPITAL...
...LETTING THE SYNDICATE FIND MIZUNA-SHI IS *UTTERLY* OUT OF THE QUESTION!
THAT'S RIGHT. EVEN IF HE DOESN'T HAVE ANY INFORMATION, THEY'D TARGET HIM JUST FOR HELPING US.
BUT HOW CAN WE SUSS OUT WHICH OF OUR SUSPECTS...
...IS THE SPY?
HMM...
CHOTARO SHINKI CAME TO THE HOSPITAL ON DECEMBER 18TH...
...WITH A BROKEN RIGHT LEG.
RIKUMICHI KUSUDA ARRIVED ON DECEMBER 19TH...
...WITH A CERVICAL VERTE-BRAE SPRAIN.
AND CHUGO NISHIYA ARRIVED ON DECEMBER 21ST...
...WITH ACUTE LUM-BAGO.

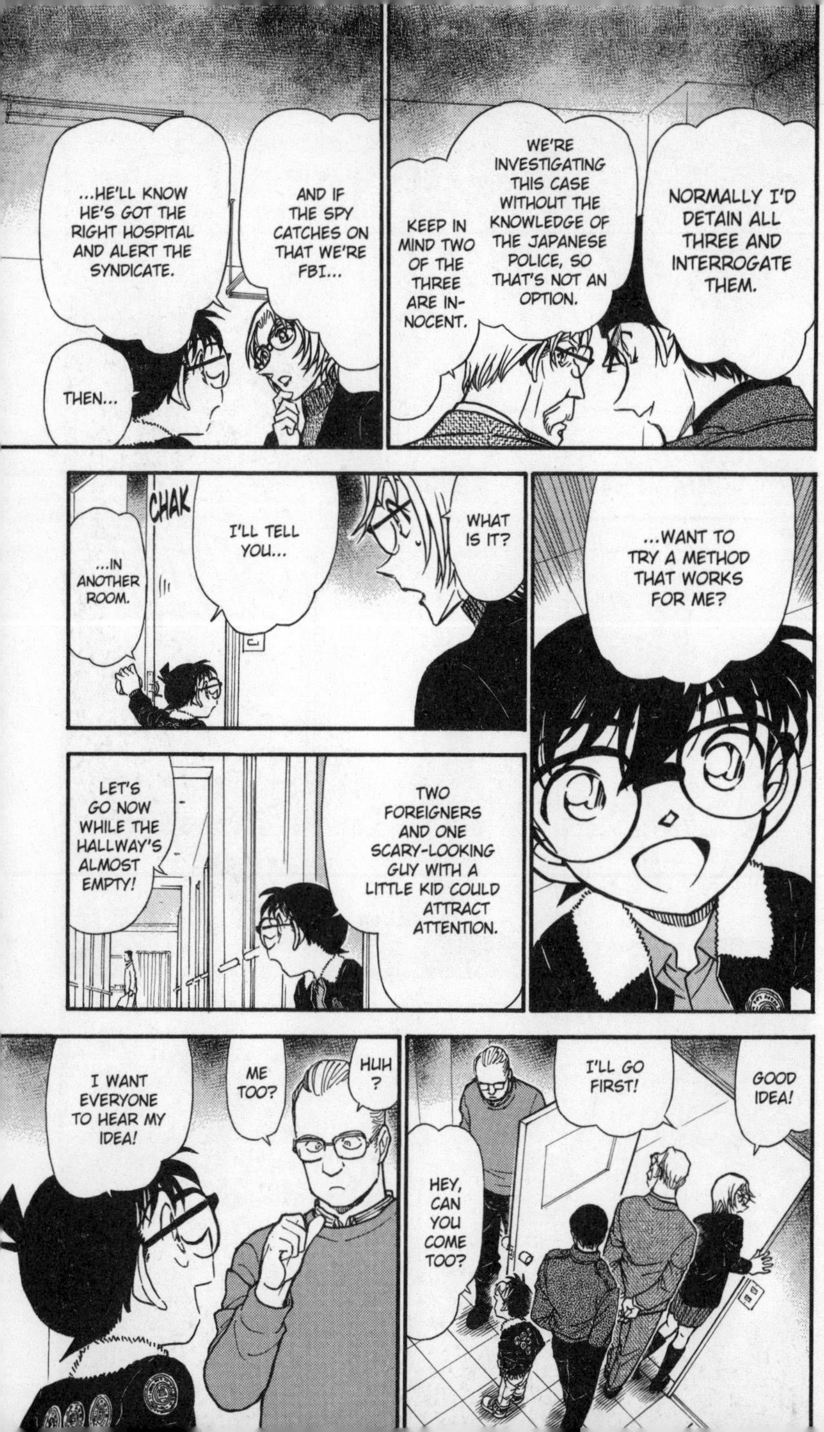
NORMALLY I'D DETAIN ALL THREE AND INTERROGATE THEM.
WE'RE INVESTIGATING THIS CASE WITHOUT THE KNOWLEDGE OF THE JAPANESE POLICE, SO THAT'S NOT AN OPTION.
KEEP IN MIND TWO OF THE THREE ARE IN-NOCENT.
AND IF THE SPY CATCHES ON THAT WE'RE FBI...
...HE'LL KNOW HE'S GOT THE RIGHT HOSPITAL AND ALERT THE SYNDICATE.
THEN...
...WANT TO TRY A METHOD THAT WORKS FOR ME?
WHAT IS IT?
I'LL TELL YOU...
CHAK
...IN ANOTHER ROOM.
TWO FOREIGNERS AND ONE SCARY-LOOKING GUY WITH A LITTLE KID COULD ATTRACT ATTENTION.
LET'S GO NOW WHILE THE HALLWAY'S ALMOST EMPTY!
GOOD IDEA!
I'LL GO FIRST!
HEY, CAN YOU COME TOO?
HUH?
ME TOO?
I WANT EVERYONE TO HEAR MY IDEA!

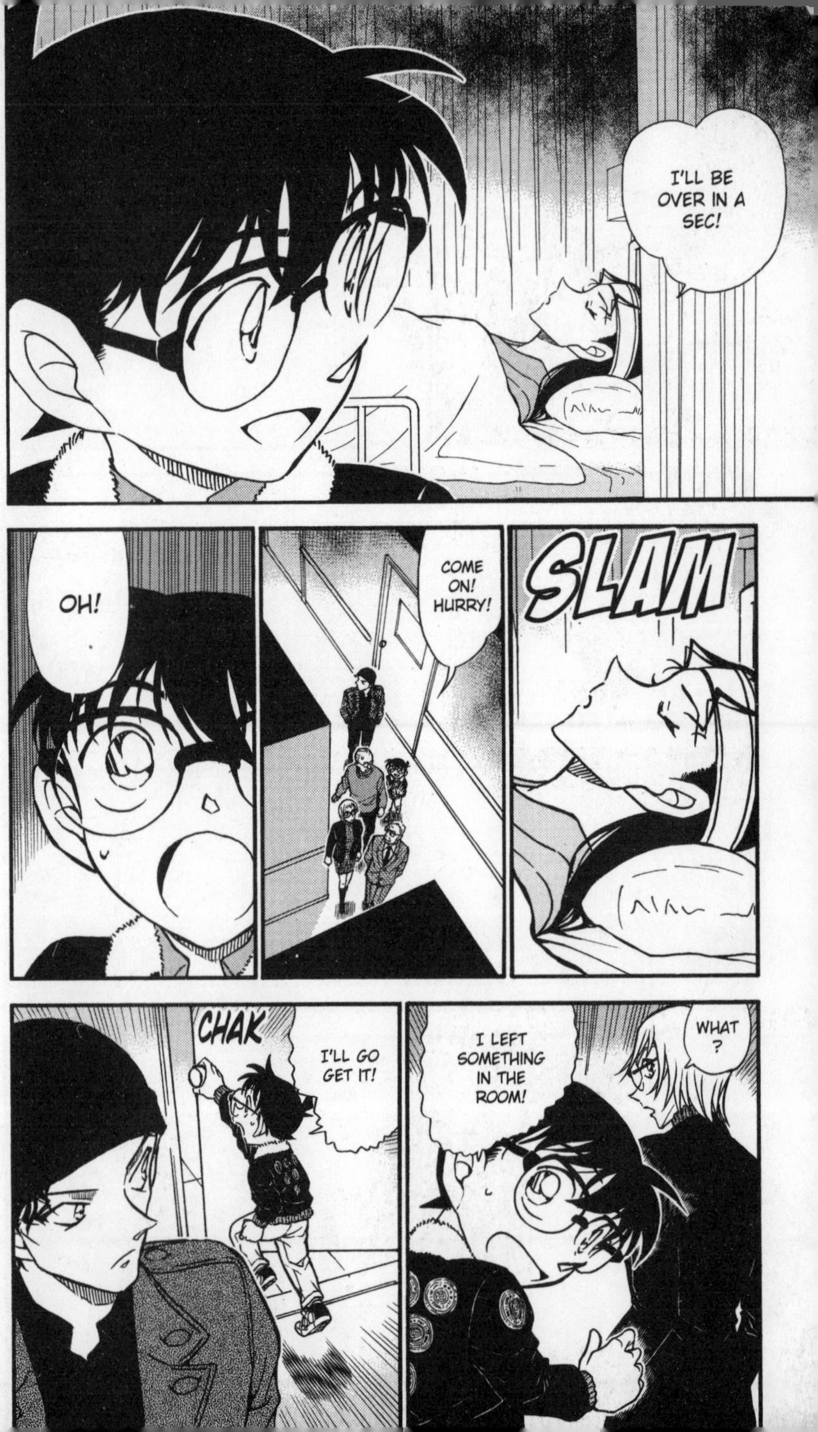
I'LL BE OVER IN A SEC!
SLAM
COME ON! HURRY!
OH!
WHAT ?
I LEFT SOMETHING IN THE ROOM!
CHAK
I'LL GO GET IT!

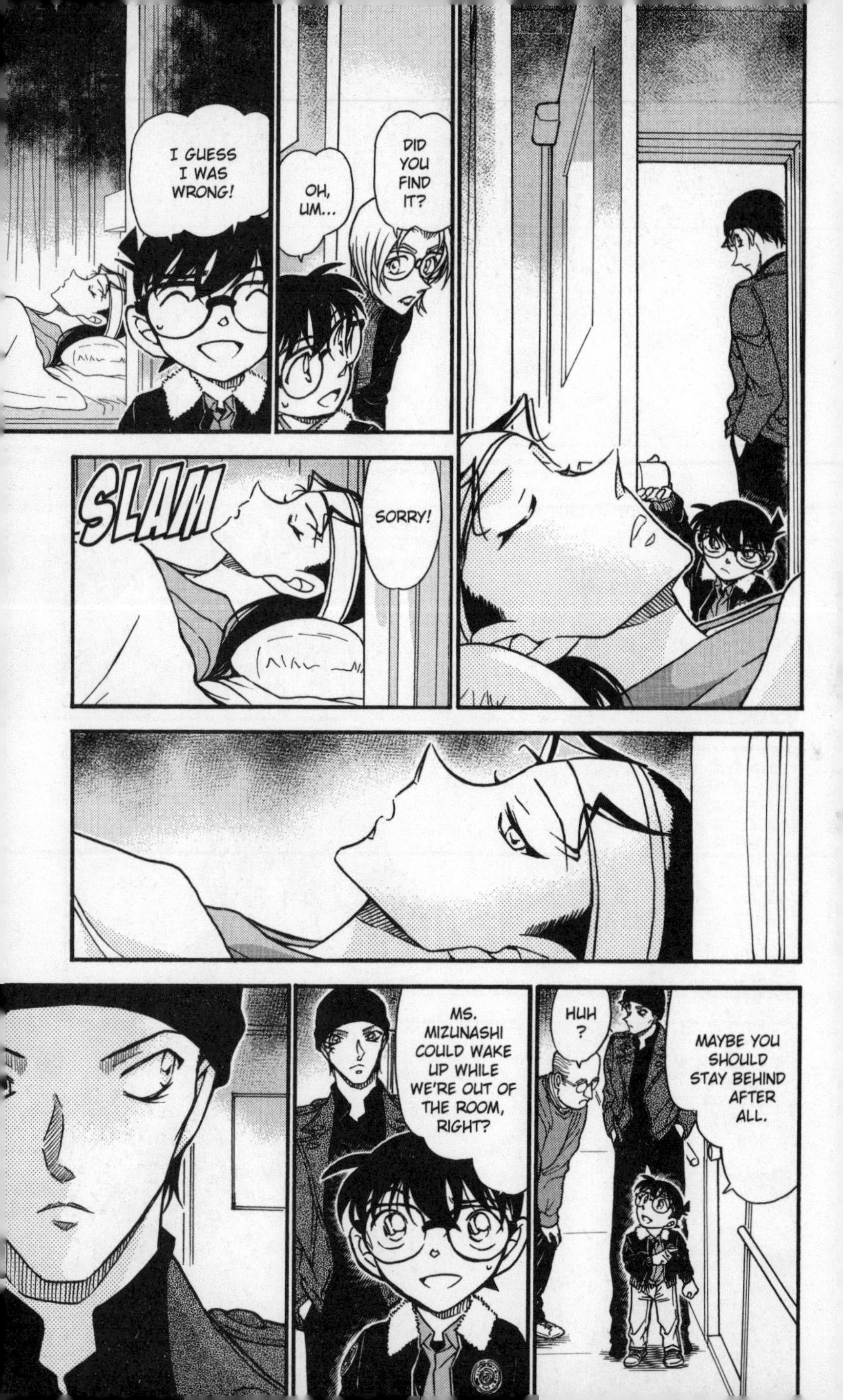
DID YOU FIND IT?
OH, UM...
I GUESS I WAS WRONG!
SORRY!
SLAM
MAYBE YOU SHOULD STAY BEHIND AFTER ALL.
HUH?
MS. MIZUNASHI COULD WAKE UP WHILE WE'RE OUT OF THE ROOM, RIGHT?

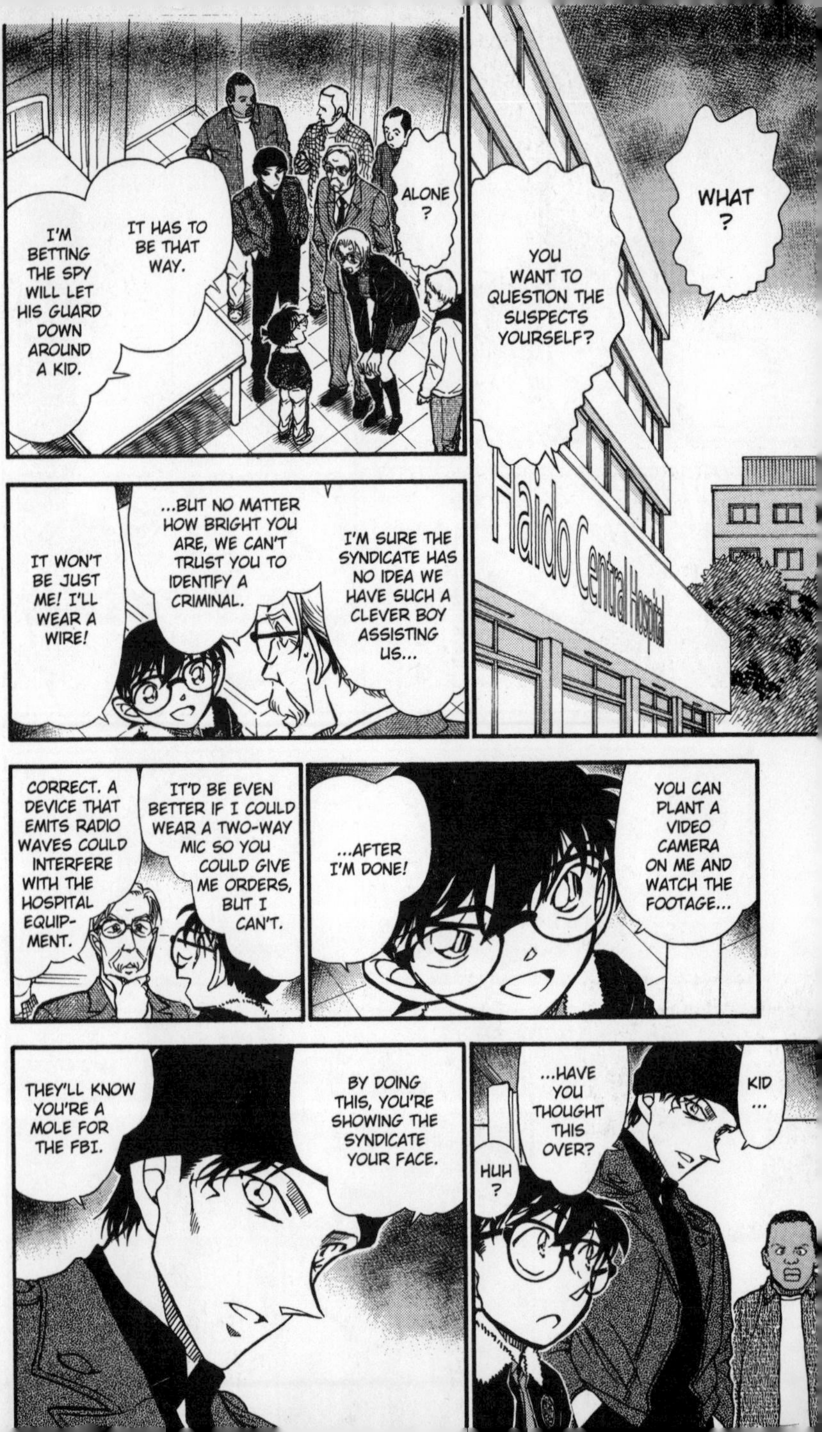
WHAT?
YOU WANT TO QUESTION THE SUSPECTS YOURSELF?
Haido Central Hospital
ALONE?
IT HAS TO BE THAT WAY.
I'M BETTING THE SPY WILL LET HIS GUARD DOWN AROUND A KID.
I'M SURE THE SYNDICATE HAS NO IDEA WE HAVE SUCH A CLEVER BOY ASSISTING US...
...BUT NO MATTER HOW BRIGHT YOU ARE, WE CAN'T TRUST YOU TO IDENTIFY A CRIMINAL.
IT WON'T BE JUST ME! I'LL WEAR A WIRE!
YOU CAN PLANT A VIDEO CAMERA ON ME AND WATCH THE FOOTAGE...
...AFTER I'M DONE!
IT'D BE EVEN BETTER IF I COULD WEAR A TWO-WAY MIC SO YOU COULD GIVE ME ORDERS, BUT I CAN'T.
CORRECT. A DEVICE THAT EMITS RADIO WAVES COULD INTERFERE WITH THE HOSPITAL EQUIPMENT.
KID...
...HAVE YOU THOUGHT THIS OVER?
HUH?
BY DOING THIS, YOU'RE SHOWING THE SYNDICATE YOUR FACE.
THEY'LL KNOW YOU'RE A MOLE FOR THE FBI.

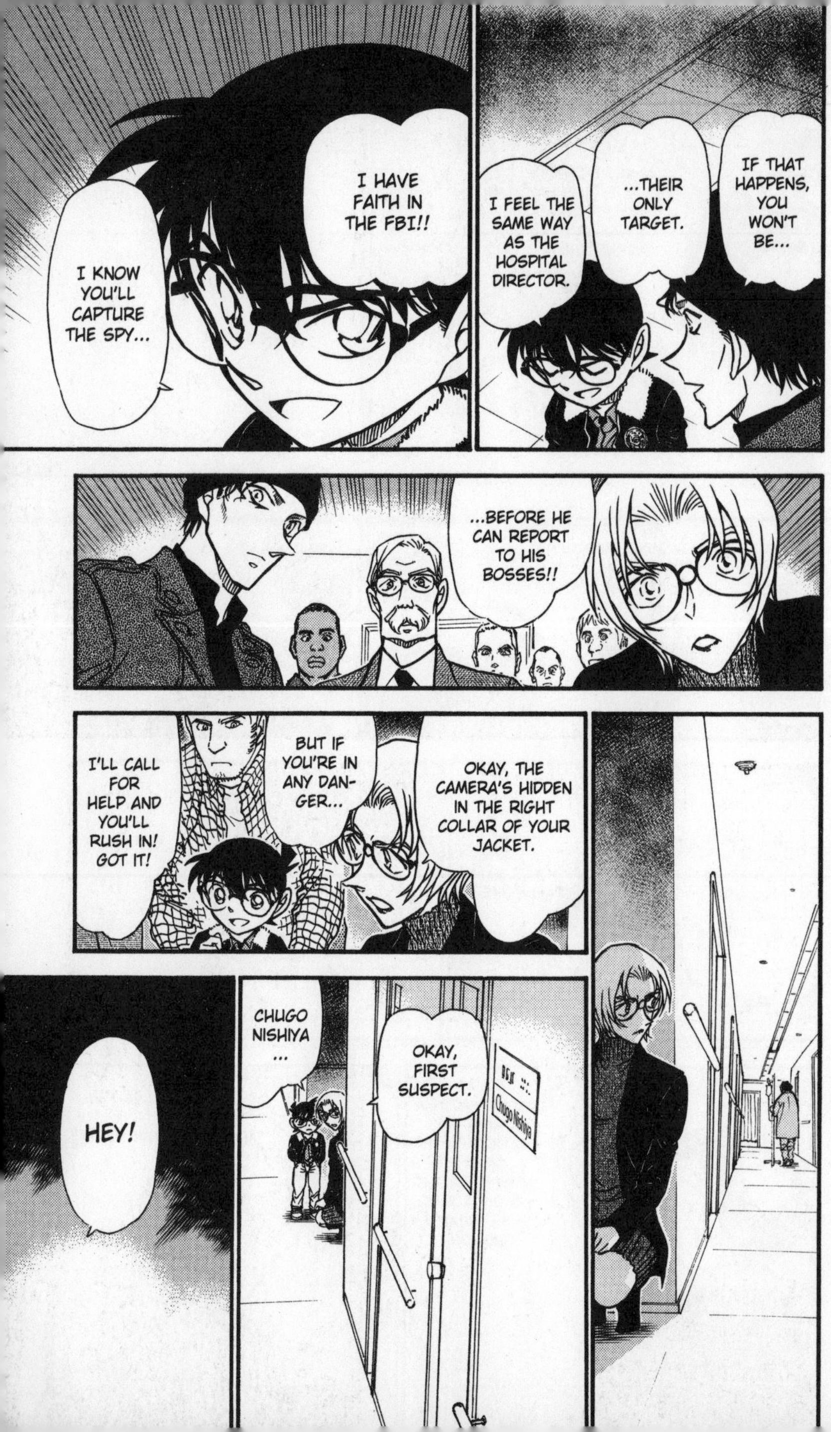
IF THAT HAPPENS, YOU WON'T BE...
...THEIR ONLY TARGET.
I FEEL THE SAME WAY AS THE HOSPITAL DIRECTOR.
I HAVE FAITH IN THE FBI!!
I KNOW YOU'LL CAPTURE THE SPY...
...BEFORE HE CAN REPORT TO HIS BOSSES!!
OKAY, THE CAMERA'S HIDDEN IN THE RIGHT COLLAR OF YOUR JACKET.
BUT IF YOU'RE IN ANY DAN-GER...
I'LL CALL FOR HELP AND YOU'LL RUSH IN! GOT IT!
Chugo Nishiya
OKAY, FIRST SUSPECT.
CHUGO NISHIYA ...
HEY!

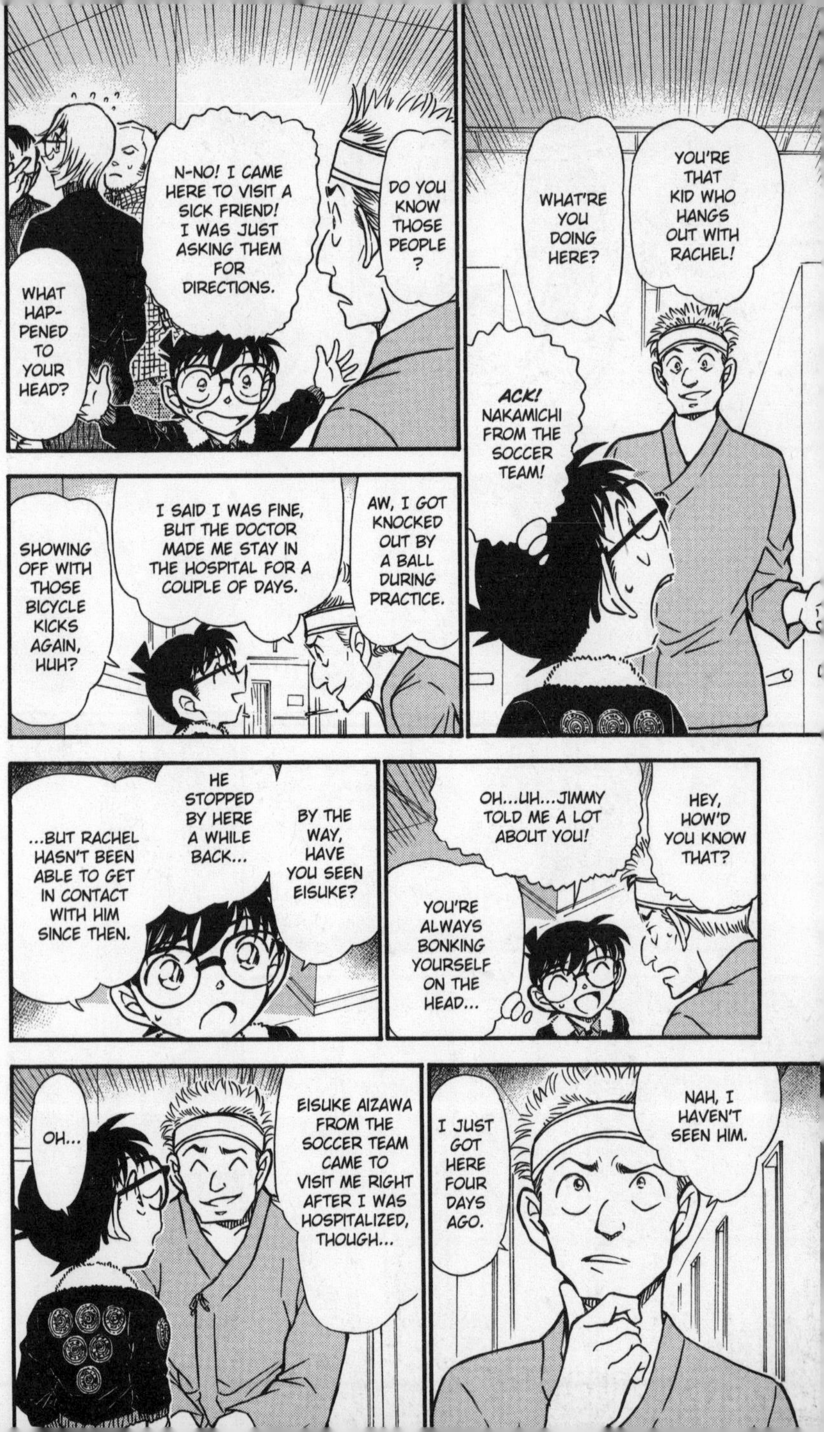
YOU'RE THAT KID WHO HANGS OUT WITH RACHEL!
WHAT'RE YOU DOING HERE?
ACK! NAKAMICHI FROM THE SOCCER TEAM!
DO YOU KNOW THOSE PEOPLE?
N-NO! I CAME HERE TO VISIT A SICK FRIEND! I WAS JUST ASKING THEM FOR DIRECTIONS.
WHAT HAP-PENED TO YOUR HEAD?
AW, I GOT KNOCKED OUT BY A BALL DURING PRACTICE.
I SAID I WAS FINE, BUT THE DOCTOR MADE ME STAY IN THE HOSPITAL FOR A COUPLE OF DAYS.
SHOWING OFF WITH THOSE BICYCLE KICKS AGAIN, HUH?
HEY, HOW'D YOU KNOW THAT?
OH...UH...JIMMY TOLD ME A LOT ABOUT YOU!
YOU'RE ALWAYS BONKING YOURSELF ON THE HEAD...
BY THE WAY, HAVE YOU SEEN EISUKE?
HE STOPPED BY HERE A WHILE BACK...
...BUT RACHEL HASN'T BEEN ABLE TO GET IN CONTACT WITH HIM SINCE THEN.
NAH, I HAVEN'T SEEN HIM.
I JUST GOT HERE FOUR DAYS AGO.
EISUKE AIZAWA FROM THE SOCCER TEAM CAME TO VISIT ME RIGHT AFTER I WAS HOSPITALIZED, THOUGH...
OH...

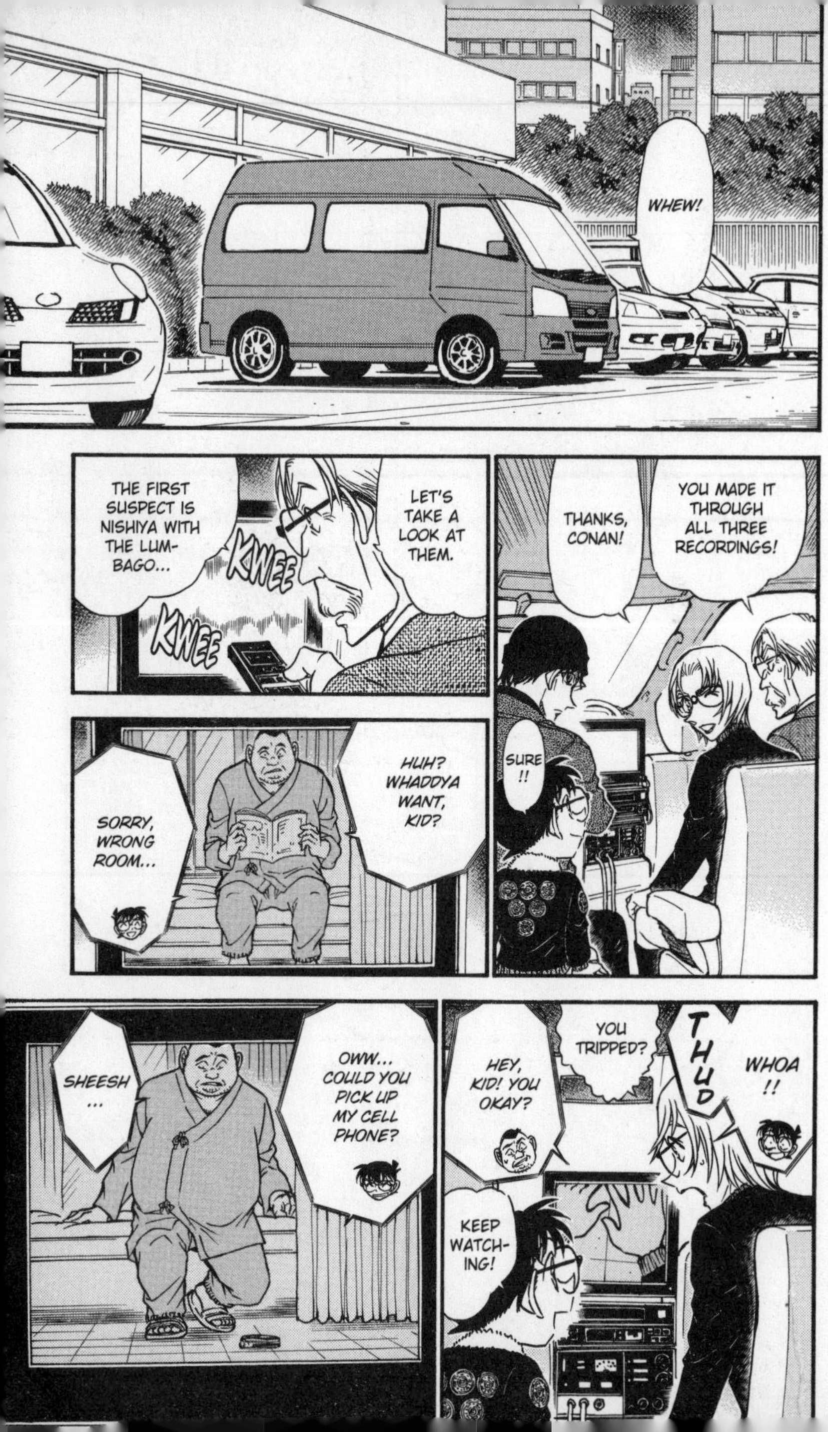

WHEW!
YOU MADE IT THROUGH ALL THREE RECORDINGS!
THANKS, CONAN!
SURE !!
LET'S TAKE A LOOK AT THEM.
THE FIRST SUSPECT IS NISHIYA WITH THE LUM-BAGO...
KWEE
KWEE
HUH? WHADDYA WANT, KID?
SORRY, WRONG ROOM...
WHOA !!
THUD
YOU TRIPPED?
HEY, KID! YOU OKAY?
KEEP WATCHING-ING!
OWW... COULD YOU PICK UP MY CELL PHONE?
SHEESH ...

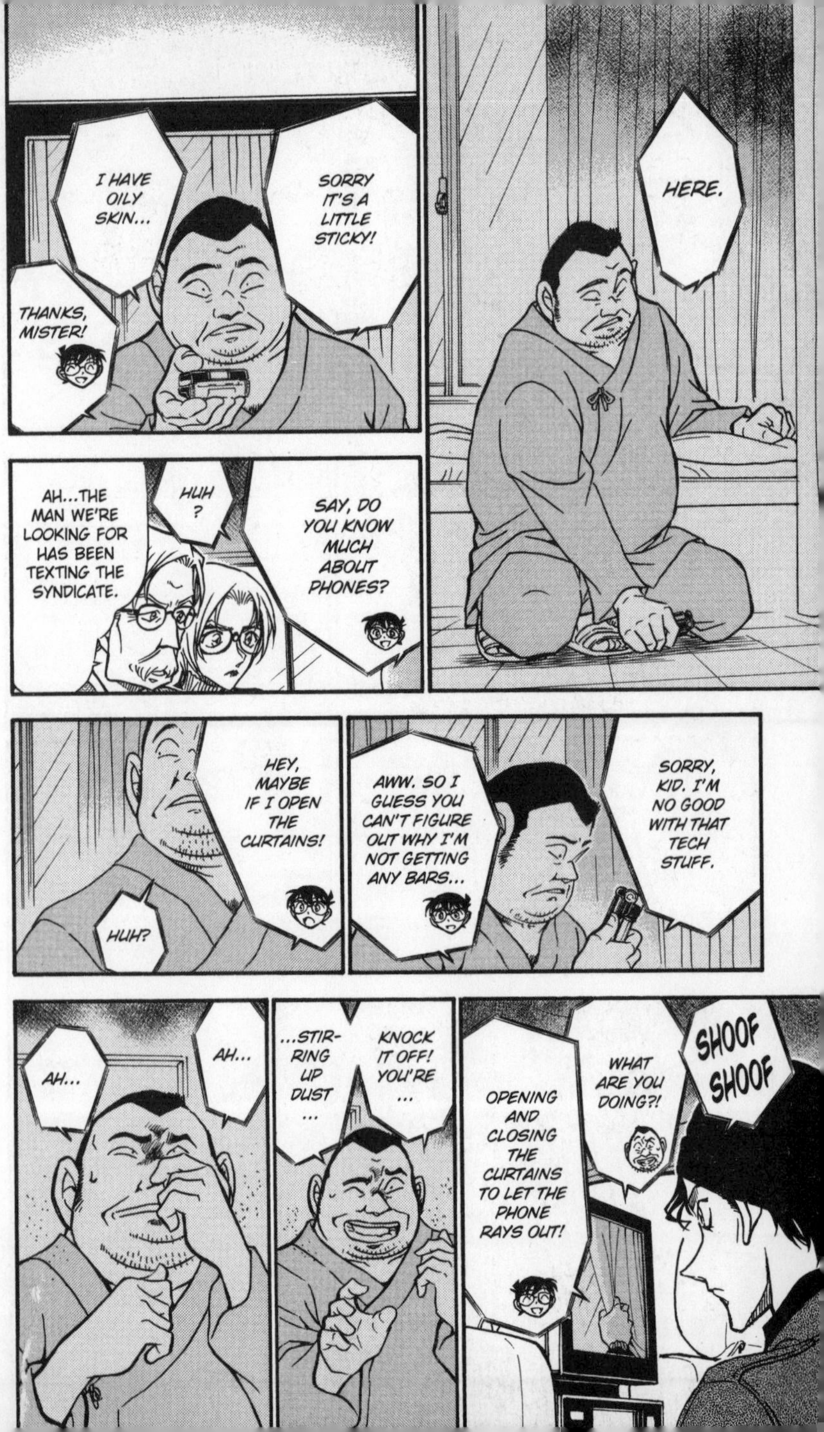
HERE.
SORRY IT'S A LITTLE STICKY!
I HAVE OILY SKIN...
THANKS, MISTER!
SAY, DO YOU KNOW MUCH ABOUT PHONES?
HUH?
AH...THE MAN WE'RE LOOKING FOR HAS BEEN TEXTING THE SYNDICATE.
SORRY, KID. I'M NO GOOD WITH THAT TECH STUFF.
AWW. SO I GUESS YOU CAN'T FIGURE OUT WHY I'M NOT GETTING ANY BARS...
HEY, MAYBE IF I OPEN THE CURTAINS!
HUH?
SHOOF SHOOF
WHAT ARE YOU DOING?!
OPENING AND CLOSING THE CURTAINS TO LET THE PHONE RAYS OUT!
KNOCK IT OFF! YOU'RE ...
...STIR-RING UP DUST ...
AH...
AH...

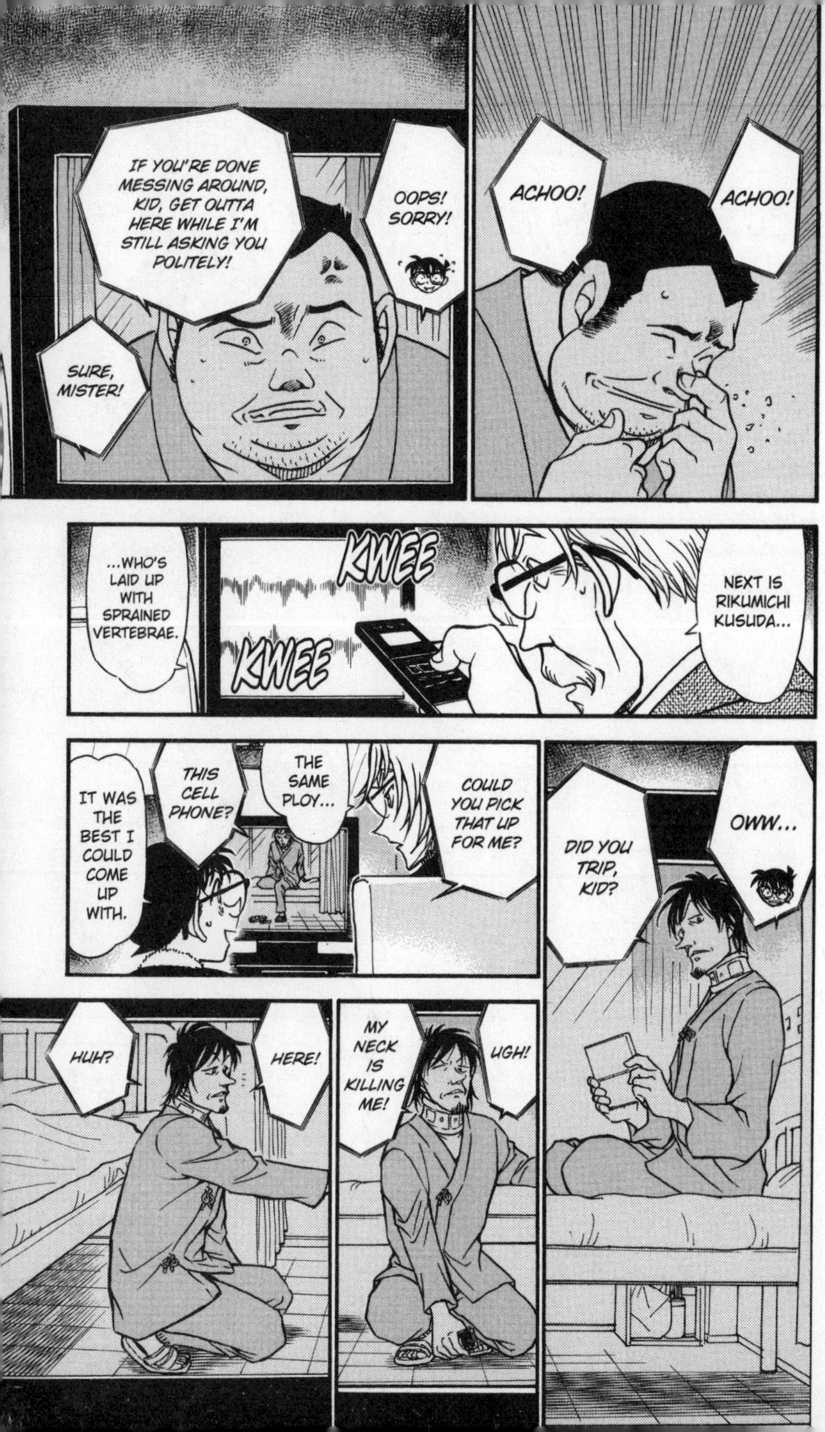

ACHOO!
ACHOO!
OOPS! SORRY!
IF YOU'RE DONE MESSING AROUND, KID, GET OUTTA HERE WHILE I'M STILL ASKING YOU POLITELY!
SURE, MISTER!
NEXT IS RIKUMICHI KUSUDA...
KWEE
KWEE
...WHO'S LAID UP WITH SPRAINED VERTEBRAE.
OWW...
DID YOU TRIP, KID?
COULD YOU PICK THAT UP FOR ME?
THE SAME PLOY...
THIS CELL PHONE?
IT WAS THE BEST I COULD COME UP WITH.
UGH!
MY NECK IS KILLING ME!
HERE!
HUH?

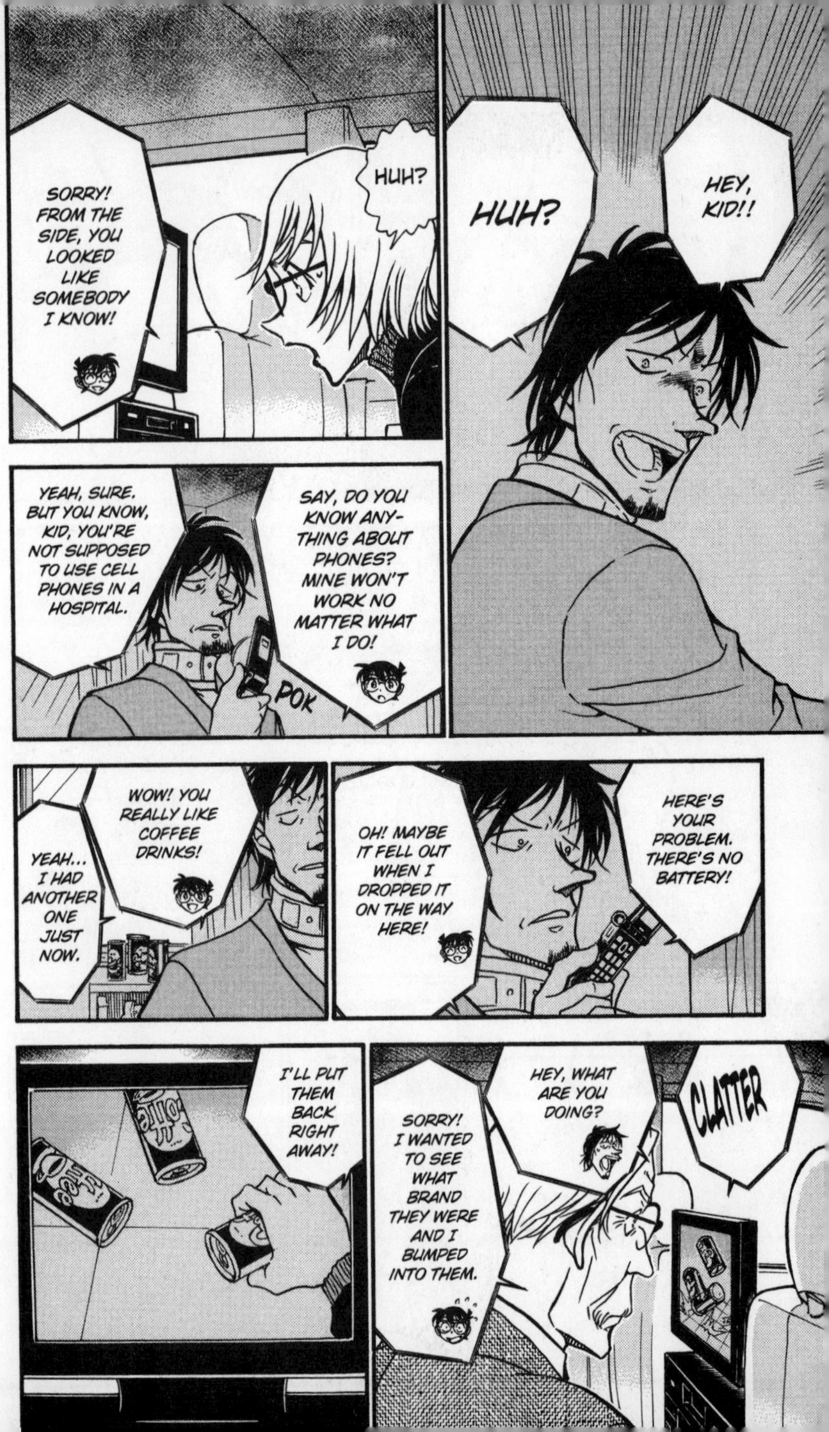
HEY, KID!!
HUH?
HUH?
SORRY! FROM THE SIDE, YOU LOOKED LIKE SOMEBODY I KNOW!
SAY, DO YOU KNOW ANY-THING ABOUT PHONES? MINE WON'T WORK NO MATTER WHAT I DO!
POK
YEAH, SURE. BUT YOU KNOW, KID, YOU'RE NOT SUPPOSED TO USE CELL PHONES IN A HOSPITAL.
HERE'S YOUR PROBLEM. THERE'S NO BATTERY!
OH! MAYBE IT FELL OUT WHEN I DROPPED IT ON THE WAY HERE!
WOW! YOU REALLY LIKE COFFEE DRINKS!
YEAH... I HAD ANOTHER ONE JUST NOW.
CLATTER
HEY, WHAT ARE YOU DOING?
SORRY! I WANTED TO SEE WHAT BRAND THEY WERE AND I BUMPED INTO THEM.
I'LL PUT THEM BACK RIGHT AWAY!

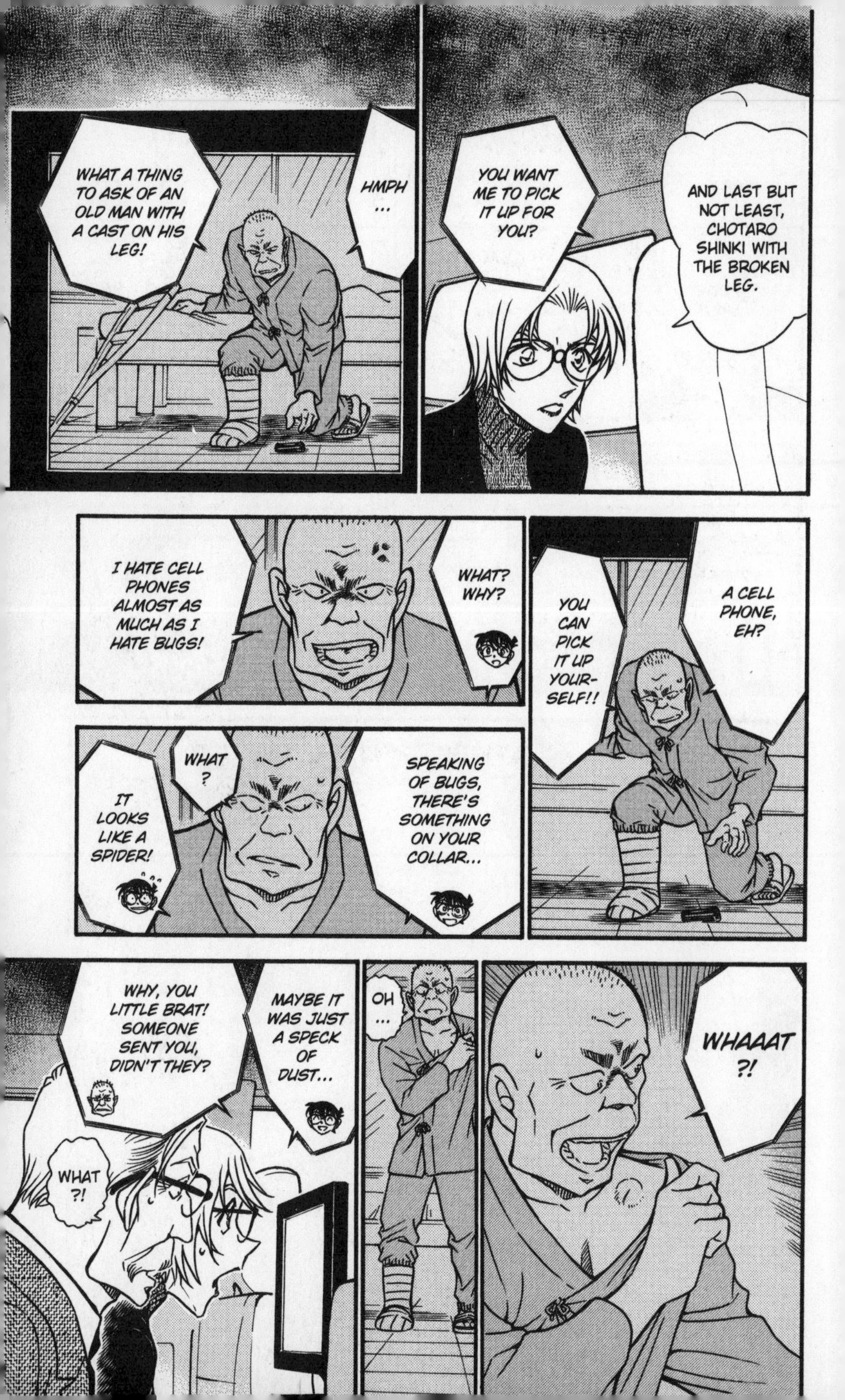
AND LAST BUT NOT LEAST, CHOTARO SHINKI WITH THE BROKEN LEG.
YOU WANT ME TO PICK IT UP FOR YOU?
HMPH...
WHAT A THING TO ASK OF AN OLD MAN WITH A CAST ON HIS LEG!
A CELL PHONE, EH?
YOU CAN PICK IT UP YOURSELF!!
WHAT? WHY?
I HATE CELL PHONES ALMOST AS MUCH AS I HATE BUGS!
SPEAKING OF BUGS, THERE'S SOMETHING ON YOUR COLLAR...
WHAT?
IT LOOKS LIKE A SPIDER!
WHAAAT?!
OH...
MAYBE IT WAS JUST A SPECK OF DUST...
WHY, YOU LITTLE BRAT! SOMEONE SENT YOU, DIDN'T THEY?
WHAT?!

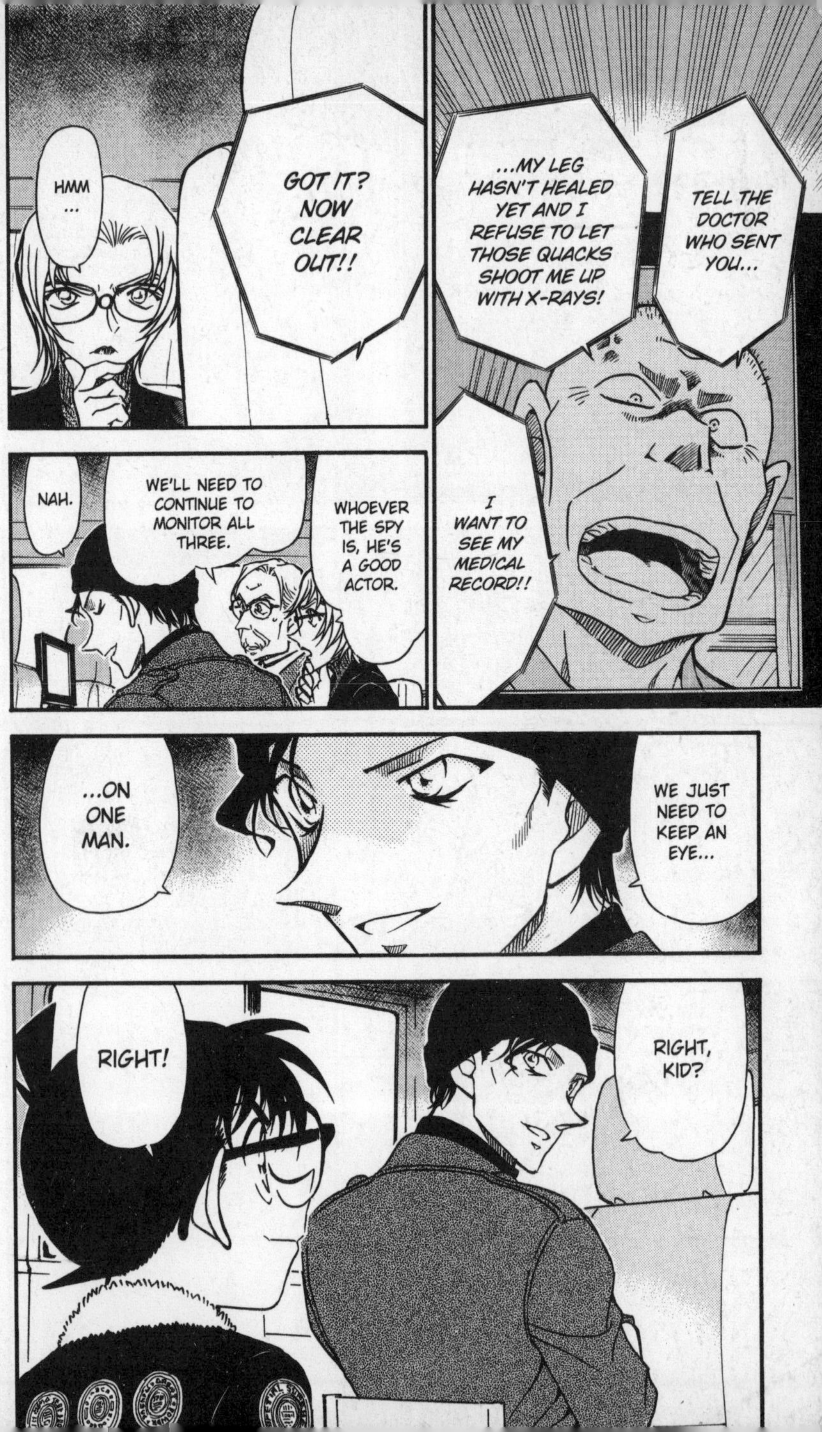
TELL THE DOCTOR WHO SENT YOU...
...MY LEG HASN'T HEALED YET AND I REFUSE TO LET THOSE QUACKS SHOOT ME UP WITH X-RAYS!
I WANT TO SEE MY MEDICAL RECORD!!
GOT IT? NOW CLEAR OUT!!
HMM...
WHOEVER THE SPY IS, HE'S A GOOD ACTOR.
WE'LL NEED TO CONTINUE TO MONITOR ALL THREE.
NAH.
WE JUST NEED TO KEEP AN EYE...
...ON ONE MAN.
RIGHT, KID?
RIGHT!

Hello, Aoyama here.

This year's *Case Closed* movie is about pirates! As it happens, back when I was an art student I had a part-time job painting the backgrounds on the Pirates of the Caribbean ride at Tokyo Disneyland. I did the "bricks" in the town the pirates are raiding before the big pirate ship appears. Drop by and take a look at my work if you're interested! Of course, it's probably too dark to see anything (heh).

Gosho Aoyama's Mystery Library

57

JOSEPH FRENCH

If you're talking about master alibi breakers, you can't forget Inspector Joseph French! A stout, middle-aged detective with Scotland Yard, he's calm and collected. His chummy attitude has earned him the nickname "Soapy Joe," but it's all part of his investigation technique. He takes great care with his questioning, analyzing every detail to reveal the truth. As you can guess from his motto, "Eliminate the impossible and whatever remains is the truth," he has great respect for Sherlock Holmes. But he has a very un-Holmes-like personality, steady and methodical.

The author who created Inspector French, F. W. Crofts, was a former railway engineer, so no wonder he was good at creating alibis and gimmicks based on timetables. I have a friend who's a train operator, but that's all we have in common (heh).

I recommend *The 12.30 from Croydon.*